Reshaping the Work-Family Debate

BASED ON THE WILLIAM E. MASSEY SR. LECTURES
IN THE HISTORY OF AMERICAN CIVILIZATION, 2008

RESHAPING THE WORK-FAMILY DEBATE

Why Men and Class Matter

JOAN C. WILLIAMS

HARVARD UNIVERSITY PRESS
Cambridge, Massachusetts
London, England

First Harvard University Press paperback edition, 2012

Library of Congress Cataloging-in-Publication Data
Williams, Joan, 1952–
Reshaping the work-family debate : why men and class matter / Joan C. Williams.
p. cm.—(The William E. Massey Sr. lectures in the history of American Civilization ; 2008)
Includes bibliographical references and index.
ISBN 978-0-674-05567-4 (cloth: alk. paper)
ISBN 978-0-674-06449-2 (pbk.)
1. Work and family—United States.   2. Working mothers—United States.
3. Dual-career families—United States.   4. Sex role—United States.
5. Social classes—United States.   I. Title.
HD4904.25.W54 2010
306.3'6—dc22
2010011122

To James X. Dempsey, with thanks for thirty years

Contents

Introduction   1

1 Opt Out or Pushed Out?   12

2 One Sick Child Away from Being Fired   42

3 Masculine Norms at Work   77

4 Reconstructive Feminism and Feminist Theory   109

5 The Class Culture Gap   151

6 Culture Wars as Class Conflict   187

   Conclusion: Sarah Palin as Formula and Fantasy   215

   Notes   221
   Acknowledgments   281
   Index   285

Reshaping the Work-Family Debate

Introduction

publicsupport +
＊ workers'rights

T HE RIGHT TOOL is half the job.
 Writ small, this book is about reframing debates about work and
family. In the press we are offered a steady stream of stories about women
who cheerfully "opt out" of high-status professional careers, but there are
few stories about discrimination against mothers who try to remain employed and still fewer about less affluent families who struggle to both
care for and support their families. And we hear almost nothing about the
central arguments presented here, that work-family issues reflect a fundamental economic problem: we still have a workplace perfectly designed
for the workforce of the 1960s. The mismatch between the workforce
and the workplace is a market failure fueled by social norms, namely, old-
fashioned and rigid definitions of masculinity and the resulting gender
pressures on men.
 Writ large, this book is about reframing American politics.[1] Work-
family issues have not been placed at the center of an analysis of U.S. politics, but it is time to rethink the assumption that they do not belong there.
The United States has the most family-hostile public policy in the developed world, and changing that situation will require reshaping American
politics in some basic ways.[2] To match today's workplace to today's workforce, we need both public supports (subsidized child care, parental leave
financed at a national level, national health insurance) and workers' rights
(mandated vacation time, proportional pay for part-time work, and the

right to request a flexible schedule). Neither is politically feasible today. For the past forty years, U.S. politics has focused on tax cuts, not new government supports; on deregulation, not workers' rights. Barack Obama, despite his stunning electoral victory in 2008, still faces a sharply divided electorate where new social programs and workers' rights remain a tenuous dream.

Building a coalition to enact policies that enable Americans to balance work and family responsibilities should be within the realm of possibility. When asked, American parents—90% of American mothers and 95% of American fathers—say that they wish they had more time with their children.[3] These levels are sharply lower in Europe.[4] Yet anything other than strictly incremental progress is unrealistic until we reshape some abiding verities of American politics that currently constrict the range of the politically possible.

Accomplishing this will require an inquiry into the deep structure of everyday and electoral politics—into the unnoticed architecture of our daily lives. This architecture channels our thoughts about work, family, and gender. In place of the insistent popular and scholarly focus on gender differences, this book shifts attention onto the masculine norms that make those differences seem so important. Because masculine norms are a prime mover of the social power dynamics within which both men and women negotiate their daily lives, feminists need to attend to masculinity.[5]

Placing masculine workplace norms at center stage challenges the long-standing assumption that the family is the "gender factory."[6] This assumption emerges whenever commentators assert that the solution to work-family conflict is for women to bargain more effectively for men to share in household work, a staple argument in both liberal and conservative circles. Conservatives argue that what keeps women back today is not workplace discrimination but the choices they make in family life.[7] Liberal feminists join in, exhorting women to "man up" and insist on equality within the household.[8] In fact, the family dynamics that drive women out of their jobs often stem from workplace norms and practices that pressure men into breadwinner roles and women out of them. Workplaces not only produce widgets. They also produce gender.

Privileged Women and Not-So-Privileged Families

This book is composed of three parts. The first explores the unspoken framework that shapes how we discuss work-family conflict, beginning with newspapers' obsession with professional women who "opt out." Lisa

[handwritten margin notes: "Masculinity" and "Workplaces produce gender"]

Belkin's famous article in *The New York Times Magazine* in 2003 reshaped the basic message that that newspaper, and many others, have been sending since 1980: they have reported, over and over, that professional women are leaving careers following their discovery that they are, after all, more traditional than they thought.[9] The basic picture is one of women discovering that they "really are" different from men, that women's priorities are different, and that the lure of children pulls them away from work and into the home sweet home—or really car sweet car, as they drive their children from one enrichment activity to the next.

This "opt-out" storyline is inaccurate in many ways. It severely downplays the depression, loneliness, and loss of status encountered by women who leave high-profile careers. In addition, by interviewing largely white professional-managerial women, opt-out stories gloss over the lives of the majority of American women. By interviewing only married women after they leave the workforce and before they divorce, opt-out stories gloss over the risks shouldered by women exiting the workforce, only to find both their economic future and their children's jeopardized by divorce. Moreover, opt-out stories gloss over the fact that contemporary career women are not returning to traditional roles but in fact are helping to invent a new, highly pressured and sped-up version of childhood—and motherhood. Perhaps most important, opt-out stories present a highly misleading picture of the long-term consequences of "taking a few years off," which typically are severe: women who spend two or three years away from work suffer a 30% drop in lifetime earnings, according to one study. Unfair as this is, women ought to know about it, but they do not—because the press does not cover it.[10]

Belkin ultimately argued that workplaces should change to accommodate women.[11] But the typical opt-out story never gets there. Little mention is made in the press of the fact that many mothers do not opt out; they are pushed out, by powerful gender bias that depicts working mothers as neither committed nor competent. Meanwhile, all-or-nothing workplaces push men out of caregiver roles as they push women out of their jobs. Last but not least, opt-out stories typically fail to note that failures of public policy are a key reason why work-family conflict in the United States is felt so much more acutely than in Europe.[12]

What happens to working-class families for whom opting out is not an option? Years of study of union arbitrations where workers are disciplined or discharged because of work-family conflicts paint a vivid picture of the impact of these conflicts on hourly workers: the bus drivers, telephone workers, construction linemen, carpenters, and welders of the working class and the nurses' aides and janitors, whose low-wage jobs place them among the working poor. These families typically have highly inflexible schedules, where they can be fired for being a few minutes late or ordered to work overtime in the middle of a shift. This scheduling instability works in poisonous combination with Americans' unusually high reliance on families for child care. Many Americans in nonprofessional jobs have crazy quilts of child care, with sometimes as many as five different child care arrangements—one for each day of the week. Or else they "tag team," where mom works one shift while dad works a different shift, with each parent caring for the kids while the other is at work. This is not an easy way to live: everyone ends up exhausted, and many parents rarely see each other awake. Moreover, if one parent is ordered to work mandatory overtime, the family has to choose between mom's job and dad's job, in a situation where they need both jobs to survive. This is a face of work-family conflict about which most Americans never hear, because it is rarely covered in the press. But we can help change today's workplaces to better fit today's workforce. We can update workplace norms and practices to save employers money. And we can redesign nonprofessional jobs so that those jobs fit into the lives workers lead today, where they are simultaneously caring not only for children but also for ill and elderly family members.

Changing the Way We Talk about Gender

The opt-out story rests on a series of unstated, and undefended, assumptions about what is good for children, how easy it is for women to return to careers they have left, whether women are conflicted or contented with the choices offered them, and whether men are even part of the equation. The ideology that ties together all these assumptions is called "domesticity," or "separate spheres." That gender system, inherited from the nineteenth century, divides daily life neatly into the mutually exclusive realms of public life and domestic life. Separate spheres imputes specific, and different, biological and psychological characteristics to men and women. Women are deemed too good for the nasty and brutish world of commerce in which men—so the story goes—thrive. From this story stems a set of interlocking assumptions: that it is natural for women to take sole responsibility for child care, that doing so fulfills women's deepest nature and so makes them happy, that men are competitive and ambitious and thus naturally suited to employment but not to caregiving, and that homemakers' economic vulnerability in breadwinner-homemaker households is no big deal. These gendered assumptions in turn shape what jobs are seen as appropriate for men and for women.

Assumptions drawn from separate spheres continue to frame today's debates about gender, work, and family. One result is that gender is commonly seen through the lens of difference, a framing that leads to the endless recycling of debates over whether men and women are the same or different.[13] The second part of the book lays the groundwork for moving up one logical level, focusing attention not on women's differences but on the masculine norms that make those differences seem so important. Masculine norms underlie the social structures within which both men and women negotiate their daily lives, yet those norms are not recognized as gendered.

To that end, in the second part of the book, I seek to reframe the ways we think about gender, beginning with an examination of the role of masculine norms in creating the workplace pressures that make men reluctant or unable to play an equal role in family life. I then examine the ways those same masculine norms lead to gender bias against women. In the face of norms framed around masculinity, women tend to adopt two broadly differing strategies. Some act the "tomboy," adapting to the roles and behaviors conventionally associated with masculinity. Others act the "femme," following more traditionally feminine roles. Both femmes and tomboys encounter, although in different ways and to different degrees, four basic patterns of workplace gender bias rooted in masculine norms: the maternal wall, double standards, double binds, and gender wars among women.[14] The end result is to police women out of good jobs and men out of caregiving. Challenging the conventional wisdom that work-family conflict stems from women's failure to bargain effectively within the family—that the family is the gender factory—I argue that workplaces also play a central role. If feminists seek to reconstruct gender on the work-family axis, they should focus as much, or more, on changing the workplace as on changing the family.

I also explain what I have termed "reconstructive feminism" and discuss its relationship to existing strands of feminist thought. For too long, feminism has struggled to come to terms with differences between men and women (the sameness versus difference debate), differences among women (the anti-essentialism debate), and the relationship of gender difference to gender dominance (the difference versus dominance debate). Reconstructive feminism reframes those debates by shifting attention away from women's identities onto the gender dynamics within which identities are forged. I discuss the relationship of reconstructive feminism to other major strains of feminist theory, notably anti-essentialism, dominance feminism, queer theory, and third-wave feminism. Reconstructive feminism also proposes an alternative to the reigning metaphor—"intersectionality"—for analyzing the interaction of gender and racial disadvantage in the lives of women of color.

Changing the Way We Talk about Class

Shifting away from a focus on gender, the third part of the book contests the conventional assumption that gender is the only crucial framework for understanding work-family issues. Here I argue that reducing work-family conflict also requires changing the way we think about class. At an everyday level, many of the dynamics that create work-family conflict stem from families' felt need to give a "class act"—a mode of living that signals class status. At an electoral level, the kinds of family supports available in Europe are unthinkable in the United States, in part because of an American politics fueled by class conflict between the professional-managerial class and the white working class.

Defusing this class conflict first requires understanding it—which entails understanding how class is expressed as cultural difference, thereby creating a class "culture gap" between reform-minded progressives and white workers. This culture gap between classes has fueled culture wars, which are best understood in this context as expressions of class conflict. Whether in a Democratic administration or a Republican one, family supports will never become politically feasible until progressives reconstruct the kind of coalition that existed in the past and led to the enactment of government subsidies (for example, Social Security) and worker protections (for example, the National Labor Relations Act). Creating a new long-term coalition will require reform-minded elites to develop a true sensitivity to issues of class. This book is designed to jump-start that process.

A growing number of American scholars document the lack of supports for working families and advocate adoption of European-style policies. This approach skips an important step: identifying how to create the political will to pass the necessary legislation. America is unusual, notes political scientist John W. Kingdon:

> In 1994, my wife and I were visiting her most pleasant and friendly relatives in Norway . . . I struck up a conversation with a niece, who was very pregnant at the time. I asked her what she was planning to do about her job when she gave birth. She replied that she would take a year's leave of absence, whereupon she would return to her job, which was guaranteed to be held for her . . . [and that] she would receive 80 percent of her salary . . . [When she heard that the United States had only twelve weeks' unpaid leave] she could barely disguise her wonder and even her amusement that the greatest and wealthiest country on earth could be so backward.[15]

Kingdon sees our lack of family supports as emblematic of the fact that "government in the United States is much more limited and much smaller than government in virtually every other advanced industrialized country on earth."[16] Prominent social welfare theorists agree.[17] Europe's basic family supports arose in the late nineteenth century: maternity leaves, comprehensive health care, and other forms of basic social insurance all developed during this period.[18] But the current comprehensive system of work-family reconciliation policies arose in Europe after 1970, during a period when new proposals for social benefits and workers' rights were going nowhere in the United States.[19]

America *is* unusual. Americans' abiding belief in limited government means that the United States always has played catch-up when compared with Europe. But in earlier eras, America managed to achieve both robust regulation and significant social redistribution. In the late nineteenth and early twentieth centuries, Progressive Era coalitions reined in Gilded Age capitalism gone amok: the Sherman Antitrust Act forced the breakup of huge industries; the Pure Food and Drug and Meat Inspection Acts improved sanitary conditions in meatpacking plants and killed off the thriving industry in patent medicines; state legislatures passed minimum-wage and maximum-hour laws; and the Sixteenth Amendment authorized a progressive income tax—all despite passionate opposition from the business elite. These and similar large-scale changes came about because progressive coalitions in the late nineteenth and early twentieth centuries successfully countered business opposition.

Similarly successful bridge-building created the New Deal coalition between workers, blacks, and the reform-minded elite. As a result, the Works Progress Administration effectively socialized employment, for many, for several years. The National Labor Relations Board gave workers the right to organize, leading to a sharp rise in union membership. The Fair Labor Standards Act brought an end to the then-standard ten-hour workday by mandating "time-and-a-half" for work in excess of eight hours a day. The elderly, then the poorest class of Americans, saw their economic status rise sharply following the enactment of Social Security and Medicare.

The New Deal coalition withered after 1970, and America-the-already-unusual was transformed into the outlier nation it is today. Beginning with Richard Nixon's presidency and crystallizing during the presidency of Ronald Reagan, the business elite engineered a sharp shift to the right in American politics. Corporations were deified while government was demonized. A highly skilled federal workforce with decades of expertise was derided, discredited, and dismantled. Workers' rights to organize constricted, and union density plummeted. New Deal–era financial regulations were dismantled, and the financial industry ran wild. This second Gilded Age ended with a financial bailout package on October 3, 2008, in which financial institutions were given $350 billion, with virtually no oversight or restrictions.[20]

Americans typically think of work-family conflict as a private issue. This is not surprising, given that American public policy to resolve such conflict is virtually nonexistent, forcing us all to cobble together individually negotiated solutions in the private marketplace. Work-family conflict is so insoluble for so many people because of a public policy environment that makes Americans' daily efforts at balance unworkable. Just compare the experience of a Swedish family with an American one. If the Swedes took full advantage of government policies, parents of a newborn could stay home together for the first two weeks after a child's birth, after which the mother could continue her year-long paid leave while the father could return to his job at an 80% schedule. Once the child turns one, the father could take the remaining six months of paid parental leave while the mother returned to work at an 80% schedule—available for one parent until the youngest child turns eight. As young as one, the child could be placed in high-quality, subsidized, neighborhood-based child care.[21] In sharp contrast, the only benefit available to the American couple is three months of unpaid leave—if the couple is lucky enough to have an employer who is not exempted from this requirement. Failures of public policy are a key reason that Americans face such acute work-family conflict.

Any inquiry into work-family conflict in the United States needs to investigate why we lack the kinds of family supports that exist elsewhere. The answer is that the dominance of the business elite has made unthinkable the kinds of supports that Europeans have nurtured. The political climate for social supports has been so hostile in the United States that it took eight years and two presidential vetoes for Congress to pass the paltry unpaid leave program that John Kingdon's Norwegian niece found laughable. By the time Bill Clinton finally signed the Family and Medical Leave Act (FMLA) in 1993, it was so compromised that the statute offered only unpaid job protection and the continuation of health insurance—and only for twelve weeks. Any employer with fewer than fifty employees was exempted, restricting FMLA coverage to just over 60% of the American workforce.[22]

Enacting paid leave has proved so intractable that advocates shifted their efforts from the federal level to the states for nearly a decade.[23] As for the other measures Europeans enacted to fit the workplace to the new workforce—from mandated vacations, to limiting the work week, to protections for part-timers—none seem remotely feasible in the United States. When Janet Gornick, a key scholar advocating adoption of European-type policies in the United States, presented her ideas at an academic conference in 2003, a commentator wrote off her prescriptions as "science fiction."[24]

Understanding the evolution of our family-hostile public policy requires a clear-eyed assessment of how the business elite gained such uncontested dominance after 1970. Work-family experts can urge adoption of new family supports until they are blue in the face, but these measures will remain politically unattainable unless and until progressives can reconstruct the kind of viable, long-term coalition that has been missing for nearly forty years. To accomplish this requires a shift away from the single-minded focus on gender traditionally used by work-family commentators. This is the reason for the last two chapters' focus on class.

Two caveats: the first concerns my focus on the white working class. Without a doubt, listening to workers of color is equally important. Yet political scientists tell us that white workers are the swing demographic of "Reagan Democrats" who have shifted Republican since 1970. For that reason, blacks are not the focus of this discussion. In part because Republicans' "Southern strategy" entailed the shameless use of coded racism to woo that region's white working class, blacks have remained firmly in the Democratic camp: 90% voted for Democrats in 1972, and 82% did so in 2004.[25] A study of the ways white and black workers are alike and differ is important and fascinating—but not our topic here.

The second caveat concerns my disproportionate focus on white men. To a significant extent, this just reflects the disproportionate focus on men in the existing studies of class, for reasons I would not defend. But in part my emphasis on men continues my exploration of the central role of masculinity in shaping social life. Commentators have noted that working-class men have abandoned the Democrats in far greater percentages than have working-class women. The men have done so, I argue, in part because of white workers' anxieties over their increasing inability to realize the conventional ideal of what it means to be a "real man," that is, to be a bread-winner able to "support his family." The ability to fulfill ideals of manliness has become a class-linked privilege.

Working-class whites, heavily Democratic until roughly 1970, began to vote increasingly Republican thereafter.[26] Class-based masculinities have played a part. Also important is that progressives abandoned their posture of respect for the working class and began belittling them, as when college kids gave the finger to the police—white working-class men with good, stable jobs. This disrespect continues to this day. "You know the hardest thing about being a hairdresser?" asked one woman quoted in a book published in 2006, "It's the way people treat you. Some people think because you're a hairdresser, you're necessarily dumb . . . They just don't respect you."[27]

The felt lack of respect by upper-middle-class people for ordinary Joe and Jane is part of a gaping class culture gap between the white working class and the professional-managerial class from which the reform-minded elite typically is drawn. Understanding these distinctive class cultures can achieve two goals. One is to take the first step in turning around the political dynamic that has made family supports so hard to enact in the United States. The second is to deepen the analysis of gender by offering a simultaneous analysis of class, because class anxieties and aspirations play a key role in making gender so unbending.

The class culture gap fuels culture wars that drive white workers into alliance with the business elite. Rebuilding progressives' relationship with white workers requires not just superficial changes in political rhetoric—it requires a profound cultural shift. Progressives need to learn more about working-class folkways and to understand how workers see upper-middle-class folkways as "class acts" that enact elite status.

Self-reflection and self-awareness never come easy. What I offer is a description of working-class life as workers see it and of professional-managerial folkways as seen through a working-class lens. The picture of upper-middle class life produced by this lens is often distinctly unflattering, powerfully powered by class anger. Describing white workers' mentalité does not mean that I uncritically endorse it. As a typical upper-middle-class progressive, I find working-class characterizations of upper-middle-class life at once illuminating and somewhat unfair.

Yet this perspective needs to be heard for several reasons, the most pressing of which is the necessity of building a more progressive future. Along with this strategic reason is an ethical one. White workers are part of the American family. Progressives' now-traditional focus on race as the key axis of inequality has shielded them from the full challenge of coming to terms with class privilege. For progressive elites, building bridges to working-class whites may well be harder than building bridges to professional-managerial blacks. It may well be harder, too, than building bridges to working-class blacks who, according to Michèle Lamont's impressive study, tend to be less antigovernment, more receptive to social programs, and less judgmental of the poor.[28] In fact, when it comes to social solidarity, working-class blacks are more like French workers than like white American ones.[29] If all workers were more like African-American workers, the progressives' row would be easier to hoe. But they are not. We live in a democracy, and we need to build a coalition with the electorate we have rather than the one we wish we had.[30]

In 2008, the Democrats finally won a presidential election, in the face of the Great Recession. But even Barack Obama, with his remarkable leader-

Focusing on race deters from larger discussion

ship skills, will be able to accomplish comparatively little unless he can build a coalition to support a progressive agenda. As he is fond of telling us, he cannot do it alone. Progressives can help by reshaping their relationship to the white working class. This book's offer of family therapy for the body politic is designed to help.

Listening attentively can help reshape not only the electoral but also the everyday politics of work and family. While workers' critiques of the professional-managerial elite lack empathy and balance, they also offer insights into the norms that create work-family conflict among the professional-managerial class. Worth taking seriously, among other things, is working-class skepticism about the intense focus in the upper-middle class on individual achievement, the intense performance pressures placed on children, and the un-self-conscious intensity of focus on enhancing social status. Treating working-class culture respectfully not only is an ethical obligation mandated by progressives' commitments to dignity and equality. Like all good family therapy, it offers news we can use about ourselves.

This book seeks to build bridges. It seeks to bridge disciplinary gaps between social psychology, gender theory, sociology, political science, and law. It also seeks to bridge the even larger gap between mainstream discourse and the specialized field of work-family studies. Bridging these gaps will require opening up difficult conversations about masculinity and class privilege, conversations in which our identities—as men and women and as progressives—seem at stake.[31] Every attempt is made to raise these delicate questions with due respect for the fragility that sometimes plagues all of us. But raise them we must, if we are to build a progressive future.

CHAPTER ONE

Opt Out or Pushed Out?

"I WAS TIRED of juggling. I was tired of feeling guilty. I was tired of hold-ing the household reins in one hand. So I quit." The cover of the *New York Times Magazine* for October 26, 2003 sends a remarkable number of controversial messages in an efficient, cagey way. While the topic is "women," the photo is of a very particular sort of woman: pictured is a classy-looking white woman, posed as a serene modern Madonna. She is gazing at the baby in her lap, ignoring the ladder that climbs behind her. The headline asks, "Why Don't More Women Get to the Top?" "They Choose Not To" is the answer. Inside, in an article titled "The Opt-Out Revolution," *Times* work/family columnist Lisa Belkin focuses on eight women who graduated from Princeton and now all belong to the same book club in Atlanta, as well as four women, three of whom hold MBAs, with children in a playgroup in San Francisco. As Belkin acknowledges, all are "elite, successful women who can afford real choice." And yet despite this acknowledgement of her subjects' privilege, Belkin's article goes on to make generalizations about all women based on this group's decisions—to use Belkin's phrase—to "opt out" of their prestigious, highly paid careers.[1]

"The Opt-Out Revolution" shifted the cultural frame for understanding U.S. women's workforce participation. Prior to Belkin's piece, press cover-age typically had focused on women who had "dropped out"—that is, those who had left the workforce altogether. Her key insight was that this was not the crucial issue, because many women who remain in the work-force nonetheless step off the fast track, by working part-time, becoming independent contractors, or working full-time on the "mommy track." She lumped part-timers with stay-at-home moms as evidence that many women who had not dropped out had, nonetheless, "opted out" of the fast track. Belkin's success in naming and framing this phenomenon reshaped and refreshed a well-entrenched story line: that women were returning home as a matter of choice, the result of their own psychological or biological pulls rather than workplace pushes.

Belkin's bottom line, that workplaces should change to fit the realities of women's lives, was largely lost in the controversy that followed. Bonnie Erbe decried "*The New York Times*' bizarre and suspiciously predetermined editorial effort to talk women out of working" as the *Times* published story after story reinforcing the opt-out theme. In a May 2004 article, the *Times* reported that black women also were opting out. That story was followed by a 2005 Labor Day op-ed by antifeminist Warren Farrell, who—using shaky data—asserted that women's disadvantaged workplace posi-tion does not reflect sex discrimination; instead the persistent wage gap is attributable to women's choices. Later the same month, cub reporter Louise Story snagged a coveted front-page spot. Her report, "Many Women at Elite Colleges Set Career Path to Motherhood," featured interviews with Yale undergraduates, including one young woman who recalled a class in which stay-at-home motherhood was discussed, prompting many of the men in the class to say, "'I think that's really great' [and] 'I think that's re-ally sexy.'" Another front-page story, later the same month, cried "Forget the Career. My Parents Need Me at Home" and went on to explain that, according to "many experts," "middle-aged women may see leaving a high-powered career as an opportunity, not a sacrifice."[2] The coverage, including another front-page story ("Stretched to Limit, Women Stall March to Work"), continued during 2006.[3]

Although it reached a fever pitch in 2005–2006, the opt-out story line has been the interpretation of choice at the *New York Times* and other newspapers across the country for decades. The opt-out narrative in Amer-ican newspapers predominates over alternative narratives that give weight to social or family pressures pushing women out of the workforce. The Center for WorkLife Law, which I direct, conducted a content analysis of 119 print news stories covering the period between 1980 and 2006. The analysis documents the press focus on a small sliver of the workforce—the 3.7% of American women who are highly educated white professionals with jobs in traditionally male-dominated occupations. Members of this group, the story goes, whether because of biology or ideology, are realizing not only that they cannot "have it all" but also that they do not want it all. The stories overwhelmingly center on factors that lure these women back into traditional roles: in 74% of the stories surveyed, the overall emphasis is on pulls rather than pushes. Take, for example, the story of Mary Ellen McCormick, a high-powered, MBA-holding marketing executive who left her "fast track job" after the birth of her first child because she discovered "the greatest love affair of all time. When you hold your baby in your arms, that's it . . . All of this 'Me, me, me, I need to do this for me,' starts melting away." Or Debbie Korkodilos, who "was just following her heart when she decided to leave her public relations job in 1998 to stay home with her baby daughter."[4] Only 6% of the articles surveyed make forces that push women out, such as workplace inflexibility, the focus of the story, and only 16% appeared in the newspapers' business sections. Over one-third (37%) of the articles surveyed appeared in the lifestyle or features sections, reflecting the trend of presenting coverage of those who opt out as "soft news." While the opt-out trend has been declared again and again, there remain few numbers to back it up.[5]

Does it really matter that stories about dropping out and opting out arise, phoenix-like, year after year? That reporters keep breathlessly announcing as news that "Many Young Women Now Say They'd Pick Family over Career" or rediscovering that there are "Mothers Who Choose to Stay Home"?[6]

Yes. It does matter. These stories both reflect and reinforce destructive stereotypes, painting work-family conflict as a champagne problem enjoyed by upper-middle-class women in white-collar jobs. Editorial decisions determine whether to cover work-family issues, how the topic of women and work is framed, and in what part of the newspaper the coverage appears.

Fuzzy data in this arena may be uncontroversial because people readily accept stereotype-affirming information but not data that challenge existing stereotypes.[7] Opt-out stories, especially when they appear and reappear in mainstream media over many years, provide reassurance that women are happily abandoning their professional/managerial positions, joyfully embracing their role as stay-at-home moms, and cheerfully giving up the luxuries their paychecks used to cover. These messages tell us that all is well. "Traditional" values can be counted on to triumph in the end. In short, nothing needs to change.

Yet one major drawback of the opt-out story line is that it is not true. In fact, it is riddled with inaccuracies. Our choice to seek shelter in its warm, fictional glow precludes us from recognizing some cold twenty-first-century

Good Quo

realities. Important stories—of our family-hostile public policy and of uneven and unregulated child care facilities—all remain submerged in newspapers. Focusing narrowly and with much fanfare on elite workers who resolve conflict between work and family by "choosing" to head home leaves in place beliefs, policies, and laws that perpetuate the mismatch between today's workplace and today's workforce. There are alternatives to the typical opt-out story line. The struggle to balance work and family life is, without question, a compelling narrative, and there is no question that the choices women face—whether truly free or forced by the conflicting pulls of work and family—deserve their place on the front page. But these stories are much more diverse and complex than current patterns of coverage would make it seem.[8]

The traditional challenge to the opt-out narrative is to deny that women are leaving the workforce in greater numbers. Many feminists, most notably economist Heather Boushey of the Center for American Progress, have argued that no opt-out trend exists. Boushey's analysis of Current Population Survey data showed that, at the same time that women's employment dipped after 2000, so did men's. Women's employment dipped more than men's—but that effect was not due to motherhood. Boushey found that non-mothers' employment dipped about as much as mothers' did.[9] Boushey's is a particularly sophisticated version of the standard feminist response to opt-out stories—a triumphalist tale stressing the sharp increase in working mothers since 1960. Yet, despite a decrease in the effect of having children on women's employment in recent decades, what economists call the "child penalty" remains substantial. A rigorous study by economist Claudia Goldin found that only about one-quarter of college-educated women who graduated between 1980 and 1990 had both families and careers.[10]

only '/4 have family work

Meanwhile, professional women who are childless at age thirty work hours and earn wages similar to men's. Women, it seems, have achieved equality as long as they die childless at thirty. Older women hit the glass ceiling that blocks them from top jobs. Yet most women never get near the glass ceiling; they are stopped, long before, by the maternal wall. The remainder of this chapter examines the impact of motherhood, critiquing the opt-out narrative and offering some alternatives. These alternatives pinpoint the factors that shape the "choices" of today's diverse group of working women. Every woman has a different story, and it is time to explore that diversity of experience instead of repeating tired opt-out clichés. Instead, I provide new angles on the work-family narrative that offer a more inclusive picture of the challenges women face today.[11]

Reality Check

The classic opt-out story line depicts women pulled into traditional roles by biology or personal predilection. Those who heed these pulls almost always are presented as happy and fulfilled. They are buoyant with the certainty that staying at home will keep their children safe and will ensure a full array of culturally and socially enriching activities. And they are giddy with the relief of having escaped the overwhelming stress of trying to simultaneously live up to the high standards of contemporary mothering and to those of their historically male-dominated occupations. This uniformly positive depiction needs a bracing dose of reality to present a more balanced picture of the dismal choices many women face.

For the most part, opt-out stories paint a picture of professional women "getting real" about their limitations and recognizing that their priorities have changed; certainly, this is one experience women have, but numbers show that such women are in the minority. Reporters, approaching the story from a particular angle, often do not ask the right questions—and do not hear the answers to the questions they do ask. Drawbacks to the traditional breadwinner-homemaker pattern have been documented over and over again since the 1950s—and nearly half (43%) of opt-out articles mention the women's depression, loneliness, boredom, isolation, or loss of identity and self-esteem that results from leaving the workforce.[12] What the coverage does not do is to take these problems seriously. Some quotes, taken from a flood of examples found in the articles surveyed, provide a sense of the problems at-home mothers face:

- "You're walking a delicate balance, trying to talk to others but not seeming desperate." Staying home is best for her two children, Laura Yamashita, 40, was quick to say. But she also said that she missed the adult interaction and the sense of accomplishment she had gotten from her career.
- "You get lonely . . . It gives you a feeling you're not worthy."
- "I had to admit I felt depressed . . . I liked being a mother, but it was hard to adjust to being just a housekeeper."
- "I was at my wit's end. I was desperate."
- "Most at-home mothers can tell stories about being snubbed at dinner parties or having friends ask when they plan to do something 'important.'"
- "Like many women who have left promising careers for full-time motherhood, Kelley Dorn of Minnesota confronted unexpected loneliness, boredom, and a daily search for identity."[13]

One troubling story is that of Patsy Wiggins, a thirty-nine-year-old Manhattan mother of three and former hard-driving attorney, who quit her job in frustration "over her husband's unpredictable hours, constant travel, and unwillingness to share domestic responsibilities." Although she embraced her new life as "fabulous" on some days, she also said:

> I feel guilt about not living up to my intellectual potential, and I feel some guilt about not bringing in money. But I think that identity has been the biggest issue for me. I always identified myself as a powerhouse, and when people talk about me as a stay-at-home mother, I feel like, "Put 'loser' in the box next to that." I feel like it's not impressive. Servicing everybody is a thankless role.[14]

Several disturbing implications emerge. First, although this mother makes clear that she quit her job in order to enable her husband to be an ideal worker, she believes she is "not bringing in money." She is bringing in money, of course, but she sees that money as "his"—as would most judges should she get divorced. Second, Wiggins clearly articulates the loss of status faced by professional women. Research documents that while businesswomen are seen as highly competent, housewives are lumped alongside the elderly, blind, "retarded," and disabled (to use the words tested by the researchers). Entire books have been written about this painful loss of status.[15]

Yet these painful moments are quickly subsumed into the traditionalist tale of women coming to love the homemaker role. An example: "Many women feel isolated and lonely when they first elect to stay home, because they are in transition between two lifestyles. They need a year of going through the seasons, getting a new rhythm to their lives. It's a temporary problem."[16] It could be, but that is not what Pamela Stone's study of highly educated opt-out women found. Study participants acknowledged that they often felt relief at escaping the hydraulic pressures of their former lives, but they also expressed real regrets. Stone concludes that many women remain profoundly ambivalent and wish they had been offered better choices. In a society where employment roles are the chief source of social status, it is little wonder that becoming "just a housewife" is associated with higher levels of depression. "When you give up a successful career to spend more time with your children, it is not just the nice clothes, the car and the holiday that have to go. It is your ego, too," said a former journalist.[17]

Press coverage typically centers squarely, and often exclusively, on women from the professional-managerial class (PMC), although the level of focus varies by region. Papers in the Northeast were the most likely to feature such women (46% of women mentioned in articles) and the least likely to feature pink-collar, blue-collar, or low-wage-worker women (40%). In the *New York Times*, over half (58%) of the women featured in opt-out stories were in high-status, historically masculine professional jobs, a figure that spiked up to 100% in the *Washington Times*. As noted above, only a tiny fraction—less than 4%—of American women hold such jobs. More than one-quarter (27%) of American women hold low-wage or blue-collar jobs, but only 2% of the women discussed in the *New York Times* opt-out articles were in these kinds of jobs. Papers in the South and West focused least on PMC women (30% and 29%, respectively) and, compared with other areas, were much more likely to focus on less affluent women (58% and 60%). Papers in the Midwest showed a similar pattern to papers in the Northeast, although they focused slightly more on less affluent women (46%) and slightly less on PMC women (43%).[18]

In addition, the mothers quoted in opt-out stories appear to be overwhelmingly white. Only 6 of the 119 articles, or 5%, mention any African-American women sourced. Latinas also are underrepresented. This is ironic given that Latina mothers are more likely than white mothers to be out of the labor force, as is shown in Figure 1. In fact, race and ethnicity

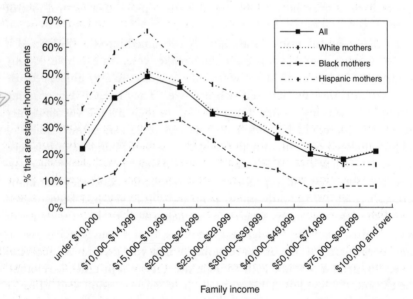

Figure 1. Stay-at-home mothers by race and family income, 2005. *Source:* United States Census Bureau, *Current Population Survey, 2005 Annual Social and Economic Supplement (Table FG8)*, available at http://www.census.gov/apsd/techdoc/cps/cpsmar05.pdf.

play an important role in who stays home full-time. Among married parents, black women have much higher employment levels than do whites; Latinas have much lower rates. These patterns may reflect that levels of work-family conflict differ by race and ethnicity: blacks feel less work-family conflict than whites, who in turn feel less than Latinas. This is the first instance of an important point that is stressed throughout this book: the experience of gender varies by race, or (to put the point more technically) gender is racialized. Focusing virtually exclusively on white women distorts the overall picture.[19]

If newspapers' focus on white women is confusing, so too is the focus on highly educated, affluent women. In fact, stay-at-home motherhood differs sharply, and increasingly, by class. Among married mothers, in 1977–1979, 55% of low-income mothers and 35% of nonpoor mothers stayed home full-time. Some thirty years later, the rate of stay-at-home motherhood had risen among poor mothers, from 55% to 60%, but fallen sharply among middle-income mothers, from 35% to 23%—and even more sharply among the PMC, from 35% to 20%. Class divergences are still more dramatic among single mothers: 27% of poor but only 4% of middle-income and 2% of PMC single mothers are out of the labor force.[20]

The accepted wisdom that highly educated women are the most likely to head home is just plain wrong. Education fuels employment—a strong and consistent finding the opt-out story ignores. Both in the United States and in Western Europe, the more highly educated a woman, the greater the chance she will be employed. In Generation X (b. 1966–1975) only 44% of all women but 55% of professional ones are employed full-time year round. The same pattern holds among slightly older women.[21]

In fact, the effect of a mother's educational level on her likelihood of remaining employed has actually increased in recent years. More highly educated mothers not only are more likely to remain in the labor force; they also average higher weekly work hours. Mothers with less than a high school education work an average of 21 hours per week, nearly 10 hours less than mothers with graduate degrees, who average 30 hours a week; mothers whose level of education falls between these two points average 27–28 hours a week.[22]

No mystery here: Better-educated women have more to lose by passing up employment. Being a waitress is not as attractive a career path as being a doctor. Women with more education have access to much better jobs and higher-quality child care than do less-educated women. College-educated women have flooded into high-paying, high-status, traditionally masculine careers, whereas female high-school dropouts are much more likely to be stuck in low-paid, dead-end, sex-segregated jobs. Figure 2

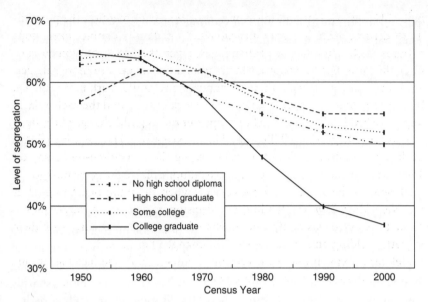

Figure 2. Occupational segregation by education. *Source:* D. A. Cotter, J. M. Hermensen, and R. Vanneman, *End of the Gender Revolution?* available at http://www .bsos.umd.edu/socy/vanneman/endofgr/ipumsoccsegeduc.html.

shows the dramatic occupational divide among women with different levels of education.

By failing to include women who work in nonprofessional jobs, working mothers of color, and those with lower levels of education, the press presents a highly misleading picture of work-family conflict.

One reason reporters keep writing and rewriting opt-out stories is because they continually interview women in one specific situation: shortly after they drop out of the workforce or, more rarely, before they enter it. For example, Louise Story's 2005 front-page *New York Times* article, "Many Women at Elite Colleges Set Career Path to Motherhood," reported that 60% of Yale women who responded to an e-mail survey expected to "opt out" and were largely unbothered that their Ivy League degrees would not mean a high-powered career. What Story's article failed to consider was that her interviewees were young—they had not yet begun either their careers or their families. What young people say they plan to do and what they actually end up doing are often quite different. In the United States, the reality is that nearly two-thirds (63%) of professional women stay in the labor force, with minimal time off, until retirement.[23]

Opt-out articles also preserve their upbeat tone by interviewing women only after they leave work and before any of them have divorced. Only 2 out of 119 articles featured stories of any divorced women. Although roughly half of U.S. marriages end in divorce, only 7 articles mention the possibility of divorce. This is highly misleading. Work-family conflict likely contributes to the dissolution of marriages, given that 58% of women consider the household division of labor unfair, and wives are more satisfied with their marriages when their husbands share family work more equally. If reporters interviewed women who left work only to find themselves later impoverished by divorce, the cheery opt-out tune would change abruptly.[24]

This tone change is well illustrated in an exception to the near invisibility of divorce in news stories of women leaving the workforce—an essay by Terry Martin Hekker. Hekker made a minor splash thirty years ago, at the height of the women's lib movement, when she published an op-ed in the *New York Times* defending her decision to become a stay-at-home mom. By 2006, devastated by her husband's request for a divorce—on their fortieth wedding anniversary—she had changed her view.[25]

Hekker is explicit about the economic vulnerability she faced as an unemployed, divorced mother in late middle age:

> "Divorced" doesn't begin to describe the pain of the process. "Canceled" is more like it. It began with my credit cards, then my health insurance and checkbook, until, finally, like a postage stamp, I felt canceled, too . . . He got to take his girlfriend to Cancun, while I got to sell my engagement ring to pay the roofer. When I filed my first nonjoint tax return, it triggered the shocking notification that I had become eligible for food stamps.

Divorced women in the United States are five times more likely to live in poverty during retirement than married women. Average alimony settlements are low; typically they last for only two to five years. When awarding Hekker temporary alimony, the judge suggested that "[she] go for job training when [she] turned 67."[26]

What happened to Hekker is absolutely standard, documented again and again in reports written by task forces on gender bias in the courts. Yet these harsh facts of life rarely rupture the rosy glow of the opt-out narrative. "Modern marriage demands greater self-sufficiency," Hekker concludes. This is another message young women are not getting. Newspapers are not telling it.[27]

A Return to Tradition?

Nearly two-thirds (64%) of the articles surveyed refer to a return to "traditional" gender roles. "Like their mothers, [women are] shifting to more traditional roles—investing in their husbands' careers rather than their own," notes well-known reporter and writer Sally Quinn (failing to note that these "investments" will be treated in divorce courts more like a gift). Claims of a return to traditionalism are supported by quotes from women who say they always knew they wanted to stay home after they had children.

- "I always knew I wanted to be a stay-at-home mom."
- Tammy Hughey said that she and her husband always knew she'd stay home when they had children. "You want them to have one parent home to give them some sense of values."
- Jennifer McNeeley, 29, refused to buy into the trend of balancing work and family. "I have always known I would stay home with my children, even before I met and married my husband . . . I want to be a part of my child's educational, social and emotional development."
- Kristin O'Hare-Blumberg's mother stayed at home with her, and although Kristin enjoyed working, she always assumed that she would do the same with her own children.

These women represent a minority. The press presents them as representative of women in general, and yet only 16% of the fifty-four women interviewed by sociologist Pamela Stone for her book *Opting Out?* said that they had always intended to stay home after they had children.[28]

Reporters frequently fail to explore the important ways in which mothering today differs from that of the past. The average time spent on child care has increased sharply for both fathers and mothers since 1985. Employed mothers spend 86% as much time with their children, and do 82% as much child care, as nonemployed moms. A 2000 study found that mothers without jobs spent only five hours a week more interacting with their children than mothers with jobs did. These are statistics rarely, if ever, found in the newspaper.[29]

The preeminent study of child rearing across classes, conducted by sociologist Annette Lareau, confirms that today's professional-managerial parents are not doing "traditional" parenting, but this does not mean that children are receiving less attention from their parents than they would have in past generations. Rather, the opposite is true; grandparents, notes Lareau, are "bewildered by their grandchildren's hectic schedules or organized activities . . . and awed by the intensive involvement of mothers in the children's schooling." Upper-middle-class mothers are doing something new. Lareau found that in working-class and low-wage families, the traditional pattern of child-created spontaneous play continues, but children in professional-managerial families now are steered toward adult-created activities. Parents in professional-managerial families "make a deliberate and sustained effort to stimulate children's development and to cultivate their cognitive and social skills," engaging in a child-rearing strategy Lareau calls "concerted cultivation." Children are guided toward "a valuable set of white-collar work skills, including how to set priorities, manage an itinerary, shake hands with strangers, and work on a team." Through concerted cultivation, professionals' children are "learning to labor."[30]

Mothers, whether employed or at home, do the great majority of this enrichment work. Employed mothers now spend as much time interacting with their children as did stay-at-home mothers in 1975. Fathers, as a group, spend about a third to a half the time mothers spend on children's enrichment activities (and even less on achievement-related activities).[31]

That this imbalance goes virtually unquestioned—by mothers as well as by others—is a tribute to the deeply entrenched belief in separate spheres. This is a way of thinking about men and women that emerged with the rise of the middle class in the nineteenth century. Its central tenet is that it is natural for women to take sole responsibility for hearth and home and equally natural for men to eschew caregiving in favor of employment. I once described separate spheres as the allocation of selflessness to mothers and self-interest to others. Under this paradigm, mothers selflessly devote themselves to home sweet home, while men pursue their self-interest in the rough and tumble of the marketplace.[32]

The opt-out narrative perpetuates separate spheres through its description of women as selfless: "It's about when you have a child, your life changes. Your need to be with your child is stronger than your desire to advance up the corporate ladder," said one women. Or, as Belkin's piece asserts, women don't succeed because they don't want to. In the nineteenth-century version of separate spheres, women's selflessness extended to their duty and desire to serve their husbands. The central rationale for homemaking shifted in the mid-twentieth century, placing children firmly at the center and the husband at the periphery. In the late twentieth century, this centering of children led to a ratcheting up of expectations—what Sharon Hays terms "intensive mothering." This new approach to child rearing, which she describes as "child centered, expert-guided, emotionally absorbing, labor intensive, and financially expensive," sets ideals of mother service so high even upper-middle-class homemakers have trouble living up to them. Intensive mothering is utterly outside the realm of possibility for less-affluent families. Nevertheless, it is widely touted as the cultural standard to which all mothers should aspire.[33]

A key aspect of intensive mothering is the intense performance pressure placed on both mothers and children: "Moms are graded by which toddlers share toys in the sandbox and who's on the honor roll. Once upon a time, adults waited until children were grown before judging how they turned out. Now they must trace a perfect trajectory of success at every age to reflect well on their parents and their employment choices," writer Ellyn Spragins pointed out in a column in the *New York Times*.

The best-known critique of intensive mothering is Judith Warner's 2006 book, *Perfect Madness: Motherhood in the Age of Anxiety*, which depicts anxious mothers who spend their days driving overscheduled kids to a steady stream of enrichment activities and working themselves into a frenzy to "be there" for their children. Child therapists have weighed in, too, as in Alvin Rosenfeld and Nicole Wise's *The Over-Scheduled Child: Avoiding the Hyper-Parenting Trap* and William Crain's *Reclaiming Childhood: Letting Children Be Children in Our Achievement-Oriented Society*. So have college counselors, pleading with parents not to overload high-school kids and convey their anxiety that their children will not get into the "right" college. Most telling is a 2009 study by two economists, Garey Ramey and Valerie A. Ramey, which contrasts the situation in Canada and the United States. Ramey and Ramey point out that the increase in time spent on child care—far from reflecting long-standing tradition—began only in the mid-1990s. That increase is twice as great among college-educated parents and is concentrated on coordinating and transporting older children to their various activities. During the same period, Canadians increased the time spent in child care very little, a difference the Rameys attribute to the very steep prestige hierarchy among American universities, which is not present in Canada. Professional-managerial families, they suggest, dedicate more time to building up their children's "after school resumés" to ensure their future in a "winner take all" economy.[34] Could it be that the drive toward ever-greater "enrichment," from baby Mozart to travel sports teams to the frenzy of extracurricular activities, stems not from children's needs but from parents' anxieties?[35]

Such critiques abound but are largely absent from newspapers. The daily press still presents concerted cultivation as the "traditional," the best, the only way to raise children.

Opt-Out Economics

Only 11% of the articles analyzed (13 of 119) discuss the long-term economic consequences of opting out. In fact, over one-third (36.8%) of the articles explicitly embrace the view that women are being realistic when they conclude that they cannot "have it all." For example, one article quoted demographer William Frey of the Brookings Institution: "Boomer moms, now generally in their 40s and 50s, 'blazed a trail, but sometimes they could not live up to their expectations of having it all. Generation X moms are more realistic.' " Another article reiterates this message, quoting a Yale professor's comment that compared women's expectations today with those of earlier cohorts of feminists, "The women today are, in effect, turning realistic."[36]

In fact, much of the coverage is supremely unrealistic about women's chances of returning to the kind of jobs they left. Mothers who have opted out are often quoted making blithe assertions such as "The skills I use in my job will not leave me. They will always be there," and "My degree is my insurance policy." Hearsay is presented again and again as indisputable truth: "People are afraid that once you get off the career track, there's no getting back on. But I know women who have returned to work after taking years off to be with their families." Few of the articles in the survey discussed the difficulty of returning to one's career, and 27% downplayed the difficulties mothers face in picking up where they left off. Other articles acknowledge the difficulties of reentry only to return immediately to the opt-out narrative. An example: an article that quotes one woman as saying "It is something that scares me. When I go to re-enter the work force, what kind of a blemish will this be on my resume?" quickly abandons this theme and ends with a reassuring quote: "I can always come back to this struggle, this [workplace] war, when my kids are older."[37]

Statistics paint a bleaker picture. One study found that women who took just one year out of the workforce sacrificed 20% of their lifetime earnings. Women who took two or three years earned 30% less. Another study found that leaving the workforce has a significant negative effect on women's wages even twenty years after a career interruption. These statistics dramatize the grim fact that women who take a career break are penalized out of proportion to any objective deterioration of their skills. Unfair as this situation is, women ought to know about these statistics— which the press does not cover.[38]

Recent studies report that many women find it much harder to reenter than they anticipated. "Many talented, committed women take off-ramps, but an overwhelming majority can't wait to get back in," notes Sylvia Ann Hewlett, director of the Center for Work-Life Policy. According to a study by that Center, of the 93% of women who want to return to work after taking time off to raise a family, only 74% succeed, and only 40% return to full-time, mainstream jobs. Despite the fact that the highly trained women in the survey averaged only one to two years off work, they lost an average of 18% in lifetime wages. Those taking off two to three years lost 37%.[39]

Another recent survey of 130 highly qualified women who had spent at least two years away from work confirms that reentry is difficult. While 70% of those surveyed reported feeling positive about their decisions to leave the labor force, 50% felt "frustrated" when they tried to return to work, and 18% became "depressed." One particularly disheartened respondent said she was thinking of taking her MBA off her resume. Said another, "Be prepared for the realization that in the business world your stepping-out time counts for less than zero. Be prepared that your stepping-out time may make potential employers think you are not as reliable as other applicants." In addition, 61% of respondents changed industries and 54% changed functional roles upon their return; only one in five found jobs in larger companies. "Companies have work-life policies, but a woman with an MBA who is out for five years, she's greeted in the workplace as if she's not that interesting, she hits a wall," explained one of the study's coauthors.[40]

Rather than acknowledging the severe economic penalties for taking time off work, many opt-out stories intimate that the key financial impact is on families' short-term inability to buy luxuries. A few of the torrent of examples:

- "We have had to tighten our belts a bit. We don't go out all the time. I used to be a shop-a-holic. Now I wear jeans and T-shirts."
- "Typically, giving up a second salary means also giving up first-class vacations, newer and fancier cars, household help, entertainment, and eating out. But most women who have done it say it's a small price to pay to stay home with their children."
- "Right now, we only have one car, and I know there are sacrifices to be made, but I also know it's better to stay home than to have another car."
- "Gone: the babysitter, the cleaning lady, the dry cleaner, summer camp for the 6-year-old, expensive vacations, the chi-chi hairdresser, the shopping sprees."[41]

Not one of the 119 articles surveyed linked mothers' opting out to women's economic vulnerability. Over their prime earning years, women earn only 38% of the wages of men. Mothers earn only 67 cents for every dollar earned by fathers. Not one news article noted that two out of three of the elderly poor are women or that only 32% of retired women have pensions (compared with 55% of men). Or that women's average pension benefit is half that of men's, and the husband's private pension is not left to his wife upon his death in 41% of couples. What economists call the "child penalty" has very real consequences. Women who leave the workforce are particularly vulnerable to poverty, relative or absolute.[42]

Push Factors and Pull Factors

While many articles mention workplace forces that push women out, only 6% of the articles surveyed made this their focus. In nearly three-quarters (73%) of the news stories analyzed, the overall tone was one of pulls rather than pushes. Yet a 2004 study suggests that pushes play a more important role than pulls in most mothers' decisions to leave the workforce. In fact, nine out of ten women in the study cited work-related reasons for their decisions to quit. Reporters need to start writing not only about family pulls but also about the workplace pushes that drive women out of good jobs they want to keep.[43]

Reporters' preference for interviewing women who have recently left their jobs guarantees a chorus asserting that opting out has turned out well. Why would one opt out for the good of the family, only to threaten the family dynamic by publicly expressing resentment that your husband helped so little at home that you had no choice but to quit?

If reporters took the time to talk with mothers who have not left their jobs, they would find a very different set of stories. The story of Julia Panley-Pagetti, for example, would require a substantial revision of the normal opt-out narrative. A mother who sought, unsuccessfully, to stay employed, Panley-Pagetti was earning a salary close to six figures before she got pregnant. She had earned three promotions and four raises in her four years and was known as the favorite employee.

> I waited to get pregnant until I was 34 years old, until my career was on track, until my income was in place, so that I had the resources to support a child . . . [When I got pregnant], I went from being the right-hand person to my boss, a very close relationship where sometimes I'd get 10 calls a day on matters of the highest priority, to not even being able to get my boss on the phone . . . I really felt it was because they didn't know how to deal with my pregnancy.

During her maternity leave, Panley-Pagetti received up to a dozen phone calls a day and into the night, as late as 11 P.M. "One of the heads of the company put it to me very plainly. He said, 'We need to know whether you're willing to give 100%, because if you're not, we will have to find a way to do it without you.'" Ultimately, Panley-Pagetti was fired, with economic consequences so dire that her family lost their house. This story was covered on CNN but not by newspapers.[44]

Workplace discrimination plays a major role in many mothers' decisions to leave the labor force. Reporters who interview women only after they have left their jobs do not pick up on this. Talking with working mothers who are trying to stay employed, in contrast, quickly reveals the "maternal wall"—the negative stereotyping and gender bias that mothers experience on the job, often beginning as soon as they become pregnant.[45] Some examples:

- "I mean, there were 2 or 3 names [of women] in the hat, and they said, 'I don't want to talk about her because she has children who are still home in these [evening] hours.' Now they don't pose that thing about men on the list, many of whom also have children in that age group."[46]
- "Elena Robinson said she believes discrimination against women and mothers certainly played a role in her getting laid off. 'After a while, women are asking: if you don't have to do it, why bother? Why should I continue to go to work and fight this battle?'"[47]
- "Even now, I have several women who say to me, 'My boss does not believe I am coming back.' 'They are changing my responsibilities where I'm working, taking the responsibilities away.' 'They're preparing to do without me, to replace me.'"[48]

The trope of separate spheres is the rebar that keeps the maternal wall strong. If women are by nature caregivers, then naturally their priorities shift away from work as soon as they get pregnant or have children, so firing them does no harm. Women themselves beg to differ. Said Ann Nolan, a former lawyer who was fired while pregnant with her second child and then fired again while pregnant with her third child:

> I call the FMLA the "Firstborn . . . Medical Leave Act" because after the first you may be working part-time or for a small employer and so the FMLA doesn't cover you. When I told people what had happened, their comment was often, "Well, at least you get to be home with your baby."[49]

In fact, Nolan did not stay home after she was fired. In order to keep her older child's spot at the day care center, she took temping work to cover child care fees while she searched for a new job. "I didn't opt out," she concludes, "I was fired . . . We really need to stop describing women who've been fired as 'opting out'—it makes us invisible."

Social scientists have now documented that workplace bias against mothers is the strongest form of gender bias in today's workplace. The leading studies find that when asked to rank identical resumes with just one difference—one but not the other listed membership in the Parent-Teacher Association—mothers were 79% less likely to be hired, 100% less likely to be promoted, offered $11,000 less in salary, and held to higher performance and punctuality standards than non-mothers.[50]

Mothers are not amused. In fact, they are increasingly likely to sue when they encounter discrimination. In a 2010 report, the Center for WorkLife Law documented a 400% increase in lawsuits involving family responsibilities discrimination (FRD) in the past decade. WorkLife Law has documented over 2,100 FRD cases, showing how mothers and other caregivers often are pushed out of jobs they want—and need.[51]

Shireen Walsh is one of these women. A top salesperson with outstanding reviews, she found the atmosphere at work changed dramatically when she returned from maternity leave. When she showed coworkers her baby pictures, she was told to stop distracting others from their work. Other employees were allowed to go to a crafts fair, but she was told to stay behind to make up for having "inconvenienced" her coworkers by taking maternity leave. Her hours, but no one else's, were closely scrutinized. When Walsh had to leave to take her son, who had persistent ear infections, to the doctor, she was required to sign in and out and to make up every minute of work she missed, despite a policy allowing for unlimited sick leave. Finally, her supervisor allegedly threw a phone book at her, telling her to find a pediatrician open after business hours. When Walsh fainted from the stress of mistreatment, the supervisor remarked, "You better not be pregnant again." The court found that Walsh faced a hostile work environment as well as discrimination based on sex and her potential to become pregnant. A federal court upheld a jury verdict of $625,000.[52]

The 2005 case *Washington v. Illinois Department of Revenue* began when a female manager complained of race discrimination. For years Chrissie Washington had worked a flex schedule, from 7 A.M. to 3 P.M., so that she could get home to care for her son, who had Down's syndrome. In retaliation for her race discrimination complaint, her employer allegedly took away her flex schedule and insisted she work from 9 to 5. The 7th Circuit held that making her work 9 to 5 instead of 7 to 3 amounted to an adverse employment action that could sustain a claim of retaliation. The U.S. Supreme Court agreed, adopting the same standard in a later case: "Context matters . . . A schedule change in an employee's work schedule may make little difference to many workers, but may matter enormously to a young mother with school age children."[53] *Washington v. Illinois* is particularly important because it established that although women may not be entitled to flexible work arrangements or telecommuting, they have the right not to have such arrangements taken away in retaliation for trying to exercise their legal rights.

Even when opt-out stories acknowledge factors that push women out of good jobs, such as workplace inflexibility, the headlines often preserve the well-entrenched opt-out story line. A few examples:

- "Most of the mothers of the Bow Road group, frankly, do not want to be home full time. They want to work, part time." (Headline: "Career Moms; They've Just Said No to Juggling Job and Family")
- "Brundage ... felt forced to quit. She and her husband, also a mail carrier, would have happily shared a job, but the postal service wouldn't allow it." (Headline: "Women Change Paths; More Choose to Stay Home with Children")
- "When other lawyers in her firm ruled out a part-time arrangement, she gave up a lucrative partnership to stay home." (Headline: "Sometimes a Career Must Be Put Aside; The New Parents")[54]

Only 2 out of 119 headlines hint that many women would prefer to work but are pushed out of jobs they want by employer inflexibility.

Many mothers are not rejecting work; they are rejecting the all-or-nothing workplace. Evidence is not hard to find: it is right there in Belkin's original article that started the opt-out craze. One of the mothers Belkin features is Sally Sears, a former TV anchorwoman in her late forties. Belkin tells us that Sears took nine years to quit and that "she did so with great regret." "'I would have hung in there, except the days kept getting longer and longer,' [Sears] explains. 'My five-day 50-hour week was becoming a 60-hour week.'" Even then, instead of quitting outright she tried to negotiate a part-time schedule, presumably so she could work something closer to a traditional full-time schedule of forty hours a week. The station refused: "They said it was all or nothing." Only then did she leave. As it happened, the same all-or-nothing employer to whom it was unthinkable to allow Sears to remain in her job on a part-time basis later offered her part-time work—but on a contingent basis, presumably at a rate far below her original six-figure salary, and without benefits. The tragic outcome of Sears's story is that, despite her talents, she ended up with a bad job (low pay, no benefits or advancement) instead of a good one.[55]

Many professional-managerial women, like Sears, have a wild and wooly dream: a forty-hour week. "They just want to have both a family life and a business life," explained Penni Naufus, director of the Women's Business Center in New Jersey. One woman who left a corporate job in favor of freelance work noted that her guiding principle was, "I like to be with my family for dinner"—a goal the forty-hour-a-week Company Man of the 1950s could readily attain.[56] What many professional women want is not to opt out but to work the traditional full-time (forty-hour) workweek.

Among Generation X professional women, only 15% work fifty or more hours a week. Highly trained mothers are 59% less likely to work fifty-plus hours a week than are their colleagues without children. Indeed, only 5% of mothers aged 25 to 44 work fifty or more hours a week. Astonishingly, the only exception is single mothers: roughly one in three (32%) professional-managerial single mothers work fifty or more hours a week.[57]

The all-or-nothing workplace affects women not only by shaping their own work schedules but also by shaping those of their husbands. Today, nearly 40% of professional-managerial men work fifty or more hours a week, in contrast to 23% of middle-income men and 9% of low-income ones.[58] "The time squeeze created by spending more hours at paid work is . . . not universal, but rather is concentrated among professionals and managers," note sociologists Jerry Jacobs and Kathleen Gerson. One sample of largely upper-middle-class families found that nearly 60% of the men worked forty-five hours a week or more. Factoring in commute time, this meant the men were away from home at least ten hours a day.[59]

When men's work hours spiral up, their household contributions spiral down, increasing the pressure on their wives to cut back or quit. The "tipping point" for many women is their husbands' unavailability, which Pamela Stone concluded is "much more a function of their husbands' jobs than it was of their values or preference for at-home wives and mothers."[60] Having a husband who works more than fifty hours a week increases the odds of a woman quitting her job by 44%. Having a husband who works more than sixty hours a week increases her odds of quitting by 112%. Stone reports that nearly two-thirds (60%) of the professional-managerial women she interviewed cited their husbands as a key reason for their decision to leave the workforce. Even in dual-career families where the wife remains employed, "men's success at work comes at the cost of not their own family success but of their wives' work success," conclude Phyllis Moen, Ronit Waismel-Manor, and Stephen Sweet.[61]

In other words, today's all-or-nothing workplaces pressure professionals toward neotraditional families, in which the husband has a high-prestige, long-hours job and the wife "opts out." Nearly 40% of dual-career professionals follow this pattern, and both parents in such families typically report feeling lower levels of satisfaction with family life. Anecdotal evidence suggests that mothers in these families often feel like single parents, while fathers feel distant from family life. This theme is rarely pursued.[62]

Many opt-out articles reflect the *Goodnight Moon* syndrome. Reread that well-known children's book and you will notice a curious absence of men. Many newspaper articles un-self-consciously reproduce the separate spheres assumption that caring for children is women's work. Among the articles analyzed, there were 315 mentions of mothers but only 25 of fathers. In nearly two-thirds (64%) of the articles surveyed, the husband's role is described chiefly as a breadwinner whose income enables the wife to stay home. That men's careers should take precedence over family life is treated as uncontroversial common sense. As one mother put it, explaining why she left her high-level job, "[My husband and I] were both working these killer jobs. And I kept saying, we need to reconfigure this. And what I realized was, he wasn't going to." This sounds like male privilege, not unfettered choice.[63]

In fact, husbands were a key influence on two-thirds of women's decisions to quit, according to Stone. Women whose husbands work long hours are 40% more likely than other women to quit. When husbands become sole earners, wives do three times as much housework as their husbands, up from a 2:1 ratio among two-job couples.[64] While the women quoted by reporters almost unanimously described their husbands as supportive, they also reported that their husbands had refused to alter their own work schedules or to do half the work at home. One woman expressed this explicitly: "He has always said to me, 'You can do whatever you want to do.' But he's not there to pick up any load."[65]

Husbands' refusal to "pick up any load" is an important driver of women's decisions to opt out. Why do men refuse? Male privilege is a common explanation and a true one, to a point. But we need to go further: men not only have the right to perform as ideal workers, they have a duty to do so. Americans overwhelmingly expect men to be providers. According to a 1997 study by Jean L. Potuchek, "both men and women attach different meanings to the employment of wives than to the employment of husbands. Eighty-three percent of American women and an even higher percentage of childrearing mothers felt their husbands should be the primary providers." Americans see being a good provider as an integral part of being a good father, according to another study; in other words, gender pressures on men to be good fathers propel them away from home, toward work. Some men also see long hours as an expression of virility. "The office was really dominated by these young macho guys who wanted to be hotshot litigators . . . [Flexibility] just wasn't in their realm of reality," said one woman lawyer. Workplaces are key sites for "doing gender."[66]

Workplaces also are key sites for "doing class." Upper-middle-class men "often view ambition, dynamism, a strong work ethic, and competitiveness as doubly sacred because they signal both moral and socioeconomic worth," according to Michèle Lamont. High-status historically male jobs demand nothing less than devotion. Mary Blair-Loy, in her study of bankers, found that high-level professionals are expected "to demonstrate commitment by making work the central focus of their lives." This requires a "manifest singular 'devotion to work,' unencumbered with family responsibilities."[67] This is a remarkable expression of how separate spheres, today, etches the breadwinner role into men's very souls.

In other words, although work-family conflict traditionally is associated with women, a prime mover of work-family conflict is masculinity. Inflexible workplaces have proved so hard to change, in significant part, because of the intertwining of masculinity with work schedules and current understandings of work commitment. Although newspapers do not discuss this, at least they are increasingly likely to mention that women leave their jobs as a result of workplace inflexibility or long hours. News stories written between 2000 and 2006 were more likely than stories written earlier to mention instances in which women left work only after being refused flexibility or part-time work. This theme appeared only three times in each half of the 1990s but in eleven articles published between 2001 and 2005.

Our Family-Hostile Public Policy

American mothers have few good choices not only because of employment discrimination and the all-or-nothing workplace but also because the United States lacks the kinds of family supports available in many other industrialized countries. One reason for this policy failure lies in the perception in the United States that women's labor participation is a personal matter rather than a major economic issue, as reflected by the fact that newspapers tend to report many of the stories surveyed in the lifestyles section. I am reminded of a major military official who, in my youth, referred to women as "little bits of fluff." I am relieved to say that when I Googled that phrase today I got blogs about kittens and knitting.

And yet the "bits of fluff" theory lives on in newspaper coverage of women's employment. No major paper would cover unemployment by having a reporter interview a handful of well-heeled acquaintances and muse on a personal period of unemployment. The idea is ludicrous; unemployment is a serious economic issue—except, it turns out, unemployment among women.

This does not make economic sense. The wage contributions of employed women in the United States are substantial and growing. Women now compose 50% of the U.S. workforce. On average, women bring home 28% of the family income. And yet the unstated assumption in opt-out articles is that women's economic lives are too trivial for the ordinary rules of journalism to apply. Anecdotes and breezy imprecision stand in for hard data. Jack Shafer's critique in *Slate* of Louise Story's 2005 *New York Times* article about Yale undergraduates' plans to opt out zeroed in on this problem. Shafer pointed out that the piece used the word "many" twelve times (e.g., "many women at the nation's most elite colleges say they have already decided that they will put aside their careers in favor of raising children"). "You could as easily substitute the word *some* for every *many*," he noted, "and not gain or lose any information. Or substitute the word *few* and lose only the wind in Story's sails. By fudging the available facts with weasel-words, Story cooks up a trend with no significant evidence." Fuzzy journalism has serious consequences. One conscientious reporter described "trend stories built on such flimsy social science [as] demoralizing, even dangerous," and went on to quote journalism professor Caryl Rivers: "These stories seep into the culture." The opt-out story certainly has.[68]

Only 12% (14 of 119) of the articles analyzed discuss the negative impact on the economy of this loss of talent, despite the fact that over a quarter (25.5%) of the articles reviewed mention one or more women who have taken a lower-status or lower-wage job because of work-family conflict. A 2006 article on mothers' employment in the *Economist* magazine is a rare example of a story that takes seriously the macroeconomic impact of this loss of skilled workers. The *Economist*, far from treating women's employment as fluff, starts from the premise that women's underemployment is an important economic issue: "despite their gains, women remain the world's most under-utilized resource." Given that "many are still excluded from paid work; many do not make best use of their skills . . . Greater participation by women in the labour market could help to offset the effects of an ageing, shrinking population and hence support growth."[69]

The *Economist,* hardly a leftist rag, takes the natural next step to examine how public policy can support mothers' workforce participation: "To make full use of their national pools of female talent, governments need to remove obstacles that make it hard for women to combine work with having children." What is needed are policies such as "parental leave and child care, allowing more flexible working hours, and reforming tax and social-security systems that create disincentives for women to work."[70]

Virtually no opt-out articles highlight the role of public policy in creating the often-unappealing choices available to American women. That needs to change. A good place to start is with in-depth coverage of the five basic elements for work-family reconciliation: short-term leaves; good, affordable child care; regulation of work hours; universal health coverage; and a tax system that does not penalize dual-earner families.

Short-Term Leaves

Other than the United States, the only countries in the world that lack paid maternity leave are Lesotho, Papua New Guinea, and Swaziland. The only federally legislated leave available to U.S. parents, provided under the Family and Medical Leave Act, is unpaid and does not cover roughly 40% of the American workforce.[71]

In Europe, the situation is different, as illustrated in Janet Gornick and Marcia Meyers's classic study of work-family policies in twelve industrialized countries. There paid leaves are financed through social insurance, which leaves European employers more competitive than U.S. employers, for two reasons. First, European businesses do not have to pay the steep 30% "benefits load"—the cost of a benefits package as a percentage of a worker's salary—that many U.S. businesses pay. Second, because European employers are not responsible for covering the cost of paid leave themselves, they can afford to replace the worker on leave. In contrast, when U.S. employers pay the wages of workers on leave, often they simply heap leave-takers' responsibilities onto their remaining workers, with no compensating increase in pay. This practice fuels workplace resentment.[72]

All European countries offer paid leave for family reasons, such as to care for a sick child. Gornick and Meyers found that in 2000, the paid maternity leave ranged from five to forty-two weeks; the United States was an outlier, offering zero weeks of paid leave. In addition to maternity leave, the European Union requires members to provide a minimum of three months of (paid or unpaid) leave for either parent's use. In the Nordic countries, most employed parents have between one and three years of paid leave, financed through social insurance. They receive roughly two-thirds of their wages while on leave, with wages of high earners subject to caps. This leave policy is structured to give families many choices about how to reconcile work and family life. In Denmark and Sweden, parents can take leave in increments until their child is eight years old. Norway and Sweden also allow parents to combine leave with part-time work. Finland and Norway allow parents to use some of their leave benefits to pay for alternative child care.[73]

Some American states, notably California, offer intriguing leave models, including the right of individuals to use up to half of their accrued sick leave per year to care for an ill child, parent, spouse, or domestic partner. Adequate leave eliminates one force that drives women out. "The worst thing in the world was waking up in the morning and having a sick child. My husband and I would look at each other and ask, 'Who's going to stay home?'" said one mom, explaining her decision to stay home full-time. California law also gives workers forty hours a year of unpaid leave to take part in activities at their children's schools. In addition, California provides a paid family leave insurance program—one of the few in the United States—that gives most workers six weeks of partial pay during unpaid leave to care for a newborn, a newly adopted child, or an ill child, parent, spouse, or domestic partner.[74]

Providing workers with more leave options would help employers keep skilled, experienced employees on the job. Gornick and Meyers's research findings leave little doubt about the importance of parental leave policies: "The evidence is clear that paid leave of several months' to about a year's duration strengthen women's labor market attachment." This holds true for fathers as well as for mothers; one reason American women take such long leaves is that American men take so little. "The fact that I could take the new six-week paid leave made it a lot easier for my wife to go back to work full time," said Stephen Brand, a professor, after his employer, the University of Rhode Island, implemented a new policy that gave six weeks of paid parental leave.[75] The most effective way to ensure that men have cultural permission to take parental leave is to make it paid and to stipulate that some portion of leave ("daddy days") must be taken by the father rather than the mother. When Norway instituted daddy days, men's use of leave rose from less than 5% to more than 70%.[76]

High-Quality, Affordable Paid Care, Including After-School Programs

Since the 1970s, surveys have reported that mothers, particularly poor ones, do not seek employment, or work fewer hours than they would prefer, due to lack of adequate and affordable nonfamily child care. Clearly, child care plays a central role in driving women into economic vulnerability.[77] That is why many other industrialized countries have been so attentive to creating a system to provide families with good options for nonfamily care.

Contrary to popular belief, adequate care for children does not require a system of vast, impersonal child care centers. Centers in countries where they are common typically are small and neighborhood-based—think public library rather than public high school. And child care centers (typically for children aged three to five) are a small but important part of the overall system of nonfamily caregiving options. As in other industrialized countries, an effective system for the United States also would include universal preschool and after-school programs.

Georgia, Florida, and Oklahoma have state-financed universal prekindergarten for all four-year-olds, and West Virginia and New York have established timelines for implementing such programs. In Belgium and France, this kind of program is available for children beginning at age three or earlier, and there are signs of progress in the United States as well. Barack Obama has signaled an intention to launch a major push for early childhood education.[78]

Child care programs end when children enter school at age five or six, but children still get out of school long before parents get out of work. The gap between work schedules and school schedules has been estimated to average twenty to twenty-five hours a week; an estimated 39 million children between the ages of five and fourteen participate in no organized system of supervised activities after school, and many of them are at home alone. In the summer, the number of hours children spend home alone increases sharply, by an estimated six hours a week. Ideally, parents would have flexible hours, so that one parent (not necessarily the same one) could be home with the kids every day, but this ideal is as yet often unattainable. The alternative is after-school programs, which are severely underfunded in the United States. Currently, 6.5 million children in grades K through 12 participate in such programs—just 11% of all children in this age range. An additional 15 million children would be likely to participate if a quality program were available in their community.[79]

Gornick and Meyers report that in countries with adequate paid leave and high-quality part-time work, few infants are in child care. Many Scandinavian families are entitled to child care at birth or by the child's first birthday (even though their mothers tend to work only part-time). In other Western European countries, children are entitled to child care at slightly older ages, between thirty months and four years old. Parents bear only a portion of the costs, typically on a sliding scale. For example, in France, parents typically pay only 17%–25% of child care costs, with the remainder split between employers and the government.[80]

By comparison, all but a tiny percentage of the lowest-income U.S. families bear the full costs of child care. Low-income American families pay an average of 22% of their total household income for child care; middle-income families pay an average of 9%; high-income families pay an average of 6%. In Europe, low-income families pay a much smaller proportion of their income for child care (8%), while middle-income families pay a slightly smaller proportion (8%), and high-income families pay a slightly higher one (7%).[81]

European systems typically require high levels of training and a high quality of care, typically in neighborhood-based programs. Child care in the United States suffers both from lack of funding and lack of quality control. Staff turnover in some centers is in excess of 100% per year, due in significant part to very low staff salaries (between $13,125 and $18,988 annually). Observational studies of child care centers rate only about 15% as "good"; 50%–69% of unregulated family care (in the sitter's home) is rated as "inadequate." Care for children under three is rated even lower: 61% of all forms of care are rated as "poor" or "fair."[82] Strikingly, even among the relatively well-heeled demographic discussed in newspapers' opt-out stories, fully one in four women interviewed cited the lack of affordable, high-quality child care as one reason they left the workforce.[83]

Workplace "Flexibility"

Today's workplace is perfectly designed for the workforce of 1960, when only 10% of mothers worked and only 10% of couples divorced.[84] Then, it made sense for employers to shape jobs around the ideal of a breadwinner available for work anytime, anywhere, for as long as the employer needed him. And it made sense to design governmental benefits around the same breadwinner-homemaker model. Today 70% of American children live in households where all adults are employed, and over 40% of marriages end in divorce. One in four Americans—more every year—are caring for elders. Hospitals let patients out "quicker and sicker." Yet employers still enshrine as ideal the breadwinner who takes care of business while his wife takes care of family. For most Americans, that is not real life. The issue is less the need for individualized workplace flexibility than the need to match today's workplace to today's workforce.[85]

Most European countries began this process long ago. In most European countries, full-time hours are set below the forty-hour week that is standard in the United States, ranging from thirty-five to thirty-nine hours a week. An E.U. directive, which caps the workweek at forty-eight hours, sets the standard for all European countries except the United Kingdom. In sharp contrast, the United States has virtually no working time regulation. The only relevant statute, the Fair Labor Standards Act (FLSA), does not cap work hours; it only imposes a higher wage rate after a certain number of hours.[86]

In the Netherlands, Germany, and Sweden, workers also have the right to part-time work (with limited exceptions). Moreover, the wage penalty for part-time is much steeper in America than in Europe (21%). And, unlike the United States, European countries mandate minimum vacation time (typically four weeks). The lack of working time regulation in the United States makes for long working hours; poor-quality part-time jobs; and, for many workers, no paid vacation time. These conditions, in turn, can make work demands on family life seem unrelenting. Given the poor quality and relative unavailability of part-time jobs, many families see no alternative but to have one partner, typically the woman, sharply cut back or quit.[87]

Women will continue to be disadvantaged if employers persist in designing the most desirable jobs around someone available 24/7—in other words, a man with a stay-at-home wife. This does not mean that women need "special treatment" in the workplace. Framing the issue that way leaves intact the old-fashioned norm of the ideal worker and calls for different, remedial treatment for women. This approach is likely to fuel a backlash—if women need special treatment, they just can't "cut it" in the working world.

Nor does it make sense to talk about work-family conflict as mothers' need for accommodation, in language carried over from the disability rights context. Individualized workplace accommodations make sense for individuals with disabilities because there is simply no way to design a norm that offers equal access to individuals with disabilities, which range from the need for wheelchair access, to bipolar disorder, to bad backs or agoraphobia. Though individualized accommodations are the only answer in that context, the same is not true with respect to motherhood. Mothers' "disability" stems from separate spheres' insistence on enshrining as ideal breadwinners without serious, long-term commitment to family caregiving. What mothers and other caregivers need is not individual accommodations but a shift in the underlying masculine workplace norms. Mothers need the same thing everyone else needs, employers as well as employees— they need today's workplaces to be designed to reflect the realities of today's family life.[88]

Universal Health Coverage

The link between work-family conflict and lack of universal health care is not immediately obvious. But it is there. The United States is virtually alone among industrialized countries in its lack of universal health coverage. Moreover, because health insurance is delivered as a job benefit, U.S. employers' benefits packages are expensive: a good package typically costs 30% of wages. For employers of hourly workers, high benefits loads mean that it is often cheaper for an employer to require longer hours from fewer hourly workers and pay the time-and-a-half wages the FLSA requires than to hire a new employee, which would trigger costly additional health insurance and other benefits.

For different reasons, the lack of universal health coverage also fuels long hours for salaried professional workers. In a system where jobs with health insurance often require a fifty- or sixty-hour workweek, and where anything under that level of work commitment is classified as "part-time" without benefits, even couples who would prefer to work two thirty-five-hour jobs rather than one fifty-hour job and one twenty-hour job may not, since doing so would mean depriving the family of health insurance.

Tax Policy

Five of the opt-out articles analyzed mention that one factor in convincing mothers to stay home was that their wages would push the family into a higher tax bracket. "Let's say the first spouse makes $50,000 per year and the second spouse makes $20,000 per year. That second income then bumps you up into the higher tax bracket," said Bob Warwick of RSM McGladrey, Inc. He used the example of a couple filing joint returns that would jump from the 15% to the 27% tax bracket. This effect would be eliminated if the United States abolished joint tax returns, as have most other industrialized countries. The alternative is to require every adult to file an individual return.[89]

The United States lags so far behind most other industrialized countries—and many less-developed ones—in supports for working families for many reasons. Distorted press coverage, with its endless recycling of stories about professional women cheerfully embracing "traditional" roles, is one of them. However, it is important to understand that the media reflects our culture as well as creating it. The primary reason opt-out articles continue to be so popular is that people read them. They are reassuring in their upbeat tone and acceptance of the status quo; we read them because they tell us that we do not need to take the difficult steps toward positive change.

But we do. As a culture, we need to stop lying to ourselves, stop pretending that the "choices" thrust on us by outmoded norms are actually choices made of free will. We need to stop ignoring the fact that the available choices are dismally inadequate.

Happily, the press has taken some steps in shifting its coverage of work-family issues away from the opt-out framework. In 2007, the *New York Times Magazine* published an article by Eyal Press about family responsibilities discrimination, featuring a mother who was fired from her job after she had a baby: "I was like, 'Please, I *need* my job—I have a premature child,'" she protested. The article concluded, "The battle about 'family values' is no longer just about gay marriage and abortion: it's also about workplace attitudes that some advocates believe do significantly more to undermine family life than those controversial practices do."[90] (Full disclosure: I am cited as one of those advocates.) In 2008, another story—this time by Lisa Belkin—examined not women opting out but couples where both parents curtailed their careers in order to play equal roles in parenting. The piece highlighted the activities of Third Path, an organization dedicated to helping couples negotiate work and family roles to share family care.[91]

These are very tentative steps. We need more definitive ones. We need to encourage the press to introduce alternative story lines. Motherhood is the strongest trigger for gender bias in the workplace today, a theme reporters need to cover. The United States has the most family-hostile public policy in the industrialized world; no hope of improvement exists unless newspapers and other media start to cover this story. Finally, the underemployment of mothers needs to be covered as an economic issue. This approach presents two questions: first, whether it makes sense in a competitive global economy to continue to refuse to match today's workplace to today's workforce; second, whether it makes sense to sit on the sidelines while the nation loses a significant proportion of its human capital, which occurs when women find themselves pushed into de-skilled jobs after they have children.

CHAPTER TWO

One Sick Child Away from Being Fired

> I've done my fair share of agonizing in print about the implacable tensions between work and family, but I'm moved this Mother's Day to feel rather sheepish about such laments. The reason for my embarrassment is [the Center for WorkLife Law's Report] *One Sick Child Away from Being Fired: When Opting Out Is Not an Option.* With that stark title, the report punctures the entitled, self-referential perspective from which journalists tend to write about working mothers . . . Guilty as charged.
>
> —RUTH MARCUS, *WASHINGTON POST*

PROFESSIONAL-MANAGERIAL WOMEN are not the only Americans affected by work-family conflict. In fact, they are the lucky ones. They can afford high-quality child care and can outsource much of the house-keeping. Or they can afford to stay home to ensure high-quality care.[1]

Not so with less-affluent families, who often face steep hurdles in balancing work and family. Thus when an employer ordered some factory workers to work overtime, they had their babysitters drop off the children at the factory. When the managers confronted the women, the women said, "I would be put in prison and my children would be taken away from me if I leave them home alone—I cannot do that. You told me to stay, so they're going to come here."[2] This is just one example of the kinds of quandaries faced by nonprofessionals. A packer was fired when she left work in response to a call that her preschooler was in the emergency room with a head injury. A newspaper press operator, who was the mother of a one-year-old as well as the primary caregiver for her own mother, came to work late because she overslept after a night spent caring for both baby and mother. Although she called ahead, she was fired when she arrived twenty minutes late.[3]

For families dealing with a child's serious illness or chronic disease, Americans' lack of child care and social services, along with job inflexibility, creates a toxic mixture that threatens the jobs of fathers as well as mothers. Consider these cases: a divorced father with custody of an asthmatic son;

the father of a severely disabled son; the stepfather of a young man paralyzed as the result of a gunshot wound; a male train operator with a diabetic
son; a male rental car shuttle driver whose son had a serious heart condition; the father of a child who needed a ventilator in order to breathe; a
father of a child with special needs; and a janitor whose son had severe
mental and physical disabilities. All were disciplined or fired due to work-
family conflicts.[4]

Twenty percent of American families are caring for a child with special
needs; 30% of these caregivers either reduce their hours or end up without
work as a result of their conflicting responsibilities. When family crises
strike, these families do not have the resources to hire help or seek out professional care for ill or troubled family members. Offering a window on
this problem are the phone company workers fired for monitoring their
own home telephones, worried over drug-dealing teenagers, family members who have threatened suicide, asthmatic children home alone, or elders
endangered by dementia and living in violent neighborhoods. These cases
reveal the lack of an important right that professional employees take
for granted: the chance to make a personal phone call at work. Especially
in the summer, when one in ten children aged six to twelve is home alone
or in the company of a sibling under thirteen, all working parents need to
be able to make a call home.[5]

The Center for WorkLife Law studied ninety-nine union arbitrations to
examine the problems working-class parents face as they try to juggle the
competing demands of their jobs and their family responsibilities. The
cases offer a unique glimpse of how these two sets of responsibilities clash
in the lives of men as well as women—bus drivers, telephone workers,
construction linemen, carpenters, welders, and others. Also represented
are nurses' aides and janitors, whose low-wage jobs place them among
the working poor. The grievants all faced a similar and deeply troubling
dilemma: their efforts to meet crucial family responsibilities jeopardized
the jobs that were essential for supporting their families. These workers
had far more protection than the average Joe: they were unionized, and
their unions chose to challenge (or "grieve") their discipline. The scenario
for the 87.6% of American workers who are not unionized is quite different. In nonunionized workplaces, employees typically have fewer rights
and fewer protections.[6]

The stories that unfold represent ripples on the surface of a deeper
struggle. This face of work-family conflict in the United States is unknown
to many professionals. It is not captured in uplifting stories of professional
mothers who "discover their inner housewife." Nor has it been a cause célè-
bre for unions. Here are important messages both for the press—which

should start covering how workplace-workforce mismatch differs across class—and for unions. Unions have mandates to serve their members, to organize more workers into unions, and to affect the political process in ways that benefit workers. Addressing workplace-workforce mismatch has powerful potential for helping achieve all three goals. Union women have long argued that work-family issues are useful in organizing women, but the fact is that work-family issues are also of pressing concern to many unionized men.[7] Unions need a new message of manly solidarity: "Just because the boss gives me a job doesn't mean he can forbid me from putting family first." "Providing," for most working-class men today, requires them to provide care as well as cash.

Stories of work-family conflict among the working class have the potential to change the national debate. This potential cuts across party lines; the Department of Labor under George W. Bush found the Center for WorkLife Law's *One Sick Child* report useful in the controversy over whether to eliminate workers' right to take federal Family and Medical Leave Act (FMLA) leave in short periods (e.g., taking time off twice a week for kidney dialysis or taking off a week three times a year to care for a child hospitalized for a serious, chronic condition). The report buttressed the position of those who were arguing that the reason workers take intermittent FMLA leave is that they urgently need it—not because they are "gaming the system," as some economists were arguing. *One Sick Child* also has played a role in the current campaign to gain a minimum number of paid sick days for American workers. Publicizing the acute work-family conflicts faced by workers is essential; helping workers to address these conflicts should be seen as a core part of the union movement—not a frill. After all, no amount of wages or benefits helps a worker who was fired for putting family first.

The New Face of Work-Family Conflict

Working-class Americans typically lack the kind of flexibility those in professional and managerial jobs take for granted.

Upper-middle-class workers can take time off to attend a child's school event, are permitted to use the telephone or even leave work to check on a sick child, and often can arrange their work day to enable them to take a family member to the doctor. Things are different for blue- and pink-collar workers. They are closely supervised. Typically they must "punch in" and adhere to rigid schedules. Arriving late or leaving work even a few minutes early may lead to dismissal. Personal business often is prohibited except during lunch and designated breaks. One study found that one-third of working-class employees—men as well as women—cannot decide when to take breaks, nearly 60% cannot choose starting or quitting times, and 53% cannot take time off to care for sick children.[8]

Nearly three-quarters of employed adults say they have little or no control over their work schedules. In addition, among the working class, 87% of families have two weeks or less of vacation and sick leave *combined*. Nearly 70% of working-class parents report having paid time off for family emergencies, but only about 34% of fathers and 39% of mothers report actually using the leave. "It's hard to get a day off," one working mother explained. "If you want a day off you put a request slip in and nine times out of 10 it gets denied because of short staff." Because only 10% of all employed mothers have paid maternity leave (apart from their sick and vacation time), they are vulnerable to discipline or dismissal if emergencies arise that require them to take additional time off.[9]

Workplace inflexibility has a particularly harsh impact on American families with children. Despite the oft-repeated idea that only rich women can afford to work part-time, many working-class women work reduced hours. One qualitative study found that in two-thirds of two-job working-class families, wives typically worked shorter hours for pay than husbands did. But, as noted earlier, American workers pay dearly for taking part-time work—the wage penalty for part-time work is a whopping 21% per hour worked. Nevertheless, one recent survey found higher demand for part-time work among U.S. hourly workers than among professionals. Given the trade-off between hours and income, this indicates the desperate hunger for family time. Fully 95% of women and 90% of men in the United States wish they had more time with family.[10]

Inflexible schedules work in combination with what are known as "no-fault" progressive discipline systems. Under these systems, workers accumulate points for absenteeism—regardless of the cause—unless the situation is specifically covered by work rules or union contract. A worker who garners a particular number of points is first disciplined and then fired, regardless of the reasons for the accrued absences. Some of the workers in the arbitrations discussed in this chapter had excellent attendance records, while many others struggled with child care, elder care, transportation, and other problems that resulted in unenviable absenteeism records. At issue is not whether employers have a right to count on employees to show up—clearly they do. Yet two questions emerge. The first is whether employees who have done everything they could to put in place dependable routine and backup family care should be fired when an emergency triggers the final point that leads to dismissal. The second issue is whether absences covered by the FMLA can be legitimately treated as garnering points under a no-fault system.[11]

Crazy Quilts and Tag Teams

The twenty-four-hour economy means that many people work what Europeans call "unsocial hours": hours outside the generally recognized working day that encroach on time traditionally reserved for family and friends. In fact, for 40% of employed Americans, most of their work time occurs outside of standard daylight hours. And 51% of two-job families with children have at least one parent working a nonday shift. Almost 30% report variable starting and stopping times, typically with the employer setting those times at will. Ten percent of Americans have schedules so unpredictable that, when asked, they tell researchers they do not know from one week to the next what their weekly schedule will be. The evening shift is the most common alternative work schedule, accounting for 40% of all nonstandard work shifts among full-time workers and more than half of those among part-time workers.[12]

Nonstandard working hours are especially prevalent in low-level service and laborer jobs and increasingly in retail, where many low-wage mothers who can least afford to pay for child care are employed. People working unsocial hours, not surprisingly, tend to have strained relationships. These schedules are associated with higher work-family conflict, lower marital quality, and reduced time spent with children. They are also associated with a lower likelihood of eating meals together, providing homework supervision, and sharing leisure. Workers with nonstandard shifts face special hardships if they divorce. One divorcing mother lost her job at a factory due to a shift change when she refused to report to work in time for her new shift because she believed she would lose custody of her children if she did.[13]

Inflexible work schedules work in poisonous combination with American workers' unusually heavy reliance on family members for child care. In the United States, child care is both expensive and of highly variable quality. Consequently, working-class families typically patch together a crazy quilt of family-delivered care that may include, in addition to parents' shift work, drafting grandparents and other family members to help with child care. These fragile, patched-together systems often break down. One study found that 30% of workers surveyed had to cut back on work for at least one day during the week in order to care for family members: nearly one-quarter of men as well as over one-third of women. These cutbacks were more frequent among lower-income workers with the most inflexible schedules, presumably because they were only half as likely to rely on child care centers as were professional-managerial workers.[14]

Among the arbitrations we examined, many that were settled in the worker's favor involved parents whose well-laid plans for both regular child care and backup care went awry. For example, in *Princeton City School District Board of Education*, a teacher requested a personal leave day when her normal day care provider suddenly became sick. Her husband was out of town, and her mother-in-law was scheduled to work. School officials denied leave in the absence of proof that she had tried to arrange for backup through a commercial day care center. She had not tried to do so on the date in question because she had learned, several years earlier, that the local centers (like most centers in the United States) did not accept short-notice, one-day clients. The arbitrator held that the personal day should have been granted because the teacher had a backup plan—relying on her husband and mother-in-law—that had worked in the past.[15]

In *General Telephone Company of Indiana*, an arbitrator ruled in favor of a service clerk who had just had a baby and was ordered, the day she returned from maternity leave, to attend a two-week out-of-town training course. Because the clerk was given less than a week's notice, she was unable to get a babysitter, and her husband was on a work assignment out of town. She asked that the class be scheduled when she had sufficient time to arrange babysitting. The supervisor suggested that she start the class several months later; she agreed. A few days later, she was informed that attending the training program was a job requirement and that she would be terminated if she did not go. After a few more days, she was given the choice of being demoted to an operator job or fired. The arbitrator reinstated this worker with full back pay, benefits, and seniority, noting that "no effort whatever was made to accommodate [her] very real child care needs," despite the fact that two other employees had been excused from the same training for compelling personal reasons. If the inability to find a suitable babysitter when neither spouse nor relatives are available "is not a compelling personal reason," the arbitrator opined, "it is hard to imagine what sort of excuse would be acceptable."[16]

An arbitrator also found in favor of the worker in *Social Security Administration, Westminster Teleservice Center*, another situation involving backup child care. The case concerned a contact representative who was treated as absent without leave when she did not report to work because her regular babysitter had car problems and her backup babysitter's husband was hospitalized with a heart attack. The worker, a single mother with no relatives nearby, made persistent efforts to reach her supervisor, expressing mounting anxiety over the cost of her long-distance calls. Her direct supervisor never returned her calls. She ultimately used foul language in frustration and remained at home. She was disciplined for her absence, a decision that was overturned by the arbitrator, who held that she was entitled to emergency annual leave under the contract because

> [she] had met the commonly understood meaning of "emergency": she had a childcare emergency. It is not disputed that the two people she reasonably and legitimately depended upon for childcare were suddenly and unexpectedly unavailable . . . Indeed, her circumstances exactly met the situation described in [the contract]; that is, there was an unexpected change in her childcare arrangements.[17]

Men as well as women are affected by child care breakdowns, in significant part because of "tag teaming," an arrangement where parents work different shifts so that each parent can care for the children while the other is at work. Among "tag teamers," fathers act as primary caregivers when their wives are at work.[18] Describing his own experience, John Goldstein, past president of the Milwaukee Labor Council, said,

> When I was a young bus driver and my children were very small (ages 4, 2, and 1), I worked the late shift and my wife went to school during the day. We couldn't afford child care, and this way one of us was always home. One day in the middle of winter, I was scheduled to work at 4 pm. The babysitter didn't show up or call to say she wasn't coming. I had to bundle up the kids and take them to work. They had to ride my bus with me. After about two hours I was lucky enough to see my wife studying in a coffee shop, so I stopped the bus and ran in and handed her the kids.[19]

Tag teaming exists in professional families, but it is far more common in nonprofessional families, especially among young, lower-income families. This way of covering child care is driven in part by simple economics. Given the lack of government subsidies, in every state the average price for child care for a one-year-old is higher than the average cost of college tuition at the state's university. Most experts estimate that more than half of paid care in the United States is "poor" to "adequate," and only about 10% of paid care is developmentally enriching. In other words, out-of-family child care is either prohibitively expensive or poor quality; tag teaming is a way to avoid inferior care. But family-delivered care can have steep costs and dangers of its own. A tag-teaming parent or grandparent who is forbidden to leave the workplace or is ordered to stay overtime faces a no-win situation. Those who leave without their supervisors' consent can expect discipline or even job loss.[20]

When faced with child care emergencies, tag-teaming families must make difficult choices as to whether the mother or the father will face discipline or discharge for taking time off to care for children. In *U.S. Steel Corp.*, a factory worker whose regular babysitter was in the hospital took off work because his wife's employer had a stricter absenteeism policy than his did. Another case involved the father of a toddler, who started his warehouse job at 7 A.M. to be available to pick up his daughter from preschool at 3 P.M.; his wife brought the child to preschool in the mornings. The father won a grievance challenging his employer's attempt to change him to a 9-to-5 schedule, on the grounds that the union contract did not allow the company to unilaterally change start times. (Without a union, the worker most likely would have lost his job.) In a third case, the arbitrator reduced a father's discharge to a one-month suspension for refusing to take an assignment because he had to pick up his daughter. In yet another arbitration, when a carpenter left work to pick up his children, the employer argued that he should have obeyed the order to stay and grieved later (that is, challenged the employer's order). The arbitrator disagreed: "the 'work now, grieve later' rule has no application. [He] could not both continue working and pick up his children."[21]

The cases we examined also revealed an unexpected finding: men's work-family conflicts stem not just from tag teaming but also from divorce. One example involved a twenty-two-year employee who explained that his stay-at-home wife had left him and their four-year-old son. He was notified that social service authorities were investigating him for child neglect. They found no grounds for the charge and subsequently tried to help him find day care for his son, but it took nearly three months of struggling with unreliable babysitters before he was able to place his son with an approved day care provider. In the meantime, he had been fired for excessive absenteeism under his employer's no-fault policy. *Interlake Conveyors* involved a material handler who was fired when he was not allowed to produce documentation that, as the divorced father of an asthmatic son, he needed to stay home because his son was ill.[22] Both fathers later were reinstated by arbitrators but would have been out of luck had they not belonged to a union.

Even when families are able to rely on child care centers or family day care, they still must cope with paid providers' often-inflexible hours and policies. Most centers close before the end of normal business hours, and most charge steep fees (often one dollar per minute) if children are picked up late. Even more important, because child-care staff become unhappy when children are not picked up on time, parents who arrive late risk losing their child care arrangement. That often means losing their jobs. In five of the arbitrations we examined, workers lost their jobs after they lost their child care.[23]

Another common scenario is when an employer unilaterally changes a worker's starting and stopping times, often without much notice, and the parent's child care provider cannot, or will not, take the child at the new time. Sometimes a schedule change affects not child care but elder care, as in *Simpson v. District of Columbia Office of Human Rights*. A secretary challenged her employer's insistence that she start work an hour and a half earlier, thereby making it impossible for her to care for her elderly and ailing father before she arrived at work. In certain jobs, an employer is not in a position to offer flexibility—obviously, one cannot stop a factory line to accommodate a babysitter. But many employers could offer far more flexibility than they do without jeopardizing business needs.[24]

Families in Crisis, Employers in Denial

The vision of families in crisis emerges strongly in the arbitration mentioned above that involved more than thirty phone company workers fired for tapping telephone lines. One reported having a mentally unstable son who had threatened to kill her, her family, and himself. Three different workers had children whom they said had threatened and/or attempted suicide. Another had a stepdaughter who was physically threatening her daughter. Another became worried and called her house fifty-two times in a single day; when she broke in to monitor the line, she heard her son acknowledging taking drugs. Two workers monitored the phones of their parents. One had a mother who was "suffering from confusion"; the other's father was ill and, according to the worker, had been threatened with harm from other tenants in the building. In another arbitration, an employee with twenty-five years' tenure was fired for monitoring her phone to check up on her young children, one of whom was asthmatic. Finally, an employee with fourteen years' service, who was on probation for absenteeism, was fired when he failed to report to work. He had stayed home because his pregnant wife, who subsequently died of a brain hemorrhage, had broken a phone in a fit of rage, and he decided he could not leave his children alone with her.[25]

In addition to child care breakdowns and family crises, family illness may lead to discipline or job loss because family members lack sick leave they can use to care for family members who are ill. Routine childhood illness is a major concern. Families with infants with special needs visit the doctor an average of eleven times a year; other infants visit the doctor an average of four to six times a year. For children aged two to four, the number of yearly doctors' visits falls to seven for kids with special needs and to four for others. In the 70% of families in which all adults are employed, one working parent needs to stay home when a child is sick—but that parent may lose his or her job for doing so. For example, in *Naval Air Rework Facility*, the grievant and her husband both worked, one as a machinist and one at an aerospace plant. Since the child care facility would not accept their child because he had chicken pox, the mother stayed home with her ill child. She was denied sick leave upon returning to work and as a result was discharged. The arbitrator held for the employer, finding that the employee did not provide the necessary documentation from the local health authorities that her child's illness required isolation.[26]

Under the FMLA, workers caring for an immediate family member (spouse, child, or parent) with a serious health condition are entitled to up to twelve weeks of unpaid leave each year, so long as they have worked for at least one year at an employer with fifty or more employees (and 1,250 hours in the year prior to the leave). Workers can take this leave in an intermittent pattern, which is particularly useful for those who need to take family members to doctors' appointments or those who have family members with chronic diseases. Yet many workers are not covered: only 11% of private-sector workplaces meet the act's minimum size requirements and fully 40% of workers are not covered. Workers who are covered sometimes fail to request FMLA leave in a manner the employer can recognize, or they fail to obtain the necessary medical documentation. In other cases, it is unclear whether the workers ever considered the FMLA.[27]

Even in the best of circumstances, FMLA leave covers only a small proportion of the time off families require in order to negotiate the joys and travails of everyday life. Children need adult attention long after they leave preschool. During children's adolescence, high parental involvement can significantly help build self-esteem and educational accomplishment. Active parental involvement and supervision also can help prevent juvenile crime and other risky behavior: most teenage pregnancies and teen violence occur between 3 P.M. and 6 P.M., when most schools have been dismissed but when parents are often still at work. Several of the arbitrations we analyzed involved workers' adolescent children (suicidal daughters; a son injured in a gang beating; a father fired for absences caused by family illnesses and "delinquent children"; a father fired for absenteeism caused, among other things, by the drug overdoses of his daughter).[28]

Grandparents, too, face workplace discipline and/or job loss when they give priority to the needs of their families. Because the average age at which Americans become grandparents for the first time is now forty-seven, three-fourths of grandmothers and almost nine out of ten grandfathers are in the labor force. Thus the more than one-third of grandmothers who provide care for preschool-aged children typically are otherwise employed. Many grandmothers tag team with their daughters, but these older family caregivers are vulnerable to the same work-family conflicts faced by parents. In *Department of Veterans Affairs Medical Center*, a grandmother was suspended from her job as a nursing assistant when she was unable to work her scheduled shift (3:30 P.M. to midnight) because she could not find child care. In another case, a grandmother bus driver lost her chance at promotion because she had been absent for a significant period caring for her adult son, who was injured. In yet another, a steel plant worker was fired when she stayed home to care for her adult daughter, who had been injured in a car accident. *Mercer County* involved a grandmother who needed time off to care for her grandchildren. She happened to have legal custody, but grandparents frequently provide regular child care even when they are not the legal guardians of their grandchildren: over one-fifth of preschool-aged children are cared for primarily by grandparents when their parents are at work. A recent study reports that 2.4 million grandparents have primary responsibility for the care of their grandchildren—and over one-fourth had cared for their grandchildren for five or more years.[29]

Grandparents sometimes ease parents' work-family conflicts, but eventually parents, as well as children, need care: one in four families care for elderly relatives. Among people aged fifty to sixty-four who need support for their health and emotional needs, 84% rely on informal caregiving networks. Almost one in five caregivers say they provide forty-plus hours of care per week, and the average length of care is 4.3 years. In *Sprint/ Central Telephone Co. of Texas*, a phone customer service representative failed to meet her sales quota because of the stress caused by caring for her mother, who had died by the time of the arbitration. Fully 57% of working caregivers say that they have had to go to work late, leave early, or take time off during the day to provide care. This is a face of work-family conflict that is not well known and is rarely reported in the mainstream press. Unions, too, may not fully grasp the range and depth of family crises that their members must balance with their jobs.[30]

The Burden of Mandatory Overtime

One form of workplace inflexibility shows up again and again in the arbitrations: mandatory overtime. The design of mandatory overtime systems can make or break workers' ability to avoid discipline or discharge when work and family conflict. The overtime issue is important, in part, because Americans work among the longest hours of any other developed economy. Long hours are largely the province of men: 95% of mothers aged twenty-five to forty-four years old work fewer than fifty hours per week, year-round. While managerial and professional men are most likely to work fifty-plus hours per week (38% do), nearly one in four (23%) men in middle-income families (with incomes between $35,000 and $101,000) do so, too. Working-class men average forty-two to forty-three hours per week, far longer than their European counterparts.[31]

Mandatory overtime leaves single parents and tag team families in jeopardy of losing their jobs. Until the union negotiated a solution, for example, members of the Amalgamated Transit Union were being fired when they refused to stay for mandatory drug and alcohol tests, which last up to three hours. Said Robert Molofsky, who was General Counsel of the ATU at the time, "They had no problem taking the tests; the problem was that they were triggered at or near the end of their shifts. And with little or no advance notice they could not stay even as paid overtime, because they had to get home to take care of their kids." In other words, they were tag team dads.[32]

Recall *U.S. Steel Corp.*, a tag team situation in which a factory worker stated that when his family's regular babysitter was sick, he took off work because his wife's employer had a stricter absenteeism policy; he was suspended for fifteen days for an unexcused absence. While his frankness was unusual, the family-care hardships mandatory overtime present are widespread and need to be addressed.[33]

Another example involved a janitor who was divorced and the mother of a seventeen-year-old son with the mental capacity of an eighteen-month-old child. In *Tenneco Packaging Burlington Container Plant*, she was fired after twenty-seven years' service for failing to report one Saturday when her son's caregiver could not work because of a sick child. All of the evidence indicated that this was an isolated incident. The janitor had worked sixty hours a week, including all but one Saturday, in the four months before she was fired, and she called in twice and left a message telling her employer she could not work on the day of the absence that led to her termination. When she returned the following Monday, she was denied her request for a vacation day to excuse her Saturday absence. Instead she was fired. The arbitrator who reinstated her said:

> The Company had been scheduling six-day work weeks for an extended period of time. This heavy work schedule was likely to have a substantial impact on any single-parent employees, and would have a particularly heavy impact on

an employee with a child in need of permanent care and assistance. [The worker] had legitimate reasons for missing two of the 23 Saturdays when she had been scheduled to work overtime.

He continued, "the demands of a regular six day work week would be a strain on a caregiver," especially given the "10-hour days . . . Under such circumstances, it is not surprising that there would be problems in persuading the caregiver to regularly work on the weekends, as well as long days, with some regularity even if her child had not become ill." The arbitrator ordered that this employee be reinstated with full back pay. Most U.S. workers, being nonunionized, would have been fired without appeal.[34]

In *State of New York, Rochester Psychiatric Center*, another arbitrator took a proactive role on behalf of a single mother. This case involved a health center that fired a mental health aide who had worked for her employer for nine years. The aide had a history of attendance problems, almost all of which stemmed from her status as a single parent. Due to understaffing and the need for around-the-clock care, aides at the center were expected to work mandatory overtime on a regular basis. If an employee refused overtime, she remained at the top of the list until she took it, which is why, after the aide refused to work overtime, she was ordered five days later to work an additional eight hours after her regular shift ended at 11:20 P.M. The aide's sitter could not stay because she had a day job. The aide asked her supervisor if she knew anyone who could watch her children at such short notice. The supervisor, while sympathetic, did not. Then the aide said she could stay at work if she could bring her children in so they could sleep at the center but that she could not leave her children alone: "If I have to stay, my kids have to stay here." Once again, she was fired; once again, the arbitrator overturned the worker's discharge, opining that the situation was

> shocking to one's sense of fairness . . . The [worker] may not be a woman of means, but she is a woman of substance . . . She does not hold a high-paying job. She would probably be better off financially if she chose to stay home, watch her kids, and go on the dole. However, instead of becoming a public charge, she has chosen to make a public contribution . . . Her recent performance evaluation indicates "she can function well on any ward she is assigned." As the parties are aware, I take a very dim view of time and attendance infractions and insubordination . . . However, [she] deserves every conceivable "break" . . . Her children were well-groomed, neatly dressed, and well-behaved. It is her efforts to be a good parent that have created her problems at work.

The arbitrator directed the aide to identify, thirty days in advance, three days a month when she could work overtime given that aides typically worked overtime two to three days a month. This is an example of how to design an overtime system that does not have a punitive impact on adults with family responsibilities—particularly if this approach is combined, to the maximum extent possible, with a system that relies on voluntary overtime. In two other arbitrations, nurses' aides were not so lucky. Both were fired, and not reinstated, when they refused mandatory overtime because they had no one to care for their children.[35]

In *GTE California, Inc.*, a single-parent telephone installer was fired when she left work in defiance of a new telephone company policy that workers had to stay until every customer who had called before 3 P.M. had been served. The installer's supervisor had a policy that only one person per shift could refuse overtime; if more than one person requested to leave without working overtime, all workers requesting to do so had to come to an agreement as to who could leave and who would stay. The installer was fired for insubordination when she left work after being ordered to stay because she and a coworker both wanted to leave without working overtime. The arbitrator overturned her dismissal, saying that the worker was entitled to leave rather than obeying the supervisor's order and filing a grievance later, because her situation was covered by a rule concerning safety. The arbitrator held that a parent could be disciplined if she left unjustifiably, but she need not "obey now, grieve later" in the face of an unreasonable system that placed a child at risk:

> I do not know what would have happened to the child if [her mother] had not arrived to pick her up. Chances are that the child would have been cared for. However, it was clear that the [worker] also did not know what would happen to the child, although she did know that she was running the risk of losing day care service. In these circumstances, the [worker] did what I believe any unintimidated parent would have done. She ran the risk of discipline.[36]

Single fathers as well as single mothers are sanctioned for refusing overtime, which makes sense, given that (outside of nursing) overtime is largely a masculine phenomenon. In *Bryant v. Bell Atlantic Maryland*, an African-American construction lineman who was the single father of two children was fired for refusing overtime. The arbitrator held that the employer lacked just cause to terminate and strongly suggested that Bryant be placed "in a position that did not require overtime" or, as an alternative, that "Bryant be scheduled for overtime in a manner that would allow him to meet his workplace and child care obligations." This arbitration was reported in a court case; the court noted Bryant's claim that child care difficulties of white workers had been accommodated, while his had not.[37]

In *Marion Composites*, a factory worker whose wife had recently left him was suspended three days for insubordination when he left after eight hours of a twelve-hour overtime shift. He was, according to the arbitrator, "an excellent employee who consistently worked overtime when asked to do so . . . He was never absent. He accepted overtime whenever the Company needed him. Indeed, his dedication to his work placed him in a situation that may have jeopardized his family responsibilities." When first asked to work overtime, he said he could not because he was "tired and worn out"—he had been so upset by his wife's departure that he had been feeling ill. Later that afternoon, he said he would help out the company but that he could only stay for eight hours because he had to get home to care for his two children. He stayed after the eight hours was up but became "distraught" after receiving a call from his wife and left after eight hours and twenty minutes. In the *Suprenant Cable Corp.* case (discussed earlier), a single father with a four-year-old son was fired for excessive absenteeism under the employer's no-fault policy as the result of the worker's inability to find child care. Said the arbitrator:

> Such policies are not best suited to dealing with long-term employees who, like [this worker], have overall good records and who run into an unusual period of bad luck and hard times. Anyone can—most of us will—experience at least one period of adversity in a lifetime. Otherwise good, long-term employees are entitled to understanding and sympathy during those rare periods. Their seniority does not exempt them from the expectations of the workplace but may require that they be applied more flexibly and sensitively.[38]

Some cases of family needs that conflict with unscheduled overtime involve care for ill spouses. In *Allied Paper,* a plant worker refused a Saturday callback because his water pump had broken, and he did not want to leave his wife, who had cancer and was severely depressed, "without water, in case of a fire." He was so concerned about his wife's cancer and depression that he had previously sacrificed thousands of dollars to avoid overtime that would have left her home alone. Said the arbitrator, "his wife had stood by him in sickness and tragedy, and he was trying to return it. He owed it to her."[39]

Caring in Secret

Roughly 55% of the arbitrations that WorkLife Law studied involved men. While we found no case involving a woman who flatly refused to discuss work-family conflicts, some men were willing to risk discipline or even discharge rather than tell their employers that they needed to leave work to care for children. This is important because employers often have rules that allow workers to refuse overtime for legitimate reasons. Even where these rules are lacking, supervisors are more likely to allow a worker to attend to pressing family needs than to accommodate a worker who refuses to disclose his reason for wanting to leave. And when employers remain staunchly inflexible, arbitrators are more likely to find in favor of a worker who communicated his reasons for needing to leave than a worker who remained silent.[40]

Yet men seem to be less willing than women to acknowledge that they need to leave work for reasons related to family care and more likely to try to "come in under the radar screen"—often with unhappy results. The classic example is *Tractor Supply Co.*, in which an employer posted notice of two hours of mandatory overtime the day before it was to be worked. Workers had the option of staying late or reporting two hours early the following day. The employer later took down the overtime notice, and a supervisor clarified that the next day's work could be handled by voluntary overtime. Then the employer changed its mind again. The overtime notice was reposted, but by that time the worker had left. Had he known of the overtime, he would have reported to work early. When he learned of the overtime the following day, he refused to stay at work past his regular shift because he had to get home to care for his grandchild. His supervisor asked why he would not stay, but the worker would only say that it was none of his business. The supervisor said that accommodations could be made for reasonable excuses and then asked again why he could not stay. The worker again said it was none of the supervisor's business. The supervisor ordered him to stay, the worker refused, and he was fired for insubordination.[41]

The factory worker in *Tractor Supply* is not alone in his willingness to risk discipline or even dismissal rather than explain that he has family care issues. In *Midwest Body, Inc.*, the arbitrator upheld the dismissal of an industrial worker who failed to report for overtime work on Saturday or for work on Monday. When asked why, "he replied he had family problems and declined to be more specific," again refusing to explain at a meeting with two supervisors and a union representative. "Reluctance to give specific information with respect to 'family problems' may be understandable," said the arbitrator, "but an employee who is unwilling to give [it] should refrain from using that sort of excuse."[42]

Another more disturbing story, is the case of the UPS package delivery driver who was fired for "theft of time" when he took off an extra hour and a quarter on two different days without telling his supervisors. He

explained that the recent birth of his second child had resulted in an exhausting wave of problems at home:

> With my new baby boy and my 2 1/2 year old, my wife was laid up . . .
> recuperating . . . I had even less sleep . . . I was taking care of my two kids
> while I let my wife rest . . . Since [then] things haven't calmed down [but] I
> returned to work . . . since I can no longer afford to be off for so long. One
> week later my wife got sick due to an infection in her breast . . . [and] ended
> up with a temperature of 104 . . . Meanwhile, my first son was coughing and
> had the flu. As the newborn is still feeding every two hours, I was getting by
> on 2–3 hours of sleep a day . . . I didn't know whether I was coming or
> going . . . [I went] home and spen[t] my lunch and breaks there to make sure
> every one at home was okay. But I lost track of time . . . My intention was [to
> be] there for my family but not to steal time, as I was accused of.

He pointed to his two years of service and said "I've always given the best
of my ability to get the job done . . . Taking away my job from me has put
my family in a financial hardship. I cannot survive with having two babies.
And my wife being out of work. I deeply regret for what I've done, but I
need my job back." The arbitrator ruled against him, and he lost his job.[43]

There are other similar cases. In *Ashland Oil*, a carpenter left work after
explaining "that he had obligations at home without specifically mentioning
child care." Another worker who needed to leave to pick up his son said
only that he needed to leave for personal reasons. Yet again in *VA Medical
Center of Indianapolis*, a pharmacy technician with a good work record
called in to request eight hours of emergency annual leave; he refused to
elaborate on the reason, saying only that it was personal. The supervisor
gave him two hours, and when he failed to report after that, he was disciplined. Only later did the technician explain to the arbitrator that the
emergency was family related. In still another case, *City of Columbus*, an
operating engineer who had been told to remain at work due to an impend-
ing snowstorm gave no reason at all when he left to pick up his son and
another first-grader from school. Company policy was that employees were
excused from overtime if they advised their supervisors of a reasonable
excuse prior to the end of their normal workday. In fact, another employee
had requested and received permission to leave for a short time to pick up
his pregnant wife from work. Noted the arbitrator, "if Benton's situation
was considered to be a reasonable excuse, then certainly [this worker's]
excuse that he had to pick up his first-grade son as well as another first-
grader from school would also be found to have been a reasonable excuse
under the contract." But the engineer did not tell the street maintenance
foreman of his difficulty. After asking for two supervisors and being told
they were not there, he simply left and was later suspended.[44]

Why risk discipline or dismissal rather than simply provide a reasonable excuse? This question takes us back to the role of masculinity in shaping men's workplace behavior. As will be explored at greater length in Chapter 5, the current generation has seen high-school-educated men's wages fall 25% since 1973. While their fathers and grandfathers could supply the "good life" on their salaries alone, or with their wives working part-time only intermittently, these men often cannot. To quote a white thirty-year-old forklift operator, "I know she doesn't mind working, but it shouldn't have to be that way. A guy should be able to support his wife and kids. But that's not the way it is these days, is it? Well, I guess those rich guys can, but not some ordinary Joe like me." Studies of working men have found consistently that their inability to "support their families" is one of the "hidden injuries of class," to use the phase from the famous 1973 study by Richard Sennett and Jonathan Cobb. Said a man quoted in a 1996 study:

> I wouldn't let my wife work. I told her, I said, "Look, you got the kids, you stay home. When the kids go to school all day, then you work." That's fine, up to a point. I tried to do it on my own. Working 20 hours a day to make everything go. She said, "Hey, look, I gotta go to work." I was against it, but it had to be done. As far as I was brought up, Pop did the work, Mom stayed home with the kids. Alright? I was raised that way, and that's the way I saw it.[45]

A 2000 study also reported that working-class men still aspire to being able to "support their families," although many no longer expect to be able to do so.[46]

An important "hidden injury of class" is the sense of inadequacy that stems from working-class men's (ever-increasing) inability to perform as breadwinners. The breadwinner-housewife dichotomy was invented in the late eighteenth century as a way of signaling the difference between working- and middle-class families. For much of the nineteenth century, being able to keep "the wife at home" remained a key dividing line between working- and middle-class families. For two brief generations after World War II, the separate-spheres ideal was democratized, but today the ability to achieve the breadwinner ideal is once again tied to class privilege. This helps explain working-class men's reluctance to admit that they need to leave work to attend to child care. Whereas middle-class men tend to "talk the talk but not walk the walk" in terms of gender equality—talking gender equality but failing to share equally in household work—working-class men tend to "walk the walk but not talk the talk"—as a group, sharing more equally in household work without espousing a verbal commitment to equal parenting roles.[47]

In addition, mothers may find it easier than fathers to discuss their need to leave the workplace to provide care because motherhood is an especially salient role for women, even if they are employed. According to Peter Richardson, an anthropologist at the University of Michigan who has both worked in blue-collar jobs and studied them,

> It makes sense to me that working class men would be less forthcoming about their family responsibilities on the job than women would. On the factory floor, the women's status as mothers is front and center. It is always part of the conversation. Men's status as fathers doesn't enter into everyday conversations in the same way. So for a mother to say she has to leave because of child care would feel natural, but for a father to say so would feel like it was coming from left field. It would be embarrassing, like making a loud fart in church.[48]

Working-class men—like higher-status ones—recognize the stigma triggered when men signal their involvement in family care. As will be detailed in the next chapter, this stigma can be severe.[49]

Men who are willing to admit they need to leave work to care for children still may be less willing than women to engage in informal negotiations in order to get permission to leave. For example, in *Southern Champion Tray*, a mechanic, after having told his supervisor repeatedly that he could not stay because he had to pick up his son, was fired for insubordination when he simply walked off the job. Asked why he did not explain to his supervisor that his family's child care backup plan had fallen through when his wife's car broke down, he replied, "I thought I did all I could and I was tired of fussing. I didn't feel anything else could be worked out."[50]

A final issue of importance to unions is that, like affluent men, working-class men often have little knowledge of their children's everyday arrangements. Even men who play an active role in providing family care often play only a little role in arranging that care or in other household management tasks. Their lack of knowledge and experience in these areas can have workplace repercussions, because both employers and arbitrators hold workers responsible for arranging backup child care if it is needed. In *U.S. Steel Corp.*, the factory worker whose regular babysitter had been hospitalized said that he phoned the plant the day before his shift in order to give them plenty of time to arrange alternative staffing. In upholding the fifteen-day suspension, the arbitrator was influenced not only by the worker's prior disciplinary record but also by the fact that he had not attempted to find another babysitter nor attempted to swap shifts to ensure that the shift was covered. As the arbitrator put it, the grievant "simply did nothing." In explanation, the worker said that since he worked two jobs, he usually was not at home except to sleep. He did not try to arrange babysitting because he was not familiar with how to make such arrangements.[51]

Lessons for Unions and Employers

The stories documented in the arbitrations suggest lessons for unions and employers. First, unions and employers need to formalize the process by which workers ask for time off to respond to legitimate family needs. A system that responds to workers' desire to preserve their privacy is essential. One possibility is a process that would allow them to state their needs on a form once, rather than out loud in public over and over again.

Second, unions and employers need to notify men that they are expected to know how to arrange backup care if necessary. That said, employers and arbitrators who insist that working-class fathers know the details of household management should ask themselves whether they are holding these workers to a standard that they themselves could meet. Moreover, employers and arbitrators should not assume that workers, male or female, have more child care options than in fact exist. Securing last-minute paid child care for an infant or young child is extremely difficult. Few day care centers accept drop-ins.

Third, a lesson just for unions: A promising approach to the problem is to reframe the issue of workers' need for time off as an issue of workers' rights rather than family responsibilities. The question, from a union standpoint, is whether employers are entitled to place profits above the welfare of workers with sick family members or small children who cannot be left alone. This reframing will help avoid situations in which working-class men are fired for insubordination when they refuse to say that they need to leave to take care of their children. If unions can persuade men to think about their need to leave for family reasons as an issue of worker empowerment, rather than as a situation that advertises their inability to be good providers, family caregiving can become an effective organizing issue rather than a key cause of worker vulnerability.

Recent studies of working-class men suggest that this approach holds promise. One, by Michèle Lamont, argues that working-class men see themselves as more moral than professional-managerial men, whom they fault for, among other things, the "poor quality of their interpersonal relationships." Lamont quotes a factory foreman: "Money isn't a big thing in my life. I don't have to be a rich man. I have riches. As long as you have the love and a tight family and that my kids grow up good, I don't need a lot of money . . . I have the respect of people who know me . . . I have those kinds of things, so I have a sense of self-worth." Asked why he likes his best friend, he says, "He's a family man. His family comes first to him as well." "Family is number one," said another worker.[52] This is the cultural context in which workers choose family over work even when they risk severe consequences for doing so. As the carpenter in *Ashland Oil* told his unhappy supervisor as the carpenter left work to pick up his children, "I must do what I have to do."[53] Unions can tap working-class pride in putting family first by bargaining for, and then by training workers to use, workplace entitlements that enable them to place the needs of their families over their employers' need for profit.

A common view among unions is that most members are not affected by work-family conflict because relatively few are women with small children, so unions are better off concentrating on issues of interest to all their members. The data and cases discussed in this chapter show the shortsightedness of that view: many different types of unionized workers sometimes need to be absent from work because of family caregiving responsibilities. Moreover, in an era of tag team families and single parents, work-family issues are key organizing issues: a crucial benefit unions offer is the ability to protect workers from disciplinary actions and job loss due to work-family conflict. After all, no wage-and-benefits package is of much use to a worker who gets fired for putting family first.

Unions also clearly need to do more to educate workers on their rights under the FMLA, including their rights to take intermittent FMLA leave. In several cases, workers were discharged when they were so overwhelmed by misfortune that they did not take the steps required by the FMLA.

Another message for unions is that the design of mandatory overtime systems is a make-or-break issue for many union members. Such systems should recognize that some members desire overtime, while others desire to avoid it. The kind of system at work in *Rochester Psychiatric,* which placed workers at the top of an overtime list until they worked overtime, is a recipe for disaster for single and tag team parents. So too is the system in *GTE California, Inc.,* which left the workers themselves to decide who would be relieved of the obligation to work overtime. Neither system offers workers or employers the necessary predictability: workers lack the notice they need to arrange for child care; employers lack predictability because, as the cases we analyzed show, these kinds of overtime systems may not be upheld by arbitrators in grievance cases with compelling facts.[54]

A final important message for unions concerns the design of no-fault progressive discipline systems. At best, such systems coexist uneasily with workers' commitment to their family care responsibilities. The most dramatic example is *Knauf Fiber Glass,* which involved a packer who had worked nine years at her company. Although she was a good worker (according to her supervisor), she had "a serious absenteeism problem," including no less than twenty-seven written warnings. But she always avoided accumulating the extra point or two that would have led to discharge. In part because of the complaints of coworkers who had worked involuntary overtime during her no-shows, she was placed on special probation, which allowed her only one excused and one unexcused absence during a three-month period. She was told she would be discharged if she exceeded two absences. She used one when she was ill without a doctor's excuse and the second when she took her daughter to the doctor. Then one day she received a call from her brother-in-law saying that her four-year-old daughter had fallen and injured her head and was being taken to the emergency room. The worker left, despite being told that her job would be in jeopardy if she did so. She was fired. The arbitrator reinstated her:

> For more than half a century, labor arbitrators have been asked to review discharges based on the "just cause" standard. Over this long history, no mechanical formula has evolved for determining whether that standard has been met. An arbitrator cannot do his job simply by programming a computer and punching in "RUN." There is judgment to be exercised solving a discharge case. But that judgment cannot be based on the subjective values of an individual neutral. The needs and interests of the parties and their legitimate expectations must control.[55]

Noting that "absenteeism is a scourge in the industrial workplace," the arbitrator affirmed that a worker's first responsibility is to be at work, on time. "A company is not a social service agency," and an "individual employee may have serious personal problems which produce an abominable attendance record, but management need not carry an employee on the rolls if prior experience proves that reasonable attendance requirements cannot be met." Yet for just cause to exist, "that final 'point' must be found to have been warranted." In assessing this, "it is important why the [packer] left the plant":

> It is fundamentally unfair to discharge an employee for leaving work because she was informed that her four-year-old daughter had fallen, was injured, and was being taken to the Emergency Room. Fair-minded people would not disagree that she was compelled to leave work. She had no real choice in the matter . . . When [she] left work on December 3, she was not continuing her pattern of regular absenteeism. She could not have prevented the occurrence or rescheduled the accident. That event was not the type of absenteeism which indicates that [she] cannot fulfill reasonable attendance requirements.

As the arbitrator highlighted, an employer need not live forever with a worker who does not show up when scheduled to work. Nevertheless, an employee cannot be discharged for doing what any conscientious parent would do for the simple reason that this kind of absence is not part of the prior pattern of absenteeism. The arbitrator, appropriately, sent a very clear message that the worker needed to address her faulty attendance record posthaste. Although he reinstated her, she received no back pay, and he put her on special probation for ninety days, with only one unexcused absence.[56]

Ultimately, the message *Knauf Fiber* sends to unions is that responsible workers need to be protected from being disciplined or discharged for acting on values that are widely shared, by management as well as by workers. To quote arbitrator Dennis Nolan, "If all attempts [to satisfy parental obligations without interfering with the employer's business] fail, the family must come first, as most employers would readily agree."[57] The case also contains an important tip for employers: if an employer wants its rules to be enforced in the event a dispute goes to arbitration, the best approach is to provide an exception to no-fault absenteeism systems for bona fide family care emergencies.

The Business Case for Workplace Flexibility

Employers are not social service agencies: they have legal obligations to their shareholders and a business imperative to attend to the bottom line. Yet this does not preclude flexibility because, in many contexts, refusing to be flexible is bad management. To quote one arbitrator, faced with a situation where a worker had been disciplined for a failure to come to work when the worker's babysitter had car trouble and her backup babysitter's husband had had a heart attack:

> On the morning of February 16 there was an employee problem (lack of a babysitter) and a management problem (need for the worker's services). [The supervisor's] actions [refusing to grant emergency annual leave] did not resolve either problem. Instead, they resulted in an angry employee and a vacant space at the [agency].[58]

A moment's thought explains why flexibility can enhance business effectiveness. The need for some level of accommodation is not yet widely accepted; an example is *Town of Stratford*, in which a police officer was suspended when she failed to report for an "orderback" (that is, an unscheduled shift). She had arranged babysitting for her three children for the regular shift starting at 4 P.M., but she could not, with no prior notice, find babysitting to cover the noon-to-4 orderback period. To quote the arbitrator:

> It is Town's position that a Police Officer's personal/family needs are separate matters from their responsibility to the job of police work. A refusal to report as a result of "orderback" is insubordination whether the reason is personal or not. The Police Department is a paramilitary organization, an "orderback" is a firm requirement of the necessary discipline that surrounds police work. [She] is expected to have her family life secured in a manner that does not conflict with her professional responsibilities.

Note that the test here is not whether the police officer made concerted and conscientious efforts to find a babysitter. Instead the message is that she was not a suitable police officer unless she had a "family life secured" so as never to conflict with work responsibilities. The only way to accomplish this is either to be childless—a relatively unusual situation in the working-class context—or to have a spouse (typically a wife) who is available to care for the children without regard to her own job, also an unusual situation in working-class families today. One might argue that the police are different—that it is so important to have police on duty that police officers should not expect family concerns to be taken into account in any way. Yet in a different case involving a police officer with family care responsibilities, the arbitrator upheld the officer's right to use her bargained-for sick leave for child care, with no sense that this would jeopardize effective police work any more than do sick leave, personal days, vacations, or leaves to address substance abuse problems.[59]

The issue is not whether the police need dependable staffing. Like other employers, they do. The issue is whether dependable staffing is best achieved by being inflexible when officers cannot report due to legitimate child or other family care issues they have taken all realistic steps to avoid. To put the matter more broadly, the issue is whether—in an economy where all adults are in the labor force in more than two-thirds of households with children—employers should operate their workplace as if responsible workers always have their "family life secured" so as never to interfere with their job. This is an entirely unrealistic assumption and one that makes no sense on either a macroeconomic or a microeconomic level.[60]

Matching the workplace to the workforce increases businesses' effectiveness and improves their bottom line. Business case literature highlights that employers need to create family-responsive workplaces not as a gesture of good will but as a way to maximize profits. "We concluded that offering flexibility and some degree of control over time is fundamental to getting a strong return on human capital investments," said Alice Campbell of Baxter Healthcare. The major elements of the business case are improved consumer and workplace safety; stronger employee loyalty and commitment, which has a direct link to profits; enhanced productivity; reduced stress, which drives down health insurance and other costs; direct and indirect cost savings due to enhanced recruitment and decreases in turnover and absenteeism; and avoidance of a loss of employer control in unionized workplaces.[61]

Improved Consumer and Workplace Safety

Workplace inflexibility can jeopardize product and consumer safety, as illustrated by *Dial Corp., Bristol, Pa.,* in which a quality-control technician failed to properly inspect carton seals when he was denied leave to stay with his wife. She had just had a miscarriage, and the hospital's discharge orders said she should not be left alone for twenty-four hours. Nonetheless, her husband was denied leave. Frantic with worry when he called to check up on her and no one answered the phone, he overlooked a product defect.[62]

In addition to the possibility that distracted workers will produce an inferior product, workplace safety is at issue when employees are not allowed to take time off for family emergencies. Consider *Piedmont Airlines,* which involved a flight attendant ordered to take an additional flight. Her husband was unavailable, and she was unable to secure babysitting for her two toddlers at such short notice. Another flight attendant flying "deadhead" (returning home from a prior flight) could have filled in, but the grievant had been so "preoccupied" with her child care crisis that she did not think to tell this to crew scheduling. How would she have reacted in an in-flight emergency?[63]

Stronger Employee Loyalty and Commitment

Employers find that increasing workplace flexibility enhances worker engagement and loyalty. "How could I not be grateful to a company that granted me this, that helped my son incredibly," asked one Bell South worker who took six months off to care for a sick child. Happy workers make for happy customers, according to a business strategy sometimes referred to as the "service profit chain approach." When First Tennessee Bank used flexibility as the centerpiece of its service profit chain approach, employee retention at the affected branch banks was 50% higher than normal, which contributed to a 7% higher customer retention rate—and $106 million in additional profit over two years. Companies that adopted the strategy of retaining customers by keeping employees happy had a larger increase in stock price over a ten-year period than average, in a comparison of companies listed by Standard & Poor's.[64]

Research by the Corporate Leadership Council, a business group, estimates that every 10% improvement in employee commitment increases employees' level of discretionary effort by 6% and employee performance by 2%, and that highly committed employees perform at a 20% higher level than do employees who are not equally committed. These findings are confirmed by a Hewitt Associates study that found that companies whose growth has been in the double digits have 39% more highly engaged employees and 45% fewer highly disengaged employees than single-digit-growth companies.[65]

Flexibility enhances worker commitment because workers care about it. When the pharmaceutical company AstraZeneca surveyed employees, it found that 96% claimed that flexibility influenced their decision to stay with the company. Allstate Insurance found that 92% of its employees rated flexibility as "important" or "very important" and that hourly employees valued flexibility as much or more than salaried managerial-professional workers. At Bristol-Myers Squibb, 87% of hourly employees (as compared with 90% of employees overall) use flexibility; and 71% say it is "very important" (78% of women and 65% of men).[66]

"The dramatic effect of flexibility on employee commitment is one of the most powerful components of the business case for flexibility," according to a report by Corporate Voices for Working Families (an industry group):

> [Hourly] workers are . . . likely to be in environments (such as manufacturing and clerical) where they must be attentive to quality and accuracy: disengaged employees are much less likely to take responsibility for making systems work and solving problems as they arise. To the extent that [working-class] jobs can be routine or tiring, it is all the more important that the company give attention to practices that will keep these employees energized and focused.

High levels of engagement and commitment are harder to achieve in hourly jobs where workers have lower levels of autonomy. Hourly workers are also more likely to be in client-facing roles, such as in retail, hospitality, call centers, customer service, and nursing (as aides), where lack of commitment can have a very direct impact on client satisfaction. Commitment and engagement also are important for hourly workers in manufacturing and clerical jobs, as noted above, because they need to be attentive to detail and quality control. In fact, according to the Corporate Voices report, the effects of flexibility on increasing commitment and decreasing burnout are "almost identical" for hourly and salaried workers.[67]

Enhanced Productivity

Businesses that offer flexibility may enhance productivity. Said one manager:

> I need 15% core workers who work regular hours or longer. If benefits for part-timers were pro-rated, there would be no cost—in money or in efficiency—to splitting one job into two, or two jobs into three, or instituting flextime. It would probably increase the plant's efficiency.

Flexible policies can improve productivity in three basic ways: by allowing employers to stay open longer hours with the same number of employees; by improving staffing during vacations, illness, and emergencies; and by decreasing "presenteeism," when a worker is present in body only and not giving his full attention to the job. For the sake of brevity, I provide only a few examples below:[68]

StrideRight added thirty hours to its workweek at only 3% additional cost when it put one of its customer service units on flexible scheduling. When PNC's Eastwick, Pennsylvania, Operations Center piloted a compressed workweek, it found a dramatic decrease in processing time for safety deposits, bond inquiries, and other banking services—while extending customer service hours by an hour and a half a day. Absenteeism also dropped from sixty days to nine, and turnover costs decreased by $112,750 over a seven-month period.[69]

Flexibility also permits better staffing during vacations, illnesses, and emergencies. One Aetna manager said he would like a whole department of job sharers, because "when one is sick or on vacation, the other one is always there." Maslon, Edelman, Barman, and Brand, a Minneapolis law firm with 15% of its clerical staff on flexible schedules, found that it never had to hire a temp. At Marquette Electronics, where a work team can stagger team members' work hours to allow individual workers to come in late or to accommodate a family emergency, employees who miss work can make up the time during another shift. The firm's philosophy is that "Everyone has bad days and days when they give 120%."[70]

"Presenteeism," a variation on the Thank God It's Friday syndrome, can also decrease productivity any day of the week. New York State, which allows flexibility for all of its 200,000 employees, found that job sharing increases productivity by decreasing the fatigue factor. A vice president at Schreiber Foods decided to allow two people to share an executive assistant job and found she got a fresh person midweek, just when others in the office were starting to tire or react to job stress. Job sharing in blue-collar jobs could provide the same benefit.[71]

Reduced Stress and Related Elements Lower Health Insurance and Other Costs

Stress is the leading cause of unscheduled absence; it is linked with higher turnover and is a major factor in productivity loss. Working evening or night shifts and rotating hours is associated with higher levels of stress and psychological distress. A study of nursing assistants, janitors, and kitchen workers found that these workers could not leave work when a family member fell ill and that this lack of flexibility correlated with increased risk of heart disease as well as with chronic sleep problems that can lead to a variety of health problems. As noted earlier, unsocial hours, which are common among blue-collar workers in protective and food service industries, and among factory workers and laborers, have negative effects on health. So, too, do long work hours. Stress is expensive for employers. Chrysalis Performance Strategies found that stress is responsible for 19% of absenteeism, 40% of turnover, 55% of employee assistance program costs, 30% of short- and long-term flexibility costs, 10% of costs of psychotherapeutic drugs, 60% of workplace accidents, and many workers' compensation claims and lawsuits.[72]

Decreased Turnover and Enhanced Recruitment

Anyone who has ever been an employer knows that hiring is a crapshoot. When employees are working out well, strong incentives exist to keep them. "Flexible policies are one way to get people to stay," said one small business owner.[73] The cost of replacing an hourly worker typically ranges from 40% to 75% of the worker's annual salary, which can add up quickly if turnover is high. For example, it costs roughly $2,100 to replace an unskilled hotel worker. Hotel chains employ thousands.[74]

The arbitrations dramatize how inflexible workplaces can lead to constant and expensive attrition. An arbitrator in *Internal Revenue Service* conditionally reinstated a typist who had been fired for persistent tardiness due primarily to child care problems, in the face of evidence that her problems began when she and her husband separated, seven years after she had been hired. She was one of the best typists in the work unit, according to the arbitrator, and the quality of her work had not been affected by the personal challenges that led to her tardiness—in fact, she had consistently received incentive pay awards. Another outstanding worker who ran into problems is described in *Miami Valley Regional Transit Authority*.[75] That case involved a bus driver whose absences were caused by child care and transportation problems and by problems with her extended family. The driver was proactive in trying to solve her problems but had not worked for her employer long enough to be eligible for family leave and was not told of a compassionate leave policy until after she was fired. Said the arbitrator (who upheld the driver's dismissal):

> During the hearing . . . I found her to be a very caring person, a people-oriented person. There is no doubt she set a good example by her demeanor on the job and in her attitude toward her passengers. She had a good driving record with no recorded complaints. Unfortunately, because of her [low] seniority position she was assigned to shifts that were difficult for her to properly service because of her family situation.

It seems unlikely that firing this driver was a good business decision, given that the demographics of the hiring pool suggest that her replacement might also encounter work-family conflicts—and be fired, leading to the hire of yet another worker with the same issues.[76] One study found that about 11% of mothers in working-class jobs, lacking maternity leave, simply left their employers.[77] The result is constant churn and burn, as one woman after another leaves for family reasons.

The growing literature on low-wage workers documents that much of the attrition that plagues employers of minimum-wage workers stems from breakdowns in child care. "Don't too many people get fired a lot," said a worker at a Chicago store. "Basically, most of 'em leave because the schedule doesn't work around their schedule. And some do have children so they come in with the intention that [their supervisors are] going to work their schedule. And when they get in, that's not the same intention." Employers who allow workers to be open about family care issues may find that, instead of calling in sick for the whole day, employees instead miss only part of the day, because they do not have to pretend they were sick. When employers encourage their employees to be forthcoming about family care crises or children's and elders' medical appointments, some have found that workers are more likely to make up time missed due to family care. One national survey found absenteeism and tardiness dramatically reduced by flextime. Another study, by the American Management Association, found that flexibility cut absenteeism by 50%. The Pella Corporation found that job sharing not only decreased absenteeism by 81% but also led to more positive performance reviews. Other businesses have also reported positive results.[78]

Flexible work also can be an effective recruiting tool. Bristol-Myers Squibb found that its flexible work options program had helped it recruit one in five of its workers—and one in three of its women. When Maslon, Edelman, Barman, and Brand, the Minneapolis law firm mentioned above, advertised a job-share clerical position, they got a "deluge" of applicants. "We had a hot ticket!" said the human resources director.[79]

Avoidance of a Loss of Employer Control in Unionized Workplaces

An employer who makes no attempt to deal with workers' legitimate family care responsibilities risks losing control over how work-family issues are treated in a unionized workplace. This occurs because, provided grievants have adequate child (or other) care and backup care in place, arbitrators often do not rigidly enforce workplace rules when workers face discipline or discharge due to family care needs. Despite the fact that arbitrators rarely make split decisions, more than a third (35%) of the arbitrations involving family care produced split decisions, typically in situations where the arbitrator refused to enforce full discipline although a work rule had clearly been broken.[80]

In this context—unlike in most others—arbitrators routinely second-guess management's disciplinary decisions, imposing less severe discipline in an attempt to balance the equities because both workers and employers lack the choices they need. To state this differently, arbitrators often treat workers' family care responsibilities as a mitigating factor (although in many cases, this is not the formulation that the arbitrators espouse). The clear message for employers with unionized workplaces is that retaining control over work-family issues requires addressing them proactively.[81]

How to Fit the Workplace to the Workforce

False maxims abound in the work-family arena. An important one is that flexible work options "just aren't possible" in working-class jobs. In reality, any job can be restructured. The key is to recognize that different kinds of flexibility are suitable in different kinds of jobs. The arbitrations highlight this point. For example, in *Sutter Roseville Medical Center*, the arbitrator was understandably vexed with a worker who insisted that he needed to refuse overtime work, leaving his coworkers to shoulder an additional burden. In ruling for the employer, the arbitrator relied in part on the point that dependable staffing is vital in medical facilities that treat seriously ill patients. For precisely that reason, however, many medical fa-cilities have elaborate backup staffing systems to ensure that if one worker is not available, a replacement can be found. In sharp contrast, the arbitra-tor in *Department of Veterans Affairs Medical Center*, faced with a more sympathetic worker but the same general situation, allowed for flexibility without mentioning the particular problems presented by staffing issues in medical facilities. Perhaps the type of facility played a role. Perhaps not.

The fact that law enforcement, medical, and other fields with a twenty-four-hour-a-day workplace need reliable staffing is not in dispute. The real issue is whether the best way to ensure reliable staffing is to disci-pline or fire workers who cannot report due to unavoidable family care responsibilities—or whether there is a more effective approach. For in-stance, cross-training workers and providing reliable backup systems would ensure that an employer's needs would be met even in circumstances when workers with normally reliable regular and backup child care cannot report. Providing such backup may be easier in medical workplaces, because they already have "floaters," on-call staff, registry, and other backup ar-rangements. Hiring halls, where workers report to see whether work is available on a given day—commonplace in the construction industry—provide another model.[82] The airline industry also has found that flexibility is not inconsistent with reliable staffing. Airlines typically staff flights through a computerized bidding system in which flight attendants bid for their flights a month in advance. Many flight attendants, male as well as female, handle child care through tag teaming; careful bidding allows them to work when their spouse will be available to care for the children.

The misconception that flexibility is not suitable in working-class jobs stems chiefly from the assumption that workplace flexibility is available only by means of individualized arrangements negotiated between individ-ual workers and individual supervisors. That model, developed for profes-sionals, is suitable primarily for white-collar jobs. Informal arrangements are most effective for high-human capital workers with unique skills that give them leverage to negotiate an individual deal—something most hourly workers cannot do. Nonetheless, both employers and workers would benefit from workplace redesigns that better fit today's jobs to today's workforce.

Below are four crucial steps toward an improved fit:

1. *Comply with the FMLA and applicable state leave provisions.* Employ-ers who are covered by FMLA and applicable state leave laws should comply with these legal mandates and publicize these rights. In some in-dustries, noncompliance is widespread. New provisions cover workers

who need to care for a spouse, son, daughter, or parent who is a member of the military or is being called to active duty, as well as workers responsible for a spouse, child, parent, or next of kin in the military who has a serious injury or illness.

2. *Create multiple types of leaves for workers with unavoidable work-family conflicts.* Offering a variety of leaves would ease workers' dilemmas. These include (a) sick leave that workers can use to care for a worker's children or parents; (b) personal days, available without notice or with minimal notice, for emergencies; (c) vacation or personal leave available in two-hour increments to address family care emergencies (such as the baby-sitter not showing up or medical appointments not covered by FMLA leave), with an expedited application process for emergencies; (d) phone breaks so that parents can call home to check on sick family members or kids alone after school; (e) gradual return to work after childbearing (a limited period of a reduced-hours schedule following childbirth); and (f) personal leaves (unpaid but with reinstatement rights) for absences in excess of twelve weeks, for care of a newborn, newly adopted child, or new foster child or for an ill family member, with family defined broadly so as not to disadvantage grandparents caring for grandchildren and others in nontraditional families.[83]

These leaves should be accompanied by backup or cross-training systems to buffer the impact of unanticipated absences. These same systems will also help ensure continuity and productivity in the case of unwanted attrition. Finally, large employers may find it worthwhile to make a contract with a child care provider to run day camps onsite during the summer and on school breaks (including snow days). Employers are already paying for many of the work absences these needs represent—they just are being counted as part of workers' own sick time.

3. *Create family-responsive overtime systems.* Overtime systems need to be redesigned to ensure effective overtime coverage for employers without driving out conscientious workers. Two principles can help guide such efforts. First, employers should rely as much as possible on voluntary rather than mandatory overtime. Allocating overtime equally among the workforce makes no sense, given that some workers positively desire overtime, while others feel a pressing need to avoid it. Second, employers should design overtime systems so that workers with bona fide child care and other family care needs may refuse overtime, and these systems should include provisions that designate specific days or other periods when workers will be on call for overtime, so that they can arrange family care coverage

in advance. This is the system developed ad hoc by arbitrators in a variety of cases, notably *Rochester Psychiatric* and *Allied Paper*.[84]

Another important principle in blue-collar jobs is that apprenticeships and other on-the-job training programs should not be offered only after working hours. That kind of scheduling potentially prevents mothers, divorced men, and men in tag team families from occupational advancement.

4. *Offer reduced hours and flexible work options.* A recent study by Allstate Insurance found that hourly workers were more likely than professional-managerial workers to want a part-time schedule. Of course, jobs with tailored schedules, if they are to achieve the business goals associated with ending workforce-workplace mismatch, should pay at least prorated benefits (in sharp contrast to the practice of switching jobs from full- to part-time in order to decrease labor costs by eliminating benefits). Examples of specific categories of working-class jobs that could accommodate reduced-hour schedules include the following:[85]

On-site blue-collar jobs in manufacturing and medical/police/emergency personnel, including medical techs, nurses, and nurses aides. In some jobs, being on site is essential, either because that is where the customers are or because the job requires extensive equipment and/or teamwork. Reduced-schedule options in these types of jobs include compressed workweeks, job sharing, and part-time work. In compressed workweeks, workers work four 10-hour days and have the fifth day off; or in the "nine-day fortnight" version, workers work eight nine-hour days and have every other tenth day off. In job sharing, two people split one job. For example, one person works two days a week and the other works three days a week. In part-time work, some workers work a four-day week; the extra days are covered by retirees who want to "keep their hand in" or by "floaters" whose jobs consist of filling in for workers on their days off.[86]

On-site pink-collar jobs, such as administrative assistants who have a personal relationship with an individual boss. When professionals work longer workweeks than support staff, compressed working time could keep administrative personnel in the office for ten hours a day, four days a week, eliminating those awkward times when the professional is working without administrative support. Floaters could cover the administrative staff's nonwork days. Another approach is to allow two administrators to job share, with each working a thirty-hour week, so that together they provide coverage for a professional's sixty-hour week. "Flexwork," which allows flexible starting and stopping times, can cut down on attrition by decreasing the number of situations in which workers have to quit because of changes in the schedules of their child care providers or because tag team partners find it impossible to continue arriving for (or leaving from) work at the originally agreed-upon time.

On-site service work, including retail sales, auto repair, computer repair, clerical jobs, and telephone jobs. In a wide variety of industries, compressed workweeks, job sharing, and flexible starting and stopping times would permit companies to increase the hours of service without paying overtime and without increasing attrition and absenteeism—if workers could choose whether to use these programs. Shifting workers' schedules without their consent plays havoc with their caregiving responsibilities, which will in turn lead to high and expensive turnover. Telecommuting is often an option for workers with clerical jobs such as billing or telephone jobs such as customer service. For example, when GlaxoSmithKline's Consumer Healthcare division implemented a compressed workweek, 89% of customers felt service had not been disrupted, and 98% said their inquiries had been answered in a timely manner.[87]

Off-site work, such as jobs in sales. Compressed working time, job sharing, and flexible starting and stopping times also are an option in off-site jobs. GlaxoSmithKline again offers an example: its Consumer Healthcare division implemented flexible work arrangements, particularly job sharing, among customer service reps as a way of retaining talent. The result was increased productivity and extra coverage. AstraZeneca found that those in job-sharing and part-time positions in its pharmaceutical sales force performed as well as sales reps with conventional schedules.[88]

Opt Out or Pushed Out, Redux?

Ellen is not the kind of opt-out mom we read about in the newspapers. Before she left the workforce, she was solidly working class. Married to a construction worker, she had worked as a cashier, security guard, day care staffer, and food preparer for an adult day care center. Then, in 1999, her husband was severely injured in a shooting. At the time of her interview by sociologist Alford Young, Jr. in 2002, Ellen had two children, aged one and two. Early in her eight-year marriage, she said, "we had gas in the car, rent paid up for the whole year, vacations, everything." But after the kids and the injury, "everything started going bad." Ultimately, she had to quit her job. She was truly upset: "It's really hard having a baby. Right now, that's what I'm going through. I had to quit my job because I didn't have nobody to watch them for four hours, and this was a good job."[89]

Ellen didn't opt out. She was pushed out, as was another interviewee, Karen. "If you're one minute late, it don't matter," said Karen, describing how she lost a prior job due to a no-fault absenteeism system. "Or, if you totally missed a day or whatever. So you got eight [absences] a year and even if say your child got sick . . . And so, you know, it comes to a point in time where you gotta say, okay, it's either this job or my kids." As these and other stories show, it is not just professional women facing the opt out or pushed out phenomenon. Working-class and pink collar women, like their professional sisters, are forced out of jobs—jobs their families sorely need—by unnecessarily inflexible, rigid workplaces. The message for newspapers and other media is that the acute work-family conflicts less affluent families face need front-page and prime-time coverage, too.[90]

For policymakers, a crucial message from union arbitrations is that work-family conflict is not just a professional women's issue. The press's overly autobiographical approach to covering work-family issues has a negative impact on public policy. "My boss is not interested in the problems of professional women," one Capitol Hill staffer confided to me around 2002. This chapter shows just how urgently public policy is needed. Once the press stops covering work-family issues as simply an occasion for celebrating the return of wholesome traditions (as documented in the previous chapter), policymakers will come face to face with a central irony. In a country where family values are an accepted part of political discourse, family members caring for children, elders, and the ill are often "one sick kin" away from being fired.[91]

The most important message is for unions. As noted above, workers need to know that just because an employer gives them a job, this does not mean their employers can deprive of their ability to do right by their families. The union movement often mistakenly views work-family issues as a luxury item. These are core union issues, particularly given American workers' heavy reliance on family caregiving.[92]

CHAPTER THREE

Masculine Norms at Work

What we know about jobs ... has more to do with [the people who inhabit those jobs] (e.g., their gender, status, lifestyles, personalities, traits, etc.) than the tasks the jobs actually involve.

—GLICK, WILK, AND PERREAULT, "IMAGES OF OCCUPATIONS: COMPONENTS OF GENDER AND STATUS IN OCCUPATIONAL STEREOTYPES"[1]

A PATIENT IS BROUGHT into the emergency room. The surgeon says, "I can't operate on this patient: he's my son." The surgeon is not the patient's father. Why can't the surgeon operate?

This classic brainteaser works—and it worked on me—because of the hidden assumption that surgeons are male. The answer: the surgeon is the patient's mother. The riddle highlights that most jobs are gendered. Only 13% of occupations are sex balanced, in the sense of integrating men and women beyond token levels.[2] And most high-paying jobs, blue- as well as white-collar, are associated not only with men but also with masculinity. Thus the personality traits commonly assumed to make for a good engineer or tool-and-die maker (good at technical subjects, not high on people skills) are considered masculine. So are the very different skills assumed to make for a good executive or factory foreman (forceful and assertive, high on people skills).[3]

No logical relationship exists between these two sets of personality traits and skills. Their relationship is historical, based on the high value placed on qualities associated with men and masculinity. Before separate spheres arose in the late eighteenth century, many women worked as blacksmiths, woodworkers, printers, tinsmiths, brewers, tavern keepers, shopkeepers, shoemakers, barbers, and shipwrights. So long as these women were wives acting as "deputy husbands" for men who were away, this seemed appropriate and unobjectionable. Women doing jobs traditionally performed by men did not yet jar sensibilities because men and women were not chiefly defined by their separate spheres.[4]

Women pre-1800 were defined not by their social role but rather by their inferiority. A nigh-unquestioned premise was that men, as heads of the household, had the right to expect obedience not only from their children but also from their wives. "God's universal law gave to man despotic power / Over his female in due awe," wrote Milton, articulating in poetry the ideology of gender hierarchy that persisted until the Enlightenment. Women needed men's guidance because they were viewed as not only physically inferior to men but also intellectually and morally inferior: morally weak and easily swayed. Fathers were the ultimate authority in child rearing as in every other arena of life, because something as important as children's immortal souls could not be entrusted to mere women.[5]

The Enlightenment's declaration that all "men" were equal destabilized established notions of women's inferiority. Very gradually, women came to be seen as equal, too—in their separate sphere. Women went from being seen as morally weak to being considered more moral than men. Under separate spheres, the "moral mother" was expected to counterbalance men's pursuit of self-interest in the market sphere. The market, still new, was painted as ruthless, "red in tooth and claw."[6]

Separate-spheres definitions of the "true natures" of men and women live on today. It turns out that our twenty-first-century common sense, our "structured sets of beliefs about the personal attributes of women and men,"[7] faithfully channels separate-spheres ideology. Thus today's typical man is seen as independent, ambitious, and competitive, naturally suited to market work and the breadwinner role. Meanwhile today's typical woman is seen as nurturing, expressive, and responsive to the needs of others, naturally suited to homemaking and emotion work required by secretaries, flight attendants, and nurses. These basic tenets of separate spheres continue to shape our default understandings of men and women, reproducing stereotypes that systematically advantage men and disadvantage women in the workplace.[8]

These stereotypes lead to powerful social expectations that link our sense of what one needs to be successful in historically male professions to masculine personality traits and traditionally masculine life patterns. "In particular, our selection procedures tend to select not only for talents that are directly relevant to success in science, but also for assertiveness and single-mindedness," noted one prominent physicist.[9] In other words, physicists are expected to have stereotypically masculine personality traits: to be forceful, proactive, assertive—"agentic" to quote social psychologists' chosen term. Social scientists have meticulously documented that men are consistently seen as more agentic, defined as "convey[ing] more assertion and control." Women, meanwhile, are seen as more "communal," defined as "convey[ing] a concern with the compassionate care of others."[10] These are just new scientific terms for the qualities assigned to men and women under separate spheres. In the early modern period, men—not women— would have been seen as more involved with communal life. "Communal" now signals separate-spheres allocation of selflessness to mothers, whose labor at home and hearth allows men to pursue their careers. Social psychologists' finding that men are seen as more agentic and women as more communal is a measure less of the way men and women actually act than of the way separate spheres continues to shape the way we see our everyday reality.

Physicists, the quote reminds us, are expected to be not only assertive but also single-minded. This is a singularly polite way of saying that, to be a physicist, you need a stay-at-home wife who allows you single-minded "'devotion to work' unencumbered with family responsibilities."[11] Not only physicists but also hard-driving lawyers, neurosurgeons, and investment bankers—indeed, all historically male high-status jobs—require some version of assertiveness and single-mindedness. In other words, they are designed around masculinity and men. "There's definitely a machismo that goes with being a corporate lawyer," said one attorney, a woman of color.[12]

Masculinity holds the key to understanding why the gender revolution has stalled. As long as men continue to feel threatened by the possibility of being perceived as wimps and wusses unless they live up to the norms of conventional masculinity, we can expect little economic progress for women. Therefore, this chapter explores masculine workplace norms, focusing first on their impact on men and then on their impact on women.[13]

Men Are Gendered, Too

It has been said that masculine norms make American society "an affirmative action plan" for men. But not for all men—only for those who play by the rules of conventional masculinity. The U.S. Supreme Court case of *Oncale v. Sundowner Offshore Services* documents how masculine norms disadvantage men such as Joseph Oncale, who do not fit into the straightjacket of conventional masculinity. Oncale, one of an eight-man crew on an oil platform in the Gulf of Mexico, did not conform to the swaggering machismo enshrined as normative in his workplace.[14] As a result, his colleagues saw him as a "girlie man," to use a famous quote by Arnold

Schwarzenegger.[15] Oncale, who was straight, was subjected to homophobic name-calling, physically assaulted, and threatened with rape. The legal issue was whether he could sue for sexual harassment. The Supreme Court held that he could.[16]

Mr. Oncale was punished by his co-workers for his imperfect performance of masculinity. This form of gender discrimination is not unusual among men deemed effeminate, who often face employment problems. Feminists need to be on the front lines of documenting how conventional masculinity disadvantages men as well as women.[17]

As noted earlier, being a good provider still is viewed as an integral part of being a good father. Fathers with child care responsibilities risk being seen as wimps, so a man who fails to perform as an ideal worker risks being seen as both a bad father and a failure as a man. Moreover, the social regard for stay-at-home fathers is even lower than for stay-at-home mothers. Stay-at-home fathers are frequently considered worse parents than are employed fathers. Think of everyday language: when mothers dream about their daughter marrying a "successful" man, most are thinking of paychecks, not Snugli child carriers. Said one upper-middle-class man, "Let's face it, most men want to build their ego by saying, 'I've made it, I've been successful.' Hell, how do you grade that success? You grade it by the amount of money you made."[18]

The literature on fatherhood sends a stark message: all fathers are not equal. Breadwinners married to homemakers earn 30% more than those in two-job families and encounter favored treatment at work. One study found that fathers were held to lower performance and commitment standards than were men without children, presumably because respondents reasoned that since a father "has a family to support," he will work hard. A second study found that fatherhood did not affect the job prospects of someone applying for a position as a management consultant. These studies reflect the normative father—a breadwinner with a wife who is responsible for children and home. In sharp contrast, a father who discloses that he has family care responsibilities faces sizable job risks. One study found that men are often penalized for taking family leave, especially by other men. Another found that men with even a short work absence due to a family conflict were recommended for fewer rewards and had lower performance ratings.[19]

So the choice is clear. Be a manly, successful ideal worker, or be a wimpy nurturing father. Blue-collar men with child care responsibilities report, "I get teased" and "The husbands think I'm pussy-whipped . . . There are friends of mine who think I'm a wuss."[20] Many white-collar men find themselves in the same position. When one young University of California professor requested parental leave, he was "met with a sneering denial by [the department] chair, who said that, while another male colleague at Berkeley may have enjoyed that 'vacation,' our department couldn't spare my teaching services."[21]

This scorn for men seeking to fulfill family responsibilities is commonplace—and unambiguously illegal. Granting parental leave routinely to women but denying it to men is a violation of federal law. So is creating an environment hostile to men who seek parental leave (or, even more bravely, demand flexible work arrangements). Illegal as well is retaliation against men who are courageous enough to ignore the sneers and play an equal role in family caregiving. A key agenda for modern feminism is to work with men to decrease the penalties encountered by those who flout the expectations that stem from conventional masculinity.[22]

When ideal-worker norms police men into breadwinner roles, this not only hurts women. It also hurts many men who cannot live up to the breadwinner ideal. Since most American families cannot live comfortably on one income, many low-wage and working-class men, as well as many middle-class men, find themselves in the painfully demoralizing position of being unable to "support their families." Men are caught between an old-fashioned breadwinner ideal and an economic era that no longer delivers the family wage and are left facing two choices: they can feel terrible about themselves, or they can help to change an outdated ideal. Feminists need to engage men on this issue.

A surprisingly high number of men who live up to the old-fashioned breadwinner ideal do not endorse it. Men who work fifty to sixty hours weekly would prefer to work an average of thirteen fewer hours a week; those working sixty or more hours would prefer to work a stunning twenty-five hours fewer. While male professionals and managers tend to work longer hours than other men, this does not reflect unfettered "choice." Their preferred schedules would be about the same as other men's: their preference is to work about forty hours a week. Only 17.6% of men report wanting to work fifty or more hours a week; about twice as many men (including 40% of college-educated men) actually do so.[23]

Ultimately, the successful breadwinner may incur personal costs that far outstrip his earnings. The typical upper-middle-class man spends fifty-five hours a week at work or commuting, spending 8 A.M. to 7 P.M. away from home each weekday or working at least one day each weekend.[24] That does not leave much time for family life. "I had the opportunity to close a business deal once," a female executive recalled. "It was a table full of men, and they all said that they never see their kids. One man said, 'I see my kids two hours a week.'"[25] This absence takes a high toll on children.

A 1999 study of two-job couples found that the children were more likely to report having too little time with their fathers than with their mothers. Not surprising, given that on average, fathers spend only one hour with their children for every three that mothers spend with them.[26]

Privileged men still regularly report regret at the sudden realization that they have missed their children's childhoods. Their perception is accurate, especially as compared with dads in the 1950s. In the classic television show *Ozzie and Harriet,* which has become emblematic of 1950s family life, Ozzie returned home at 5 o'clock. Men's midlife crises are at once an expression of gender privilege—when they walk away with their wallets and "marry a newer model"—and an expression of gender pain. In midlife, men who have lived work-centered lives often feel a vast, unquiet emptiness to their lives, fueled by an (often accurate) sense that they are marginal to family life. "Fathers [are] a poor source of information about their children's daily lives," reports one researcher, although many report "high levels" of involvement. "Many fathers," one study reports, "appear to be ideologically committed to the idea that they should play an active role in their children's lives" but overreport their household labor by 149%.[27]

Men's gender role attenuates their social relationships in general. Said one father, when asked which of the parents he knew from among his children's friends, "My wife will tell you who I know."[28] Women, thanks to the long reach of separate spheres, are assigned responsibility for "the conception, maintenance, and ritual celebration of cross-household kin ties: including visits, letters, telephone calls, presents and cards to kin; the organization of holiday gatherings; the creation and maintenance of quasi-kin relations; decisions to neglect or to intensify particular ties; the mental work of reflection about all these activities."[29] Without women, many conventional men—particularly, one suspects, shy ones—become lonely and isolated.

Think of Warren Schmidt, played by Jack Nicholson in the film version of Louis Begley's novel, *About Schmidt.* After Schmidt retires, his life's work—actuarial calculations—is unceremoniously thrown in the trash. When Schmidt's wife dies, he tries, and fails, to persuade his daughter to give up her career and move back home to take care of him. When she refuses, his once-immaculate house becomes dirty and his refrigerator empty. He comes to realize that he hardly knows his daughter and that, indeed, he hardly knew his wife. He has only one close friend, from whom he becomes estranged. His life is so empty that his emotional center becomes an African orphan to whom he pours out his innermost feelings, so long withheld from everyone in his family, including himself. Gender privilege is not all it's cracked up to be.[30]

Breadwinners, even affluent ones, also feel the pressure of being a family's sole support. "My husband feels it's a huge burden to support all of us," said a stay-at-home mother with a Harvard law degree and a home in an affluent Connecticut suburb. "He's definitely stressed out."[31] This is not to suggest that men are not privileged by gender. They clearly are. But the straightjacket of conventional masculinity hurts not only men unable to live up to socially accepted male roles but also the many men who play those roles well but ultimately feel imprisoned by them. Deconstructing masculine norms—both workplace norms and norms that link masculinity with stunted personal expressiveness—is an agenda that should hold attraction for men as well as women.

Masculinity at Work

In 1985, Sarah Fenstermaker published an influential book called *The Gender Factory*, in which she argued that family dynamics are the anvil upon which gender roles are forged. The book is a formal expression of the accepted wisdom among American feminists that the key to women's equality lies in having women bargain more effectively at home.[32] "The thickest glass ceiling is at home," notes Linda Hirshman, urging women to engage in "reproductive blackmail," if necessary, to get their men to do half the housework.[33]

Shifting the focus through what I have termed "reconstructive feminism" offers an alternative argument and leads to a different solution. The family is a gender factory, but so is the workplace.[34] Consider the comment of Scott Webster, a Silicon Valley engineer:

> Guys try to out-macho each other, but in engineering it's really perverted because out-machoing someone means being more of a nerd than the other person . . . It's not like being a brave firefighter and going up one more flight than your friend. There's a lot of see how many hours I can work, whether or not you have a kid . . . He's a real man; he works 90-hour weeks. He's a slacker; he works 50 hours a week.[35]

Men's felt need to prove their masculinity at work sharply limits women's ability to negotiate gender equality within the family.

To flesh this out further, let's begin with Robin Ely and Debra Meyerson's astute study of oil platforms, a blue-collar workplace "that traditionally has rewarded men for masculine displays of bravado and for interactions centered on proving masculinity."[36] The management of one company undertook a large-scale effort to change the company culture, in order to decrease accidents on their deep-water oil-drilling and production platforms in the Gulf of Mexico. Oil platforms are masculine through and through. The predominantly male workforce typically works and lives together offshore for two weeks on duty, two weeks off. The standard shift is twelve hours, and everyone is on call twenty-four hours a day, so the structure of the job requires workers to have someone else caring for their children. Ten years ago, the dominant script at the company in question was masculine in other ways as well. At its core was a "masculine identity centered on appearing physically tough, technically infallible, and emotionally detached."[37] Then management decided that the workplace culture was not cost-effective: "We were more and more frustrated with the fact that people kept getting hurt . . . In the early nineties we made the commitment [to reduce injuries] that became known as Safety 2000."[38]

The before-and-after contrast was stark. An offshore installation manager who had worked for the company for twenty-seven years described a shift away from a bullying form of masculinity:

> [Back then] the field foremen were kind of like a pack of lions. The guy that was in charge was the one who could basically outperform and out-shout and out-intimidate all the others. That's just how it worked out here on drilling rigs and in production. So those people went to the top, over other people's bodies in some cases. Intimidation was the name of the game . . . They decided who the driller was by fighting. If the job came open, the one that was left standing was the driller. It was that rowdy. But it's not like that at all now. I mean we don't even horseplay like we used to. There's no physical practical jokes anymore. Most stuff now is just good-natured joking.[39]

An electrician described a shift away from the "strong silent type" persona:

> Ten, twelve years ago I just couldn't imagine sitting down with somebody like you and talking about these kinds of things. It was way more macho then than it is now. It was like, "Hey, this is a man's world. If you can't cut it here, boy, you don't need to be here." Now there's a little bit more of, "Let's learn what people are about," a little bit more about the personal and interpersonal relationship and that kind of stuff.[40]

Definitions of competence and leadership also changed. Under the new regime, an admission of doubt, error, or caution was no longer seen as a sign of weakness. Before the culture shift, the most valued workers had been the "biggest, baddest roughnecks" who gave no thought to the safety of themselves or others—much less any thought to people's feelings or to team building. Any expression of vulnerability, any acknowledgement of physical limitations, any admission of a need for help, or even for information, had been interpreted as a sign of weakness. A forty-year-old production worker described the cultural shift that changed this paradigm:

> I started working offshore when I was seventeen. Back then, there was much more profanity, much more posturing. If you didn't posture yourself in a position of power, then you set yourself up for ridicule. But over the years, with company training in the personal and interpersonal areas, people have learned that you don't have to present yourself in that fashion in order to gain power. You don't have to use profanity to make a statement that carries power.[41]

Another worker admitted having found the culture change "very hard" at first:

> [We were taught] how to be more lovey-dovey and more friendly to each other and to get in touch with the more tender side of each other type of thing. And all of us just laughed at first. It was like, man, this is never going to work, you know? But now you can really tell the difference. Even though we kid around and joke around with each other, there's no malice in it. We are a very different group of people now than we were when we first got together— kinder, gentler people.[42]

Note the association of masculinity with malice, and collegiality with "lovey-dovey" femininity. The new model of leadership defined "mission-driven" employees according to a new set of ideals: as people who "care about their fellow workers," are "good listeners," and are "thoughtful"— all qualities management saw as crucial to driving down the incidence of workplace injury. These qualities map onto the stereotype of the "typical woman" (nurturing, expressive, and responsive to the needs of others) far better than onto the stereotype of the "typical man" ("more confident, less sensitive").[43]

Under the old regime, it was seen as unmanly to admit mistakes. And since admitting a mistake could lead to job loss, a culture of cover-ups resulted. Under the new regime, workers were trained to acknowledge their own physical limitations, to ask for help when they needed it, and to openly attend to feelings, their own and others'. A production operator described the new ideal worker as someone who "knows what he's doing, or if he doesn't, he'll take the time to do the research to understand what he's doing . . . They take time to learn."[44] The new culture also encouraged workers to talk things through and learn from past mistakes, as when a seventeen-year-old accidentally shut down all production by throwing a switch, on the advice of a coworker. The coworker was a six-foot-four former Chicago cop. During an investigation of the incident, the younger man admitted that he had thrown the switch against his better judgment, acknowledging that he was intimidated by the older man's imposing presence. "This exchange led to a larger team discussion about the need to watch out for one's potential to intimidate—however unwittingly—or to be intimidated."[45] Brute strength had come to be seen as a potential work-place detriment. As a production operator explained, when problems arise, the goal is no longer to find a suitable scapegoat but instead "to get to the root cause to prevent this from happening again. Was it a lack of knowledge, a lack of skill, or improper equipment? Was it an engineering issue where engineering needs to come in and take a look at this? We go through the whole thing."[46] The new message is that when mistakes are made, management is chiefly concerned with avoiding them in the future, rather than meting out punishment.

Note how masculinity was redefined as the ability of working-class men to work things out for themselves, without the need to call in management. One leader held "fireside chats"—on-site meetings where he fielded questions from workers and listened to their concerns. "People talk about how brave he is to do this."[47] This is quite a change from the old definition of bravery as the ability to take physical risks without thinking twice—and one far more useful to the company.

If the traditionalist blue-collar work culture is inefficient, what about the white-collar version? Marianne Cooper's brilliant study, "Being the 'Go-To Guy,'" answers that question by closely examining the paradigmatic white-collar workplace of the twenty-first century: Silicon Valley.[48] The quote with which this section begins shows that white-collar men also feel pressure to enact their chosen masculinity on the job. Silicon Valley engineers internalize an image of themselves as "pencil pushers" ("It's not like being a brave firefighter"). Whereas blue-collar work is suffused with masculinity—it is dirty and requires strength—white-collar work is clean, gender-neutral knowledge work unrelated to physical strength. This leaves white-collar men searching for ways to imagine their work as proving their manliness. In Silicon Valley, Cooper finds, they do so by interpreting long work hours as a heroic activity. Recall the Silicon Valley engineer, who commented that to be a "real man" required working extremely long hours: "He's a real man; he works 90-hour weeks. He's a slacker; he works 50 hours a week."[49] Another engineer elaborates on the workplace culture that equates manliness with "putting in wild hours":

> Even under normal circumstances, when there are no extraordinary demands, you see people working 36 hours straight just because they are going to meet the deadline. They are going to get it done, and everybody walks around being proud of how exhausted they were last week and conspicuously putting in wild hours. It's a status thing to have pizza delivered to the office. So I don't know why it happens, but I really feel like it is kind of a machismo thing: I'm

tough. I can do this. Yeah, I'm tired, but I'm on top of it. You guys don't worry about me . . . The people who conspicuously overwork are guys, and I think it's usually for the benefit of other guys.[50]

"There's this kind of machismo culture among the young male engineers that you just don't sleep,"[51] said a father of two who ultimately left his job to work from home. Denying oneself sleep is a way to turn a sedentary job into a test of physical endurance. "The successful enactment of this masculinity," Cooper writes, "involves displaying one's exhaustion, physically and verbally, in order to convey the depth of one's commitment, stamina, and virility."[52] This norm is policed through language of community and mutual responsibility: one's refusal to sleep proves one's commitment to the team. As one engineer explained, "You have to be part of the team. You can't fall out. If you get injured, you come back as fast as you can or you play with your injury whether it's emotional or physical."[53] Cooper concludes, "A prerequisite for being a committed team player is a devotion to work that borders on addiction." She quotes one man who admitted, "I was just anxious as hell unless I was working."[54] Ultimately, it took that man "years and 12-step programs" to escape a situation he had come to see as unhealthy. "Time becomes a proxy for dedication and excellence," notes sociologist Cynthia Fuchs Epstein. People literally forget that it is possible to be both talented and dedicated to their careers while also refusing to mistake their job for their life.[55]

Despite the assumption that working people hard makes more money, Cooper shows how the norm of work devotion can detract from the bottom line.[56] Much of the time, she points out, the need for the Silicon Valley engineers to stay late reflects a lack of planning. "Remarkably, poor planning is reinterpreted as a test of will, a test of manhood for a team of engineers," she observes.[57] Along with poor planning, failure to delegate is tolerated or even admired. "They have no idea how to delegate," one informant remarks of his colleagues.[58] Also accepted is working oneself so hard as to undermine productivity: "My god, I mean, talk about sweatshops, I mean, they are oblivious. The managers have no idea what an altered state they are in all the time while they are managing these guys."[59] Extensive research documents that sleep deprivation corrodes performance, and that constant stress leads to higher health insurance costs.[60] "Wild hours" are not likely to translate into steep profits. The business case for a more family-friendly workplace has been documented extensively for decades.[61] Yet this evidence has had relatively little impact because stereotypes and unspoken norms either cause people to overlook the business case or to refuse to credit it. For example, the Project for Attorney Retention (which

I direct) documented over a decade ago that law firms that fail to offer non-stigmatized flexible schedules experience high rates of attrition, which creates steep costs. It costs between $200,000 and $500,000 to replace a single associate—so five associates who leave to escape 24/7 schedules cost a firm $1 to $2.5 million.[62] Yet many law firm partners remain convinced that "we can't afford part-timers." Attrition costs are seen as unavoidable costs of doing business and so fade easily from consciousness. Yet every penny associated with part-time schedules is noticed, and deeply felt, because it is seen as an "extra," avoidable cost.[63]

Because workplaces are gender factories where men forge and enact their masculinity, a worker's manliness may be called into question when a man calls attention to his family care obligations. Recall the union men in the previous chapter who would rather be fired than admit they needed to leave early to care for children.[64] Professional men, too, often avoid taking time off work, or they hide the fact that they are doing so, to preserve their "Go-To" status.[65] Consider the case of Rich, a young engineer with a growing family. When his boss spoke enthusiastically of the need to hold a particular meeting as soon as possible, he reacted with panic. "Sweating like a horse," he called his secretary. "Hey, you gotta get me out of this, because my baby is getting christened and if I don't meet with the priest it's not going to happen and my family is going to kill me and my wife will divorce me and I won't have any kids and my life will be terrible."[66] Rich resented his manager's demands, noting that the manager "doesn't have two kids and a wife, he has people that live in his house, that's basically what he has."[67] Despite the fact that Rich appears not to share his manager's views, confronting this issue directly apparently seemed out of the question: he was dependent on his boss for good assignments and a future with the firm.

The conventional wisdom—that the stalled revolution is best addressed by insisting that women negotiate more effectively with their husbands—is utterly unrealistic. That wisdom rests on the assumption that family is "the gender factory." In many situations, the salient gender factory is in fact the workplace, which sets the nonnegotiable terms within which men and women bargain in family life. Take the example of a young couple, both of whom worked for the same law firm. After they had a baby, the wife was sent home promptly at 5:30—she had a baby to take care of—whereas her husband was kept later than ever—he had a family to support. Negotiating hard with her husband would not have helped this woman at all, unless her husband was willing and able to find another job.[68]

An additional factor feeds the dynamic of masculinized workplace devotion: the role of continually occurring status negotiations among men. This aspect of conventional masculinity is astutely observed by Deborah

Tannen, who notes the importance, for many men, of maintaining "the one-up position."[69] Historians point out that when masculinity first became associated with breadwinner status in the nineteenth century, anxiety became men's heritage. "Sons had to compete for manhood in the market rather than grow into secure manhood by replicating fathers," a commentator remarked in the 1920s.[70] "The birthright of every American male is a chronic sense of personal inadequacy," added another twentieth-century author.[71] The bulwark against inadequacy is to be "successful"—which again means to be successful at work. "Despite men's differences, breadwinning has remained the great unifying element in fathers' lives. Its obligations bind men across the boundaries of color and class, and shape their sense of self, manhood, and gender," concludes historian Robert Griswold.[72] This makes it difficult for men to challenge the felt mandate to live up to workplace norms. "I was talking to a friend of mine, a partner at a major San Francisco law firm," Derek Bok, former president of Harvard University, told me in 2001. "He was always complaining about how hard he worked, so I asked: 'Then why don't you just work 3/5 as hard and take 3/5 the salary?' He was tongue-tied. But of course the real reason he couldn't is that then he feared he wouldn't 'be a player.' "[73]

The dictates of conventional masculinity often make men wary of situations that might result in losing face. "Men are more likely to be on guard to prevent themselves from being put in a one-down position," Tannen notes. Social psychologist Joseph A. Vandello and his coauthors help explain why: "whereas womanhood is viewed as a developmental certainty that is permanent once achieved, manhood is seen as more of a social accomplishment that can be lost and therefore must be defended with active demonstrations of manliness." Consequently, men respond to a threat to their status as "real men" with greater anxiety than women respond to a threat to their status as "real women."[74]

Because caregiving is not high-status—whereas having a wife who takes care of all that is—many men are reluctant to admit at work that they have caregiving responsibilities. This is true of both blue- and white-collar men. In unionized jobs, it appears that more men than women are fired due to work-family conflict at least in part because men are extremely reluctant to admit that they need to leave work to care for children.

Some younger men, however, are less willing than their elders to play by the old rules. The literature on Gen X and Gen Y men suggests that a critical mass of younger men—though by no means all—are seeking something different.[75] Rich, the man who went into a panic at the possibility of missing his child's baptism, explicitly questioned his boss's priorities:

The CEO of this start-up company had three kids—4, 7, 10—nice kids but he never ever sees them because he's at work 7 days a week . . . And I'm thinking, his kids aren't going to have any idea who he is. He doesn't think these little moments matter, but they do. I mean, the guy was a real shit when it came to his kids. I'm sorry. He's 40, and he's bound and determined that he's going to make his multimillions, and he thinks he is doing the right thing for his kids, because he thinks he's doing all this for them, since one day they will be rich. They will be rich with money, but poor as people.[76]

Rich makes short work of the traditionalist rationale: that workaholic fathers are selfless, doing it all for their children. He found obvious flaws in this version of masculinity, but recall that he felt powerless to challenge this ideology at work. He put his foot down only when his supervisor threatened to deprive him of attendance at a "set piece"—his child's baptism. As Arlie Hochschild pointed out long ago, ideal-worker men tend to think of childhood not in terms of day-in, day-out care but in terms of set pieces such as children's theatrical performances or soccer games.[77]

This is a long way from playing an equal role in a child's life. But it is a start. Americans now work longer hours than workers in most other developed countries (including Japan, where there is a word, *karoshi*, for "death by overwork"), and American elites work longer hours than other Americans.[78] If feminists can learn to engage elite men, their workplace dissatisfaction could be a powerful force for change. Herein lies the challenge, as Cooper makes clear in the conclusion to her study of Silicon Valley working fathers. She ends by discussing Kirk, a Gen Xer who at one point "personified the Silicon Valley warrior." His log-in moniker, "Ali"—a reference to the boxer—aptly reflected his initial commitment to the work ethic required to knock 'em out. He took off only a few days when his second child was born, which was "a sore point" with his wife but taken for granted by his colleagues at work. Eventually, Kirk recognized, "They need the job to come first, and I had spent a year letting a really crappy job come first. The family really suffered." He decided to quit, but in order to do so, "he had to renegotiate aspects of his identity." Specifically, "I had to convince myself that it was okay to fail." He had to let go of being a player—the go-to guy.[79]

Feminists can admire this kind of courage, but we cannot depend on all men to have it. Which means that we must ally ourselves with men like Kirk and bring about nonstigmatized career tracks that offer Gen X and Gen Y men good careers and time for family life. Otherwise, women will continue to do the bulk of family and household work and will also continue to pay a steep economic price for doing so.

Femininity has changed a lot since 1960. True, the old schemas of reassuringly nice and soothingly feminine women persist, but they exist alongside more capacious understandings of femininity that include room for "deference-challenged" women. Hillary not only bakes cookies; she also runs for president—with high negatives but a credible campaign. But changing femininity is not enough. Masculinity has changed comparatively little. Feminists need to work with men to deinstitutionalize "go-to guy" masculinity in the workplace. Following up on the trend in employment law that prohibits employers from using stereotypes as job requirements is a good place to start. Similarly, we need to make more systematic use of federal laws that prohibit employers from penalizing people who take family leave to which they are legally entitled. Also needed is a cultural component aimed at helping men invent a wider range of masculinities, so that refusing to conform to the orthodoxy will not require so much raw courage. Recall that many men are fired when they act on family values— and that unemployed men have higher rates of impotence than men in general. Traditional gender roles are literally inscribed into men's bodies. There is a lot at stake.[80]

One reason that allying with like-minded men is so important is that feminists seeking to restructure market work cannot assume that all women will join the fun. Women who perform as ideal workers often have paid a higher price than men for doing so: most either gave up having children or struggled with the dual demands of work and motherhood, facing daily challenges and abiding fears that they were being "bad moms." Many of these women have a lot invested in the view that being an ideal worker is what the job takes: otherwise, why did they sacrifice having children or having time with them? These women cannot realistically be expected to join with younger generations of women to change the workplace. Although some will, it is not fair to demand that of them. Conversely, men like Kirk and Rich can be expected to join with mothers and others to insist on workplaces that allow people to reconcile work and family commitments.

The Effect of Masculine Workplace Norms on Women

Spontaneous classifications of jobs are dominated by what we know about the gender and the social status of job occupants. Both blue-collar and high-prestige white-collar jobs are gendered masculine, although in different ways. Blue-collar jobs are associated with masculine traits that include physical strength and mechanical and special ability; feminine personality traits are a distinct negative in these jobs. High-status white-collar jobs also are gendered masculine, but the class-based differentiation of masculinities emerges clearly: these jobs are seen as requiring analytical ability and personality traits traditionally coded as masculine, such as ambition, competitiveness, and leadership abilities.[81]

When good jobs are associated with masculinity, gender stereotyping arises in everyday workplace interactions. Thirty-five years of social science document these patterns: this section summarizes the findings of over 200 social psychology studies, schematizing them into four basic patterns of gender bias.[82] The strongest and most open form of stereotyping, "maternal wall" bias, reflects the separate-spheres assumption that jobs (or at least good jobs) are best suited to breadwinners, not mothers. The second pattern, "Prove it again!", reflects the perceived "lack of fit" between historically male jobs and women who behave in traditionally feminine ways.[83] The third pattern, the "double bind," is summarized by a female professor at the Massachusetts Institute of Technology: "To get ahead here, you have to be so aggressive. But if women are too aggressive they're ostracized . . . and if they're not aggressive enough they have to do twice the work."[84] A final pattern of "gender wars", rarely studied, occurs when gender bias against women feeds conflict among women.

The Maternal Wall

Of all the triggers of stereotyping in today's workplace, motherhood triggers the strongest bias. As noted earlier, when researchers gave subjects identical resumes that differed in only one respect—one, but not the other, mentioned membership in the PTA—the mothers were 79% less likely to be hired and 100% less likely to be promoted. They also were held to higher performance and punctuality standards if they were hired. The mothers were assumed to have lost their commitment to work—they could not live up to the norm of work devotion. Mothers often are assumed to be less competent, to have "pregnancy brain," as one San Francisco official heard herself accused of at a public hearing. "I had a baby, not a lobotomy," protested a Boston lawyer, who found that she was given the work of a paralegal once she returned from maternity leave. Earlier studies found that while "businesswomen" are seen as highly competent, on a level comparable to businessmen, "housewives" are lumped alongside the most stigmatized groups in the economy: the elderly, blind, "retarded," and disabled. Mothers have to work harder to overcome the powerful negative competence and commitment assumptions triggered by motherhood. Bias against mothers is much stronger than "glass ceiling" bias against women in general.[85]

The maternal wall reflects the continuing hold of separate-spheres imagery that mothers belong in a domestic sphere set apart from the world of work. Separate spheres lives, too, in the family realm: "the good mother"—but not the "good father"—is seen as "someone who is always available to her children," according to another study.[86] Separate-spheres imagery of selfless motherhood continues to structure social intuitions in ways that systematically disadvantage women at work.

Maternal wall bias differs by race, creating double jeopardy for women of color. While white stay-at-home mothers are viewed more positively than white employed mothers, black employed mothers are viewed more positively than black stay-at-home mothers. One study reports that black mothers do not encounter the maternal wall until they have more than two children, while another study finds no difference between black and white mothers. No motherhood penalty exists for Latina women, according to another study. Perhaps the assumption that all Latinas will have children means that maternal wall bias is built in to the racial stereotype of Latinas.[87]

Fathers, as long as they signal an immunity to household work, are held to lower performance and punctuality standards than mothers: in the default mode, they are seen as breadwinners who receive an automatic assumption of competence and commitment. In sharp contrast, men who refuse to enact the breadwinner role, by signaling that they have caregiving responsibilities, encounter harsh workplace penalties. The bottom line is that anyone—male or female—who signals that he or she does not fit the breadwinner norm, either because of sex (she is a woman) or because of gender performance (he or she is a caregiver), can encounter harsh bias on the job.

Prove It Again!

When job competence is intertwined with masculinity, women find it harder to establish themselves as competent.[88] As a result, women find themselves having to work twice as hard to achieve half as much, an aphorism confirmed by a quarter-century of social science.[89] For example, a study that asked male and female psychology professors to evaluate identical application packages for a professorship found that the man was preferred over the woman by two to one. Remember, the applications were identical.[90] Another study found that women who applied for postdoctoral fellowships had to be 2.5 times more productive than male applicants in order to receive the same rating as men from the application reviewers.[91] In the corporate world, women often have to provide more evidence than men of job-related skills to be seen as competent.[92] Senior male executives "freely admitted that women in upper level positions were subject to competency testing much more often than their male counterparts."[93] Successful women "counter the 'competency barrier'" by "deliver[ing] more than people expect."[94]

Judgments about competence—including performance reviews— routinely reflect unexamined assumptions about differences between men and women that advantage the former and disadvantage the latter. Here are some examples:

1. Men's successes reflect skill. When the task at hand is seen as masculine, men's successes tend to be attributed to stable personality traits, while women's tend to be attributed to transitory situational factors.[95]

2. Women's mistakes reflect incompetence. Conversely, men's mistakes tend to be attributed to transitory situational factors, while those of women tend to be attributed to stable personality traits. This pattern is sometimes summarized as "what is luck in a woman is skill in a man."[96] Because stereotype-consistent information is recalled better than stereotype-inconsistent information, women's mistakes (confirming their lack of competence) may be remembered long after men's are forgotten.[97] "A man takes a big risk and makes a mistake, that's considered risky, but he's taking a chance; a woman does it, then it's just a big mistake," said one woman professor.[98] As a result, women can make fewer mistakes than men before they are judged incompetent.[99]

3. Men, but not women, are judged on their potential. The assumption that men but not women "have what it takes" may lead men to be judged on their potential in situations where women are judged strictly on what they have already accomplished.[100] "They were saying, 'We don't know her book of business,'" yet they let the males slide through," reported one woman law firm partner. "The scrutiny of a woman's book of business is harder.'"[101] (A "book of business" means that a lawyer has clients.) When men are judged on their potential, while women are judged on their achievements, men's job prospects are powerfully accelerated as compared with women's.

4. Objective rules are applied rigidly to women but leniently to men. Objective rules are no guarantee of objectivity when they are applied leniently to men but rigidly to women, a pattern called leniency bias.[102] Said a woman professor, "When it comes to equipment orders, we have a budget, and men just go out, make purchases, hand in the receipts and get reimbursed. But when [my woman colleague's] computer crashed, she had to haggle and go through procedures to get her one desktop replaced, even though a man in the department just bought two computers without prior protocols and was reimbursed."[103] Merit reviews have been found to be particularly vulnerable to leniency bias—and a lot of promotions depend heavily on "merit" reviews.[104]

5. Women who are excellent but not stellar are judged much more harshly than comparable men. While women who are superstars tend to get even higher evaluations than comparable men (who knew a *woman* could do it?), women who are merely excellent tend to get sharply lower evaluations than comparable men.[105] Negative information about a woman tends to be given greater weight than it would be if the information were about a man, since men benefit from a reflexive presumption of competence.[106] This pattern of polarized evaluations is especially common in workplaces with few women, because in those cases women's performance tends to be more closely scrutinized than men's.[107]

6. What's important? Whatever credential the man has. Evaluators shift standards in ways that advantage men. In a pattern called "casuistry," when a male candidate applying for a professional job had stronger educational credentials than women against whom he was competing, evaluators tended to value education. But when a woman had stronger educational credentials, evaluators tended to value experience over education—and still favor the man.[108]

7. Double jeopardy: merit standards differ by race. Glass ceiling stereotypes differ by race, putting women of color in double jeopardy. A substantial literature documents racial inequality in the labor market.[109] When evaluators were shown two identical resumes with just one difference— one had with a European-American name ("Greg"), the other an African American name ("Jamal")—white candidates got as many callbacks as blacks with *eight additional years of job experience*. The higher the qualifications of the applicant, the larger the race gap.[110] Another matched-resume study showed that when race was indicated on a resume, whites recommended the white candidate 76% of the time but the black candidate only 45% of the time.[111] In a national survey of law firms conducted in 2006, women of color reported being perceived less favorably than their white male counterparts in almost every one of the fourteen categories covered.[112] Yet another study found that a favorable letter of recommendation for a black job candidate was interpreted as evidence of weaker performance than the identical letter written in support of a white candidate.[113] White women are seen as significantly more competent and more intelligent than black women.[114]

Because black women trigger two sets of negative competence assumptions, they may well have an even harder time than white women at establishing competence. This double jeopardy has predictable workplace detriments. One black lawyer summed up the situation this way: "White [lawyers] are not expected to be perfect. Black [lawyers] . . . have one chance and if you mess up that chance, look out. There is no room for error. Who's perfect coming out of law school?"[115] A twenty-three-year-old science major and student government leader at a Texas university reports that she "invests huge amounts of time and energy trying to disprove the myth of inferiority," working herself to exhaustion to perform as the "optimum African-American."[116]

The evidence on Asian-American women is scanty, and the evidence on Latinas and Native Americans is scantier. An informal exploratory study I conducted suggests the following hypotheses. At least on the West Coast of the United States, with its long history of discrimination against "lazy Mexicans" (who are so diligent they "steal our jobs"), negative competence assumptions against Latinas are powerful.[117] The situation with Asians is more complex. On the one hand, Asians are stereotyped as "too competent, too ambitious, too hardworking." This "model minority" stereotype can mitigate stereotypes of Asian-American women as less competent— although the downside of the model minority stereotype is that Asians are seen as having technical but not leadership skills.[118] On the other hand, Asian-American women are sometimes stereotyped as deferential and passive: the "golden flower."[119] Said one Asian-American lawyer, "I've had opposing counsel treat me like a little girl and part of that is the Asian thing because they see a little Asian doll."[120] Asian-American women who encounter this stereotype will encounter negative competence assumptions even stronger than those encountered by white women.

Double Binds

Although women who behave in traditionally feminine ways often have trouble being seen as competent, women who do not "act femmy" may encounter gender bias of a different sort. Recall that the typical woman is seen as nurturing, expressive, and responsive to the needs of others.[121] "Tomboys" who act in ways traditionally associated with men and masculinity often find themselves faulted for having personality problems that boil down to their failure to act femmy. Said Kim Campbell, a former prime minister of Canada:

> I don't have a traditionally female way of speaking. I don't end my sentences with a question mark. I'm quite assertive. If I didn't speak the way I do, I wouldn't have been seen as a leader. But my way of speaking may have grated on people who were not used to hearing it from a woman.[122]

A tomboy's possibilities for advancement may evaporate if her demeanor "grates on" coworkers. Said one male lawyer, "There were women who did well but were just despised. And I think I would say that the same personality in a man was not nearly as despised. There were many more male partners who were just complete jerks, and people kind of laughed it off a little bit."[123]

Consider the experiences of Ann Hopkins, a senior manager at Price Waterhouse, who received outstanding evaluations from her clients, billed more hours, and brought in more business than any other partnership candidate in one year. She was judged by the partners in her office as "an outstanding professional" who had been performing "virtually at the partner level."[124] Clearly Hopkins was competent, but she was denied partnership on the grounds that she lacked "interpersonal skills."[125] Hopkins swore like a sailor and did not suffer fools lightly. She was told to "walk more femininely, talk more femininely, dress more femininely, wear make-up, have her hair styled, and wear jewelry."[126] The Supreme Court responded that femininity could not be treated as a job requirement: "An employer who objects to aggressiveness in women but whose positions require this trait places women in an intolerable and impermissible Catch-22: out of a job if they behave aggressively and out of a job if they do not."[127] In other words, women find they have to choose between being a bitch or a bimbo— and are judged as unqualified either way.[128]

The technical name for this pattern is "ambivalent sexism," which describes the situation in which women who play traditionally feminine roles receive benevolent approval, while women who do not play these roles encounter hostile disapproval. In workplaces affected by ambivalent sexism—which is common but by no means universal—women who self-present in traditionally feminine ways will find it hard to progress, because they will be penalized if they make uncomfortable those men who prefer them to remain in their femmy, supportive role. Yet deference-challenged tomboys are equally unlikely to progress, because job advancement depends "not only on competence but also on social acceptance and approval."

This is the double bind: women have to choose between being liked but not respected or being respected but not liked, in contexts where workplace advancement requires being both liked and respected.[129] Other patterns that stem from ambivalent sexism include the following:

1. She's a bitter, selfish, effective manager. Some women are unpleasant, and others lack interpersonal skills. Yet behavior that is accepted in men often is considered unacceptable in women. Career women in general are seen as "aggressive, selfish, greedy and cold."[130] Said one woman professor, "I've had students lodge complaints about me, for perceived rude behavior that was nothing compared to what some of my male colleagues would do to their students."[131] A woman in a traditionally masculine job may be called a "bitch" or "too ambitious" in situations where a man would be seen as "hard-driving," "having a temper," or "not suffering fools lightly." She, but not he, may be required to be helpful rather than challenging, warm rather than commanding.[132] One study found that women managers who were judged effective also tended to be seen as "bitter" and "selfish," reflecting unspoken expectations stemming from scripts of self-sacrificing motherhood.[133] One Latina lawyer observed, "It's really hard for a woman to ask for what she should be able to ask for, and not be perceived as a bitch."[134]

2. She's aggressive, he's assertive; she's abrasive, he's direct.[135] One study found that the "same critical remark was found to be abrasive coming from a woman, but incisive and direct coming from a man."[136] The unspoken message is that women should be demure and retiring, in keeping with their assigned role in separate-spheres ideology. Note that women who "choose" to play traditionally feminine roles may be responding as much to unspoken messages about what is expected of them as to their own preferences. An example:

> When I started, I was ... the only female [faculty member], and I was expected to help with the filing and sorting mail and some of that stuff. And I just kind of took it because I was very low-level faculty. A new faculty woman came in and she insisted that the staff all refer to her as doctor and she wasn't going to do any of the filing, and everybody was like, who the hell is she?[137]

3. She's a shameless self-promoter; he knows his own worth. That people who engage in self-promotion enhance their performance ratings and thus improve their job evaluations is hardly breaking news. Yet women who self-promote often are seen as distasteful by men and judged even more harshly by other women.[138] Self-promotion in women flouts the norm that "women cooperate, men compete, yet another expression of separate spheres' allocation of selflessness to women."[139] It is not surprising, then, that researchers found that women in a traditionally masculine job who "spoke in a direct, self-confident manner, highlighted past accomplishments," and attributed their success to skill rather than to luck were viewed less favorably than women who spoke modestly about their accomplishments and included disclaimers ("I'm no expert") and hedges ("Don't you think?").[140]

4. Femi-nazis. Studies show that feminists are seen as high in competence but low in warmth.[141] The hostility expressed toward women who advocate for women often is very open. For example, a woman lawyer was faulted in her performance review for being "too involved with women's issues." When she told her supervisor she felt she was not getting high-quality assignments, in part because she was a woman, he replied, "Nancy, don't say that around here. They don't want to hear it."[142] Although it is completely socially unacceptable to fault a black person for being "uppity," faulting women for being feminists—which reflects a similar sentiment—remains permissible in some workplaces.

5. Double jeopardy for deference-challenged minority women. Although studies of the racialization of glass-ceiling bias are scanty, anecdotal evidence is suggestive. "The perception of Black women as complaining, overbearing, bitchy . . . has affected my relationships with men, Black and White," a Chicago attorney stated. "For example," she continued, "if I challenge my White supervisor or coworker, I'm viewed as aggressive, and Black men view my ambition and independence as overbearing and bitchy."[143] Assertive black women risk triggering not only the "bitch" stereotype but the stereotype of "angry blacks,"[144] which conveniently deflects whites' responsibility for racism by faulting blacks' outrage at it. Black women, perhaps particularly those in less-powerful positions, sometimes feel they have to give the "bitch" stereotype such a wide berth that they end up feeling muzzled. "Instead of being the strong black woman that I am by voicing my opinion and saying how I feel, sometimes I back down so as not to seem like I've got an attitude, which is discouraging,"[145] said a twenty-two-year-old executive assistant. As for Asian-American and Latina women, even anecdotal evidence is scarce. The stereotype of Asians as deficient in sociability[146] may make it more likely for Asian-American women to be seen as cold "dragon ladies."[147] The situation for Latina women remains unclear.

Gender Wars

In some workplaces, ambivalent sexism may create a dynamic in which women can succeed only by stepping into one of a limited number of conventionally feminine roles: the princess, who aligns with but does not threaten the dominance of a powerful man; the mother, who seeks to ensure everyone else's welfare; the cheerleader, who applauds male achievements; the efficiency queen, who cheerfully accepts the ministerial tasks; the daughter, who looks up to the men around her.[148] These workplaces may also reinforce status differentials by limiting women employees to traditionally feminine roles. "Women who were more acceptable have a gift of making everybody in the room feel good," said a lawyer in one such workplace. "They are no threat."[149] "Early in my career," a female manager recalled, "I ran into the stereotype of the woman who always needs to be the nice one, smiling and accepting and nurturing."[150] Gender-based status differentials "foster expectations that men are controlling, assertive and directive and that women are supportive, sympathetic and cooperative."[151]

Social psychologists Susan Fiske and Peter Glick note that "The ideal subordinate is one who happily defers . . . listening attentively to and expressing support and admiration" for the dominant group.[152] In this context, deference-challenged women may encounter push back for not knowing their place. Expectations grounded in status differentials may manifest themselves in subtle ways. For instance, modesty often is expected even in highly accomplished women. Deborah Tannen recalled a faculty meeting in which a woman professor who was extremely well-known was up for promotion. A male colleague commented with approval, "'She wears it well.' In other words," noted Tannen, "she was praised for not acting as successful as she was."[153]

Where women are pressured into a narrow range of feminized roles, they may be separated into liked and disliked subtypes, with men expressing positive feelings toward the good girls (who meet their expectations of femininity) and negative feelings toward the bad girls (who do not and are thus seen as selfish, aggressive, and cold).[154]

The next step is often bad blood between these two groups of women, as the different strategies each group adopts pit them against the other. For example, one academic institution employed a relatively high number of female professors—but had trouble keeping certain kinds of women. When one professor received a coveted offer at a higher-ranked institution, word on the street was that she "sucked up to people at elite institutions"; a male colleague who received an identical offer was, quite simply, brilliant. At the same institution, one of the "good girls," who rose to a position of substantial power, rarely supported female candidates, making it very difficult to hire additional women. Consequently, women who were hired typically filled quirky positions with far greater "service" obligations than others had, requiring the incumbents to spend much more time on devalued administrative and counseling tasks. Some astute women raised their political capital by carrying out unsavory tasks such as speaking up in support of a male colleague with a history of sexually harassing students. Other women who survived and thrived would never have considered playing that role, but they were very much attuned to men's comfort levels. One highly accomplished woman turned to her male colleague in admiration at a dinner party: "Let's ask [name]. He knows everything," she said. "He is my role model," said another women professor, introducing her colleague at a conference.[155]

Discrimination can create additional levels of mistrust and hostility within disadvantaged groups in the workplace. Legal scholars Devon Carbado and Mitu Gulati, who have explored the tendency of employers to embrace minorities who conform to majority norms, posit that corporate employers may favor black women who relax their hair and act "country club" over identically qualified black women with cornrows who act "black."[156] When assimilation becomes a job requirement, Kenji Yoshino points out, minority members feel the need to "cover" their default identities in order to survive; when this covering is required, whether implicitly or explicitly, it becomes a civil rights violation.[157] The resulting conflict among minorities is a common, if often unrecognized, symptom of workplace bias.

Another pattern of conflict among women, often called the "queen bee" syndrome, occurs where one woman is taken into the in-group and fails to support, or even targets, other women. Queen bees tend to emerge in contexts of tokenism. "If you're used to being the one woman, and you've had to be that much smarter and that much better, then all of a sudden . . . it's almost like you can't work with other women because you're so used to being the only woman," said a woman science professor.[158] This is one interpretation. Another is that a politically savvy woman gets the message that there is room for only one woman. The resulting struggles are not "cat fights." They are symptoms of a sexist environment.

In the maternal wall context, gender wars often are expressed as generational conflicts. Older women, who entered the workplace when they had to conform to ideal-worker life patterns in order to survive, may see things very differently than younger women do. The latter expect to be able to both succeed at work and live up to the ideals of intensive motherhood that preclude them from outsourcing their children's lives. Women who played by the old rules, including those in my generation (I am fifty-seven), sometimes try to enforce those rules against younger women who seek to change them by taking maternity leave, working part-time, or interrupting their careers. The older women typically assert that these younger women "just don't understand" what it takes to be a doctor/lawyer/banker/chief, to which the younger women typically respond, "We don't want your lives."

In generational divisions, identities are at stake. The older women, joined by younger tomboys, typically fall into three identity groups: ideal-worker mothers, childless women, and child-free women. Ideal-worker mothers, who accepted the "hard truth" that the only way to be a serious contender in their chosen field is to work like a man, have a lot invested in proving that the sacrifices they made in order to combine work and motherhood were absolutely necessary. Their sensitivity is a response to gender stereotypes: women who take no time off from work for child rearing are viewed in society more negatively than those who do.[159] Childless working women, in contrast, are often referred to as the women who "forgot to have children." This is absurd. They did not forget; rather, many felt that having children would jeopardize their chances of career success. Of this group, many are successful but regretful. They look at a younger woman and ask why she should "have it all," given that they gave up so much.

The final group, child-free women, never wanted children. As cultural entrepreneurs trying to invent a new template of a full female life without children, they may well have encountered another type of gender discrimination. Since the "typical woman" norm maps tightly onto the "mother" norm, those who are childless often are seen as defective women and perhaps as flawed human beings. This is especially ironic, given that dual-earner couples without children report the most satisfaction with their family lives.[160]

Conversations become difficult and freighted when the participants feel their identities are at stake. In the contexts described above, the reaction of these groups of women reflects the fact that each woman finds her own identity—as a good worker and/or as a good mother—threatened.[161]

Talking about these kinds of gender wars is controversial. But just because a message is unwelcome does not mean it is unimportant. Feminists must offer an explanation for these conflicts. Otherwise, they will continue unabated, prompting others to conclude that workplace flexibility is not worth the candle, because "even the women can't agree." The better course is to acknowledge these painful battles and to recognize that they arise from masculine norms that force women to play the femme or the tomboy and then penalize each group. After all, what working women—mothers and others—want is simply what men have always had: access to both conventional careers and conventional family lives. Reconstructive feminism aims to spread the message that ending the gender-based economic vulnerability of both femmes and tomboys requires replacing masculine norms with more inclusive ones that embrace a much broader range of the life patterns and gender performances of women—and of men.

Femininity and Masculinity
as Problematic Packages

Let's return to the typical man and typical woman. The typical woman is seen not only as nurturing, expressive, and responsive to the needs of others. She also is seen as less confident and influential than the typical man—a powerful indication of the ways nurturance and emotional expressiveness are devalued. The typical man is less sensitive, more analytical, and less warm than the typical woman: the strong silent type or, less flatteringly, an individual purposely out of touch with his emotions. "My father was never very good at personal relations of an intimate kind," Katharine Graham tells us. "The feelings were there, but they went unexpressed."[162] Lack of emotional expressiveness as an enactment of masculinity cuts across class lines. Said Lillian Rubin, of working-class men: "After a lifetime of repressing his feelings, he often *is* a blank, unaware that he's thinking or feeling anything."[163]

Are these healthy packages? Is it healthy to associate responsiveness to the needs of others with lack of confidence and influence? Of course not. If adults caring for children and elders lack confidence and influence, everyone will suffer. Is it healthy to associate responsiveness to the needs of others with self-erasure? Again, no. This is the Giving Tree Mother, so endlessly selfless she ends up as matchsticks.[164] Celebrations of women's "focus on relationships," and of mothers' decisions to opt out, tend to overlook the framework within which women make these highly constrained choices. The ideal-worker standard and norm of work devotion push mothers to the margins of economic life. And a society that marginalizes its mothers impoverishes its children. That is why the paradigmatic poor family in the United States is a single mother and her child.

With those assumptions challenged, let's turn to conventional masculinity. Is it healthy to associate sensitivity to the needs of others with lack of manliness? Warmth with being a wuss? To assume that one can be analytical only by keeping emotions in check? Neither masculinity nor femininity, as conventionally defined, is a recipe for a centered life that balances sensitivity to the needs of others with a healthy respect for one's own self-development.

So the conventional gendering of emotions is unappealing. Moreover, men and women who refuse to conform often encounter behavior that is downright punitive. "What-a-witch" gender bias, which disciplines women who are insufficiently selfless and responsive to the needs of others, is matched by "what-a-wuss" gender bias, which disciplines men who are "inappropriately" warm and insufficiently commanding. Men who are "too" sensitive—artists are a good example—may feel the need to act out exaggerated forms of masculinity so as not to fall into the "girlie man" abyss. Think Jackson Pollack, who died in an acceptably macho manner—at age forty-four in an alcohol-related car accident. Nonartists are affected as well. It is not uncommon for blue-collar and low-income men, or young men of all classes, to put themselves in harm's way in order to prove their masculinity. For the same reason, men also often feel under pressure to insult or devalue women and things feminine (including emotional expressiveness and attentiveness to workplace safety).[165] Moreover, in the United States, the workplace strategies blue-collar men adopt to establish their masculine credentials also tend to undercut their ability to organize effectively.[166] Similarly, in the upper-middle class, the felt need to be a "go getter" puts even relatively powerful men in a poor position to demand a reasonable work-life balance. Not a great system.

Our gender system also distorts U.S. politics in ways that are easier to see in the wake of the 2008 election. Hillary Clinton's campaign had to struggle mightily to dodge the "what-a-witch" bias—that much is obvious. But let's dig deeper and ponder the political implications of the widely held view that women are more "communal" whereas men exercise more agency.[167] First, we should note the oddness of assuming that someone whose orientation is communal does not exercise agency. I suspect that Europeans would find this assumption truly odd. Their welfare states are communal but their people are hardly passive. It is a peculiarly Anglo-American assumption that orientation toward the community is somehow feminine, expressed concisely in the epithet "the nanny state." That expression aptly captures how solidarity—so robustly masculine in France—is feminized in the Anglo-American political tradition, precluding the need to make an actual argument as to why we should not have universal health or child care. The mere suggestion that such softness would castrate our society has long been sufficient to silence public debate before it begins.

Returning to the individual level, why do we continue to believe in an arbitrary allocation of personality characteristics by sex? We all know, after all, that some women are high in analytical intelligence (think Marie Curie) while some men are high in emotional intelligence (think Bill Clinton). We also know that, in order to succeed in all except the most technical jobs, one needs not only analytical competence but also people skills, a key factor in job success for executives as well as others. How is it that the current highly artificial gendered allocation of intelligences does not collapse from the weight of its own implausibility?

Part of the answer is that language helps. A primary-caregiver father is "Mr. Mom." We code him as a woman in order to avoid destabilizing our deeply held association of nurturance with possession of a vagina. When men are sensitive and supportive, they "show their feminine side." That formulation starts with information that undermines the hypothesis that emotional expressiveness is a strictly feminine trait and then turns it into reinforcement of the link between emotion and femininity.

An alternative formulation would be that being nurturing and sensitive is one way of being a man. This alternative does not surface, though, because of the tendency for stereotype-consistent information to be noticed and retained, while stereotype-inconsistent information is overlooked, forgotten, or attributed to personality.[168] Here is another example, common in the workplace: when a mother comes in late, others notice, assume it is related to her child care, and remember it later as evidence that she cannot arrange her life to fulfill her obligations at work. But when a man comes in late, either no one notices, or he is slapped on the back and asked if he had a wild night.

This kind of mental sleight of hand is normal. We all are bombarded by a mass of stereotype-disconfirming information every day. So, for cognitive comfort, we need a methodical process for preserving our stereotypes, protecting them from too much challenge. One way we do this is by using different words to describe much the same behavior. If a traditionally masculine job requires a personal characteristic associated with femininity (good people skills), that characteristic is then seen through a masculine lens. Thus a male executive who helps others along is demonstrating his leadership potential by mentoring, while a female executive who does the same thing is nurturing, which is a sign that she lacks sufficient steel to be a leader. The tool-and-die maker's close attention to detail is seen as manly precision, not as evidence that men are "just naturally" good at detail work. Similarly, a courageous man just proves once again that men are brave, while a courageous woman is like a lioness protecting her children—she proves not that women are brave but that mothers are devoted. A sensitive man is a great artist, while a sensitive woman is just a typical woman.

The gender contortions involved in these routine linguistic somersaults are a highly underdeveloped arena of inquiry. That is especially unfortunate because they are highly consequential in the workplace. I once read over 1,500 performance evaluations from a large employer and found that many more women than men received the comment that "clients love" her/him. Funny thing, though: men who received that comment tended to get high scores, with evaluators often citing these men's potential as future rainmakers. The comment did not yield high scores for women, nor did it prompt notations that they stood to enhance the employer's client base. Why? One expects a woman to be personable and responsive to others' needs. Being so does not prove she is a business asset. It just proves she is a woman.[169]

Deconstructing gender is a task to which neither social psychologists nor feminists have devoted enough attention. The goal is not an ungendered world. Whether that goal is desirable or not is irrelevant, since it is impossible. Gender is too firmly established as a metaphor of self-expression to be simply abolished; it is just too useful a way of expressing aspirations, anger, humor—you name it. The goal of reconstructive feminism is to decouple gender from the key habits and conventions that impoverish too many men and women—and brutalize others who cannot fit within the simple masculine-feminine dichotomy.

As we attempt to reshape gender, piece by careful piece, we would be wise to remember that gender is always in flux. In the 1940s, if a man did the dishes, he might well pull the curtains, so as not to be unmanned before the neighbors. In the 1950s, when I was young, men who took care of their kids for even an afternoon were "babysitting." Today, washing dishes does not threaten manliness, and many (though not all) fathers walk around with Snugli child carriers without feeling their dignity threatened.[170]

Gender flux is constant; what we need to do is catalyze and direct it. Reconstructive feminism seeks to identify the key levers for encouraging this process. Articulating this goal raises interesting questions. Are we seeking, ultimately, to eliminate the need for workplace "softeners" that dilute the dominant masculinity with injections of femininity? I think not. Instead, I believe our goal should be to require softeners of both men and women, replacing spike heels with warmth and macho one-upmanship with social skills. One aim of reconstructive feminism is to recognize that all healthy people have both a cooperative dimension and a competitive one. And apart from a few hermits happy on top of a pillar, all healthy people need both meaningful work and a web of intimacy. We all need to recognize that healthy relationships do not rest on one partner's promise of permanent self-erasure on the grounds that selflessness is her "true voice." Nor do healthy relationships enshrine in one partner a sense of entitlement at the expense of the other. Healthy relationships involve give and take. Healthy living does not consign men to a life of strategic self-seeking at the expense of the women who selflessly support them. Nor does it consign men to a life of endless work, outsourcing their children's childhoods to women and abandoning any hope of nonstrategic social connections. Feminists need to return to the early feminist insight that our current gender system impoverishes the lives of men as well as women. We need to deconstruct gender, in order to allow men more room for caring, connection, and communality and to allow women more room for an entitled sense of self-development, assertiveness, and competition.[171]

A key goal of reconstructive feminism is to replace both the selfless-mother model and the breadwinner model with the model of a balanced worker, one who combines serious work commitments with serious family commitments and also with serious commitments to long-term self-development and enriching community life.[172] The notion that having a child is a private frolic that does not deserve community support is implausible. There is no reason to expect that society should be able to privatize the costs of raising the next generation of citizens—from which all society will benefit—onto the backs of the women who bear them. This habit impoverishes women economically and men emotionally. "The person whom I damaged most by being away when [my children] were growing up was me," observed one man sadly. "I let my nurturing impulses dry up."[173]

Placing Masculinity at the Center of a Feminist Analysis

Placing masculinity at the center of a feminist analysis is not the same as placing men there. Instead it involves recognizing that workplace gender bias against women stems from masculine norms in jobs that historically were held by men. These masculine norms not only create the maternal wall, the glass ceiling, and gender wars—they also create hydraulic pressures on men to perform as ideal workers to the extent their health and social advantage allow them to do so. Gender pressures come from the family, but they also come from work sites that produce not only gems, genes, and jars but also gender.

Feminism is caught in the trance it seeks to break. The assumption that women will join in automatic sisterhood reflects an unwarranted premise: that women are inevitably bound together by their experience of womanhood. The experience of gender divides women as often as it unites them. Unlike critical race theorists, who generally have been savvy about the need to build coalitions, mainstream feminists often seem stuck in a time warp, still speaking of "women" as though all women will "naturally" agree on issues of gender.[174] Critical race theorists have the better argument. Gender, like race, is nothing more than a single axis of social power, readily available to carry diverse social meanings. Race can bind people together, which is the way Martin Luther King, Jr. used it. But it can also divide people. Think of the divisions and hurt feelings sparked by Bill Cosby's (and Barack Obama's) comments about responsible fatherhood, which deeply express what it means to be a black man in America.

Feminists need to do what we are always urging others to do. We need to recognize that gender is nothing more or less than a social toolkit and that women use those tools in a wide variety of ways. If feminists are to mold a coalition of women, we need to carefully tap into what different groups of women care about passionately. Women do not all agree just because they are women. To assume so is to take as a premise the error feminists have united to defeat: that biology determines destiny.[175]

CHAPTER FOUR

Reconstructive Feminism and Feminist Theory

I got into this work because I'm a tomboy . . . If you try to do
your share and don't come off really femmy you're all right.

—Kathy Shaughnessy, phone line repair staff

A common but regrettably underexamined assumption is that feminism's goal is to illuminate identity. The canon of second-wave feminism reflects many explorations of personal identity, from Betty Friedan's
1963 *The Feminine Mystique* (based on interviews of Friedan's college
classmates) to Leslie Bennetts's 2007 *The Feminine Mistake* (which begins
by telling the story of her mother and grandmother). Explorations of personal identity also predominate in the writings of many second-wave feminists of color. An early example is the 1984 collection *This Bridge Called
My Back*, but there are many later examples as well. Younger third-wave
feminists have been, if anything, even more focused on personal identity
than the generations that preceded them, beginning with Jennifer Baumgardner and Amy Richards's *Manifesta* in 2000.[1]

Here is a controversial statement: despite the profusion of personal narratives it has produced, feminism does a poor job of illuminating identity.
The reason is simple—no woman is only a woman. Women are affected by
many forces other than gender. Consider me. I am a white, professional,
able-bodied, anxious, earnest, Jewish-Episcopalian, heterosexual woman.
Feminism captures some, but only some, of the social forces that have
served as the anvils on which I have forged my identity.[2] Other social
forces, including religion and ethnicity, are rarely discussed; still others—
race, class, and ability status—are more a source of guilt and guilt-tripping

than of sustained analysis. Feminism never talks about genetics, psychology, and family history, the most basic shapers of identity.

If the bad news is that feminism is flawed as a way of exploring the full contours of individual identity, the good news is that it does not matter. Ultimately, feminism is useful for exploring not "women" but rather the gender dynamics that disadvantage them. This news should alleviate feminist angst (called "anti-essentialism") about how to accomplish the task of taking into account all the differences among women. This kind of inclusiveness is impossible. An analysis of gender dynamics can never be a "view from nowhere"—but neither can any other intellectual tool.[3] Analysis of the ways that racism disadvantages people of color is not any less limited than feminism is; just as feminism examines only gender, race analysis examines only race. Each is a tool designed for a certain job. It really should not shock us that a screwdriver is an inefficient hammer.[4]

Do We Need a Trowel or a Backhoe?

Given that my goal is to theorize gender, the threshold question, which must be resolved before going further, is to ask what level of generality is required for the analysis at hand. If the right tool is half the job, do we need a trowel or a backhoe? Gender theorists typically fail to ask this question. As a result, most have proceeded to analyze in depth a relatively narrow range of gendered interactions, all the while proclaiming grandly to be explaining "gender"—presumably all of it. Two examples are the two most prominent gender theorists of the last quarter century: the law professor Catharine MacKinnon and literary theorist Judith Butler.

For MacKinnon, gender is all about the eroticizing of dominance. MacKinnon sees the violation of women as "the meaning and content of femininity,"[5] writing, "What is called sexuality is the dynamic of control by which male dominance . . . eroticizes and thus defines man and woman, gender identity and sexual pleasure."[6] Note MacKinnon's assumption that a single dynamic (apparently alone) explains all of gender dominance. Butler avoids such sweeping statements, yet she explains "gender trouble" (again, presumably, all of it) by reference to queer sexualities. This focus leads her to see gender identity as fluid; she overlooks the gendered experiences of people who feel comfortable in their conventional gender skins. "[A] feminist view," according to Butler, "argues that gender should be overthrown, eliminated, or rendered fatally ambiguous precisely because it is always a sign of subordination for women." It is clear in this and innumerable other instances that when Butler refers to gender, she means something quite specific: the intersection of compulsory heterosexuality and what anthropologists call "gender display," namely, clothing and body language.[7]

Although gender theorists commonly assume they are explaining all of gender, in fact they focus on quite different topics. From the mid-1960s until the early 1980s, U.S. feminism focused primarily on deconstructing and deinstitutionalizing the cultural mandate that women become homemakers and men breadwinners. *The Feminine Mystique* critiqued the housewife role, as did much of feminism that followed. In 1966, the National Organization for Women (NOW) was founded on the premise that the old-fashioned approach of safeguarding women through protective labor legislation should be replaced by a framework in which men and women were treated the same.[8] The Equal Pay Act of 1963 and Title VII of the Civil Rights Act of 1964 both followed this new equal treatment template.[9] Feminists' assault on the homemaker-breadwinner dichotomy had implications for the family as well as for workplaces. The "divorce revolution" of the 1970s saw divorce courts undermine the legal infrastructure undergirding the breadwinner-housewife system. So, for example, short-term alimony replaced permanent alimony for wives who had kept house and raised children while their husbands went to work.[10]

By the mid-1970s, feminists had divided into those who believed that women should be treated the same as men ("sameness feminists") and those who believed that women were, in fact, different from men and that courts and legislatures should recognize and act on that fact ("difference feminists"). Conflicts over the design of public policy resulted and became intertwined with the debate over Carol Gilligan's 1982 book, *In a Different Voice*. Gilligan's followers advocated reshaping various institutions around women's voice, using as a starting point her contention that women have a different moral system from men; Gilligan's critics took issue with the basic premise of her work, namely, that women had a unified voice.

By the mid-1980s, U.S. feminists' attention had shifted away from work-family issues onto issues related to eroticized dominance: sexual harassment, pornography, and domestic violence. In 1980, a year after Catharine MacKinnon published *Sexual Harassment of Working Women*, the Equal Employment Opportunity Commission adopted guidelines that established sexual harassment as gender discrimination. In 1986, the Supreme Court, in *Meritor Savings Bank v. Vinson*, held that sexual harassment was a violation of Title VII.[11] Sexual harassment went from being seen as something any woman worth her salt could handle to being considered illegal gender discrimination. (Despite this, today nearly 60% of employed women have experienced sexual harassment. In the military, the reported figure is nearly 70%, followed by colleges and universities [nearly 60%], the private sector [45%], and the government [42%].)[12]

Meanwhile, MacKinnon, along with Andrea Dworkin, shifted her attention onto pornography, which she and Dworkin both viewed as violence against women. Together Dworkin and MacKinnon advocated antipornography ordinances, which did not fare well as public policy. The 1983 Minneapolis Anti-Pornography Ordinance was vetoed by the mayor.[13] The 1984 Indianapolis Ordinance was struck down as unconstitutional.[14] The antipornography campaign lost steam after 1990, as the result of opposition from civil libertarians and queer activists, who argued that pornography plays a vital role in reassuring gay youth that they are not alone.

The third basic thrust of feminism in the late 1980s has proved the most enduringly galvanizing: domestic violence. Anti–domestic violence advocacy led to a massive worldwide movement, as funding for programs poured into both national and international nongovernmental organizations, and domestic violence went from being seen as a private matter to being seen as illegal assault. In the United States, this movement led to passage of the Violence against Women Act of 1994.[15]

Then, in the 1990s, the center of gravity shifted once again, away from sex-violence issues toward an examination of gender identity and compulsory heterosexuality. Here Judith Butler, who published her highly influential *Gender Trouble: Feminism and the Subversion of Identity* in 1990, was a central figure.[16] Butler's book helped spark the field of queer theory, which focuses on the complex interrelationships of biological sex, sexual orientation, and gender display. Queer theory influenced intellectuals through such cult film classics as *The Adventures of Priscilla, Queen of the Desert,* and influenced mainstream culture through such films and plays as *To Wong Foo Thanks for Everything, Julie Newmar; The Birdcage; Rent;* and, most recently, *Transamerica.*

Each new wave of gender theory has been seen as a critique of, and an improvement on, the prior wave. A closer analysis reveals this idea of progress as inaccurate. In fact, each new wave, in large part, simply changed the subject—from work-family issues during the initial period, to sex-violence issues from the late 1980s to the mid-1990s, to the construction of sexuality thereafter. Once we recognize this, we are in a position to formulate our threshold question about how general our analysis of gender should be.

A Unified Theory of Gender?

Gender is one of the central organizing principles of social life. Consequently, gender theory that seeks to address all the social meanings of gender perches on such a lofty plane that it offers little but platitudes. Each era of second wave U.S. feminism focused not only on a different topic but also on a distinct set of social mechanisms through which gender structures social life.

The assumption that all three of these gender dynamics can be theorized simultaneously is just that—an assumption. In fact, analyses of gender have proved it untrue. In practice, theorists have concentrated on one of these three axes while ignoring the other two. The alternative to continuing the assertion, and the assumption, that one's particular area of interest is *the* central gender dynamic is to make explicit what the last forty years of feminist theory have shown in practice: that gender permeates many different arenas of social life and that the work-family axis, the sex-violence axis, and the queer axis need to be theorized separately, as do any number of other axes that have not yet been conceptualized. What follows, then, is a retheorizing of the work-family axis. This retheorization has significant implications for the other two axes but is best analyzed apart from them.

The work-family axis of gender traditionally is framed in terms of the "sameness-difference debate." This debate seems old hat, yet it continues to haunt us because it translates separate spheres into theoretical terms. The separate-spheres allocation of agentic, competitive men to the public sphere and nurturing, communal women to the home defines men's economic dominance as a natural and uncontroversial outcome of gender difference. Interpreting gender through the lens of difference continues to dominate how we talk about work and family today, both in the press and in theoretical discussions, where this pattern of argument is called the sameness-difference debate.[17]

That debate has concrete consequences for the design of public and workplace policies.[18] Consider a workplace policy that grants family leave to any new parent, male or female. I designed such a policy for my law school in the 1980s when I, in keeping with the times, was wary of treating men and women differently. The result: while women used the leave for child care, men took a different tack—one went to Mardi Gras during his leave (without the baby); another published a long article he wrote during his leave. "That's the problem with treating men and women the same, when they really are different," some said.

The sameness-difference debate shapes not only public and workplace policies but also mainstream discussions of work and family, intimating that women's economic subordination is a natural result of women's difference. In "The Opt-Out Revolution," for example, Lisa Belkin presented the "revolution" as the natural result of women's choices, driven by their difference. Thus she makes the "dangerous" (her descriptor) argument that women "leave [work] more easily and find other parts of life more fulfilling." She notes, "There's nothing wrong with money or power. But they come at a high price." Belkin's argument is that the steep price for professional success is not one women are willing to pay, perhaps for biological reasons (she quotes one woman noting that "women's brains light up differently") or perhaps for moral ones (Belkin argues that she and other women simply have different values than men). "Why don't women run the world?" asks Belkin. "Maybe it's because they don't want to."[19] Thus in keeping with separate-spheres ideology, she argues that women's difference explains their absence from positions of power and authority. Her opt-out moms are too centered (and perhaps too moral) to put up with the lack of personal balance required for workplace success.

Belkin ultimately sought to flip separate-spheres ideology—originally designed to show why women should stay home—to explain why the workplace needs to change in order to "fit" women. But the "difference" argument can be readily flipped back again to explain that employers need not worry about changing the workplace because the paucity of women in good jobs reflects only that women do not want those jobs.

To escape this fruitless loop, a good start is to recognize that two distinct debates have been lumped together inadvertently. The first is a debate over policy design, namely, whether workplace and public policies should treat men and women the same or differently. The second involves not policy but psychology and asks the question of whether "real psychological differences" exist between men and women. Merging these debates has caused massive confusion, for they involve quite different issues. Some "sameness" feminists do not believe in the accepted description of the psychological differences between men and women or that women just naturally have a "different voice" centered around an ethic of care. But these same people may ascribe to the "difference" thesis in the sense that they believe there are serious flaws in public policy that blindly treats women the same as men. I am one of these and, as a result, have been called both a sameness feminist and a difference feminist over the course of my career.[20] I have also been called a radical feminist, which no doubt has contributed to my dim view of the usefulness of these traditional categories.[21] In their place, I introduce two new categories, assimilationist feminism and reconstructive feminism. These offer the promise of busting out of the frame of the sameness-difference debate.

Assimilationist Feminism

In theory as in everyday life, separate spheres has the effect of enshrining masculine norms. This forces women to choose between assimilating to those norms or seeking to empower their traditionally feminine roles. The assimilationist strategy, which seeks access to traditionally masculine rights and roles, dates back to the nineteenth century. First-wave feminists Elizabeth Cady Stanton and Susan B. Anthony sought to win for women the right to vote. They and others fought for married women to have the same rights to property as men had. Access efforts continued in the twentieth century, when the Supreme Court required proportionate gender representation on juries and Congress passed the Equal Pay Act of 1963, guaranteeing equal pay for equal work in the higher-paying jobs that were traditionally held by men.[22]

In the 1970s, the Supreme Court began to articulate women's rights more systematically, as the result of a concerted litigation strategy orchestrated by Ruth Bader Ginsberg (then American Civil Liberties Union general counsel). In landmark cases in the 1970s, the Supreme Court invalidated an Idaho law that favored men over women as estate administrators (*Reed v. Reed*), a federal law that required breadwinner wives (but not breadwinner husbands) to prove that their spouses were in fact dependent in order to receive certain medical and dental benefits (*Frontiero v. Richardson*), and a federal law that gave survivors' benefits automatically to homemaker wives of breadwinner husbands but not to homemaker husbands of breadwinner wives (*Weinberger v. Weisenfeld*).[23]

Often these are called the "formal-equality cases," but this is a misnomer. Mere formal equality was never Ginsberg's goal. Instead her goal was to deconstruct separate spheres, by enabling women to gain access to roles traditionally reserved for men and enabling men to gain access to roles traditionally reserved for women.[24] Her strategy was to get judges to prohibit legislatures from designing benefits around the breadwinner-homemaker roles. From early on, it was clear that Ginsberg's goals went beyond the capacity of her litigation strategy.[25]

A look at Ginsberg's nonlitigation writings shows clearly that her goal was to deconstruct gender by undermining the institutional infrastructure undergirding separate spheres. For example, in a 1975 law review article, Ginsberg advocated part-time schedules "for students unable to undertake full-time study because of family obligations (notably, care of preschool children) that cannot be met by customary financial aid."[26] Thus Ginsberg signaled that access was not enough, arguing that true equality required reconstructing career tracks and passing additional supports for working families. "If Congress is genuinely committed to the eradication of sex-based discrimination and promotion of equal opportunity for women, it will respond to the uneven pattern of adjudication by providing firm legislative direction assuring job security, health insurance coverage, and income maintenance for childrearing women."[27] Ginsberg, from the beginning, was focused on reconstruction. We can see her as the first reconstructive feminist.

The early cases Ginsberg litigated did not necessarily reflect her future ambitions. Their goal was simply to gain for women access to the rights, privileges, and benefits of the breadwinner role. This is a strategy that is effective for a particular group of women: those who are seeking to replicate the social roles traditionally reserved for men. "Formal equality works best in situations when men and women are enough alike that the same rule operates equally well for both," notes a leading law casebook by Katherine Bartlett and Deborah Rhode.[28]

Paving the way for women to assimilate into traditionally masculine life patterns is undoubtedly an important feminist goal. Yet to call this "formal equality" is confusing: no feminist would describe herself as committed to empty, merely formal, equality. Indeed, "formal equality" is more a charge of wrongheadedness than a description any feminist would adopt for herself. Feminists focused on gaining access for women to historically male jobs and roles are more fairly termed assimilationist feminists, given that their chief goal is to enable women to assimilate into arenas traditionally reserved for men.

When we use this alternative formulation, it seems to work. The "formal equality" cases in the Bartlett-Rhode casebook all involve women who seek to enter historically male spheres. Recall the 1989 *Price Waterhouse v. Hopkins* case, which involved a most un-femmy senior manager who brought in more business than any of the men in her partnership class but whose partnership was deferred because her evaluators felt she ought to first learn to walk and talk more "femininely," to get her hair styled, and to wear makeup and jewelry.[29] Other formal-equality cases involve women who wanted to be prison guards or factory workers, women who wanted Rotary Club membership, and girls who wanted entry into the Boys Club. The goal of these legal challenges is assimilation. If you are a tomboy, all you need is to be allowed to play ball with the boys.[30]

Assimilationist feminism works well to help the tomboys whose goal is to assimilate into masculine roles, but it offers little to feminists focused on women whose gender inequality stems from their insistence on "acting femmy." One such group is homemakers who are divorced after decades out of the labor force. A second is employed women who do femmy things like getting pregnant. Assimilationist feminism carries distinct risks for these women. Not surprisingly, these are the two major foci of critiques of assimilationist feminism. The single most forceful critic of "formal equality" is DePaul law professor Mary Becker. She argues that using a formal equality standard "is unlikely to effect much real change without seriously risking worsening the situation of many women, especially ordinary wives and mothers."[31]

The most systematic critique of formal equality in the family law context is by Emory law professor Martha Fineman. Some background is required to understand her analysis. Under the paradigm established under separate spheres, displaced homemakers were entitled to automatic child custody, ownership of the marital home, and permanent alimony (at least in theory; in fact, only a small percentage of women have ever received alimony, and a precondition was that the homemaker in question was not found to be "at fault," typically through adultery).[32] This legal regime ended in the 1960s, when courts and legislatures increasingly embraced the new ideology of the "clean break." Overlooking the small matter of who would care for the children, courts began offering husbands a no-strings-attached chance to begin life anew, awarding ex-wives, at most, temporary alimony and ordering sale of the home so that "both parents" could get their equity out.[33] The strong presumption in favor of maternal custody also was eliminated, leading many husbands' lawyers to demand custody strategically, thereby forcing mothers to trade off economic claims in order to ensure continued custody of children for whom they were— and had always been—primary caregivers.[34] These trends, in conjunction with sharply higher levels of divorce, meant a sharp increase in maternal and child poverty resulting from divorce. Many mothers found they had to move the children to a cheaper part of town and pinch pennies to enable their husbands to get their clean breaks. Fineman attributes displaced caregivers' newfound vulnerability to misplaced efforts from feminists entangled by the "illusion of equality." Fineman argued that feminists committed to formal equality insisted on treating women the same as men after divorce. In *The Illusion of Equality* and subsequent work, Fineman called on feminists to end their willful blindness to the "real differences" between men and women. Decrying "formal equality," she favored "substantive equality" and argued that courts should address women's "true needs."[35]

The second major feminist battleground, over maternity leave, came to a head in the 1987 case *California Federal Savings and Loan v. Guerra*.[36]

In "*CalFed*," as this case is called, the California Chamber of Commerce and its allies challenged California's maternity disability leave on the grounds that it conflicted with, and so was preempted by, the Pregnancy Discrimination Act (PDA), an amendment to Title VII that required that pregnant women be treated "the same" as other workers.[37] West Coast feminists, including Christine Littleton and Linda Hamilton Krieger in law review articles, defended California's maternity leave law.[38] East Coast feminists attacked it. The assimilationist position was best articulated by Wendy Webster Williams in the law review article "The Equality Crisis."[39] Williams's article, published at the height of the internal strife among feminists over assimilationism, opposed the California statute. She compared maternity leaves to protective labor legislation and argued that, like the latter, maternity leave would redound to women's detriment.[40] Williams maintained that "the equality approach to pregnancy creates not only the desired floor under the pregnant woman's rights but also the ceiling . . . If we can't have it both ways," she warned, "we need to think carefully about which way we want to have it."[41] The implication was clear: feminists should insist that women be treated the same as men. No maternity leaves. This assimilationist position predominated for decades among feminist groups inside the Beltway. One prominent feminist confided to me in 2006 that women's groups in Washington could have gotten maternity leave a decade before the passage of the Family and Medical Leave Act in 1993. Historical study documents that California congressman Howard Berman wanted to do for the country what he had done for California: pass a four-month maternity leave.[42] When he approached inside-the-Beltway feminists, they refused to support the measure. Instead they fought on for ten more years, insisting that the right to maternity leave be folded into the right of workers to take leaves for their own health reasons. During that conversation in 2006, all I could think of were the women who, in that decade, had gone without maternity leave. That included me.

"Formal Equality" as Assimilationist Feminism

To understand these fights among feminists, it helps to begin with gender wars at work. Workplace conflict often arises between assimilationist tomboys and anti-assimilationist femmes. Consider the following quote, from a woman science professor:

> I've seen lots of women, senior women, behave that way. And even not just as far as the working long hours, but even adopting male mannerisms. I don't know how to describe it, but sort of really aggressive and not putting up with

any crap and almost having a chip on their shoulder and also going out of their way to not mentor young women. You would think that women above you would be the ones that would be the obvious people to really help the next generation of women and it usually turns out that they're the worst . . . I mean not everyone, but I've found that my best mentoring comes from men that are sensitive to the issue.[43]

The speaker describes colleagues who have assimilated into masculine norms, both in terms of behavior (acting assertive and direct) and time (working long hours). Women whose default modes are masculine (the tomboys) in a given context are bound to view gender equality as a somewhat different project than women whose default modes are feminine (the femmes) in that context. To quote another science professor:

One of the things that I think I'm on kind of a backlash mission almost. I purposely don't [behave as a man]. I wear dresses, I bake cookies for my group meetings, I bring my child to class with me . . . I guess I've just kind of really stuck it out there and said look, this is you know, this is me, I'm a woman, I'm someone's mother. And you get the whole package. Nobody's really commented on it in particular . . . But it is kind of a conscious choice on my part that I'm not going to compete as a boy because I'm not a boy.[44]

Workplace conflict between femmes and tomboys is an inevitable consequence of masculine norms that require women to choose between standing up for feminine traditions or assimilating into masculine ones. These gender wars, as I have called them, are a symptom of workplace gender bias.

In feminism on the work-family axis, the issue is not whether the femmes or the tomboys are committed to real equality. Both sides are. It is just that each feels the pinch of masculine norms in a different place. For femmes, the chief injury is the devaluation of feminine traditions. For tomboys, the chief injury is their barred entrance to masculinity. Once we shift away from the terminology of "formal equality," we see what are commonly known as the sameness-difference debates as gender wars between femme feminists (difference feminists) and tomboy feminists (assimilationists). These continue up to the present day.

Columbia law professor Katherine Franke is a prominent example of the assimilationist approach. She scolds feminists who focus on motherhood as "heteronormative" (that is, unjustly centering on the experience of heterosexuals). First let me respond to the merits of this charge. A key problem is that it overlooks the fact that separate spheres affects gay as well as heterosexual couples.[45] A study of census data reports that gay male couples are slightly more likely than heterosexual couples to have a stay-at-home parent (26% as compared with 25%), and lesbian couples are only slightly less likely (24%).[46] Gay fathers, another study finds, "remain very judgmental of parents who don't stay home."[47] Surveys often report that lesbian couples are more egalitarian than heterosexual couples and more likely to share housework equally.[48] Yet these studies rely on self-reports, which are notoriously unreliable in this arena.[49]

A well-known qualitative study of gay families in the San Francisco Bay Area by Christopher Carrington contradicts these egalitarian claims.[50] "Families hide much of domesticity, closet it, and drape the door with the ideological veneer of egalitarianism," says Carrington in a study of lesbigay families, cautioning against the "myth of egalitarianism."[51] He found "rough parity" of sharing of household work in about one-quarter of households, which included wealthy families that outsourced much of the housework; female couples where both partners held historically feminine jobs with "a *real* 40-hour week"; and male couples that did little housework. In the remaining 75% of couples, one partner tended to do most of the household work, with paid employment exerting the most influence on the division of household labor, a finding confirmed in another study.[52] The dynamics surrounding housework appear remarkably similar in some lesbigay couples and straight ones. Said one gay male of his partner, "Sterling never cleaned toilets, he still doesn't clean toilets; he intends to clean the toilets, but right about the time when he gets to it, I have already cleaned the toilets."[53] Carrington found that although in gay couples, as in straight ones, one partner typically carries a disproportionate load of housework, this tends to be denied; in fact, this pattern holds true for straight families as well, with both partners insisting that the division of labor is "fifty-fifty around here," even when it clearly is not.[54] And the domestic partner in gay male couples often encounters the devaluation, economic vulnerability, and self-blame faced by female homemakers.[55] Carrington describes Henry Zamora, who had recently broken up with his partner of fourteen years, Joe Solis, when Joe had an affair with his secretary. Joe worked sixty to seventy hours a week and earned $110,000 as an attorney; Henry worked thirty hours a week and earned $28,000 as a nursing assistant. After the breakup, Henry had few personal belongings, no health insurance, and no savings or retirement and was having trouble paying his rent on a modest apartment. When Carrington recalled the lavishly furnished home in upscale Marin County where Henry had lived with Joe, Henry noted, "Much of that really belonged to Joe. He did buy it, after all." "What truly perplexes me," Carrington notes, "is that Henry felt no sense of entitlement." However, Henry's devaluing of his own household contributions reflects that of many stay-at-home wives who struggle to start in-home businesses on the grounds that they want to "contribute something"—as if raising children, buying and cooking food, furnishing, cleaning, and perhaps overseeing the renovation of a house, or a succession of houses, does not constitute a "contribution."[56]

Franke is not focused on the Henrys of this world. In fact, she shows little interest in femmes, male or female. She is a tomboy with respect to workplace roles, whose goal is access for women to a traditionally masculine way of being. She embraces as a truly liberated agenda for women one that validates a lifestyle centered on sexual pleasure and sexual fulfillment. "Perhaps we can find the most liberated and exciting forms of sexual experience through a kind of hermeneutic vampirism, whereby we rummage through past and present sexual iconography and suck what life we can out of the unsuspecting world around us," she writes.[57]

I agree with Franke that this is a lifestyle that should be as open to women as to men. And I embrace her implicit worry that women who do not have children, and who seek instead the kind of sexual striving that has traditionally been the province of men, will be seen negatively. Yet I cannot help noticing that she is arguing that true liberation for women lies in adopting a hypersexualized self-definition traditionally reserved for men, gay and straight. (Think notches in the belt; "scoring"; gay bathhouses.)

Yale law professor Vicki Schultz proposes that women assimilate into a different arena of conventional masculinity. In *Life's Work*,[58] Schultz criticizes "joint property" advocates whose goal is to empower women in their traditional roles by giving dependent women additional economic rights upon divorce. This approach, she argues, simply lures women back into homemaker roles, which she sees as a recipe for continued social and economic marginalization. Schultz argues instead for an agenda that treats paid employment as the centerpiece of the life well lived.

Far be it from me, admittedly a strikingly work-identified woman, to decry the joys of hard work. And far be it from me, who understands the risks of poverty faced by women who "take a break," to decry the importance of employment for women. Yet massive documentation, and common sense, remind us that to recommend that women treat employment as the key to identity is to recommend that women embrace conventional masculinity. One recent study, one of hundreds, documented that three times as many men as women describe their lives as "work-centered."[59]

The third example of a contemporary assimilationist is Harvard Law School's Janet Halley. Like Franke and Schultz, Halley has made important contributions to this debate. These include her explorations of the ambiguities of gender identity, her recognition that conflicts within feminism provide a key to understanding gender dynamics in society at large, and her clear articulation of the divergences between the queer and the sex-violence axes. Yet what has made her work so well known and controversial is her exhortation to feminists to "take a break from feminism" for "fun."[60]

This is not a play date that women subjected to domestic violence, rape, impoverishment upon divorce, sex discrimination at work, and other subjects at the center of feminism would care to attend. Indeed, Halley's focus is not on the perils of Pauline but the lure of being John Malkovitch, or (to be more precise) her Harvard colleague Duncan Kennedy: "if I could click my heels and become a 'gay man' or a 'straight white male middle class radical,' I would do it in an instant—wouldn't you?" Halley asks. Her attraction to masculinity as a life form could not be more explicit.

It's a free country, and Halley's entitled to call it as she sees it. But it is intriguing that Harvard has chosen a gender theorist who makes a name for herself by telling women not to make demands on men. Also intriguing is that three of the country's top gender theorists, teaching at three of its most prestigious universities, all focus their work on celebrating various aspects of masculinity. Is there a message here about institutional comfort level? Are there politics at elite institutions that tend to lead to the selection of assimilationists?

Halley is an extreme example. Most women engage in delicate, ongoing negotiations both with masculinity and femininity, participating in both traditions in different melds that vary in different social contexts, as when a woman dresses in a hard hat and acts tough at work but changes into a dress and flirts at dinner. Tomboy, remember, is one way of being a woman—the whole point is that being a "tomboy" is different from being a boy or a man. Though most women adopt some masculine strategies, very few perform conventional masculinity top to bottom. Doing so, outside of a few mandarin academic environments, would trigger social sanctions, informal but severe. Hillary Clinton is a good example. Throughout her professional life, she has struggled to project an image that is feminine enough to avoid turning off a lot of people. Said one commentator, "They are casting Hillary Clinton as an Angry Woman, a she-monster melding images of Medea, the Furies, harpies . . . This gambit handcuffs Hillary: If she doesn't speak out strongly against President Bush, she's timid and girly. If she does, she's a witch and a shrew."[61] "Should Hillary Pretend to Be a Flight Attendant?" asked Maureen Dowd, in a column that quoted a grandmother who advised her doctor daughter, in 2005, to "never let a man think you're smarter. Men don't like that."[62] And it is not just grandmothers. A 2006 study of speed dating found that men valued intelligence in a woman "but only up to a point . . . It turns out that men avoided women whom they rated as smarter than themselves. The same held true for . . . ambition—a woman could be ambitious, just not more ambitious than the man considering her for a date." "We males . . . [have] fragile egos in search of a pretty face and are threatened by brains or success that exceeds our own," concludes the study's author, economist Ray Fisman.[63]

Hillary entered the White House with a severe hairstyle featuring a black hair band. The press pounced, and gradually her appearance got femmier and femmier. As noted, successful women typically mix masculinity with feminine "softeners."[64] Arguably, the most effective softener Hillary ever found was to "stand by her man" after he publicly humiliated her by first having an affair and then by putting her in a position of claiming (falsely) that he had not. By the time Hillary ran for president, she had long since settled on pantsuits (tomboy) but a much softer hairstyle and clothes with bright touches of orange and pink (femmy). She flirted openly with the femmy when she gave her campaign a boost with a PDE (public display of emotion), getting teary eyed about how much she loved this country.[65]

Hillary's masculinity-plus-softeners approach is a common strategy among successful professional women. Amanda Burden, New York City planning commissioner, noted that her "soft-spoken demeanor is a terrific foil for a will of steel." An executive, ironically named Dawn Steel, described her persona as combining "the best of men and women—tough and compassionate, aggressive and morally and emotionally responsible, decisive and creative." High-powered women in conventional arenas typically offset masculine life patterns and personality traits ("hard-driving," "ambitious") with strong signals of femininity. Perhaps the most commonplace strategy is to wear high heels. These signal femininity without requiring women to adopt deferential behaviors that would undercut their authority and credibility. Classic shows of deference common in women include talking less than men, using more tentative speech patterns ("don't you think?), making fewer task suggestions, and using fewer gestures that display dominance and assertiveness. All of these would directly undercut status, credibility, and perceived competence. High heels do not. Instead they draw on the association of women's sexuality with power, as crystallized in the stereotype of the vamp. High heels are bad for one's feet— women have 80% of the foot operations carried out in the United States— but they allow women to signal femininity while sending messages of power (additional height, sexual confidence) rather than deference.[66]

Michelle Obama has avoided the Hillary trap. After being burned by early campaign experiences that depicted her as an angry black woman, including the *New Yorker* cover that depicted her as a terrorist, she has gone out of her way to signal femininity, identifying herself as "first mom," whose focus will be on her children, and spending much of her first hundred days giving interviews to women's magazines and looking elegant. As one prominent academic, an African-American woman, explained,

> African American women . . . are put in all these different boxes and I remember feeling that really strongly again when I heard Michelle Obama speak at the Democratic National Convention . . . I found it really hard to watch because she had to stand in front of America and make sure she wasn't too threatening to America and she was the requisite lady to be the first lady . . . I don't know if I would have done something different. I think she probably correctly gauged the American public . . . Hilary Clinton didn't play society's game and it cost her.[67]

If prominent feminist public figures go out of their way to signal respect for feminine traditions, mainstream feminist authors are less cautious. Two leading examples are Linda Hirshman, in *Get to Work: A Manifesto for Women of the World*, and Leslie Bennetts, in *The Feminine Mistake: Are We Giving up Too Much?* Hirshman and Bennetts make the important point that women need to stay in the workforce to protect their economic futures: as noted, women who take even two or three years out of the workforce encounter a 30% drop in lifetime earnings.[68]

The pressing question is not whether this message is an important one—it clearly is—but whether the means Hirshman and Bennetts use to convey it are persuasive to their intended audience. Hirshman's argument that women should not leave work to stay home with children is clearly deeply felt, by someone who identifies very strongly with her work, yet her advocacy becomes less effective because of her harsh criticism of stay-at-home mothers. Hirshman sees homemakers as living lives that indulge "a bit too much of the inner child for any normal adult": dressing like children and inhabiting a "private world of laundry and kissing boo-boos." "It does not take well-developed political skills to rule over creatures smaller than you are [and] weaker than you are," she writes. Hirshman consistently belittles traditionally feminine roles (she calls one homemaker "a merry maid") and embraces the breadwinner role, dismissing the "canard, 'I never met a man who wished on his deathbed he had spent more time at work'" as "manifestly false." Of the long hours required in extreme jobs, she remarks, "Obviously, longer is not the same as soul destroying."[69] Hirshman's work would be more persuasive, and less divisive, if she maintained her focus on the economic vulnerability associated with homemaking rather than veering off into a devaluation of it.

Leslie Bennetts's argument is equally heartfelt: that women who leave employment are highly vulnerable if they divorce. This is an important point, as is her welcome reassurance to younger women that sharing of household chores is possible and her interviews with women who found it extraordinarily hard to "opt back in" after a career break are a welcome antidote to the newspapers, who so often gloss over how hard it is for women to reenter the workplace.[70]

Yet these important messages need to be delivered in tones her intended audience can hear. Bennetts's reporting taps into very real divisions women feel about the home-versus-work divide—the question is whether reporting women's harshest judgments about each other will help her cause. I suspect not. Bennetts reports on women referring to "the infantilizing effects of female dependency," comparing a homemaker to a "husband's unpaid servant," and noting that "the smart ones are bored." She quotes a hedge-fund manager opining that most homemakers turn a blind eye to extramarital affairs because they "are . . . happy with the affluence." She reports stories about women whose husbands use money to control and abuse them, noting that "financially independent women are frequently appalled by such self-degradation."[71]

Many homemakers, I suspect, would be equally appalled. These harsh judgments reflect the fact that both sides feel their identities at risk when it comes to issues of work and family. But that is exactly the point: women face a no-win situation—those who perform as ideal workers are faulted for being bad mothers, while women who live up to the ideals of the mother ("always available to her children") are faulted for failing to be ideal workers. Feminists need to interrupt this pattern if we are to persuade across the femme-tomboy line. Tomboys need to avoid calling femmes bad workers. Femmes need to avoid calling tomboys bad mothers.

This message is particularly important if assimilationists' goal is to reach younger feminists. As third-wave feminists have made very clear, they find their mothers' assimilationism distinctly off-putting. The third-wave *Manifesta* shouts "femme" long and loud, in explicit rebellion against the tomboy ethic of older feminists.[72] While older feminists scold about high heels, younger feminists note, "maybe we *should* be painting our nails in the boardroom," and insist, "I can still access the 'girly' parts of feminine identification," from wearing thongs to crocheting.[73] While older feminists are chary of stay-at-home motherhood, younger feminists often embrace it, calling for greater opportunities for part-time work and "valuing (monetarily) stay-at-home parents."[74] Said Rebecca Walker, a leader of third-wave feminism and the daughter of second-wave feminist Alice Walker, "I'm supposed to be like this feminist telling them, 'Go achieve, go achieve.' And I'm sitting here saying, 'For me, having a baby has been the most transformational experience of my life.' "[75]

Assimilationist feminism alienates not only many younger women but also homemakers who do not appreciate being called infantilized servants. Moreover, an unhelpful racial dynamic can arise, given "that black women hold less egalitarian attitudes towards female-typed domestic work, even though they hold more favorable attitudes towards women's labor-force participation."[76] Tomboys would do well to remember that black middle-class women may want to stay at home—a role traditionally reserved for white women. For African Americans, the homemaker role may be viewed as a way to ensure the health and longevity of their marriages. The larger social and economic context in which black middle-class families raise children also plays a role. "Although middle-class white children are themselves highly likely to become successful members of the middle class, the same assumption cannot be made about black children." Thus the homemakers' role in ensuring the transmission of cultural and human capital to the next generation is likely to be a pressing concern.[77]

Assimilationist feminism is very strong in the United States, but "equality" means something quite specific. When Americans discuss equality, they typically mean equality of opportunity—equality to fit into society as currently structured.[78] As a result, the United States is probably the best industrialized country in the world for tomboys, since these women need only equal opportunity to perform on the terms traditionally available to men.

Reconstructive Feminism

Conversely, the United States may well be the worst industrialized country in the world for women living traditionally feminine lives: levels of maternal and child proverty are wildly higher here than in Europe.[79] This uncomfortable fact shapes the contours of reconstructive feminism, whose fundamental precepts have been around a long time. Yale law professor Reva Siegel articulated the basic thrust of reconstructive feminism while still a law student, in a student note published in 1978 arguing that maternity leave is required by a commitment to basic equality tenets.[80] In the 1987 *CalFed* case, Supreme Court Justice Thurgood Marshall agreed: "The entire thrust . . . behind [the Pregnancy Discrimination Act] . . . legislation is to guarantee women the basic right to participate fully and equally in the workforce, without denying them the fundamental right to full participation in family life."[81]

Reconstructive feminism picks up on Justice Marshall's insight that what women need is equality—but that equality first requires changing masculine norms to allow women, as well as men, to have both conventional careers and a conventional family life. Two more recent cases make much the same point. Reva Siegel argues that the recent United State Supreme Court case of *Nevada Department of Human Resources v. Hibbs* moves away from the notion that pregnancy regulation responds to "real physical differences"—which locates difference in women's bodies—to a more modern view of pregnancy regulation as a response to gender stereotypes, which as we have seen stem from masculine norms (although the *Hibbs* opinion does not amble down that particular path). Another case makes much the same point. Decided by the conservative Seventh Circuit Court of Appeals, *Washington v. Illinois,* upheld a cause of action by a mother whose employer retaliated against her for filing a race discrimination complaint by rescinding her flex schedule. Her 7 A.M. to 3 P.M. schedule was essential to enable her to be home when her son with Down's syndrome returned from school. Judge Frank Easterbrook ruled that taking her flex schedule away constituted retaliation, adopting a broad interpretation of what constitutes an "adverse employment action" required to sustain a retaliation claim. Citing that great legal authority *Dilbert*, Easterbrook voiced a suspicion that "the Illinois Department of Revenue may have a Catbert in its management." "Catbert, the Evil Director of Human Resources in the comic strip *Dilbert*," the judge explained, "delights in pouncing on employees' idiosyncratic vulnerabilities." Easterbrook reasoned that the change in schedule might not have been materially adverse for every employee but that the plaintiff was not a normal employee. "She has a vulnerability: her son's medical condition. Working 9-to-5 was a materially adverse change for *her*, even though it would not have been for 99% of the staff."[82] Workers have children, and employers have to take account of that in designing their employment practices. By ruling that requiring someone to work 9-to-5 could amount to an adverse employment action, Easterbrook's opinion signals an early shift from the old-fashioned ideal-worker norm to the new norm of the balanced worker. Reconstructive feminism aims to help tomboys gain access to workplace structures designed by and for men, but it also aims to help women who do the femmy things women conventionally do, like getting pregnant and caring for children, by locating the source of work/family conflict in the fact that "workplace norms" are masculine norms.

Reconstructive Feminism and
Difference Feminism

The accepted—and flawed—approach of feminists focused on femmes is to speak of the need to recognize "real differences" between men and women. Argues Mary Becker,

> formal equality is based on a counterfactual assumption; because of this assumption formal equality will, in practice, actually mean inequality. Formal equality assumes that it is possible to ignore an individual's sex. Both common sense and empirical data suggest that we cannot and do not ignore sex in dealing with an individual.[83]

Note how Becker locates the relevant "real" differences in women. In this piece and elsewhere, it is clear that Becker is thinking of "real physical differences," such as pregnancy; "real social differences," such as the fact that women still handle a disproportionate load of family work; and "real psychological differences," generally described as the view that women embrace an ethic of care and nurturance.[84]

Reconstructive feminism starts from a simple premise. People have thousands of "real differences" that lack social consequences. The question is not whether physical, social, and psychological differences between men and women exist. It is why these particular differences become salient in a particular context and then are used to create and justify women's continuing economic disadvantage. If I were writing in the 1980s, I would baldly deny that differences exist between men and women. Less confusing is to point out that women's differences have to be measured against something—what are women different from? The answer: from unspoken masculine norms.

Feminists whose goal is to empower women in traditionally feminine roles typically are called "difference feminists." Thus in Bartlett and Rhode's casebook, the sections on difference feminism involve women in traditionally feminine roles that are socially devalued and economically vulnerable, such as pregnant women and homemakers.[85] In the workplace context, difference feminism focuses not on historically male jobs but on historically female ones, as in the fight for "comparable worth" (that is, to give women in historically female-dominated jobs pay equal to that in comparable jobs historically held by men).[86] Indeed, in discussing difference feminism, the Bartlett and Rhode casebook lumps together a hodgepodge of cases in which courts treat men and women differently. Some cases involve "real physical differences" such as pregnancy leaves ("Eliminating the Consequences of Women's Differences") and women's longer life spans

("Recognizing Sex-Linked Average Differences"). Other cases involve "real differences in women's lives," notably their disproportionate load of family work and consequent economic vulnerability upon divorce. All of these "differences" are treated as uncontroversial, in contrast to the supposed psychological differences between men and women, which are acknowledged to be "controversial."[87] Reconstructive feminism rejects the view that *any* of these differences, whether physical, social, or psychological, are inherently meaningful by shifting attention away from women and onto masculine norms.

How Masculine Norms Create "Real Physical Differences"

The key drawback with formulating the inquiry as one of "real differences" is that this approach locates the "difference" in women's bodies. In fact, the gender trouble stems not from women's bodies but from masculine norms.[88]

Let's begin with pregnancy. The only reason pregnancy represents a problem for employed women is because the ideal-worker norm is designed around someone with a man's body (no time off for childbearing) and men's traditional life patterns (no time off for child rearing or other care work). Once again, the issue is not whether men and women are really different; the issue is why this particular difference matters in this context. As Martha Minow pointed out long ago, men are as different from women as women are from men. What gives women's difference salience in the workplace is the weight of unstated masculine norms.[89]

The approach of reconstructive feminism is nicely illustrated through an analysis of *Los Angeles v. Manhart*, a 1978 Supreme Court case that involved a constitutional challenge to the Los Angeles pension system.[90] L.A.'s system was challenged as a violation of Equal Protection because it required women to make greater contributions than men, on the theory that women live longer than men as a group and would therefore receive greater pension payouts than men. The Supreme Court struck down the pension system as a violation of Equal Protection. Is this just a "politically correct" refusal to acknowledge that men and women really do have physical differences?

No. The fact is that Los Angeles city employees were, and are, divisible into a potentially infinite number of categories: men and women, people with long and short noses, smokers and nonsmokers, whites and people of color, couch potatoes and the physically fit. And yet sex was the only "real difference" the city chose to build into its pension system actuarial tables.

The tables ignored all sorts of unhealthy behaviors, such as smoking and lack of exercise. They ignored the reality that people of color tended (and still do tend) to die earlier than whites, though it would be equally logical to offer lower premiums to people of color—an option never considered. The tables also ignored differences in age, although an actuarial analysis no doubt would have shown that older workers cost a pension system more than do younger ones.

But L.A.'s system acknowledged the difference only between men and women. Because women were newcomers to the workforce, their presence in the labor pool seemed contingent. Having old workers and young workers, ill workers and healthy workers, smokers and nonsmokers, seemed like unavoidable "costs of doing business." But the costs associated with women seemed different because of the unspoken sense that the default worker was a man. Thus any costs associated with women were seen as "extra," avoidable costs—and any insistence that employers treat those costs as ordinary costs of doing business seemed to undermine the natural functioning of the market. In a very specific sense, it is true that accepting women's role in the market disrupts its natural functioning. After all, the beauty of the market is its ability to transmit socially created preferences efficiently—including racism and sexism. What the Supreme Court did was to interrupt the efficient transmission of those well-documented social preferences.

Due to the lack of a suitable theoretical framework, the Supreme Court's rationale for striking down the Los Angeles pension system was weak. The Court argued that Equal Protection required women to be treated as individuals, overlooking the fact that the whole point of actuarial tables is to draw inferences from demography to structure decisions about how to pool risk. The Court's inability to supply a cogent explanation for its decision resulted from a flawed theoretical apparatus—precisely the kind of ellipsis that gives rise to charges that political correctness is prohibiting us from acknowledging "basic realities." Reconstructive feminism provides a solution to this quagmire. By shifting attention from women's bodies onto social norms, it avoids fueling the common pattern in which the "real differences" between men and women are used to justify continuing sex discrimination.

How Masculine Norms Create "Real Differences in Women's Lives"

In addition to the "real physical differences" between the sexes, a second set of controversies surrounds "real differences in women's lives."[91]

Martha Fineman has been influential in articulating the view that while formal-equality feminists insist on denying difference, substantial-equality feminists are more realistic and willing to acknowledge the real differences in women's lives. "The application of equal treatment assumes that those subjected to the rules are in fundamentally the same position," Fineman writes.[92]

One drawback of Fineman's analysis is her focus on the division of marital property as the key issue regarding women's economic disenfranchisement upon divorce. In fact, no legal rule regarding the division of marital property would matter much, given the meager savings of most divorcing couples.[93] Marital property rules are important only for women married to very wealthy men, as they seek a fair share of millions, or billions, of dollars. For most women facing divorce, the key economic issue is not marital property. Instead it is whether they can assert a claim on the chief family asset—the husband's wage, given that husbands earn 72% of the family income in families with children.[94] This topic is referred to commonly, although inaccurately, as the need for "a new theory of alimony."[95]

As explained earlier, during the 1970s alimony was eliminated in many cases, and in many others, it was limited to a temporary period of "rehabilitative" alimony, typically two to five years. The new clean-break approach was seen as a recognition that the traditional support-for-services swap was a thing of the past.[96] The only problem was that the support-for-services swap was alive and well. It still is: the average American father still earns three dollars for every dollar earned by mothers.[97] And the most common family form in the United States remains the neotraditional one, in which the husband is the breadwinner and the wife's labor force participation is marginalized, because she shoulders the lion's share of family work.[98] Child support does not help divorced wives much, both because it is not fully paid in most families and because it is typically lower than what it costs to raise a middle-class child. Consequently, men's standard of living rises sharply after divorce, while women's and children's falls.[99] Doesn't all this prove that women should abandon the siren song of sameness and acknowledge once and for all (as Fineman argues) that women's needs are different from men's?[100]

A key problem is that most Americans do not believe in the Marxist tenet "from each according to his abilities, to each according to his needs." What they believe in is concisely summarized by a quote from Bill Clinton: "The American dream that we were all raised on is a simple but powerful one—if you work hard and play by the rules you should be given a chance to go as far as your God-given abilities will take you."[101] Demanding "substantive equality" sounds less like asking for a place at the starting line and more like asking for a guarantee that women will win the race. Put another way, Patricia Williams pointed out long ago that subordinated people have been talking about their needs forever, without noticeable results. "For blacks, describing needs has been a dismal failure as political activity . . . The history of our needs . . . has never been treated by white institutions as a statement of political priority."[102] In short, the coin of the realm in the United States is not "to each according to his needs;" it is equality of opportunity and the elimination of bias. Perhaps Fineman's ideas have found so little purchase outside of the academy because they are, alas, out of sync with what most Americans believe.

What divorced women need is not substantive equality but the elimination of bias. Numerous task force and commission reports on gender bias in the legal system issued in the 1980s and 1990s document that gender bias in divorce courts was rampant.[103] Again not much has changed. Sometimes bias takes very obvious forms, but the core of the problem is subtler. Divorced women's key problem is not too much equality but too little. When women who have marginalized their workforce participation in order to support their partners' ability to perform as ideal workers are treated "the same" as men, this is not equality. Equality entails treating likes alike, and men and women are not similarly situated with respect to workplace and legal norms designed around men's bodies and traditional life patterns. Equality requires first deconstructing the masculine norm.

The relevant masculine norm is a property rule so taken for granted by divorce courts that it invariably remains unstated. The "he-who-earns-it-owns-it" rule assumes that the husband's wage is his sole personal property. Given that most husbands earn the bulk of the family income, the he-who-earns-it-owns-it rule means that divorcing women will remain largely reliant on courts' willingness to redistribute what they see as the husband's wage.[104] But is it really "the husband's" wage? Not really. Recall, first, that the ideal-worker wage embeds not only the husband's market work but also the wife's family work, without which he could not perform as an ideal worker. Fundamental property principles suggest that a family asset jointly produced by the labors of two family members should be jointly owned. Treating a jointly produced asset as the sole personal property of the husband makes no sense—except as an expression of the old-fashioned rule that husbands own their wives' labor as well as all property that stems from it. This rule was rejected in the Married Women's Property Acts, over a century ago. But it lives on, uncontested, in divorce courts today.[105]

American divorce courts need to replace the he-who-earns-it-owns-it rule with a new rule that recognizes the role of women's work in creating men's human capital. Once that happens, men and women should in fact be treated the same at divorce. If the marginalized caregiver is the husband, the joint property rule will benefit him. If the caregiver is the wife, she, too, will be protected from artificial impoverishment upon divorce. The key point is that divorcing women do not need substantive equality or equality of results; nor do they need courts to "meet their needs." All they need is equal treatment—after the elimination of masculine norms.

Women's Supposed Psychological Differences

Advocates of the notion that women have different values, or a different voice, are on the defensive. A flood of studies, across a wide range of fields, discredit the thesis that women have a "different voice," reflecting an "ethic of care," while men are focused not on relationships but on hierarchy.[106] And yet the different voice thesis arises again and again, in legal texts like the Bartlett and Rhode casebook, in the scholarly literature, and in the popular press.[107] Thus Lisa Belkin attributes women's choice to their different biology and also tells us that she and others rejected ambition when their values changed after they had children.[108] She quotes one woman: "I don't want to be on the fast track . . . Some people define that as success. I don't." Belkin attributes her own decision to give up her dream of becoming editor of the *New York Times* to a lack of ambition:

> I decided to leave the full-time job in the newsroom for a more flexible free-lance life writing from home, and I must admit that it was not a change I made only because my children needed me. It's more accurate to say I was no longer willing to work as hard—commuting, navigating office politics, having my schedule be at the whim of the news, balancing all that with the needs of a family—for a prize I was learning I didn't really want.[109]

Antifeminists make arguments remarkably similar to Belkin's. Kingsley R. Browne asserts that "much of what we call the glass ceiling and the gender gap is the product of basic biological differences in personality and temperament" between men and women. He claims that these differences stem from men's and women's different reproductive roles,[110] arguing that women do not reach the C-suite because they lack the qualities that get men there: "aggressiveness, ambition and drive, strong career orientation ('a passion for success'), and risk-taking."[111] Remember the typical woman? Nurturing, expressive, and responsive to the needs of others.[112] "Combined with women's greater commitment to families, these temperamental differences have a powerful effect," concludes Browne, explaining women's failure to reach the top rungs in the world of work as reflecting women's choice rather than a glass ceiling.[113]

If feminists like Belkin and antifeminists like Browne agree, there must be some powerful gravitational force pulling them in the same direction. There is, but this force is not biology itself. It is separate-spheres ideology. The description given by both Belkin and Browne, of women as less aggressive than men and focused on care rather than personal ambition, describes not women but social norms: the way women are expected, and often required, to behave—namely, as femmes who conform to the expectations that surround conventional femininity. Commending women for their caring nature is an example of the benevolent prescriptive stereotyping; social psychologists have documented that both men and women hold benevolent stereotypes of women—indeed, women hold them more strongly than men.[114] Different-voice feminists certainly do. Their endorsement of conventional femininity as a celebration of "women's strengths" is a warm embrace of benevolent stereotypes. To understand why this is so, we need to circle back to Carol Gilligan's work in the 1980s, recording the self-descriptions of (upper-middle-class, predominantly white) women.

Gilligan described women's "different voice" as the view that the "moral person [is] one who helps others; goodness is service, meeting one's obligations and responsibilities to others, if possible without sacrificing oneself."[115] Note the "if possible": Gilligan's acute ear picked up the abiding influence of separate spheres. Her subjects describe the influence of their mothers, whom they saw as "endlessly giving" and "selfless," terms that perfectly capture nineteenth-century conclusions that women's natural proclivities suit them to the private rather than the public sphere.[116] This is why the stereotypes constructed as part of this old but enduring gender system—and now endorsed by different-voice feminists, among others, as indicative of women's strengths—are so readily flipped into an explanation for why women's failure to achieve economic equality merely reflects their psychological indisposition, their lack of "a passion for success." As one astute commentator has pointed out, "Praising women's sensitivity and emphasizing the importance of mothers' nurturing of children . . . may be a less incendiary way of invoking the notion that women are suited for domestic life, but not for business."[117]

The tricky part is that stereotypes have "a social kernel of truth"—again because gender pressures push women toward femininity.[118] The gender trouble emerges when we hold a mirror up to the world, find separate spheres reflected, and then describe separate spheres as the true voice or nature of women. Ultimately, the claim that women have different values, or a different voice, boils down to a claim that women as a group are more feminine than men. This is no revelation. Women are under hydraulic pressure to conform to the social norms of femininity. But saying that "women as a group are more influenced than men by the norms of femininity" is very different from saying that "women have different values," which is a claim that all women act consistently femmy all the time. The conflation of *women* with *conventional femininity* may not bother those who do act femmy or adopt stable identities as femmes, but it is greeted with howls of outrage by the tomboys. Said one:

> I *literally* recognized myself in [Gilligan's] . . . book . . . When I was a college student I participated in one of the psychological surveys discussed . . . I was one of the women who gave the "archetypical" masculine response . . . My "different voice" and the voices of the other women in the study who gave similar unladylike responses (and the male subjects who gave "sissy" answers) even if we were in the minority, apparently were not worthy of discussion.[119]

Fortunately, there is a straightforward way to heal divisions between tomboys and femmes. Feminists can avoid feeding into antifeminist blame-the-victim arguments that women's disadvantaged economic position reflects their own choices—and feminist femmes can avoid deeply offending feminist tomboys—by framing different-voice claims as statements about *the voice of femininity* rather than about *the voice of women*.

This shift will help in practical debates as well as theoretical ones. Take, for example, the debate over why women continue to do so much more family work than men. Some women feel they do more housework and child care because they want to. A theoretical expression of this position is law professor Naomi Cahn's article arguing that women do more than men because family work is a way of enacting and realizing their femininity. Women, argues Cahn, are "gatekeepers." They take over, and they push men aside when men try to engage in family work.[120]

No doubt some women do gatekeep; and no doubt those who do so believe they are doing a disproportionate load of family work by their own choice. Other women, however, resist a disproportionate load—presumably because they do not see household chores as a way of enacting and expressing their femininity. These tomboys discover something the femmes never see: that when women do insist that men carry an equal share, often they encounter resistance, if not outright refusal. This is why it is so misleading to explain women's disproportionate share of household work as simply the result of gatekeeping (an explanation, perhaps not surprisingly, that was immediately picked up in the newspapers).[121] Here, too, the key is to recognize that, in this context as in so many others, women's experiences differ. Femmes will see unequal sharing as the result of women's preferences; tomboys will see unequal sharing as the result of men's behavior. Acknowledging that femmes and tomboys experience the world differently offers a much more useful framework than recycling old disagreements about whether women and men are "really" the same or different.

Using Past Discrimination to Justify Future Discrimination

The risk of continuing to conflate the voice of women with the voice of femininity is aptly illustrated by the hoopla over *Women Don't Ask: Negotiation and the Gender Divide*, by Linda Babcock and Sara Laschever. The book remains important because it plays a major role in debates over whether women have failed to make substantial progress toward a proportionate share of prominent positions because of discrimination or because of their own inadequacies.

The book was a media hit, like so many others that have recycled benevolent stereotypes of women (for example, John Gray's *Men Are from Mars, Women Are from Venus*). *Women Don't Ask* was discussed on CNN and covered or reviewed in newspapers ranging from the *New York Times* to *USA Today* to the Montreal *Gazette* and in journals ranging from the *Economist* to *New Zealand Management*. Articles about the book make it clear that many read the authors as proposing that women have only themselves to blame for their failure to achieve economic equality: "Women Could Get More, Just by Asking," "Fear of Negotiating Can Keep Women behind on the Payroll," "Economic Scene: Women Are Less Likely to Negotiate, and It Can Be Costly to Them," "Ground-Breaking Study: Women's Negotiating Style Leads to Lower Pay Offers than Men," "Selfless Women too Backward in Coming Forward for Promotion," "Women Need to Learn the Art of the Deal; Pay Gap Linked to Negotiation."[122] What wimps women are! No wonder the pay gap persists. As the *Washington Post* explained, Babcock and Leschever "cite hundreds of studies and present scores of revealing anecdotes to explain why women's reluctance to negotiate leads to lower salaries and job positions."[123]

Descriptions of women in the media coverage of *Women Don't Ask* consistently overlook the difference between women and femininity. An example: "Babcock said a woman's approach to negotiating—when she actually does negotiate—is more collaborative. That's good, she said, because it helps maintain long-term relationships in the workplace and at home."[124] Yet again we see women conflated with the ethic of care. "Women need to acknowledge that they often have dual goals in any negotiation—substantive goals and relationships goals. They need to find ways to achieve both."[125] Separate spheres again, with women depicted as selfless and focused on relationships. "[Linda Babcock] argues women are reared to be selfless—and that this may be a reason why they are not smashing the glass ceiling."[126] "We fundamentally haven't changed the way we raise our kids," notes another article. "Girls are taught to focus on the needs of others, not on themselves."[127] "While detractors might rubbish the idea women are naturally more retiring—and suggest instead that the lack of female advancement in the workplace is down to inadequate childcare," observes a British writer, "the book argues that women's psychology and upbringing turns them into caring, selfless adults."[128] In other words, separate spheres ideology forms the basic architecture of *Women Don't Ask*. The book jumps from a discussion of "Real Differences"[129] to its proposed solution, that we need to recognize that "Women Are Better"[130] and act on "The Female Advantage." Separate spheres again: selfless women were viewed as more moral than men.[131]

Many of the articles about *Women Don't Ask* provide self-improvement tips, as when Babcock is quoted urging "women to read trade journals that publish salaries."[132] "Researchers Linda Babcock and Sara Laschever," says another article, "also maintain that women could make up some ground if they'd simply learn how to ask for raises and negotiate for higher pay, rather than waiting for a reward unbidden."[133] Get with it, gals! The *Economist* develops this theme with abandon, lumping its coverage of *Women Don't Ask* together with a discussion of research findings from three economic studies. One, from the London School of Economics, found that only one-third as many women as men regard themselves as "work-centered." The other two, by two American economists, showed that "the average man did about 50% better" than women when experimental subjects were paid sharply more for winning a game and that boys run faster if paired with girls. Lest readers fail to get the point, the *Economist* includes a helpful quote from one of the study authors, who concluded that "if men try harder when competing, they will disproportionately win the top jobs."[134]

Now let's take a look at a more recent social psychology study, co-authored by none other than Linda Babcock, a few years after she published *Women Don't Ask*. In a series of four experiments, Hannah Riley Bowles, Linda Babcock, and Lei Lai looked at whether and how women negotiate for compensation.[135] The first experiment investigated whether subjects were willing to hire candidates who initiated a salary negotiation. The results showed that both male and female evaluators penalized female candidates who initiated salary negotiations more often than men who did so. The second experiment measured subjects' willingness to work with women who negotiated salary. The results: women, but not men, incurred a large penalty for attempting negotiations—women's penalty was 5.5 times as steep as men's—and women as well as men were less willing to work with other women who initiated salary negotiations. The third experiment involved a video of the candidate's interview rather than a resume. In that experiment, male evaluators (but not females) penalized women for salary negotiations, and they insisted on a greater degree of likeability from women job candidates than from men. The final experiment manipulated the sex of the interviewer. The results showed that when the evaluator was male, women were more reluctant than men to negotiate compensation, but this difference did not exist when the evaluator was a woman.

The researchers posed the question of whether women's greater reluctance "to initiate negotiations over . . . compensation could be explained by the differential treatment of male and female negotiators" and concluded "the answer is yes."[136] In the first three experiments, the authors pointed out, male evaluators punished women more than men for attempting to negotiate salary. In the third, women's reluctance to negotiate salary disappeared when negotiating with a woman. "We show with this research that women's disinclination relative to men to initiate negotiations over resources, such as compensation, may be traced to the higher social costs that they face when doing so."[137] The authors point out that their results indicate that society rewards women for living up to the feminine ideals of modesty, niceness, warmth, and sensitivity to others and often penalizes women for engaging in the kind of competitive, self-promoting behaviors that are accepted as appropriate for men.[138] "As lower-status group members making claims to the privileges of higher-status group members, women are likely to appear inappropriately demanding if they attempt to negotiate for higher levels of compensation,"[139] especially (but not only) if the evaluator is a man. Other studies confirm that women's inability to negotiate disappears when negotiating for others; it is only when they negotiate for themselves that they falter, for fear they will transgress the separate-spheres mandate of selflessness.[140] This conclusion is further supported by the findings of a meta-analysis of sixty-two different studies.[141]

Why don't women ask? Often because they sense that they will face steep social costs if they do. As previously pointed out, women whose behavior or personality traits seem beyond the bounds of conventional femininity risk being perceived as bitchy and treated accordingly, by other women as well as by men. A second reason women don't feel that they can negotiate hard is that they don't feel as entitled to good jobs as men do. When one researcher simulated a job interview with MBA students, she found that 85% of the men felt that they knew their own worth in the negotiation, while 83% of the women felt unsure of their worth. While 70% of the men felt entitled to above-average compensation, only 30% of the women did. The men, but not the women, also felt they could use self-promotion to justify a higher salary.[142] Why don't women feel entitled? Because traditionally they have been blocked from most good jobs. Once again, past discrimination against women can easily be used to justify future discrimination—their lack of entitlement translates into a failure to negotiate.

When *conventional femininity* is characterized as the *voice of women*, past discrimination against women (that is, norms that punish women for negotiating) is used to justify future discrimination against women (that is, workplace gender bias that imposes a steep price on women who negotiate). The media's enthrallment with *Women Don't Ask* provides a particularly clear example of this neat loop. The *Baltimore Sun* notes, "[The authors] suggest that [women don't ask] because women have lower expectations of what they can achieve, are grateful for the job offer in the first place and have less knowledge of the job market and what they are really worth."[143] Why women have lower expectations is, alas, a question the *Sun* reporter did not ask, although the answer is simple: gender discrimination in the past is all-too-frequently used to justify gender discrimination in the future.

To their credit, Babcock and Laschever tried to forestall criticism that they were conflating femininity with women in general by asserting that they were not offering a "fix the women" argument.[144] But in interviews they often offered suggestions about how women should change, and the book repeatedly cites women's attitudes and behaviors as the fundamental loci of their workplace problems. The preface begins, "Women don't ask. They don't ask for raises and promotions and better job opportunities. They don't ask for recognition for the good work they do. They don't ask for help at home."[145] The introduction tells a story about women PhD students who came to Babcock when she was director of their program, complaining that male grad students were teaching courses of their own, while they were relegated to teaching assistant positions. When Babcock asked the relevant dean why, he explained, "More men ask. The women just don't ask."[146] This comment is followed by more talk about women's socialization. There is not a glimmer of a suggestion that unspoken messages sent by the dean and others in the department may well have played a crucial role in creating the women students' reluctance to speak up.

Why would two feminists embrace traditional stereotypes that can be used against women—and regularly are? I assume they did so because they felt those stereotypes to be true: "Women often worry more than men about the impact their actions will have on their relationships."[147] This is certainly true of some women, but what about deference-challenged tomboys, who worry not a bit and pay the price for their confidence? Babcock and Laschever quote a woman architect as "working and working until I fell apart," stating that "asking [for help] didn't seem like a possibility, but I'm sure it was."[148] But for every woman who tries to power through, there is a woman who actually asked her husband to make career sacrifices, only to find out that he refuses to help. The authors then discuss women who do not negotiate because "they are satisfied with less": less money, less status, an unequal division of household chores. There is not a word about the women who do demand more and are subsequently written off as lacking in interpersonal skills. Only one of the book's eight chapters features tomboys chafing against the mandates of feminine niceness. The other seven overwhelmingly feature femmes reluctant to negotiate, for their own psychological reasons. It is a book about women who feel that descriptive stereotypes aptly describe them and are baffled when their attempts to meet other people's expectations do not pay off.

Gender Wars Revisited

Difference feminism's embrace of conventional femininity raises acute problems for coalition building. This emerges clearly in the *Women Don't Ask* debate. During a recent interview, Babcock recommended that women should use a "cooperative negotiation" style to get what they want. "The trick is not to say to your manager, 'I have another job offer and I'll leave if you don't match it.' That approach would be threatening from a woman, even if it could be accepted from a man, Babcock said. So instead, reframe it: 'I have this other offer, but I'd like to find a way to stay here. Can you match it so I can stay?' "[149]

That may be good advice for women whose hesitancy comes from within. But to tomboys, who may comply with feminine niceness reluctantly or not at all, this is sure to seem like a recommendation that they conform to a sexist insistence that they act femmy. Ultimately, why does it matter whether the woman has adjusted her behavior wholesale or retail to the mandates of conventional femininity? The fact is that masculine workplace norms often make it politically risky for women to negotiate.

The surest way to preclude a feminist coalition is to insist, as the only true path, either on assuring women unfettered access to masculine gender performances (the tomboys' access-to-masculinity agenda) or on assuring women's opportunity to make the world safe(r) for conventional femininity (the femmes' femininity-empowerment agenda). This either-or approach also creates generational rifts. A recent study of lawyers found that younger women work fewer hours and years and do more child care than did women in the cohorts that preceded them.[150] This may be because women who entered the legal profession between 1996 and 2000 were more conventionally feminine than the pioneers who entered the profession before then. Generational differences also emerge in attitudes toward feminism. Two recent studies found that women born between 1936–1955 and 1946–1959 are more likely to consider themselves feminists than women born afterward.[151]

Building effective coalitions will require feminists to frame issues in ways that appeal both to tomboys and to femmes. For example, both groups can agree on the need to displace masculine norms—in this case, the practice of determining salary by individualistic hard bargaining. Hard bargaining is costless for most men. In fact, hard bargaining enhances their masculinity, and as we have seen, masculinity is an implicit job requirement for most high-status jobs—so men have little to lose, and much to gain, from bargaining hard. In sharp contrast, women—femmes and tomboys alike—face a debilitating catch-22 when faced with the need to bargain: if they act femmy and do not negotiate, they get lower salaries and look ineffectual; if they act like tomboys and do negotiate, they may get a higher starting salary, but they are also likely to trigger negative responses stemming from ambivalent sexism in the workplace, thereby jeopardizing their futures.

The solution is not to advise tomboys to negotiate in a deferential, reassuringly femmy way. The solution is (again) to notch the analysis up one logical level and change the masculine norm. It is perfectly possible to design a compensation system—or a system for selecting which graduate students teach their own courses—so that it does not systematically disadvantage women. But to do so requires jettisoning a system that gives good starting salaries, and good raises, only to those people who negotiate hard and self-promote well and replacing it with a system that does not systematically reward masculinity. That is the direction we need to go, because that is the only direction that will offer true opportunity—not just for tomboys, or for femmes, but for the broad band of men, gay and straight, who are not comfortable with "hard-hitting," self-promoting, conventional masculinity.

A start has been made in the academic world. For example, at the University of Michigan, some department chairs negotiate start-up packages for new hires rather than leaving new hires to negotiate for themselves. This procedure allows women scientists to ask for the lab space, equipment, and staffing they need to conduct their research effectively without having to bargain hard after they are hired. The system of bargaining after hire often leads to start-up packages that are more generous to men than to women, because women sense that hard bargaining could brand them as "difficult" even before they begin their new jobs.[152]

Does Reconstructive Feminism Play Well with Others?

This section seeks to explain the relationship between reconstructive feminism and three other strains of feminist theory: queer theory, dominance feminism, and anti-essentialism.

Queer Theory

Reconstructive feminism is a "queer eye for the straight guy" (and girl).[153] It applies the intellectual tools developed by queer theorists—most famously Judith Butler—to conventional masculinity and conventional femininity (note the use of the singular). Reconstructive feminism draws inspiration from queer theory's explorations of "gender trouble": the way people try out, and play with, femininities and masculinities.[154] Queer theory uses the metaphor of "gender performance" (or performativity). I have avoided that metaphor because it overlooks the way gender is embodied into dispositions, so that "doing gender" rarely feels like a performance—that is precisely its power. More useful, I believe, is queer theory's core insight that gender does not reside naturally in people's bodies. Rather, it is a set of social scripts that people follow or resist, or do a little of each. Gender is a cultural resource all of us use to shape our personas and our social interactions. It is not something we *are* but something we *do*. It involves "crafting conduct that can be evaluated in relation to normative conceptions of manly and womanly natures and assessing conduct in the light of those conceptions—given the situation at hand," to quote the influential formulation of sociologists Candace West and Don Zimmerman.[155] As a specific example, my use of the term "femme" is meant to communicate that not only do lesbians in butch-femme relationships enact femininity as a strategy of self-expression; so do women in conventional contexts.

Despite its debt to queer theory, reconstructive feminism focuses on the center rather than the margins. Emblematic of queer theory is the wonderful Australian film *Priscilla, Queen of the Desert*, a road trip movie whose central character is a man struggling to come to terms with his gender identities as a drag queen and a father.[156] Emblematic of reconstructive feminism is the film *About Schmidt*, with its sensitive portrayal of the ways conventional masculinity constrains and distorts the lives of conventional white male breadwinners.[157] While queer theory stresses the manipulability of gender identity, reconstructive feminism stresses that gender is unbending. Queer theory celebrates marginalized sexualities and Madonna's "cunning stunts";[158] reconstructive feminism places at its analytical center the yearning for, and performance of, hegemony.

These differences in focus lead queer theory and reconstructive feminism to develop different tools and to use different terminology. Queer theorists, whose goal is to explore the complex relationships between biological sex, gender performance, and sexuality, often find work-family feminists' insistence on distinguishing between biological sex and socially constructed gender counterproductive. Making that sex-gender distinction, queer theorists argue, sends the message that sex is natural rather than socially constructed.[159] Yet the distinction between sex and gender is vitally important on the work-family axis, as a way to highlight that people with vaginas do not always behave in the ways the separate-spheres paradigm describes as feminine. Not all women share an ethic of care or embrace the homemaker or mother role.

These differences do not need to be divisive. Recognizing the logical independence of the three different axes of gender analysis—work-family, sex-violence, and queer—leads to an awareness that the tools for analyzing the queer axis of gender are, and in fact *must be*, different from the tools necessary for analyzing the work-family axis. Reconstructive feminism's call to distinguish (at least) three distinct feminist agendas aims to help keep things sorted out.

Dominance Feminism

Reconstructive feminism also shares many of the premises and conclusions of dominance feminism, which is widely associated with Catharine MacKinnon. Most notable is a focus on masculinity as a source of social power. More than two decades ago, MacKinnon wrote insightfully about the prevalence and the influence of masculine norms: "men's physiology defines most sports, their needs define auto and health insurance coverage, their socially designed biographies define workplace expectations and successful career patterns."[160] She even mentions what I later named the ideal-worker norm, noting that jobs are "structured with the expectation that [their] occupant would have no child care responsibilities."[161]

From there the divergences begin. One is MacKinnon's undefended, and fundamentally indefensible, claim that the eroticizing of dominance is the central (or only?) dynamic of gender.[162] A second is MacKinnon's claim that her approach is "feminism unmodified," intimating that other feminisms do not deserve the name; similarly, her often-harsh judgments, such as charging that sex-positive feminists are just "procuring for men,"[163] are not characteristic of reconstructive feminism. Yet another difference is MacKinnon's consistent failure to distinguish between *masculinity* and *men*. Just as many women do not buy into the least attractive parts of femininity, so, too, many men do not buy into the profoundly unattractive parts of masculinity that MacKinnon's work so thoroughly plumbs.[164] Last but not least, reconstructive feminism takes issue with MacKinnon's understanding of the social processes that link men with power. Her simple model of men enforcing gender privilege with their fists works well in the domestic violence context, but the workplace dynamics that block women from good jobs reflect processes more subtle than men's "foot [on] our necks."[165] Workplace gender privilege stems from the ways gender is built into time norms and work devotions that systematically disadvantage not only women but also many men.

Anti-Essentialism

Reconstructive feminism shares with anti-essentialism a commitment to inclusion. The classic anti-essentialist text critiques white feminists for reflecting white privilege when they describe gender problems from their own perspective, thereby erasing the perspectives of women of color, lesbians, and other women disadvantaged by more than one axis of social power.[166] Some white feminists, notably MacKinnon, go further and insist that all women are united by gender oppression—even over the protests of women of color, who insist that their experience of social oppression does not invariably elevate in importance their experience as women over their experience as people of color.[167]

The accepted metaphor for responding to these concerns is Kimberlé Crenshaw's concept of intersectionality.[168] Black women, she argues, exist at the intersection of race and gender, and it is time to "demarginalize" their experience. The idea of intersectionality has proved a useful tool for highlighting the need for feminists to discuss the experience not only of black women but of other women of color and of lesbians.[169] Yet today we find ourselves bumping up against its limitations. First, intersectionality as a metaphor itself reinforces white privilege and heteronormativity, by erasing the fact that women of color are no more and no less at the intersection of race and gender than are white women, and gay women are no more and no less at the intersection of sexuality and gender than are straight women. Second, the metaphor of intersectionality does not provide a language that allows us to separate the experience of black women from the experience of blacks in general—to avoid changing the topic from black women to black men—and the experience of black women from the experience of women in general—to avoid changing the topic from women of color to white women.

What we need is to jump-start the study of the racialization of gender bias: the ways the experience of gender differs by race. This is a process I sought to begin in the previous chapter. That discussion aimed to impart two important facts. The first is that women of color often encounter gender bias. The second, captured by the metaphor of double jeopardy, is that women of color's experience of gender sometimes differs from that of white women. This literature is in its infancy. Social psychology studies of "women" produce conclusions that apply largely to white women, given that lab studies are performed predominantly on white college students and audit studies are performed predominantly on white employers.

In-depth qualitative studies on the racialization of gender in the work-family context have just begun to emerge.[170] The 2006 report *Visible Invisibility: Women of Color in Law Firms*, is a pathbreaking investigation of race and gender in the workplace. More studies exploring how glass-ceiling biases (double standards and double binds) differ by race are sorely needed. The maternal wall literature is less insular. Despite the fact that this area of study began only in 2004, initial studies have explored maternal wall bias against black women, Latinas, and lesbians.[171]

Anthropologist Riché Jeneen Daniel Barnes's pioneering study of black stay-at-home mothers focuses on the role race plays in work-family conflict. Barnes documents that the homemaker role takes on different implications among blacks and whites. White women's angst focuses on their children, as they worry about whether they can remain employed and be good mothers. In the black community, breadwinning has been seen as a normative element of the mothering role since slavery, and black wives are one-and-a-half times more likely than white wives to be employed full-time.[172] In fact, black women are taught to fear economic dependence, on the grounds that one cannot count on a man to be around forever ("a man is not a plan"). Thus Barnes found that the chief work-family conflict among black stay-at-home mothers was their anxiety over their economic dependence on their husbands. "Each of these women discussed their predicaments as the daughters of 'strong black women' who expected them to be independent" rather than economically dependent.[173] "I was raised to be independent," said one. "I did not know who would be there for me and so it was very important for me to have my own money and my own everything. Depending on my husband now is just so contrary to how I think of myself."[174] In sharp contrast to white stay-at-home mothers, who typically report that their mothers laud their decisions to leave the workforce, black stay-at-home mothers feel called out: "I don't know why you doing all that," one woman's mother told her, after the woman, a former doctor, had been a stay-at-home mom for three years, "they ain't gonna appreciate it."[175]

The small sample of black stay-at-home mothers Barnes studied saw the desire to protect and maintain their marriages as a chief motivation for their decisions to stay at home full-time. Few had grown up in two-parent households sustained by good marriages, leaving them with the sense they were ill-equipped to be good wives. "Our mothers did not know how to be wives," said one.[176] Barnes notes, but does not highlight, that there is only one marriageable black man for every two marriageable black women, due to high levels of incarceration, drug abuse, and unemployment among black men, which places black men in a powerful position to bargain for family support.[177] Her interviewees express understandable concern over sustaining their marriages amidst sky-high levels of divorce—two-thirds of all married black couples will divorce.[178]

Barnes's important study highlights the need to understand the different meanings of the homemaker role in different racial contexts. The flood of research and popular commentary on the homemaker role is already racialized: it focuses on that role among white wives whose articulated rationale for their decisions to stay at home typically focuses on the needs of their children, not on those of their marriages.[179]

Generating a literature on the ways the experience of gender differs by race is a vitally important step for designing remedial action. In the public policy arena, initiatives designed to reach stay-at-home mothers will not work if they are premised on the assumption that children are the chief reason women leave employment. Moreover, understanding how gender bias differs by race is vital to family law courts that step in to define ongoing economic entitlements when out-of-the-labor-force wives divorce their husbands.

Equally important, documenting the racialization of gender bias is vital for feminist coalition building. White feminists have often alienated women of color when their supposedly generic descriptions of gender unwittingly reflect gender as experienced by white women. Thus far, feminists of color have relied on self-referential autobiographical essays to provide that shiver of recognition that their lives have been described. Such writing is a good first step—feminists often begin with consciousness-raising—but the literature on white women that now provides "objective" and "scientific" studies of gender bias carries considerably more cultural authority than do personal essays. Social psychology can be cited in court, in legislative hearings, in the press—in other words, in ways that consciousness-raising essays cannot. Feminist thinking will always be led by a frisson of self-exploration, but feminism will be far more effective if it does not stop there. The metaphor of intersectionality is fine for consciousness-raising essays, but in other contexts, it may have outlived its usefulness.

The need for a new framing emerged in sharp relief when the Project for Attorney Retention discussed a project on women lawyers we had been asked to undertake. The conversation was confusing to everyone involved. I kept insisting that we would discuss only gender dynamics. The response: "So you are going to discuss only white women?" "No, of course not," I said. "I am going to discuss the workplace experience of *women*. That includes women of color." At which point, someone said, "So you're going to include all diversity issues? That would be great. My firm really needs that." "No," I said. "I am not qualified to discuss all diversity issues. And that would be too unwieldy. I am just going to discuss women." At which point, I was asked again whether I would be discussing only white women. It was the classic anti-essentialist moment—and frustrating for us all.

As we completed the project, I developed the methodology deployed above to explore the racialization of gender bias, relying on *Visible Invisibility*, which extensively documents how women of color are affected by double standards, double binds, and the maternal wall in ways that sometimes differ from the ways those patterns affect white women.[180] The hope is that the methodology will spark a new generation of studies that explore how the experience of gender differs by race.

The importance of studying how gender experiences are racialized is highlighted by a current study by psychology professor Maureen Perry Jenkins. Jenkins found marked differences by race in the psychological effects of work-family conflict. Immigrant Latina women were most likely to experience depression when they returned to work after the birth of a child, reflecting strong norms against employed mothers in Latin American cultures. African American mothers experienced the lowest levels of depression upon their return to work, reflecting their cultural norm that paid work is an integral part of responsible motherhood. White women were in the middle—no more at the intersection of race and gender than either of the other groups of women.[181]

The crucial point is that to study gender responsibly, one must study how the experience of gender differs in different racial groups.[182] On the work-family axis in particular, it is not useful to conflate the important distinctions between different groups of women of color. When it comes to motherhood, for example, the experience of Latina women differs as much from that of African American and Asian American women as from that of white women. Recall Figure 1, which shows that white and Latina mothers are more alike with respect to their tendency to be out of the labor force than either group is like African American women. The category "women of color," so important for coalition building, is downright unhelpful in the work-family context.

A study of the racialization of gender is not—and should not purport to be—a study of race. Just as a responsible analysis of gender will include the racialization of gender bias, so will a responsible analysis of race. But the race and gender studies will differ. While a gender study will compare the experience of women of color to white women, a study of race will compare the experience of people of color to white people. These two different points of reference will lead to different emphases and perhaps to different findings in some contexts.

The next obvious issue is that gender and race are not the only categories of social power, which also include class, sexuality, and ability status. How are we to account for them all? This has been a key stumbling block for anti-essentialism. The solution is to recognize, once again, that the right tool is half the job, and what tool we pick will depend on the job we wish to do. One can only account for race, class, gender, disability, sexuality, and every other category of social power at once in the way anti-essentialism typically does: with an exhortation to take everything into account, always. This works well as an exhortation but poor as a matter of practice. In practice, studies ultimately examine specific social locations (Latina working-class mothers, black professional women, white lesbians). Note the word: *locations*, not identities. Recall that what we are talking about are the social norms and forces within which people negotiate their individual identities.

Third-Wave Feminism

A very brief word about the relationship of reconstructive and third-wave feminisms. One significant divergence has already been addressed: third-wave feminism is intensely focused on personal exploration. Therefore, it seeks to play a very different role than does reconstructive feminism, which is oriented toward bringing about institutional change. Yet a significant overlap between third-wave and reconstructive feminism is that third-wave feminism is intently committed to explorations of the values associated with the traditions of femininity. Unlike the tomboys of early second-wave feminism, who so often focused on gaining access to roles traditionally limited to men, the femmes of the third wave share with reconstructive feminism a focus on, and respect for, the traditions of femininity.[183] Younger feminists, whether or not they self-consciously identify with the third wave, may well reject assimilationist feminism. (Recall the cookie-baking, dress-wearing science professor discussed above.)

Reconstructive feminism seeks to plot a course different from either sameness or difference feminism. While seeking to value the traditions of femininity, it does not do so by "recognizing real differences." What are so often accepted as "real physical and social differences" appear real only by reference to unstated masculine norms that make women's differences seem to carry weighty explanatory power. "Real psychological differences" reflect only the unsurprising fact that, given hydraulic social pressures to conform to societal expectations surrounding gender, women as a group tend to behave more femininely than do men as a group. Conversations focused on how women, more than men, act in conformity with the mandates of femininity need to replace loose talk about "women's voice" or "values." Women's "different voice" must be recognized as the voice of conventional femininity—not the voice of women. This voice has some elements we need to preserve, as does the voice of conventional masculinity, but each also has some elements we need to lose.

The seemingly laudable "ethic of care" has a dark underside. First, confusion between women and the mandates of femininity often leads to a situation where past discrimination is used to justify future discrimination. Second, the ideology of separate spheres forges a strong link between caring and self-erasure. Surely caring for family, friends, and the world is an important value, but the version of caring enshrined in conventional femininity is seriously flawed. Care work is not logically linked with an inattentiveness to one's own needs: that is an aspect of the "ethic of care" enshrined by separate spheres. In fact, raising children, to take the paradigm case of care work, is not best accomplished by someone who ignores her own needs. The "ethic of care," to the substantial extent that it is associated with self-erasure, reflects a cultural linkage between caregiving and the selflessness that stems from the societal devaluation of caregiving.

Since care work is not considered real work, it is not linked with the kinds of entitlements that seem to "flow naturally" from work. The point is not that caregiving is unimportant. The point is that it is too important to continue to occur within a cultural framework that associates it with economic vulnerability and social devaluation—celebrated as saintly self-denial.

CHAPTER FIVE

The Class Culture Gap

Within U.S. feminist theory and cultural studies, *class* as a topic
seems tainted, perhaps perceived as outdated and unfashionable.

—JULIE BETTIE, *WOMEN WITHOUT CLASS*

IT'S NO MYSTERY how the New Deal Coalition died: white working-
class voters left. Most commentators date this exit from the 1960s or
1970s. The percentage of the white working class who identified as Democrats fell from 60% to 40% between the mid-1970s and early 1990s, according to one study. Another found that Democratic presidential voting
among the white working class declined precipitously between 1960 and
1996.[1]

The trend continued through the next election cycles in the 1990s and
early 2000s. Workers who described themselves as painters, furniture
movers, servers, and sewer repairmen were more likely than managers and
professionals to report that they were going to vote for George W. Bush in
2004. Another study found that working-class women backed Bush, but
by a lesser margin than had working-class men—among working-class
women without a four-year college degree, Bush had a seven-point lead
over Al Gore in 2000.[2] Bush won among white working-class men by
landslides: he received roughly two-thirds of their votes in 2000 and again
in 2004. In 2008, despite his clear victory, Barack Obama still lost big
among white working-class voters, with an eighteen-point deficit, larger
than even Gore's in 2000 (seventeen points).[3]

"By and large, when Democrats win the White House, it corresponds
with a greater proportion of working class whites in their coalition," concludes John McTague, whose measurement of class is the most elegant and

convincing of any political scientist I have read. "In fact, JFK was the only Democrat [since 1948] to win the White House without winning more lower-middle-class votes than his Republican opponent." Middle-class voters, whom McTague defines via a complex formula that includes both income and education, are more predictably Republican than are working-class ones. But both groups "grew decidedly more Republican over the last half of the twentieth century and into the 2000s." McTague cautions against concluding, based on his results alone, that the white working class is a crucial swing vote for Democrats, but his analysis, combined with others', certainly suggests that Democrats need to pay attention to the "Missing Middle."[4]

Scholars are agreed that class, as well as gender, has played a role in recent American politics, but less consensus exists about the role of class, probably stemming from the different proxies used to define who is working class. Ruy Teixeira found a decline of 21% among men and 9% among women in white working-class votes for Democratic presidential candidates between 1960 and 1996. Support for congressional Democrats fell, too, during this period, by 20% among white males with high school degrees and by 15% among those with some college. Support also fell among the women but by less: 10% for both high school graduates and those with some college. David Brady, Benjamin Sosnaud, and Steven M. Frank, using job categories as a proxy for class, found that white working-class men have moved dramatically and consistently away from the Democrats but that the evidence for women was more mixed. They found "some evidence" to suggest that working-class women were significantly more likely to vote Democratic in 1996 and 2004, although not in 2000.[5]

The accepted wisdom attributes working-class whites' defection from the Democratic Party to race and religion. Both no doubt have played important roles. But race and religion do not tell the whole story. Understanding the alienation of the white working class is not only about race and religion but also about class—about a deeply patterned series of class conflicts between socially conscious progressives and working-class whites. These conflicts, expressed as cultural differences, have fueled "culture wars" that have cemented a long-standing alliance between working-class whites and the business elite. The most refined fuel for class resentments is the culture of casual insults leveled by progressives toward the white working class. Changing U.S. politics will require an embargo on such insults.[6]

Rebuilding an alliance with the white working class also will require that progressives learn a lot more about their potential allies. This is vital because food, sports, vacations, and other practices and habits of the upper-middle class often are seen by working-class observers as expressions of class privilege. The resulting culture gap between classes—what I call the "class culture gap"—has political consequences because the progressive center of gravity is upper-middle class. We need to lay the groundwork for the new cross-class sensitivity necessary to rebuild an alliance between progressives and the Missing Middle.

I Can't Get No Respect

During the New Deal, working-class men were often romanticized. The murals in San Francisco's Coit Tower, painted in 1933, of farmers and policemen, factory workers and strikers, dramatize the role white working-class men played in the reform imagination. Race had not taken center stage in the understanding of social power differentials: most of the workers were white. Nor had gender: most were male. Like many Works Progress Administration murals across the country, the Coit Tower paintings dramatize the respect reform-conscious intellectuals accorded working-class men. From Tom Joad in John Steinbeck's *Grapes of Wrath* (1939) to Marlon Brando's Terry Malloy in *On the Waterfront* (1954), white working-class men were celebrated as noble and oppressed. When intellectuals thought about social disadvantage, class—not race or gender— typically emerged as the central theme.[7]

With a few notable exceptions—Bruce Springsteen comes immediately to mind—the last quarter of the twentieth century saw a sharp reversal in the way progressive elites depicted the working class. Emblematic of that reversal is the groundbreaking *All in the Family*, one of the most popular shows on television from 1971 to 1979. Archie Bunker, the patriarch who dominated his dingbat housewife Edith, was painted in sharp and unflattering contrast to his long-haired, liberal-and-enlightened, college-going son-in-law. Archie Bunker represented a new, and strikingly different, image of workers: narrow-minded, ignorant, racist, and sexist. Moreover, that image came from the heart of the progressive elite—Norman Lear, the series' producer, subsequently founded People for the American Way, a pillar of progressive activism and left-wing thinking.

With *All in the Family*, Lear aptly captured a cultural trend. By 1971, a government report concluded, "Today, there is virtually no accurate dramatic representation—as there was in the 1930's—of men and women in working-class occupations . . . Research shows that less than one character in ten on television is a blue-collar worker and that these few are usually portrayed as crude people with undesirable social traits . . . lawyers are clever, while construction workers are louts."[8] Archie Bunker was a rocket scientist compared with that icon of the 1990s, Homer Simpson. Homer "embodies several American working-class stereotypes: he is crude, over-weight, incompetent, clumsy, thoughtless and a borderline alcoholic"—the class implications are obvious to the author of the show's Wikipedia entry. Homer represents a critique of masculine privilege but one comfortably distant from elite masculinity. He is emblematic of the shift in cultural status of white working-class men. Far from having their lives celebrated, as in the Coit Tower paintings, they became the butt of jokes. Even if they laughed at Archie and Homer, they noticed this change.[9]

The pervasive disrespect emerges loud and clear in the memoirs of class migrants—individuals born and raised working class, who join the upper-middle class through access to elite education. Said one, "It is striking to me and many other working-class academics that faculty who would never utter a racial slur will casually refer to 'trailer trash' or 'white trash.'" Said another:

> When I began to teach in the Northeast, I discovered to my surprise that many people—even some enlightened academics who would staunchly fight the stereotyping of other minorities or "fringe" cultures in American society—pretty much accepted the stereotype of the southern redneck as racist, sexist, alcoholic, ignorant, and lazy . . . redneck jokes may be the last acceptable ethnic slurs in "polite" society.

Still others have noted: "Academia barely acknowledges working-class existence"; "Where I live and work, white Southern working-class culture is known only as a caricature." Workers' children who go to college, often at lower-status (and lower-cost) institutions, may find that their professors treat them with condescension:

> Many of the professors resented having to teach us. One of them once described in class the mission of the school as "teaching the first generation of immigrant children how to eat with a knife and fork." We knew we were being insulted, but in order to get as far as college we had learned that school was the one place in our experience where we couldn't get in somebody's face, specifically the teacher's. So we took it. A lot of my friends who did not make it to college were those who would not stand for that kind of treatment; they insulted back.

The first step in building bridges between progressives and white workers is to stop these insults, by instituting and rigorously enforcing the sort of taboo that now exists against using racial innuendo, jokes, and insults.[10]

Is the Upper-Middle Class in the Middle?

The next step is to forge a new vocabulary. The powerful taboos against acknowledging class in America result in a vocabulary that makes it diffi-cult to talk intelligibly about class. Both washing-machine repairmen and corporate lawyers commonly refer to themselves as middle class, making it difficult to describe class conflict between them. In fact, things get even more confusing. The group professional-managerial people call "working class" or "lower-middle class" calls itself "middle class." Although the professional-managerial class calls itself (upper-)middle class, less affluent Americans tend to see manager and professionals as an elite. Colliding vocabularies dramatize with eerie precision the lack of consensus on class.

Forging a new vocabulary starts with some demography. Let's begin with the simple class array from a standard college textbook, by Dennis Gilbert. Although income is widely acknowledged to be a highly imperfect proxy for class, it can at least help clarify who is not in the middle. Ac-cording to Gilbert, as of 2003, roughly one-quarter of Americans were "underclass" (median income $12,000) or "working poor" (median income $22,000). Then come the "working" and "middle classes," with 30% of Americans each, and median incomes of $35,000 and $55,000, respec-tively. The "upper-middle class"—whose median income is $120,000—is not, in fact, in the middle: it is an elite, the top 15% of American earners, just below the "capitalist class" (median income $2 million). A particularly dramatic example of the upper-middle-class confusion over who is middle class was Harvard's decision to offer financial aid to "middle- and upper-middle-income families" earning as much as $120,000 to $180,000 a year; a similar program at Yale offered aid to families earning as much as $200,000.[11] Clearly, confusion about who is middle class can have very concrete consequences.

How you define class depends on the problem you are tackling. If, as I have said before, the right tool is half the job, then no tool is suited to every job. For the first job at hand, which, though a highly imperfect proxy for class, serves just fine to make the point that the "upper-middle class" is not in the middle: it is an elite. I use both the group's self-description of "upper-middle class" and the more accurate term "professional-managerial class."

Defining the groups just below it is more difficult. In the discussion that follows, I abandon the distinction between "working class" and "middle class." That made sense only when it tracked onto blue- versus white-collar jobs. In today's service economy, working-class men are as likely to sell auto parts as to make them, and trying to decide whether the many routine white-collar jobs land one in the working or middle class is a futile exercise. On the ground, the circumstances of a "middle-class" small business owner may well be more similar to those of a "working-class" family employed as a nonunionized power plant worker and a receptionist than either is to the family of a corporate lawyer or business executive. The blue-collar/white-collar distinction also erases working-class women, who have remained sex-segregated in pink-collar jobs, chiefly clerical and retail, even as professional-managerial women have entered historically male careers in large numbers. Common jobs for working class women are secretary, hairdresser, receptionist, cashier, and retail saleswoman.[12]

Consequently, I combine the groups Gilbert calls "middle" and "working" class and refer to them either as the "Missing Middle," a term coined by political scientist Theda Skocpol. I also sometimes use the terms "working class" or "workers," following the usage of sociologists such as Michèle Lamont, who argues that working class is "best defined negatively, in opposition to the poor and to professionals and managers who have completed college."[13] Yet I try to avoid that terminology, except where I am relying on texts that use it, both for the reasons stated above and because academics often confuse the "working class" with low-income Americans.

In this chapter and the next, I avoid using the term "middle class" to define any specific income group. That term is best reserved for the very broad group that sees itself as having achieved access to the core symbols of the settled life: a single family house, one car per adult, ownership of major household appliances, and some access to consumer goods—at a level defined by one's friends and neighbors, that is, by one's class status. For this reason, who is seen as "middle class" differs by class. The group the upper-middle class calls "the working class," in my experience, typically calls itself "middle class" and refers to the upper-middle class as rich. Class demarcations also differ by race: upper-middle-class blacks are likely to see police as "middle class," whereas similarly situated whites tend to see them as "working class." For our purposes, however, it appears that what Americans mean when they say they are middle class is that they have the basics and are neither poor nor rich. "Middle class" is best understood as a symbol of arrival rather than a designation of a particular demographic group.

As always, allowance must be made for the specious precision of categories. When I talk about the characteristics of social groups, I am describing cultural norms and centers of gravity, not rigid templates to which people conform in lockstep. Individuals have complex relationships with social norms and cultural tropes. And individual members of a class sometimes depart from class norms. Class culture (like gender conventionality) is not a straightjacket but a default mode. Michèle Lamont reflects this with great precision when she informs us, for example, that 49% of white and 43% of black blue-collar men define success in moral terms (for example, "being a good father and a faithful husband"), while 38% of each group stresses socioeconomic achievement. Thus to say that working-class men are more likely to define success in moral as opposed to socioeconomic terms is at once true of the group as a whole and not true of many individuals.[14]

A final caveat is that, unlike many who examine the working class, my focus is not on unions nor the working-class solidarity expressed and nurtured by them. The reason is simple. As of January 2009, only 12.4% of private-sector workers belong to unions.[15] Most unions have remained loyal to the progressive agenda, and unions have often done a yeoman's job of mobilizing support for Democratic candidates. Yet the focus here is on the working-class people who are neither members of unions nor have a politicized sense of themselves as working class.

Gender Performance as a Class Act

The worst insult suffered by the Missing Middle in the years since the 1970s is the sharp decline in their standard of living, fueled by losses suffered by working-class men. At the time of the first oil shocks of the early 1970s, the typical working-class man had a unionized blue-collar job that allowed him to provide his family with the basics of middle-class life (car, house, major appliances), perhaps drawing intermittently on part-time work by his wife. Thus, Baby Boom men grew up with a very specific image of what to expect from life: the typical working-class household in 1973 was more than twice as well-off as the equivalent household twenty-five years earlier. But beginning in the mid-1970s and continuing for the next quarter century, the typical working-class family's income fell—diving 12% in real dollars.[16]

The dip in family income, though large, is considerably less dramatic than the huge drop in men's wages. (A sharp increase in wives' work hours helped slow family income's free fall.) The wages of white working-class men fell 15% between 1979 and 1998.[17] Wages in the "good" working-class jobs stalled. Technicians' earnings, which climbed $15,000 in the thirty years before 1979, rose only $2,000 in the eighteen years thereafter. Wages of police, firefighters, and other protective workers rose $13,000 during the earlier period but only $1,000 in the later.[18]

Wages in the most desirable working-class jobs at least kept up with inflation; this is not so in more modest jobs. Wages of sales staff, administrative support workers, and skilled blue-collar workers fell by $1,000 to $3,000. The typical fifty-year-old white male high-school graduate made $2,000–$3,000 less in 1996 than he did ten years earlier. He also was 10% less likely to have health insurance and unlikely to have a defined benefit pension, which meant that he lacked the economic safety net his family enjoyed while he was growing up.[19]

Supported by labor unions, working-class men attained the "family wage" (that is, a wage level sufficient to support a wife and children) for two short generations following World War II. They lost it again after 1970. Thus men who grew up in families on an escalator to solid middle-class lives find themselves unable to earn wages that would allow their families a middle-class standard of living. Women whose mothers had worked only intermittently and part-time now find themselves ironing at 10 P.M. and waking up at 5:30 A.M. to make breakfast and lunches, drop the kids off at child care and school, and rush to jobs where they could be fired for being a few minutes late. For both spouses, the inability to sustain the traditional breadwinner-homemaker split may be the subject of regret. Because gender analysis typically is not melded with an analysis of class, the extent to which traditional gender performances are driven by class aspirations has rarely been explored.[20]

The breadwinner-homemaker family has been emblematic of middle-class status since the emergence of the notion of separate spheres in the early nineteenth century. Class aspirations give both men and women a stake in conventional gender roles. The accepted mantra is that these roles persist due to socialization, but that begs the question of why successive generations still are socialized to construct their identities around conventional roles. Melding analysis of class and gender suggests an answer. Because breadwinner-homemaker families have signaled middle-class status since the 1780s, successful performance of these roles is seen as vital among working-class families who aspire to upward mobility. Conventional gender performance, in short, is a class act.

Sociologist Francine Deutsch shows that many working-class men continue to take the separate-spheres division of responsibilities very seriously. In the working-class "tag-team" families she interviewed, in which parents work different shifts to cover child care responsibilities, she found that the husbands often regretted that their wives had to work. If finances permitted, they said, their wives would stay home. This finding is confirmed by many other studies documenting relatively traditional gender ideology among working-class men.[21]

Interestingly, many wives told Deutsch a different tale, confiding that they would continue in their jobs, although perhaps part-time—an intention they had not necessarily shared with their husbands. Note that the wives'· aspiration to part-time work can be seen as an aspiration to attain the neotraditional pattern that predominates among the professional-managerial class. Although working-class men contribute more hours to child care than do upper-middle-class men who espouse egalitarian values, Deutsch notes, typically they have "not changed their view that mothers are ultimately responsible for childcare and fathers for breadwinning."[22]

A more recent study by Carla Shows and Naomi Gerstel presents a different picture. Shows and Gerstel interviewed EMTs and physicians in Massachusetts. They found that the doctors, but not the EMTs, had lives shaped around the norm of work devotion and defined fathering as participation at public (typically sports) events. In contrast, the "EMTs emphasized private fathering in ways that the physicians did not. They talked about routine involvement in the lives of their children—picking them up from day care or school, feeding them dinner, or staying home with them when they got sick." Some (though not all) EMTs turned down overtime: "I will totally refuse the overtime. Family comes first for me," said one. The EMTs were not begrudging in their willingness to swap shifts to accommodate family responsibilities. Indeed, many "seemed *happy* with their schedules *because* they allowed the EMTs to participate in childcare."[23]

These findings may signal a generational shift, but caution may be in order. As Shows and Gerstel acknowledge, the EMTs work in a job with a hypermasculine work culture and long hours (averaging forty-five hours a week). "We did not hear protests from them about threats to their masculinity. Perhaps this is because they work in highly masculine jobs and do not need to use family relations to shore up their identity as men." It seems likely that despite their self-image as caregiver fathers, the EMTs saw themselves as breadwinners in neotraditional families, who worked longer hours (two-thirds had second jobs) and brought home more money than their wives.[24]

The good news is that men can be quite happy with family caregiving so long as they feel their masculinity is secure. The bad news is that many non-elite men do feel their masculinity threatened, by jobs that are insecure or are (they feel) beneath their dignity. Three-fourths of the jobs lost in the Great Recession of 2008–2009 were men's jobs, many in industries such as manufacturing and construction; if past trends are any guide, many of these men will end up in lower-paying jobs once they return to work.[25]

Since the 1970s, even as non-elite men's wages fell and their futures faded, reformers' attention shifted away from class, onto race and gender.

Progressives tend to depict working-class white men as privileged—privileged as whites, privileged as men, "relatively privileged" as more affluent than the poor. Many of these men have a different perspective. When they compare their current situation with what their fathers and grandfathers could expect—and deliver—they do not feel privileged. Many feel cheated.

The Poor, the Privileged, and the Missing Middle

After 1970, the reform-minded elite shifted its attention away from the economic issues that had bound it in alliance with the working class, focusing instead on civil rights, the environment, peace, feminism, and alternative energy. This shift away from class had repercussions not only in politics but also in academics' interpretations of politics. A strong consensus emerged in political science that class was playing a decreasing role in American politics after 1970. The most prominent strain of this "class is dead" literature is the "post-materialist thesis," which cites Democrats' shift of attention away from economic ("material") issues onto cultural ones as evidence of class's diminished role.[26]

Among political scientists, the only prominent dissenter to the "class is dead" theory is Jeffrey Stonecash. Ironically, his analysis perpetuates the erasure of the Missing Middle. Stonecash compared the voting patterns of the bottom third and the top third of the income distribution, literally omitting the middle. Stonecash's analysis reflects the assumption that a discussion of the poor and the privileged suffices as a discussion of class.[27]

I have encountered this assumption time and again. When I told someone I was writing about class, the common assumption outside of union circles was that I was writing about the poor. This is not surprising: people in poverty play a central role in the moral imagination of progressives. Floods of studies document the lives of Americans in poverty, both as a cause and an effect of this phenomenon. When I searched Amazon.com I found 349,303 books listed under "poverty," with a large percentage about public policy initiatives to help the poor. When I searched "working class," I found less than one-half as many books (140,790); the top hit was titled *The Working Class Majority: America's Best-Kept Secret*. Most of the books I did find on the working class were on how to get their votes; very few focused on public policy initiatives. "Poverty in America" was a particularly popular categorization; the parallel in the literature on the working class, "working class Americanism," was focused largely on historical studies rather than on contemporary society.[28]

Public policy studies' lopsided emphasis on poverty reflects a long and rich tradition dating back to the Progressive era. Jane Addams, who founded the settlement house movement and helped found the profession of social work, wrote early sympathetic studies explaining the poor to the privileged. This tradition has persisted, reenergized by Michael Harrington's tremendously influential 1962 work, *The Other America: Poverty in America*. No similar tradition of studies of the Missing Middle exists in the United States, in sharp contrast with Europe and Australia. American studies of the working class are more likely to focus on the history of the union movement or other historical topics than on the importance of class in the United States today.[29]

I call this the problem of the poor and the privileged. Educated Americans can easily find masses of information about people in poverty. But the average educated American knows comparatively little about the nurses, secretaries, ticket agents, factory workers, mattress salesmen, and X-ray technicians of the Missing Middle. As Theda Skocpol pointed out nearly a decade ago, progressives tend to focus so intently on poverty that they miss Americans in the middle of the income distribution. Skocpol finds it "puzzling" that "our policy debates deal so little with the fate of working families of modest means." She recommended "a new family-oriented populism" that offers support for working families of the type that exists in Europe, namely, universal programs, rather than means-tested programs that are limited to the poor. Her analysis has been largely ignored.[30]

Once attention is focused on the Missing Middle, the central role of class in recent American politics emerges loud and clear. But to reveal this dynamic, education—not income—needs to be the relevant proxy for class. Three astute Dutch political scientists note, "Any number of studies point out that it is not so much those with low incomes who are socially conservative but rather those who are poorly educated." Less-educated workers tend to hold liberal views on economic issues but conservative views on cultural issues. Thus when education is used as a proxy for class, we find an increase since 1945 in what the Dutch authors call "cultural voting": voting driven by cultural issues. In fact, cultural voting accounts for most of the working class's shift to the right, not just in the United States but also in Europe. Thus, as a result of cultural voting, "class voting has not declined during the postwar era but has become even stronger." Whereas many American "post-materialists" assume that a cultural analysis of voting patterns provides an alternative to class-based explanations, the Dutch authors recognize that cultural differences are an expression of class differences and a key language of class conflict.[31]

Class and Cultural Differences

An Iowa attack ad decried Howard Dean as a "tax hiking, government-expanding, latte-drinking, sushi-eating, Volvo-driving, *New York Times*-reading, body-piercing, Hollywood-loving, left-wing freak show."[32] Note how this characterization forges the class culture gap into a potent political weapon. The first step toward defusing this weapon is for progressives to understand how their taken-for-granted habits and predilections differ from those of the Missing Middle. This information is not easy to gather because, as noted, while it is easy to learn about the daily lives of Americans in poverty, it is much harder to learn about daily life in the Missing Middle. Here I describe in detail the differences between the upper-middle class and the Missing Middle, who express very differently their fears of falling out of their current class status, their preferences for child rearing, networks, food, and entertaining and leisure, and their moral visions. The underlying message is that "class is an 'identity kit', equipped with the proper mask and costume, along with instructions on how to act."[33]

A key point to inform this discussion: class is expressed as cultural difference. The French sociologist Pierre Bourdieu and the ethnographic literature on class that he influenced demonstrate how. Bourdieu urges us to examine workers' "cultural repertoires," rather than "focusing solely on explicit class conflict or on position in the system of production." He emphasizes the importance of paying attention to "the taken-for-granted categories [that groups] mobilize for interpreting and organizing . . . without predefining specific dimensions of identity as particularly salient." People raised working class who become socially mobile can, of course, learn new cultural skills and habits later in life, but these acquired tastes and dispositions rarely become second nature like those learned in childhood. Bourdieu argues that our set of taken-for-granted organizing principles— our dispositions—gives us different values and tastes, and that these values confer—or deny—social status.[34]

"Culture shapes action by defining what people want," notes Ann Swidler.[35] Bourdieu argues that an accurate understanding of class needs to focus not just on jobs but on "cultural capital," which consists of "attitudes, preferences, formal knowledge, behaviors, goods and credentials" used to attain and to signal class status. Artists and graduate students, for example, typically lack economic capital but often have the kind of cultural capital needed to negotiate the upper-middle-class world.[36] Workers lack it, which they signal (often inadvertently) in many different ways:

The use of nonstandard grammar, parents who cannot help with homework, who may not know the distinction between college-prep and non-prep courses, who may not know about college entrance exams, who might feel they have to devalue themselves and their own lives in the process of encouraging their children to go beyond them, who may wrongly assume that the school will adequately prepare their child without their participation, who might desire to avoid the school themselves, because it is a familiar site of failure and intimidation where they are required to interact with . . . professionals like teachers and administrators.[37]

Cultural capital is class specific: the kinds of cultural capital required to survive and thrive in non-elite circles differ from the kinds required in professional-managerial contexts. To get a professional-managerial job, for example, requires a degree at a four-year college—the more elite, the better—and often a graduate degree as well. This looming entrance requirement profoundly shapes elite culture. Upper-middle-class parents' child-rearing strategies seek to develop an intense achievement orientation in children with the goal of self-actualization. Everyday life is carefully designed to allow upper-middle-class children to develop, and adults to display, their class-specific cultural capital. Examples include dinners full of teachable moments; food preparation stressing novelty and book learning (cookbooks); and European vacations and eco-retreats that require, develop, and display not only book learning (guidebooks) but also the characteristic upper-middle-class broad-but-shallow networks (webs of connection that help them find that perfect little hotel in Paris).[38]

Other requirements of professional-managerial jobs shape professional-managerial folkways. Professional-managerial jobs require people skills, which are essential for building and exploiting networks and for enhancing opportunities to advance as a lawyer, doctor, or "organization man." Moreover, these jobs are not rote. Typically they require verbal adeptness and a delicate combination of independent judgment and conformity (because nonconformity can be seen as lack of people skills). Among professionals, being able to think things through for yourself and to adapt to changing circumstances are vital concomitants of success, given that professionals and managers are order givers.

The cultural capital required of workers is quite different. While questioning authority and thinking for yourself might get you a promotion in an upper-middle-class job, in a lower-status job it is more likely to get you fired. (Truck drivers and small-business owners are the exception, which is why both jobs are highly prized.) Both because of economic constraints and cultural ones (recall the painful sense of class dislocation expressed by class migrants in academia), working-class kids generally get only a high-school education or a two-year associate's degree. Only 29% of Americans have graduated from a four-year college, and even four-year colleges are highly class stratified.³⁹ Harvard has some non-elite kids, but most are upper-middle class; UMass Amherst, Temple University, and UC Riverside all are proudly working class—and lower in status. A recent study of selective colleges found that students from families in the top 25% (as measured by a combination of income, education, and occupation) are twenty-five times more likely to attend a "top tier" institution than are students in the bottom 25%. As the Great Recession of 2008 showed, many less affluent families are only few paychecks away from "hard living": losing their homes and sliding into a chaotic life. This specter dominates their approach to child rearing, where the focus is on raising a "good kid," defined as one who finishes school and lands a stable job. Self-regulation, not self-actualization, is the underlying goal of child rearing in the Missing Middle. Workers place a high value on comfort and predictability, as opposed to innovation and openness to change.⁴⁰

The Fear of Falling

In *Fear of Falling*, Barbara Ehrenreich, writing about the professional-managerial class of the late 1980s, observed, "If [this] is an elite . . . [it] is an insecure and deeply anxious one." Ehrenreich argues that the only way upper-middle-class parents can pass their elite status on to their children is by ensuring that their "children are disciplined enough to devote the first twenty or thirty years of their lives to scaling the educational obstacles to a[n upper-]middle-class career." The child-rearing strategy Annette Lareau calls "concerted cultivation" can be seen as an expression of upper-middle-class anxiety that, with a few poor choices or a dip in the stock market, their children could end up being house painters or taxi drivers, rather than the doctors or lawyers their training and education meant them to be.⁴¹

Few commentators have noted that workers' fear of falling is even more angst ridden. Their fear is of falling from "settled living" into "hard living." This distinction, introduced in 1972 by Joseph T. Howell in *Hard Living on Clay Street*, has received far too little attention. In her 2003 study of working-class high-school girls in California's Central Valley, Julie Bettie found that, generally, in settled-living families, both parents had finished high school and between them held at least one stable job, with health care benefits. Settled families live lives that are "very routine." They are very conscientious about house upkeep and neighborhood respectability. They maintain strict control over their children and expect them to graduate from high school and perhaps to attend a local college.[42]

Maria Kefalas's study of settled working-class families in Chicago explains why the "lace-curtain Irish" and other settled families are so house-proud and starch-happy. Much more is at stake than dust bunnies:

> I came to see the Beltway from the viewpoint of its full-time inhabitants. I took note of the elaborate lawn decorations, manicured grass, color-coordinated kitchens, fastidiously cared-for American-made cars, and the graffiti-free alleys and streets. Such displays require the solicitous care of local activists and property owners. The people of Beltway willingly dedicate themselves to the care of the neighborhood landscape with an unquestioned, nearly spiritual devotion.

Residents described their modest neighborhood as "the last garden spot in Chicago," epitomizing "the two things the residents of Beltway want most to cultivate in their lives: . . . order and abundance." Beltway residents worried that not having a well-maintained home would make them seem like "white trash"—that is, as people who had fallen into hard living—to their neighbors.[43]

Whereas settled families insist on order and self-regulation, hard-living families tend toward drugs or heavy drinking, marital instability, and flightiness. Hard-livers would—if they had trust funds—be the sort of people who drop out of college to travel the world. Free spirits not born into money cannot count on the second and third chances granted to free spirits born elite. A joy ride by a prep school kid may end with daddy paying a lawyer to get junior's record erased, while a less privileged kid in the same situation could end up with a police record that would permanently bar him from a desirable job.[44]

Thus settled working-class families stress routine and "keeping your nose clean" as a way to protect their children's future. Bettie reports that children of settled Mexican American families in California's Central Valley hoped to go on after high school to vocational business or technical programs, or community colleges, to complete certificate programs; a few hoped to transfer to four-year universities. Their white counterparts typically planned to go to community college, with the explicit goal of transferring to four-year universities. Children of hard-living families generally dropped out of high school and had little to look forward to. As one put it succinctly, "My life is shit."[45]

Understanding the settled working class is impossible without an appreciation of the specter of hard living. This specter is what anchors working-class culture to stability instead of novelty, to self-regulation instead of self-actualization. The specter of hard living also shapes the moral vision of American workers in ways that fuel culture wars.

Learning Class at Your Mother's Knee

The ideology of concerted cultivation discussed is largely an elite phenomenon. *Unequal Childhoods*, Annette Lareau's eerily insightful study of class-based differences in child rearing, details how upper-middle-class families' focus on developing "children [who] are above average" leads to a frenetically paced family life. Lareau described one family this way:

> They rush home, rifle thorough the mail, prepare snacks, change out of their work clothes, make sure the children are appropriately dressed and have proper equipment for the upcoming activity, find their car keys, put the dog outside, load the children and equipment into the car, lock the door, and drive off. This pattern repeats itself, with slight variations, day after day.[46]

Children's activities determined the schedule for the entire family, and at times "everyone—including ten-year-old children—seemed exhausted." These children's Taylorized leisure time helps them develop the skills required for high-status white-collar jobs: how to "set priorities, manage an itinerary, shake hands with strangers, and work on a team." And more: multiple leisure activities help them develop time-management skills, "gain poise and learn how to 'negotiate institutions,'" work smoothly with acquaintances and adults unrelated to them, and "handle both victory and defeat with grace." In upper-middle-class households, television typically is sharply controlled, and unstructured time is so rare that children have trouble handling it.[47] Also in keeping with the felt need to develop the skills required in professional-managerial jobs, upper-middle-class parents

> actively fostered and assessed their children's talents, opinions, and skills. They scheduled their children for activities. They reasoned with them. They hovered over them and outside the home they did not hesitate to intervene on the children's behalf. They made a deliberate and sustained effort to stimulate children's development and to cultivate their cognitive and social skills.[48]

The contrasts with childhood outside the elite are stark. The working-class approach is succinctly summarized by class migrant and journalist Alfred Lubrano, whose father was a bricklayer: "In the working class, people perform jobs in which they are closely supervised and are required to follow orders and instructions. [So they bring their children] up in a home in which conformity, obedience, and intolerance for back talk are the norm—the same characteristics that make for a good factory worker."[49]

In sharp contrast to Marxism's insistence that class relations are forged in the workplace, other recent authors point to family life as a crucial site "where cultural capital is acquired and where class identity is formed."[50] Less affluent families, whose goal is to raise a "good kid," follow what Lareau terms the "accomplishment of natural growth." They view "children's development as unfolding spontaneously, as long as they were provided with comfort, food, shelter" and other basics. Given the often difficult economic circumstances faced by less affluent families, the steady provision of "the basics" for their children presents a "formidable challenge . . . and they are proud when they accomplish it." Lareau describes the natural growth approach as involving clear boundaries between adults and children, with prompt obedience expected; relatively few structured activities; little adult intervention in children's TV watching or their unstructured play; social encounters chiefly centered around a small circle of family and close friends, in activities that tend to involve both adults and children; and feelings of unease and constraint during encounters with professionals such as doctors and teachers.[51]

The differences between child-rearing philosophies of white workers and the upper-middle class, along with their differing financial situations, lead to differences in children's organized activities. White professionals' kids participated in an average of 4.6 organized activities a week; black professionals' kids, even more (5.2). Working-class kids, black and white, had 2.8 and 2.3 organized activities each week (of which at least one typically was church-related). Lareau tried hard to find an upper-middle-class child who did not participate in any organized activities. She could not find a single one.[52]

Professional-managerial kids' busy schedules are a testimony to the importance accorded to self-actualization in upper-middle-class life. Non-elite families rarely mention self-actualization as a goal. "The sense of an obligation to cultivate their children that is so apparent among [upper-middle class] . . . parents is uncommon among their poor and working-class counterparts." Their focus is on self-regulation: "That their children do well in school and stay out of trouble are what most fathers wish for." Few professional-managerial families would embrace natural development, for fear that their kids would not gain the kind of cultural capital required to attain and sustain an upper-middle-class life. Yet commentators raise questions about concerted cultivation that are worth considering. One class migrant, who grew up in a "hillbilly" family, describing the children she babysat in an upper-middle-class family, said: "I just kept thinking these kids don't know how to play. When I went to [their] rooms, it didn't seem like [they] had a whole lot of toys . . . it just seems like there were mostly books and more educational things."[53]

Lareau agreed that working-class kids seemed more relaxed. The lack of restrictions on television and video games highlights the lack of performance pressures like those placed on elite kids. Because working-class kids participate in far fewer organized activities, children in these families learn how to structure their own time, how to construct and sustain friendships on their own, and how to organize and negotiate with peers. They also are less likely to rely on adults to keep them amused. They watch TV; play on their own with siblings, cousins, and neighborhood kids; and generally "hang out," unguided by a specific agenda of activities.[54]

Non-elite parents "see adult life as hard and pressured, and want their kids to spend time happy and relaxed before the pressures of life set in." From their perspective, the children of professional-managerial parents are pressured to achieve. When Lareau's team recited the schedules of professionals' kids, her less affluent informants were dubious: "I think he doesn't enjoy doing what he's doing half the time (light laughter). I think his parents are too strict. I think he's not a child (laughter)." Others felt that the busy schedules would "pay off 'job-wise' " but still expressed serious reservations: "I think he must be a sad kid," and "He must be dead-dog tired"— perspectives worth pondering. Lareau also suggests that the intense performance pressure on upper-middle-class children seems to lead to more, or at least more acrimonious, sibling rivalry.[55]

Also worth noting is the shock registered by class migrants at the disrespectful way upper-middle-class children talk of and to their parents. Noted bell hooks, whose father worked for thirty years as a janitor, "we were taught to value our parents and their care, to understand that they were not obligated to give us care."[56] I think often of the contrast with upper-middle-class motherhood. "My children see me as part of the furniture," said a mother in an upper-middle-class neighborhood in Washington, D.C.

A final perspective on concerted cultivation stems from Lareau's observation that upper-middle-class kids, but not less-affluent ones, are allowed to miss family events and visits, including those involving relatives whom they rarely see, in order to "be there" for their teammates or other peers. Lareau quotes one upper-middle-class parent, explaining why his son would not be attending a family gathering: "Soccer is more of a priority." Such relative valuing of individual achievement over family ties would likely strike non-elite parents as offensively wrongheaded. To what extent is concerted cultivation another name for intense performance pressure that sends children the message that human connection is less important than giving a class act?[57]

Class and Social Networks

The social networks of workers and elites differ in ways that provide significant insight into some unspoken truths about each group. Workers' networks are smaller and denser (that is, relationships are more intense), facilitating access to local jobs and making possible the exchange of neighborhood favors that play a central role in life in the Missing Middle. Professional-managerial networks are larger but less intense, facilitating access to a greater number, variety, and geographic range of jobs. Elites generally get jobs through "the strength of weak ties": acquaintances rather than close friends. Elites' broad networks also provide access to recommendations for high-quality service providers (elites are more likely than workers to hire help versus turning to family or neighbors).[58]

"In the world of the working class, the world of reciprocal invitations, spontaneous or organized, is restricted to the family and the world of familiars who can be treated as 'one of the family,' " notes Bourdieu. DeVault agrees: "working-class families live relatively close to their relatives and spend a large part of their social time with kin. Husbands and wives often have separate social groups, and their friends tend to be local people they have known for many years." Workers, Lamont reports, "are often immersed in tight networks of sociability, in part because their extended family often resides within a few miles (the children appear to spend considerable time visiting cousins)." And Lareau describes close connections among relatives in poor and working-class families, noting that adults "speak daily with their brothers and sisters and their parents. Cousins play together several times a week."[59]

Their small, dense networks allow these families to count on each other for help, in an environment where they are far less likely to be able (or perhaps willing) to commodify their needs for such things as backup child care or short-term use of a heavy-weight truck. The reciprocal exchange of favors is sex specific, which may explain why one study found that half of working-class women and most working-class men place a high value on same-sex socializing (guys' basketball night, girls' night out). In addition, family members and close friends passed along the news when a desirable factory was handing out applications or "put in a word" with a foreman on behalf of a friend or family member, since this kind of personal recommendation could help them land a desirable job. At best, these small, intense networks offer warmth, comfort, and intimacy. At worst, they can be suffocating—or can lead to the kind of tense relationships that characterized families in earlier periods in which family ties were inescapable.[60]

Traditionally, network scholars have characterized workers' networks as impoverished, given that studies consistently show that network size and diversity increase with education and social status. Yet each class creates the kind of networks that fits its material and social conditions. "People in higher positions work more with people instead of things, span boundaries within and between work organizations, and take part in more social settings away from work, so their contacts are more wide-ranging," notes one network scholar. Not only do professionals typically get jobs through acquaintances rather than close friends or family, but markets for professional-managerial workers often are nationwide. The paradigmatic example is the professor who moves 3,000 miles to take a job.[61]

Nationwide job markets clash with the "cultural obligation to remain near the clan," presenting acute problems for class migrants who seek to relocate to take the professional jobs for which they have trained. Class migrants report that their parents still expect that family ties "involve regular and close association with nuclear and extended members in the same geographical area." Socially mobile adult children get caught in cultural cross fire. Relocating for one's career is an accepted fact of life in the upper-middle class, but the same is not true in less privileged families. "My parents had been delighted that I had been accepted [to Stanford] and [simultaneously] adamantly opposed my going so far away from home [Kentucky]," said bell hooks. "In 1980 . . . I was offered my first job on a now-dead paper in Columbus, Ohio," said another class migrant. "I broke the news in the kitchen, where all the family business is discussed. My mother wept as though it were Vietnam. My father had a few questions: 'Ohio? Where the hell is Ohio?'" "How can you live so far away from your people?" asked the family of one class migrant, who noted that his middle-class friends "would marvel at the frequency of my trips home. 'I don't see my family as much as you do yours,' said a pal whose relatives lived within 20 miles. It's a blue-collar thing, I tried to explain. Middle-class kids are groomed to fly away, and they do. The working class likes to keep its young close to home." This avoids social isolation, though perhaps at the price of social mobility.[62]

Friendship patterns also reflect a class culture gap. Workers are more likely to name kin as friends. In one study, 80% did so, while less than 50% of college-educated respondents did. More affluent couples are far more likely to name their spouse as a close friend (half versus one-third). Managers and professionals are much more likely to socialize as couples, going out to dinner, having friends over to dinner, or going out as a couple or with friends to cultural events. All provide opportunities to further enhance one's cultural capital and bond with shared commitments to sophisticated cooking or sophisticated tastes for high-brow culture. Workers may see this as showing off—a class act. Those who do it probably just see it as pleasurable, further demonstrating that society shapes personal dispositions.[63]

Food as a Class Code

Consider the class structure of coffee. "His wife brings us coffee with amaretto-flavored creamer," writes Lamont on the first page of her book, signaling to elite readers that her subjects are people who favor flavored creamer.[64] Whereas in my parents' generation, a cup of coffee was a cup of coffee, today what coffee you drink signals class status. Starbucks is for the upper-middle class, who can afford $6 for a latte and biscotti. Dunkin' Donuts signals working class, where you can get a dozen donuts for $6 or less. Of course, you can now get lattes at Dunkin' Donuts: elite foods always filter down the social scale, at some point becoming universal although typically changing in the process.

That's just the tip of the iceberg lettuce. Sociologist Marjorie DeVault, in her brilliant study *Feeding the Family,* examines the distinctive food cultures of the settled working class and the professional-managerial class: "The contrast is between a taken-for-granted expectation that good will be good because [it is] familiar, and an elaborated standard based on an expanded (and constantly expanding) field of knowledge about food that links pleasure with novelty and entertainment." Non-elite women tend to develop standard repertoires, with little felt need for experimentation. Said one wife, "I cook all my meats the same, you know. And as long as he doesn't complain, why should I change it? He likes it, so there's no reason for me to change it." Even women who collected recipes still served their families a "steady drumbeat" of menus that were tried and true; none relied on recipes for everyday cooking. Instead, they sought to reproduce the kinds of meals they grew up with. "I would always be on the phone when it was right around supper time. 'Ma, I have this and this. What do I do?'" Even women who would like to experiment more are "restrained from doing so by their husbands, who were 'hamburger and hot dog type' or 'meat and potatoes' people." "Thus the new petit bourgeoisie of middle or working class origin more often offer 'plentiful and good' meals, which is *never* the case with those of upper class origin, who, by contrast, are very inclined to the 'original and exotic.'"[65]

People who voted for Hillary Clinton, the favorite among Missing-Middle voters in the Democratic primaries of 2008, preferred Red Lobster, with its large portions of standard dishes.[66] The settled working class celebrates its settledness by serving the tried and true and celebrates its success through abundance. Thus Maria Kefalas reports on celebrations in Chicago where food was served "'family style,' which means massive platters are passed around so the guests may have a choice of three or four entrées" that are "popular staples."[67]

On the other side, elite restaurants, like Alice Waters's Chez Panisse in Berkeley, offer sophisticated, novel tastes in small portions. The home cooking of the upper-professional-managerial class also stresses novelty and sophistication. Upper-middle-class women tend to repudiate their mothers' cooking in favor of new dishes that seem original or exotic. They talk about trying out different "cuisines" and are more likely to rely on recipes. Children learn that good food should be different and interesting. Said one upper-middle-class woman: "I get a lot of feedback for experimenting. Even my little one will say, 'Mom, this is fantastic.' And he's very diplomatic, you know he came up to me and he said, 'I know you tried your hardest, but this doesn't have any zing to it.'" Creativity, novelty, and experimentation—the high value placed on self-development, self-actualization, and "talent"—all are expressed in upper-middle-class food. Upper-middle-class food also provides an opportunity to express personal success, not through abundance but through sophistication.[68]

The elite sees working-class food as boring. And the Missing Middle often sees elite food—when they are not adopting it—as pretentious. Time to declare a truce. Both can be delicious.

Entertaining, Family Meals, and Leisure

Transforming food into class acts continues after guests arrive. The paradigmatic non-elite get-together is a barbeque with the extended family. No one is time disciplined: these are people with closely supervised jobs where they can be fired for being a few minutes late. Time discipline is associated with work, not leisure. The atmosphere is informal: no one need put on airs. One silver-spoon spouse in a cross-class marriage asked her husband: "What is your idea of entertaining?" To which he replied, "Having people over for a barbeque on Labor and Memorial Days, and an open house at Christmas." Period. "These gatherings are comfortable precisely because they are familiar," notes DeVault. Working-class social events often involve only family and people the hosts have known since childhood.[69]

"In sharp contrast to these informal gatherings is the upper-middle-class dinner party, with its myriad of rules: don't start until everyone is served, talk to the person on either side of you, don't clear until everyone is finished," notes DeVault, And the full day of cooking: "It's almost an unspoken law, you know. You have to think up a really acceptable menu, with a fancy dessert. It has to be beautiful, and it has to be platters, and it has to be served in a certain way." Family rarely is among the guests, who are more likely to be people whom the couple "wants to get to know better." Relationships often mix the simple desire for friendship and company with anticipated professional advantage (a.k.a. networking).[70]

As opposed to the informality and comfort of the barbeque, creativity, novelty, and experimentation are expected at an upper-middle-class dinner party: one arrives ready to be impressed. Even if the hostess dislikes experimenting, she may well feel pressure to do it:

> I used to subscribe to *Gourmet* magazine when I was married, and I used to—if I had people over for dinner—really try to go all out. My friends were into it too, so—but I hated it . . . I don't know why I did it. I guess I felt like people wouldn't like me, you know, there was part of that too, that I had to show how good, how talented I was.[71]

The emphasis on talent comes in sharp contrast to the ideal of what Bourdieu calls "Plain speaking, plain eating: the working-class meal is characterized by plenty (which does not exclude restrictions and limits) and above all by freedom." Restaurants that cater to ordinary Joes and Janes feature large portions, menus a mile long, and an informal atmosphere. In working-class homes, notes Bourdieu (sounding very French):

> The strict sequencing of the meal tends to be ignored. Everything may be put on the table at much the same time . . . so that the women may have reached dessert, and also the children, who will take their plates and watch television, while the men are still eating the main dish and the "lad," who has arrived late, is swallowing his soup. Informality is the rule of the game, amongst any guests as well as the family itself. The common root of all these "liberties" is no doubt the sense that at least there will not be self-imposed controls, constraints, and restrictions—especially not in eating, a primary need and a compensation—and especially not in the heart of domestic life, the one realm of freedom, when everywhere else, and at all other times, necessity prevails.

Some of this sounds dated, but the basic point—that the working-class meal enacts workers' escape from their rigorously time-disciplined, closely supervised jobs—still rings true. "Since informality is the order of the day, there is no reason not to keep an eye on the television."[72] TV during dinner is a dead giveaway that one is not in a professional-managerial household. Another is the different role of talk. Workers assume that boys will end up in closely supervised jobs with a narrow range of responsibilities, in which promotion depends on strength or technical skills.[73] These skills can hardly be taught at dinner. In working-class households, Lareau observed, life "does not revolve around extended verbal discussions." Though the amount of talk varies, typically there is considerably less than in upper-middle-class homes. "Family members talk about relatives and friends, tell jokes, and make comments about what is on television . . . Short remarks punctuate comfortable silences."[74]

In sharp contrast, among the bourgeoisie the meal enacts "a habitus of order, restraint, propriety," to quote Bourdieu. No TV here. Because elite jobs are "open-ended, with wide-ranging responsibilities that involve ambiguity, problem solving," and networking, dinnertime is full of teachable moments—opportunities to develop kids' cultural capital. The *New York Times* quoted one reader recalling how "at dinner, we would discuss current events . . . During each holiday season, the discussion included an article about The New York Times Neediest Cases Fund." "A Sense of Duty Takes Shape during Dinner Table Conversations," shouts the title.[75]

When Flor, a working-class high-school girl, was asked what she wanted to be, she replied, "I don't know. Maybe a lawyer or a receptionist or something like that. Somethin' in an office." One cannot imagine an upper-middle-class teenager conflating the social status of a lawyer and a receptionist. This is class-based knowledge, imparted, in part, at the dinner table. So is knowledge about how to manipulate bureaucracies to one's advantage. "Manipulating the system is a given for the [upper]-middle class," said one class migrant. "If there had been magnet schools when I was a child, we wouldn't have known about them." Important lessons also emerge about the function and origin of rules: that it's okay to "question them and reshape them to make them fit ever-changing situations—and, further, that in this other world, rule-bound thinkers get poor grades." Lareau found that upper-middle-class parents tend to use "reasoning [as opposed to directives] as their chief method of control." Children are expected to supply evidence for their opinions; part of the "steady stream of speech" that includes not only extensive and sometimes exhausting negotiation but also verbal play, banter, and jousting. The development of curiosity, not obedience, is the goal. Said one class migrant, class affects "what we tell our children at the dinner table (conversations about the Middle East, for example, versus the continuing sagas of the broken vacuum cleaner or the half-wit neighbors); whether we even have a dinner table, or a dinnertime." Once again, attention to life outside of the elite encourages progressives to think hard about the performance pressures we sometimes find ourselves placing on our kids.[76]

Class-based differences also shape other forms of leisure. "Did your family take you on mind-expanding, Machu Picchu vacations, or were they plot-at-the-beach, two-week affairs in summer rentals," asks one class migrant.[77] Upper-middle-class families often go on vacations that simultaneously reflect and enhance cultural capital. To plan a trip to Europe or Asia requires both economic and cultural capital, as does eco-tourism to Costa Rica or Africa. Such vacations can be highly stressful, they broaden life experience (self-actualization again), and they can be discussed at dinner parties or become fodder for children's school presentations. Another commonplace upper-middle-class option is to spend time at the family's vacation home, signaling that the family can afford not one house but two, and while there perhaps they develop sports skills useful later in life (golf, sailing, tennis).

Vacations for less affluent people, of course, are less elaborate. At the low end, when Julie Bettie asked one girl about her vacation, she replied, "oh yes, once a year my mom and I go to Discovery Park," a local amusement park.[78] Families in less straited circumstances may travel to a Disney resort, or to Club Med, which offers a low-pressure atmosphere of plenty. Disney World is a major vacation destination for adults: grown-ups outnumber children by 3.5 to 1.[79] If the Missing Middle goes abroad, packaged tours make up for their inability to find that perfect little place in Paris on their own. But they are much more likely to go to Las Vegas. At one level, it is ironic that both Disney World and Las Vegas offer recreations of European landscapes. At another level, it makes sense that such resorts would offer the aura of Europe without the expense and in the context of an entirely predictable environment. Las Vegas also offers the (largely illusory) chance of striking it rich.

Even sports are class-coded. Bowling and NASCAR are working class; windsurfing, tennis, backpacking—all of which require expensive equipment and/or training—send off distinct upper-middle-class signals. An important challenge is for progressives to understand the class signals they send as they go about their daily lives.

A Clash of Moral Visions

Another important challenge is to understand where voters get their values. To answer the question requires an understanding of the moral logic of settled working-class life and how it conflicts with the moral logic of the upper-middle class. (Note that many in what Lamont calls the "settled working class" would call themselves middle class. Nonetheless, for clarity's sake I preserve her terminology.) When Michèle Lamont studied upper-middle-class men, she found that they were more likely than workers to define their own worth in terms of socioeconomic status, as opposed to morality. While this may be true of the professional-managerial class in general, it is far less true of progressives. Progressives tend to define themselves in opposition to the business elite, whom they view as people whose lives revolve around money. They define themselves, in contrast, as people whose deepest commitments are to "issues," such as human rights, social justice, environmentalism, or feminism. Workers and progressives find themselves at odds because both groups define their identities in terms of moral commitments—but they define morality very differently. Culture wars emerge because the two groups' sincere and deeply held moral visions clash.[80]

Lamont stresses that the central spring of settled working-class life is the desire to maintain the "world in moral order." Although Lamont does not frame it as such, the settled working class often defines moral order in opposition to hard living. Lamont's workers carefully distinguish themselves from "those below," who are not (as Lamont often initially assumes) the poor; rather, they are the hard living. Thus a stage technician at a Broadway theater contrasts himself with "people who whine and complain . . . people that are chronically late and people that go out and have a couple of drinks and come back a little lit up . . . I am cursed with a strong work ethic." "Lazy parasites" are despised, while people who hold more than one job are objects of admiration.[81]

Note that the distinction drawn is between different members of the working class, rather than between the working class and the poor. One worker stressed the importance of responsibility in work, family, and community life: "he views it as essential to the well-ordered world he is striving to maintain," concludes Lamont. Another worker expressed disapproval of those who are not "forward-looking"—such as the guy who "just doesn't care about life and the future and everything." This echoes commentators' observation that hard-living families are so overwhelmed by the present that they plan little for the future. Indeed, settled white families, who see themselves as "middle class" or "from good families," often judge the hard living harshly, as "lower class" or "white trash."[82]

Lamont pinpoints the "disciplined self" as the goal of the settled life. Her informants admire men who "don't let go, they don't give up, and it's largely through work and responsibility that they assert control over uncertainty." They take pride in having "proper management of [their] impulses, time, and budget." One informant disapproved of a coworker who "would eat off a lunch truck and he had no money. That's $50 a week . . . He can't send his wife to the store and buy some cold cuts?" (Note the "send.") Lamont's explanation:

> These workers value responsibility . . . because they are highly dependent on the actions of others . . . The physical conditions in which they live and work and their limited financial resources make it difficult for them to buffer themselves from the actions of neighbors, coworkers, kin, and friends. They have no private space at work and live in neighborhoods where houses are set very close to one another . . . They can less readily escape crime, drugs, and undesirable people by moving to high-income suburbs.[83]

All true, but this ignores the symbolic dimension of settled life—of the disciplined self as a bulwark against hard living. "Sometimes, I wish I could be more carefree. And then I say no, I like the way I am . . . I like people who are responsible," remarked a printer from Rahway, New Jersey. Professional-managerial progressives who celebrate ambiguity and associate change with opportunity often forget that change feels (and is) far riskier without a safety net. Professional-managerial families teach their children to be more open to risk and change because they have the human, cultural, and economic capital to recover if a risk taken leads to failure. "I associate change with loss," said one class migrant, struggling with the upper-middle-class love of novelty.[84]

Lamont's informants are all men. I have noted where her conclusions probably are unrepresentative of women. Yet I suspect both men and women share Lamont's four basic tenets: commitment to hard work; belief in the importance of perseverance and personal integrity; strong commitment to religious principles; and an emphasis on "family first." Below, I discuss each of these in greater depth, highlighting contrasts between workers' worldview and that of upper-middle-class progressives.

Hanging in There

"My father made a religion of responsibility," notes one class migrant whose father was a bricklayer. He was possessed of "a well-developed work ethic, the kind that gets you up early and keeps you locked in until the job is done, regardless of how odious or personally distasteful the task." "Workers are acutely aware that 'hanging in there' depends above all on their capacity to work," says Lamont. "Their labor is often painful and time-consuming, yet underpaid, physically demanding, or psychologically challenging because repetitive. Being able to stick to it demands emotional energy and moral fortitude." Jonathan Rieder adds, "All the adages of the lower-middle-class life celebrated the values of get up and go, busting chops, doing for yourself." As Paul Willis pointed out long ago, "working class kids who had really absorbed the rubric of self-development" would face a "terrifying battle" when greeted by "meaningless and unfulfilling jobs." "I just figure I get paid from the shoulders down, if you know what I mean," said a construction worker. The lack of opportunities for self-development highlights the need for the "disciplined self."[85]

Intertwined with workers' religion of responsibility is their pride in hard work. Again, a key dimension is symbolic: "work signals a form of moral purity." Blue-collar men distinguish themselves from those above by stressing that theirs is heavy, manly work: "You have to keep going . . . and it's heavy work, the managers couldn't do it . . . there's not many strong enough to keep lifting the metal." Working men's focus on strength "is vastly out of proportion to the number of people actually involved in heavy work," as Willis observed long ago. A firefighter told Lamont that he was able to do things that "99 percent of other people in this world can't or won't do." For this reason, "he views himself as part of an elite."[86]

From a gender perspective, this looks like working-class men's celebration of a form of masculinity to which they have realistic access. The dark underside of this class-specific masculinity is that women's presence in blue-collar jobs is seen as a threat to masculinity, leading their male coworkers to harass them, sexually and otherwise. Progressives need not endorse this to acknowledge that the undercurrent of masculine pride in blue-collar jobs is a part of American politics they cannot afford to ignore.[87]

Working-class men and women alike differentiate themselves from "the suits" by defining working-class jobs as "real work," in contrast to the "pencil pushing" of the upper-middle class. Class migrants, self-chastised, see themselves as pencil pushers, recalling "with what scorn my parents and their friends used to talk about pencil pushers, who included anybody in a white-collar job . . . We disrespected pencil pushers, considered them lesser people who nonetheless had all the power." This form of class resentment turns "servitude into honor," as settled workers assert that their work represents more of a test of character than the work undertaken by managers and professionals. For the daughter of a carpenter, being an academic "doesn't feel like work because it isn't hard, it isn't unpleasant, it isn't boring or frustrating."[88]

Although workers' identities are bound up with their capacity for hard work, they differentiate themselves from work-identified professional-managerial men. As workers see it, professionals care more about showing off to other professionals . . . I mean like "I've got a Jaguar," drive by to see his friends. As for me, I would not care less what the other guy thinks of me. Because if I feel good about myself, and my wife thinks good about me, and we're all happy, that's what matters. My family is what I center myself around. I'm not trying to keep a race with the Joneses, like that.

While upper-middle-class men "often view ambition, dynamism, a strong work ethic, and competitiveness as doubly sacred because they signal both moral and socioeconomic worth, one-third of the white workers view it with suspicion." This suspicion helps explain the difference workers see between the brand of work-centeredness among the Missing Middle and the norm of work devotion among professional-managerial men. Working-class men are committed to "keeping [their] nose to the grindstone" because they see a stable job as the necessary infrastructure to settled living. Unlike managers and professionals, however, their identities are not tied up in moving up the ladder. Thus a bank supply salesman decries overly ambitious people who "have blinders on. You miss all of life . . . A person that is totally ambitious and driven never sees anything except the spot they are aiming at." An electronics technician criticized people who are "so self-assured, so self-intense that they don't really care about anyone else . . . It's me, me, me, me, me. I'm not that kind of person at all, and that's probably why I don't like it." In short, non-elite men often dismiss the norm of work devotion as a symptom of narcissism.[89]

Workers also contrast their ability to work hard and deliver the basics with what they see as the cushy lives of those in the classes above them. One class migrant described the suspicion he faced when he showed up for a summer job as a mechanic. "My co-workers tolerated the 'college boy' when they saw I could work and would work." Another "college boy" earning summer money in an oil field found that "the gang delights in assigning me tasks that either I cannot do or cannot do well, or that cannot be done by anyone."[90] When another working-class college boy reported for work in the mines, his supervisor made it clear that he thought that "college kids don't like to get their hands dirty." Then the supervisor found out he was the son of a former miner. "Now your daddy, *he's* a worker. Everybody likes to work with Charlie. He always does his share . . . plus some."[91]

"A person felt lucky to be working . . . To them, any kind of work was noble," said one class migrant. Describing his mother's complex split shift and her crushing responsibilities for paid work and family work, he said, "I still don't know how she did it, but she often said she was glad to have the work. We needed the money." He concludes:

When I was employed in corporations, [my working class work ethic] helped me continue to give what I promised to my employers (a full day's work for a full day's pay) . . . And now that I am a freelancer, my working-class background helps me deliver on my word to meet deadlines, to put in extra work when the project calls for it, whether it's in the budget or not. The way I live my life and write my fiction will continue to reflect the most important lesson I learned [as a mineworker] 2200 feet underground.

Workers' pride in their own hard work also fuels their disdain for the hard living who—in their eyes—fail to rise to life's challenges. This view affects their opinions about, and responses to, social programs that are narrowly targeted to the poor. These programs are often seen as taking money out of the pockets of settled families to give to the poor who, in workers' view, do not deserve their hard-earned dollars.[92]

Respect for Religion and Traditional Morality

In the Missing Middle, respect for traditional expressions of ethics and spirituality does not always take the form of being religious. Of the white working-class men Lamont interviewed, only 25% called themselves very religious and only 18% picked "religious" when asked to choose qualities important to them. But a far higher percentage (60%) belonged to religious organizations, and roughly half participated in religious activities—strikingly higher percentages than among higher-status men.[93]

Religion is part of the quest for stability and clear-cut answers in a cultural context where intellectualism is neither valued nor attainable. "High school graduates generally uphold more rigid moral norms than college graduates: they are less supportive of freedom of choice and self-expression, especially in the area[s] of sexual morality, divorce, abortion." Lamont quotes a man who drives commuter trains, who tells her that his goal is to raise his three daughters to

believe in God, and you know, all the rights and wrongs, no grays. I don't believe in gray. Truth, honesty, responsibility, that's what I believe in . . . Believe in God and believe in parents. Must have two parents in the family. I don't believe in divorce . . . Without religion, there's nothing. Without religion or some sort of background, we would have anarchy, total breakdown. We have to put religion in children. I'm Catholic and proud to be Catholic. Honesty and morals. I am worried about this country [especially] groups that are trying to break down our morality . . . [like] lesbianism and gayism. [The world is] going to hell.[94]

He also expressed strong support for capital punishment. The concern for moral rectitude is intermixed with wanting others to behave themselves. Many in the settled working class cannot buy themselves out of proximity to misbehavior. This trainman had been robbed at gunpoint twice and had had his jaw broken by drug addicts. For some, moral absolutism is a bulwark against what they see as upper-middle-class relativism. "Absolutes are a way to get in the face of and stick up the [apertures] of managerial/professional classes. Commitment to a different moral order is itself a form of resistance and an important one," notes one insightful commentator.[95]

Religion often provides a language for self-regulation. The trainman praised religion for helping him move beyond the womanizing of his past. Both Howell and Lamont interviewed workers who had turned to religion to help them stop drinking or otherwise get their lives in order. In fact, in this context, religion and the military are the key institutions for turning individuals' lives around. "When hard-living people talk of changing their ways and of getting their lives straightened out," notes a pastor, "the image of what they considered a good life looked a great deal like" settled living.[96] Elites, facing a life crisis, pay high fees to a psychiatrist to work in a collaborative way to create an individualized interpretation of the patient's past, matched with a new plan for ever-more-perfect self-actualization. For the hard living, adherence to traditionalist religion, with its emphasis on absolute truths and a transcendent moral authority, sometimes offers a path back to settled life. The practice of traditional faith also can express hopes for a better future, as articulated by the teenage mother quoted at the beginning of this section. She brought her baby to a local priest to be baptized, seeing that as the first step in her plan to build a better life for her child than the life she had.[97]

Settled families' insistence on self-regulation may seem heavy-handed to the upper-middle class. But these families live close to the edge. In the upper-middle-class context, children are encouraged to experiment, with the secure knowledge that any "scrapes" they get into will often pass without a trace. Money can buy second chances, something professionals often take for granted. While an insistence on self-regulation may stifle creativity and spontaneity, these may seem worth sacrificing in order to maintain a foothold on the settled life.

Religion also offers an alternative to the elite metric of success as possession of a high-status job. A letter carrier said, comparing himself with his brother, who was a congressional representative, "I'm successful now because I know Jesus Christ . . . I don't put success on a monetary level." The trainman quoted above "feels that being very religious gives him authority." He explained, "there is a certain aura when I walk in. They really listen to what I say, you know. I like that." Religion offers a source of status some workers use "to put themselves a notch above others."[98] Workers' commitment to traditionalist morality ("all the rights and wrongs, no grays") has become a major axis of class conflict, focused on issues such as abortion and gay marriage.

Directness as an Expression of Personal Integrity

To settled working-class men, integrity is everything. People with integrity, said one, "skip the b.s., and don't jerk me around." As Jonathan Rieder found when he talked with Jewish and Italian men in Brooklyn's Canarsie neighborhood in the 1970s, straight talk and toughness carried more weight with them than did middle-class gentility. "Directness is a working-class norm," noted one class migrant. Lamont confirms this, quoting a worker: "If you have a problem with me, come talk to me. If you have a way you want something done, come talk to me. I don't like people who play these two-faced games." Howell's Clay Street informants, too, valued genuineness and saw themselves as being able to "call a spade a spade." "I can always find another job," said a postal worker. "I can't always recoup my pride and my own dignity." Straight talk is seen as requiring manly courage, not being "a total wuss and a wimp," to quote an electronics technician.[99] Note the way class resentment is expressed through a gender affront to upper-middle-class men. One need not condone this to accept the power of "straight talk" as a fact of political life.[100]

The value working-class men place on "straight talk" signals class-based differences in masculine sociability. The blue-collar jobs traditionally held by these men involved specialized, technical skills rather than social skills. Professional-managerial jobs, by contrast, typically require the ability to get along with people and place significant value on the social skills required to avoid testy confrontation. Career success in professional and managerial jobs depends in part on tact, friendliness, conflict avoidance, and teamwork; on making coworkers feel comfortable; and on "conforming" (at least with regard to "cultural matters"). A manager's failure to "fit in" typically results in suspicion and career stall and may result in getting fired.[101]

Yet what many professional and managers see as basic social skills, many non-elite men see as a distasteful requirement for being fake or playing workplace politics. A firefighter who left his job as a messenger on Wall Street told Lamont of his new job, "It's more friendly, open, not as conservative. In big business, there's a lot of false stuff going on. A lot of people are, 'How are you doing?' And then you turn your back and they are like, 'He's a jerk.' At least at the job in the firehouse, if you're a jerk, someone is going to tell you you're a jerk." A car mechanic expressed a similar sentiment:

Oh! You know what I hate? Two-face. I can't stand that. You're a fake, you're a fake. Why be a fake? Like with this person, they are snobby, and with this person, they are a regular down-to-earth person . . . Well, if you have to become snobby for them to want to be around you, well, then screw this person.[102]

Managers' and professionals' success often requires impressing colleagues with the extent of one's skills and "potential," which calls for behaviors that workers see as insincere. A policeman decries "Barbie and Ken people," whom he describes as "people with facades or snotty people. I just like regular people. I don't try to hang out with lawyers or doctors." "Net-working," beloved of professionals, strikes workers as evidence of a lack of authenticity and the presence of a strategic dimension that makes them distinctly uncomfortable. A pipe fitter criticized "shirt and tie types" for "too much politicking." He said, "They are jockeying for jobs and worry-ing about whether they are making the right moves and stuff. I feel I don't have to get involved in that. Their hair is turning gray, and they look older than I do. That's the way I would measure [my happiness], where I can come home and enjoy myself where they are sweating things out." Julie Bettie's high-school girls agreed: "working-class girls' interpretation of [upper-middle-class] preps was that they were 'fake'; their friendships were considered phony and insincere, always working in the interests of social ambition."[103]

Class migrants also describe with distaste the kind of self-promotion that is routine in elite circles. White-collar work "doesn't always speak for itself," Lubrano observes, adding, "Lots of blue-collar people are taught as kids that boasting and self-promotion and credit hogging are wrong and unseemly; but that's precisely what's needed to succeed in the office, as long as it's deftly and subtly done." Another class migrant decried the "middle-class game-playing bullshit" endemic to academic life. "One element that continues to amaze me," a third wrote, "is the obsessive attention grabbing." And a fourth concluded that "The desire to be unique, to be on the cutting edge, is central to academic culture."[104]

Workers' appreciation for plain talk presents challenges for upper-middle-class individuals in public life. Talk that seems no more than thoughtful and intelligent may be seen as an arrogant display of cultural capital and a class affront. Note that Ronald Reagan, George W. Bush, and Sarah Palin all affected a bluff, direct style and presented themselves as down-home folks. Ironically, after 1980, the Republican Party became "the party of ideals," managing to articulate their paradigm shift in ways that sympathetically connected with voters in the Missing Middle. Progressives need to learn to speak to non-college-educated people in language they can relate to, bearing in mind that just because people have not graduated from college (or from a fancy college) does not mean they are unintelligent. Barack Obama has a nice way of not hiding his light under a bushel, while simultaneously managing to not talk down to less-educated people. He has thought a lot about this since his years as an organizer in Chicago. His example is worth emulating.[105]

Family Comes First

Asked why he likes his best friend, the foreman at a New Jersey tin factory replied, "He's a lot like me. He's got high standards for his kids and his family, very protective." Says Lamont:

> Blue-collar men put family above work, and find greater satisfaction in family than do upper-middle-class men. Family is the realm of life in which these workers can be in charge and gain status for doing so. It is also a realm of life that gives them intrinsic satisfaction and validation—which is crucial when work is not rewarding and offers limited opportunities.[106]

"Family comes first" is a truism of working-class life. Consider Thomas Fell, who worked for five years in a classic new-economy working-class job, selling auto parts in a car dealership. When he asked for a raise, his manager told him he could have one, if he quit the union in which he was an active member. The following month, Fell's thirteen-year-old son called shortly before the end of the workday, asking his dad to pick him up at school. His sports practice had finished and his coach and teammates had left. The boy was frightened to be alone at the school because shots had been fired through the windows the previous week. Fell immediately locked up and left work fifteen minutes early. That night, when Fell called to explain his actions to his manager, the manager told him he had done the right thing, saying, "Family is number one." (Nonetheless, Fell was fired the following day, perhaps because of his union activism.)[107]

As noted before, many working-class men associate the enactment of "family comes first" with the breadwinner gender role. "Many equate a high quality of family life with 'being able to keep the wife at home' ":

> My wife was always there for [the kids], which I thought was right . . . I'm old-fashioned that way, where I feel my mother was home, my wife's mother was home and I feel that a mother should be home to raise her child in most circumstances. I know things are rough.

Working-class white men—more than blacks—hold themselves to the breadwinner ideal. For both groups this ideal typically is unattainable. "The husband should take care of the family but, realistically, it's hard. Hard to support a wife," said a Bayonne, New Jersey, firefighter in his thirties who worked two jobs to pay his mortgage. Remember that men of his father's generation could pay the mortgage with a single job and only intermittent part-time work by their wives. Working men today typically cannot, but many continue to believe they should.[108]

The mantra "family comes first" also signals the different relationship workers typically have with their jobs. While both professional and non-elite men are job focused, jobs mean something different in each context. For professionals, "work is the means by which they develop, express, and evaluate themselves." Professional men's sense of personal growth is related not to their perceptions of the quality of family life but to their workplace success. Non-elite men are more likely to view jobs as a way to provide for their families: "My father's job was a means to an end . . . a way to put food on [the] table," said one class migrant who ultimately opted out of work-obsessed upper-middle-class masculinity. Working-class men "measure the success of their lives by having good productive children and grandchildren . . . Jobs are just the means that allow you to provide the best you can for your children," noted another class migrant. For these men, the settled life and the disciplined self that gives rise to it are the true measures of success.[109]

The Missing Middle often sees the upper-middle class as having priorities that are seriously misplaced. "Writing is what makes me happy," Alfred Lubrano told his father. "No, you're happy with your family," his father corrected, "uttering a key blue-collar rule." Psychologically robust people put their eggs in baskets they can fill. "How much money can you spend?" asked one working-class man. To him, what mattered is that "I'm cared for by a lot of people." Said another: "Family is very important in my life. You need to work to support your family. So, I don't worry about a job. I mean, I don't care what I have to do, I'll go out and do it to support my family."[110]

Working-class families and friends rarely talk about work. "What do you do?" is a quintessentially upper-middle-class question. Note the built-in assumptions: that one's job defines one's essence and that reciting one's job category puts everyone at ease. "Work is the place I feel most empowered" and "competent," said an engineer. "It's just a place where I've been recognized as a star . . . and that means a lot to me."[111] Among the upper-middle class, stating one's occupation adds to one's gravitas (except for homemakers, whose jobs are of painfully low status). But to non-elite men, the question is an affront. My husband forgot this crucial cross-class tidbit at his thirtieth reunion at the Catholic high school in the Rustbelt factory town where he was raised. "What do you do?" he innocently asked a class-mate. The classmate put his face close and said, angrily and very loudly, "I sell *toilets*."

Workers' attitudes about family may provide some purchase for progressive reformers who seek to rethink the norm of work devotion among upper-middle-class men, who typically see their long hours on the job as an expression of family commitment. Workers' skepticism of that viewpoint and their view of the norm of work devotion as an unseemly devaluation of family life points to another path.[112]

Class, Cultural Difference, and Politics

Cultural conflicts often take on a political dimension. An astute analysis of this phenomenon is David C. Leege and his coauthors' *The Politics of Cultural Differences*. "In speaking of a cultural approach to politics," they note,

> we wish to emphasize not just the *subject matter* of a political debate—
> particular issues involving abortion, women's rights, school prayer—but rather
> *any political controversy that turns on conflicts about social values, norms,
> and symbolic community boundaries.* As we understand cultural politics, the
> phenomenon is woven into argumentation about public policy on a wide
> range of subjects . . . We recognize a *style* or manner in which politics is con-
> tested that incorporates cultural argument.[113]

In the next chapter, I take this concept a step further. Because class often is expressed as cultural difference, I argue, what is often referred to as "culture wars" are really an expression of class conflict.

CHAPTER SIX

Culture Wars as Class Conflict

Anybody gone into Whole Foods lately? See what they charge for
arugula?

—Barack Obama

THE DEMOCRATIC PARTY has a long history of putting its foot into
its collective mouth when it comes to class issues. A picture of John
Kerry windsurfing provoked a furor of class anger rather than a surge of
admiration for his hip fitness; Barack Obama was ridiculed for his poor
bowling score. Howard Dean was decried as a "latte-drinking" elitist.
Dukakis got into trouble with Belgian endive, Obama with arugula.[1]

The reform-minded elite have been singularly clueless about how these
and other taken-for-granted elements of their lifestyle serve as class acts.
Note how often Democrats' gaffes involve food. When Obama tried to
connect with an Iowa audience during the 2008 presidential campaign by
remarking on the price of arugula, he signaled his lack of awareness that
ordinary Jane has never heard of arugula. "I don't know what it is," a hospital clinic assistant told a reporter. "Maybe it's a Hawaiian thing." It's not
a Hawaiian thing, but it is an upper-middle-class thing. Democratic candidates who talk about endive and arugula send an unintended message—
that they possess sophisticated tastes that set them apart from the iceberg
lettuce eaters of the world. Democratic candidates need to become more
self-aware about the ways their everyday speech and actions signal a specific class location.[2]

Democrats sometimes act mystified about why the Missing Middle re-
sents them. As Democrats often see it, they have such good intentions,
whereas the Republicans' chief goal is to protect the capitalist class. And

yet Americans in the Middle often see liberals, not conservatives, as out of touch with their values. The literature suggests that workers generally distrust professionals but admire the very rich. Class migrants report hostility toward college students and that "professional people were generally suspect." Managers, they feel, are college kids "who don't know shit about how to do anything, but," as one worker put it, "are full of ideas about how I have to do my job." Professionals are no better. Barbara Ehrenreich's working-class father "could not say the word *doctor* without the virtual prefix *quack*. Lawyers were *shysters,* as in *shyster-lawyers;* and professors were without exception *phonies*." Many of Joseph Howell's informants agreed. They felt that lawyers had cheated or overcharged them (typically in divorce cases). Though lawyers were most disliked, doctors fell not far behind. "Doctors will screw you every time. Prescribe medicine for you you don't need and then charge you double for not helping you one goddamn bit."[3]

Annette Lareau also found tremendous resentment against professionals. She writes of a child with learning disabilities who never gets properly diagnosed; a college student who ends her career prospects because no one tells her how to drop a course she is failing; and a seriously ill woman who refuses to go to the doctor because she feels she and her family are treated like "white trash" and never told what illness ails them. People with less education often see professionals as exercising arrogant, unchecked power over their lives.[4]

In sharp contrast, researchers find little resentment of the rich. "[I] can't knock anyone for succeeding," a laborer told Michèle Lamont. "There's a lot of people out there who are wealthy and I'm sure they worked darned hard for every cent they have," opined a receiving clerk. "You can't associate money with happiness, but I would sure like to give it a try," joked an electronics technician.[5]

This makes sense in context. First, workers, black as well as white, tend to dream not of professional credentials but of the independence that flows from owning a business. "To many American workers, self-employment—however remote a possibility—seems to offer a more realistic chance to escape from working-class subordination than does a socialist revolution." A machine operator put it this way: "The main thing is to be independent and give your own orders and not have to take them from anybody else." "The dream of self-employment is one *expression* of his class consciousness, not a denial of it," astute sociologists Reeve Vanneman and Lynn Weber Cannon point out.[6]

Workers are expressing the common longing (shared by members of all classes) not to have to take orders, particularly from people who seem to lord it over them. This longing translates into class resentment of the professional-managerial class but not the rich because most workers have little direct interaction with the rich but do spend time with doctors who speak over their heads, with teachers judgmental of parents who cannot help with homework, and with lawyers who cut corners or even prey on the uneducated.[7]

Workers' selective resentment also reflects a desire to avoid losing their own distinctive class culture, as expressed through food choices, leisure activities, child rearing styles, and values. While the upper-middle class is seen as having a different culture, the rich are seen as just having more money. Thus workers (black as well as white) rank income above education in evaluating people's worth. "While I often needed more money, I never needed a new set of beliefs and values," said one class migrant. A Harvard-trained public interest lawyer told me that his working-class parents saw his career choice as mysterious. "What did they expect?" I asked. "Isn't this what they wanted?" "No," was his quick reply. "What they wanted was for me to stay in [the Rust Belt town where he grew up], and buy a big car and a big house. Sort of like the real estate agent my mother used to work for." What they wanted was to keep him home, in body and mind—just with more money. That's not what they got.[8]

Sunburn

On Ash Wednesday of 2003, I lay bleeding in a hallway in the Yale Hall of Graduate Studies, with a gash from my eyebrow to the crown on my head, huge enough to require more than thirty stitches. In true upper-middle-class fashion, I had multitasked my way to injury—thoroughly engrossed in a high-tension cell phone conference call, I tripped over a doormat and smacked my face, very hard, against a door jamb. From a gurney in the emergency-room hallway at Yale-New Haven Hospital, I called my sister, who taught at Harvard and knew lots of people at Yale. Fifteen minutes later, Yale's chief of plastic surgery was on his way from his home to the hospital, where he proceeded to sew me up. Today you can see my scar but only if you are really looking for it: class privilege etched into my flesh.

Outside of the elite, people lack this kind of social capital. They live with scars. These have been called the hidden injuries of class, but, in truth, they are not all that hidden. Class migrants provide eloquent testimony of injury, as they reveal their haunted sense of being guilty of "betrayal and treachery in some nebulous way."[9] A few of the flood of examples:

My grandfather, who had completed grade school, told me gruffly, "Now that youah goin' to college, you'll be too good t' talk to us anymoah." I protested but he shook his head; it was the last thing he ever said to me.[10]

Practically any journey home for a [class migrant] is going to inspire pain and nostalgia, guilt and ambivalence. Being class-mobile means you're rejecting at least some part of the past, of your kith and kin. Otherwise, you would have stayed.[11]

As soon as I brought up college, or my work, my mother literally changed the subject. She was out of school by the time she was 14, and I think she just feels insecure.[12]

I could not bring myself to talk about books or ideas that never intersected with the lives of my mother and brother, my cousins and extended family. To talk about my studies seemed ridiculous and stuck-up at best in a context that appeared to be as mistrustful of academia as academia was condescending to it.[13]

When I mentioned to my mother [that I was leaving for a more distant, higher-status job], she said to me, "Education destroys something."[14]

"I feel like I have changed sides in some very important game," noted one class migrant. Another, a woman who had grown up in an ethnic neighborhood in Chicago and worked as a carhop to make money for college, remembers treading carefully at her summer job. "Admitting to ability or intelligence was a great sin and indicated that you were 'stuck on yourself,'" she knew. She worked hard not to appear stuck up and thought she had succeeded when the handsomest of the boys who hung around the drive-in asked her out:[15]

I spent a long time getting ready for the date and had trouble even hours later accepting the fact that I had been stood up. Still later, I had even more difficulty realizing that the incident was deliberately planned. Perhaps, in their view, it was retribution because they were somehow stood up by me. I was deserting my class; they knew their place.[16]

The injuries of class are like sunburn so painful that the slightest touch makes you pull away, wincing. That is why Obama got into trouble when he tried to explain the less affluent to a well-heeled audience at a San Francisco fundraiser:

You go into these small towns in Pennsylvania and, like a lot of small towns in the Midwest, the jobs have been gone now for 25 years and nothing's replaced them ... And they fell through the Clinton administration, and the Bush administration, and each successive administration has said that somehow these communities are gonna regenerate and they have not ... And it's not surprising then they get bitter, they cling to guns or religion or antipathy to people who aren't like them or anti-immigrant sentiment or anti-trade sentiment as a way to explain their frustrations.[17]

Hillary Clinton and John McCain immediately decried Obama's comments as "condescending," demeaning," and "elitist."[18] "It was my biggest boneheaded move," Obama said later.[19]

Two rules emerge for Democrats. A presidential candidate should never get into a situation of explaining the less privileged to the elite. The risks of sounding condescending are just too large.[20] (Note that I am explaining the working class to the elite. It's a risky business even for an academic.)

The second rule is subtler. The elite habit of self-analysis and its commitment to the therapeutic model themselves are class acts. Consider Maureen Dowd's column on Obama's Bittergate. She grew up working class, Dowd tells us, "in a house with a gun, a strong Catholic faith, an immigrant father, brothers with anti-illegal immigrant sentiments and a passion for bowling." She reminds us that Obama did not; that his mother "got her Ph.D. in anthropology, studying the culture of Indonesia." Then Dowd lights in: "And as Obama has courted white, blue-collar voters in 'Deer Hunter' and 'Rocky' country, he has often appeared to be observing the odd habits of the colorful locals." Americans do not mind some "elitism," Dowd remarks, "the great tradition of the millionaire who was cool enough to relate to the common man—like Cary Grant's C. K. Dexter Haven in 'The Philadelphia Story.'" In others words, we admire the rich. "What turns off voters is the detached, egghead quality that they tend to equate with wimpiness, wordiness, and a lack of action—the same quality that got the professorial and superior Adlai Stevenson mocked by critics as Adelaide." Be rich and you are manly. Intellectual? What a wuss.[21]

As Dowd's column signals, what upper-middle-class circles see as thoughtful self-analysis may look very different to workers. Self-analysis, fueled by the upper-middle-class logic of self-actualization, is itself a class act. Said one class migrant,

> I asked Pop if he was ever going to die. His retort was consistent with family practice: "Shut up!" A cousin got slapped in the face during dinner because he had asked his father a question . . . it was very different at school, where I was praised for asking and telling.[22]

Said another, a carpenter's daughter, "There's . . . an absolute dictum that you don't talk about your problems in public. This includes going to any sort of counseling or therapy—or, indeed, what I do constantly, talk about my background and my differences from my colleagues." "While working-class people are not without self-insight and concern about their inward states, nevertheless they are not typically occupied with their 'innards' on the scale of the middle class," observes a theology professor who recalls talking with a woman who had left her church because of her upper-middle-class pastor's use of therapeutic language: he "thinks he's a shrink," she noted with disapproval. Lareau reports that when school personnel recommended therapy for a boy with behavioral problems, the boy's father was outraged and the mother resisted. Said the school counselor, "The mom has had some real resistance to his being involved in group therapy . . . I think she had the idea, as many parents have, that therapy means you're saying your child is crazy." "Hyperactivity," one law-and-order civic leader informed Rieder, "is just a fancy term for a bad kid."[23]

In other words, while many people in the professional-managerial class view therapy as a necessity for a well-lived life, the therapeutic model is just a local custom at a specific class location. "Hey, Yale kid, you know who writes books? Liars and squealers. Throw the books out the window, get out on to [the] streets and learn something!" an informant instructed Rieder. The idea that just trying to understand someone could be perceived as irritating and disrespectful is nearly incomprehensible in the upper-middle-class context, where the need to analyze things and talk them through is taken as a given. But because "shrinking" itself is a class act, it is best handled with extreme caution.[24]

Obama, one suspects, immediately regretted his use of words like "cling." Hillary Clinton was all over this: "People embrace faith not because they are materially poor but because they are spiritually rich." Clinton, married to a good ol' boy from a hard-living family (and a man who has never quite shed his own hard-living ways), got the tone exactly right.[25]

Culture Clash and Class Affronts

Far be it from me to deny that gender, race, generation, and other factors play an important role in contemporary American politics. Yet while commentators widely acknowledge the influence of these factors, the role of class typically is overlooked. Bill Clinton sensed this:

> The Democrats limped out of Chicago divided and discouraged, the latest casualties in a culture war that went beyond differences over Vietnam . . . The kids and their supporters saw the mayor and the cops as authoritarian, ignorant, violent bigots. The mayor and his largely blue-collar ethnic police force saw the kids as foul-mouthed, immoral, unpatriotic, soft upper class kids who were too spoiled to respect authority, too selfish to appreciate what it takes to

hold a society together, too cowardly to serve in Vietnam ... Much of my public life was spent trying to bridge the cultural and psychological divide that had widened into a chasm in Chicago.[26]

The "cultural and psychological divide" Clinton describes is a class divide. The New Deal coalition, under which Democrats won the presidency seven out of ten times between 1932 and 1968, was anchored by unions and blue-collar workers, bound in coalition with white Southerners, Catholics, intellectuals, and blacks. Circa 1970, Democrats moved away from the old electoral coalition and replaced it with a new one. George McGovern, the first presidential candidate to move away from the party's traditional blue-collar base, sought instead to appeal to young upper-middle-class activists who already supported his opposition to the Vietnam War. He consolidated this relationship by staking out liberal ground on issues of abortion and legalization of marijuana.[27]

Whereas the New Deal coalition had been organized around class lines and economic issues, the new coalition focused more on social issues, such as civil rights and women's rights, the environment, and resistance to the Vietnam War. "Although this well-educated, culturally libertarian, relatively affluent progressive elite forms a minority [40%] of the Democratic Party," notes liberal commentator Thomas Edsall, "it is this activist stratum that sets the agenda for the Democratic Party."[28]

As liberal attention shifted away from economic issues and toward cultural ones, class warfare erupted within the Democratic Party. Let's examine the lines of division by assessing the charge, initially made by McGovern's more conservative Democratic opponent, Henry (Scoop) Jackson, and used to "devastating effect" by Richard Nixon, that McGovern was a candidate of "acid, amnesty and abortion."[29]

Acid

Why did hippies make many Americans so hopping mad? Because they not only rejected settled living; they derided it and took all kinds of chances with drugs and sex. To many workers, they were nothing more than spoiled rich kids. One class migrant reports that her mother "called the would-be hippies 'trust-afarians.' " "Their safety net is their bank account," another noted dryly. Hippies acted out the freedom available to upper-middle-class kids whose parents could support them while they were out sailing the world or saving it, whose parents' cultural capital could rescue them if their hippie ways put them on the wrong side of the law. It did not help that hippies scoffed at policemen—working-class men with good, stable, high-status jobs—referring to them as "pigs." In short, hippies acted out brazen (if entirely innocent) class privilege. Note that "acid" came first in the trinity of insults.[30]

Amnesty

Amnesty was even more explicitly class tainted. During much of the Vietnam War, rich kids got college deferments while less affluent kids were drafted and sent to Vietnam, only to be spat on when they returned home as veterans. The idea that draft dodgers would get amnesty added insult to injury: the social, cultural, and economic capital of upper-middle-class families protected young adults who were openly defying the law, in ways that might well have permanently extinguished the life chances of a non-elite kid.

Amnesty brings into focus other dimensions of class conflict surrounding patriotism and the military. Patriotism of the flag-waving variety used to be a given among all classes of Americans. Among the white working class, it still is: "Being an American is one of the few high-status signals that workers have access to . . . For this reason, workers might be particularly proud of their manly protective mission and their national status." Lamont links workers' patriotism with their sense of moral mission: "workers are busy keeping moral order not only in their home and neighborhood but also in the world at large."[31]

Upper-middle-class progressives love their country, too. President Obama has sought to forge an inclusive language of patriotism that avoids pitting the Missing Middle against upper-middle-class progressives. Yet Obama has had to work hard to accomplish this, reversing his initial decision not to wear that ever-popular political accessory, the flag lapel pin, and overcoming Michelle Obama's widely quoted comment that the first time she was proud of her country was when its citizens showed support for her husband during the primaries.[32]

Patriotism and the military lost prestige among large segments of the upper-middle class during the Vietnam War. Meanwhile, the military continues to serve as a crucial class escalator by which children of settled workers can move up the class ladder. In fact, the military serves as an ever-more-important path to settled life, given the contraction of manufacturing and the increased importance of a college education. "Specialist Alexis Hutchinson was gung-ho in 2007 when she enlisted in the Army straight out of high school in East Oakland," reported a story in the *San Francisco Chronicle*. "She'd done three years in the ROTC." Her motivation? "This was her ticket to rock-solid stability." In today's volunteer army the bulk of soldiers are from the working and middle classes, often entering the service to finance college. In addition, the military is a key institution where hard-living youth can get their lives together and gain access to the settled life. Ironically, for many Americans, entering the military provides the only route to the kinds of social supports European countries offer all citizens: health insurance, a college education, and low-cost, high-quality child care. The reform-minded elite does not need the military either to pay for college or to provide a career path. Disapproval of militaristic U.S. foreign policy has bled over into disapproval of the military for decades now, beginning during the Vietnam War. An early example was a parody of a Vietnam-era army ad. The original ad, designed to stress how the military offers wider horizons for non-elite kids, urged recruits to "Join the Army and see the world." The parody countered: "Join the Army. Travel, meet new people, and kill them." During the wars in Iraq and Afghanistan, progressives—to their credit—have bent over backward to combine disapproval of war policy with messages of respect and appreciation for the troops. This is an important improvement. It is worth recognizing that belittling the military fuels class conflict. The troubling challenge today is to assess how to respond to the likelihood that prohibiting recruiters from high schools and other campuses as an expression of opposition to "don't ask, don't tell" fuels class frictions.[33]

Abortion

Abortion trips many triggers fated to engage and enrage the settled working class. To explain why requires us to back up and analyze the 50 percentage-point differential between homemakers, who trend strongly Republican, and business and professional women, who trend strongly Democratic. Business and professional women began to leave the GOP after 1980 because they were upset by the Reagan and George H. W. Bush campaigns' use of racial code words. The GOP's increasingly conservative positions on family and gender issues fueled this defection, as the GOP moved away from Rockefeller Republicanism toward the Religious Right. "By the 1990s, [upper-middle-class women's] defection was huge," notes political scientist David C. Leege and his coauthors.[34]

The class dimension of the abortion debate has long been evident. Kristin Luker's 1984 study of abortion activists in California found that "almost without exception pro-choice women work in the paid labor force, they earn good salaries when they work, and if they are married, they are likely to be married to men who also have good incomes." She found that most pro-choice activists were college graduates and over half had incomes in the top 10% of all working women. Pro-life women, in sharp contrast, were less likely to be employed and earned less money when they were. And "they are more likely to be married to a skilled worker or small businessman who earns only a moderate income." Pro-life women typically had only a high-school education.[35]

In other words, Luker found that the abortion debate was a fight between pro-choice upper-middle-class business and professional women and pro-life working-class homemakers. Why does the divide run across class lines? To the settled working class, the need for abortion may signal a lack of self-regulation—another clash between what workers see as elites' insistence on coddling the hard-living, in contrast with their own commitment to keeping the world in moral order. Thomas Edsall, who expresses the clash between self-regulation and self-actualization as the "discipline versus therapy" dichotomy, observes that many Republican voters (evangelical and not) insist on the need for "behaving responsibly." They link their positions on abortion, crime, and "the gay lifestyle" to their insistence on personal responsibility, which can be seen as a political code word for settled living.[36]

Abortion rights advocates have inadvertently exacerbated the class dynamic, by giving women's autonomy, premised on the elite norm of self-actualization, as the reason for abortion rights. As noted before, self-actualization takes a back seat for workers, who "make a religion of responsibility": abortion rights is a lightning rod channeling the sparks that fly between workers' ideal of self-regulation and elites' ideal of self-actualization. The caricature of the professional woman aborting her baby to pursue her career should be viewed in this context. That specter reflects workers' suspicion that elites are job obsessed and fail to understand that family comes first. Dig deeper and one finds class resentment over the fact that not only elite men but even elite women have opportunities less privileged men lack. What elites see as gender progress, workers may see as a consolidation of class privilege. It is both.[37]

Welfare Reform, Crime, and Affirmative Action: Euphemized Racism?

Both regression analyses and common sense show that race continues to influence voting among whites.[38] Let me say clearly that progressives will not, and should not, pander to racism. In one of the most insightful of the many studies of racism among the white working class, David Roediger argues that in the South, white workers assuaged the hidden injuries of class by embracing white privilege. This is part of a larger pattern, in which social groups attempt to compensate for social disadvantage by seeking to emphasize their membership in a group that enjoys privilege. This tendency is troubling but commonplace. When I described this pattern to a friend, she replied, "You know, you're right. That's why when I go on an important job interview, I go dripping with pearls"—a class act designed to overcome gender disadvantage.[39]

Simple racism doubtless plays a role in the animosity between the white workers and their black counterparts, but there is also an undercurrent of class conflict. White workers associate morality with "individualism, self-reliance, a work ethic, obedience, and discipline, and they believe that blacks violate these values. Thus, they say their racism is motivated not by a dislike of blacks but by a concern for key American values." When Rieder interviewed working-class Italians and Jews in Brooklyn's Canarsie neighborhood in the 1970s, he found that residents drew a distinction between "blacks" and "niggers." "It's really a class problem," said an educated Jewish housewife in Canarsie. "I don't care about the color of a person if they're nice people. The black parents in the school programs I work with are beautiful and refined people. They're like us." "I can't help thinking of the immigrants," said another, speaking of white ethnics. "I mean, they tried to make a living, they sacrificed so the next generation could live a better life. They gave their family values. Don't shit where you eat." What drove Canarsians crazy was "ghetto" blacks: "Flashy cars, booze, and broads is all they care about. They don't even want to get ahead for their families," said one. Rieder's Canarsians, like Lamont's subjects twenty years later, saw "moral failings" in the black populations they disdained; like most Americans of all classes, they lacked a structural analysis that would have opened their eyes to the ways that social disadvantage produces hard-living behaviors they disdain. "Beneath the surface of racial judgments was the ineluctable reality of class cultures in conflict," Rieder concludes.[40]

Here is a hypothesis: when justifying the lack of racial diversity in privileged positions within their own class, both elite and non-elite whites may interpret racial differences according to their specific set of values in ways that land whites on top. Settled working-class whites, whose claims for privilege rest on morality and hard work, may stereotype blacks as deficient in morality (by conflating hard living with race). Upper-middle-class whites, whose claims for privilege rest on merit, may stereotype blacks as deficient in merit (by means of the kinds of double standards described earlier, which operate to disadvantage people of color as well as women).

This is not to deny outright racism; social psychologists show that it is persistent, as does sociologist Monica McDermott's sensitive study in its explorations of race's contours among working-class whites. But it is a bit too convenient to displace racism onto the working class, on the assumption that elite whites are immune—especially when the representation of people of color in high-status jobs is as every bit as minuscule as is their representation in the good (blue-collar) working-class jobs. "One marker of progressive politics is displaying oneself as antiracist, and this can, at times, unfortunately manifest itself as a demeaning of and distancing from white working-class people, who are constructed as stupid and racist," to quote Bettie.[41]

Republicans from Nixon on have used racial code words in a self-conscious way as part of the Southern strategy to capture the formerly Democratic South. This history makes it easy to write the white workers off on the grounds that Democrats should not sink to racism in order to win votes. But it is a reaction worth resisting. Enthusiasm for law-and-order legislation, for welfare reform, and for scaling back affirmative action all are commonly cited as evidence of working-class racism. Let's look more carefully at each.[42]

Law and Order

Again there is no doubt that "law and order" was used, by Nixon and others, as a code for racist sentiments that could no longer be openly expressed. Yet it is worth considering whether non-elite whites were also, quite simply, deeply concerned about crime. Between 1965 and 1975, the murder rate more than doubled. It rose again in the late 1970s after only a few years' stall. While upper-middle-class families lived in white neighborhoods far from the crime wave, many less affluent families were in the midst of it. Many working-class jobs—as bill collectors, deliverymen, cabbies, firefighters, utility workers, and repair personnel—take their occupants into tough neighborhoods. In addition, homeowners, such as those in Canarsie, sometimes found themselves unable to sell homes they had worked all their lives to buy, and they were sharply apprehensive about changes in their neighborhoods. "Who are the Canarsie people?" asked one neighborhood resident. "They're not rich. They bought a home in a sanctuary, and they're afraid they're going to lose it. They are saying, 'Don't tread on me.' They want to protect their turf." Many did not want to move because they had a rooted sense of place and neighborhood. Remember that the geography of working-class social networks is highly localized. In the period directly before Rieder's study began, the percentage of the population on welfare soared; in one neighborhood the figure went from 8% to 31%. This is not the kind of situation the upper-middle class has ever faced.[43]

Rieder reported that when he spoke with Canarsie residents in the 1980s,

> I met few residents who were strangers to street crime. If they had not been victimized, usually only one link in the chain of intimacy separated them from the victims—kin, neighbors, and friends. Canarsians spoke about crime with more unanimity than they achieved on any other subject, and they spoke forcefully and often. Most had a favorite story of horror.[44]

One "trucker remembered defecating in his pants a few years earlier when five black youths cornered him in an elevator and placed a knife blade against his throat." They threatened to kill him if he went to the law, but he did anyway. "The judge gave them a fucking two-year probation." This experience, Rieder tells us, "left an indelible imprint," the trucker "still reliv[ing] the humiliation of soiling himself." "It's all in danger: the house you always wanted is in danger, the kids are in danger, the neighborhood is in danger. It's all slipping away."

Fifteen years later, Lamont found her informants still apprehensive about keeping their families safe. Many of the men Lamont interviewed "perceive their environment as threatening." Iron bars adorned many windows; attack dogs were tied in workers' small backyards. A 2006 study again documented the prevalence of crime and its role in fueling racism. Fast forward a bit and find Hillary Clinton seeking to solidify her appeal to the Missing Middle through a $4 billion anticrime program. There are no easy answers here—just the point that less affluent people's concern with crime should not be written off as mere racism by upper-middle-class people who live in safe neighborhoods.[45]

Welfare

Workers may conflate hard living not only with blacks but with the poor. This conflation is partly true: some people are poor because of their hard-living ways. It is also partly false: many others are poor because they were born into or fell into poverty and lacked the skills or means to get out; or they pursue hard living because they judge their chances of getting ahead as so slim that self-medicating or settling for immediate gratification seems the better course.

While no doubt people sometimes turn to hard living because the cards are stacked against them, settled-living whites feel that the cards were stacked against them, too, but they persevered and achieved a decent life.

Maintaining that life is both deeply meaningful and a daily struggle, as is clear in the testimony of a woman quoted by Lillian Rubin:

> Mike drives a cab and I work in a hospital, so we figured one of us could transfer to nights. We talked it over and decided it would be best if I was here during the day and he was here at night . . . So now Mike works days and I work graveyard. I hate it, but it's the only answer; at least this way some-body's here all the time. I get home at 8:30 in the morning. The kids and Mike are gone . . . I clean up the house a little, do the shopping and the laundry and whatever, then I go to sleep for a couple of hours until the kids get home from school . . . Mike gets home at 5; we eat; then he takes over for the night, so I go back to sleep for another couple of hours. I try to get up by 9 so we can have a little time together, but I'm so tired that I don't make it a lot of times. And by 10, he's sleeping because he has to be up at 6 in the morning. So if I don't get up, we hardly see each other at all . . . It's hard, very hard; there's no time to live or anything.[46]

People whose commitment to fulfilling their work and family responsibili-ties leaves them "no time to live" may have very little patience with needs-based social programs, since these typically deliver services to hard-living families, leaving settled families to fend for themselves. Such allocations and expectations tend to alienate voters of the Missing Middle.[47] Said one union activist:

> When I talk to working women and ask them, do you have flexibility, and they say, oh yeah, I've got a flexible schedule; I work nights and my husband works days. [What they mean is] I don't have to pay a baby-sitter because somehow we manage but I haven't seen my husband in four years.[48]

Missing-Middle couples who pay for child care are similarly stressed. Those who tag team or struggle to pay for inadequate child care may well be outraged that low-income families get free child care, health care, and a steady income that enables mothers to stay home with their children—even if that income is extremely low. To some extent, their viewpoint is understandable. Low-income families are more likely than families in the middle to have mothers at home full time: 60% of poor mothers but only 23% of middle-income ones are stay-at-home mothers. Furthermore, child care subsidies are available for poor families but not for middle-income families who also find themselves stretched to cover child care costs: 30% of poor families that use child care centers but only 5% of those in the middle receive subsidies. To a professional-managerial policy analyst, fur-ther analysis shows that poor families still pay a larger proportion of their income for child care, that the subsidies available to them are low and sporadic, and that poor mothers tend to remain out of the labor force because the wages available to them are so low that after paying for child care, their gross pay would be tiny.[49]

None of this is readily apparent to nonspecialists. "The taxes go to the poor, not to us," said one Canarsie homemaker. "And the rich have their tax accountants. The middle-income people are carrying the cost of liberal social programs on their backs. The rich can afford to be liberal. They won't be touched by liberalized programs."[50] More recently, a conservative Head Start teacher made a similar point:

> They don't care if they pick up their kids late. Why should they? They're not paying anyway. So they show up late, and I have to pay my babysitter because I'm late picking up [my son]. Sometimes they show up with shopping bags. They've been at the mall. I'm just sick of it.

So did a liberal law student:

> I'll admit I resented it. I was working really hard, waitressing and going to school, and *I* couldn't afford health insurance. Some of the girls I went to high school with, they had had kids and were on welfare. *They* had health insurance.

When my husband suggested to his mother—the wife of a former factory worker and a lifelong Democrat—that she see whether a government program existed to help pay for the care of her ailing husband, she dismissed the suggestion. "It's not worth it. The government doesn't care about people like us, who have worked all their lives. They only care about the poor." "Who's feeling sorry for me?" a Canarsie man had demanded thirty years earlier. "The colored have gotten enough. Let them do for themselves like we do!"[51] To quote Theda Skocpol:

> Americans in the missing middle are not exclusively "the poor" on whom many liberals and conservatives debating welfare chiefly focus. Still less are they the biggest market winners . . . These Americans are, above all, people who put in long hours to earn a living and make a decent life—coping with rising pressures in their workplaces, while trying to raise children in solo-parent or dual-worker households.[52]

Skocpol argues, "Successful social programs have built bridges between more and less privileged Americans"—through such resources as Social Security, public schooling, and early social programs for mothers and children. Republicans have recognized that needs-based programs are unpopular and politically vulnerable, which is why they now push legislation toward tightly targeted programs. Democrats need to be attentive to the class dynamics of social program design. Needs-based programs may seem easier to pass because they cost less, but past experience suggests that needs-based victories will often be pyrrhic. A Canarsie lawyer said it best:

> We never join the have-a-littles with the have-nots to fight the haves. We make sure the have-a-littles fight the have-nots. That's the shame of it. The have-a-littles, the Canarsie people, they don't see the have-a-lots. They can only see the have-nots. So the have-a-little Canarsieite says, "Don't deny me, don't take my future away from me."[53]

Better to design programs as universal, and to control costs, if necessary, by limiting them on some basis other than income. An example is the Obama campaign's approach to health coverage. The proposed limitation was not based on income but on age. Offering all children health coverage is a way to take a first step toward universal coverage without pitting the have-a-littles against the have-nots.[54]

The irony is that Medicare did help my mother-in-law. Quickly and efficiently, the government began to cover the costs of my father-in-law's sorely needed day care program. But note that the reach of Republican rhetoric is long because it has an element of truth. The Head Start teacher quoted above makes a valid point: the government paid for child care for poor families and not for working class ones. Head Start clients did not charge for late pick-ups, but the teacher (then making $14,000 a year) not only had to pay for her own child care provider but also had to pay them $1 for every minute she was delayed in leaving her job because her pupils' parents showed up late. Needs-based programs can create and sustain resentments that ultimately undercut the programs' effectiveness even for the very poor. To quote a now-common saying, "A program for the poor is a poor program." Theda Skocpol articulated this important principle a decade ago; the sentiment since has crystallized into an aphorism. It is time to pay closer attention to it.

Affirmative Action

"If you close schools on Martin Luther King Day, or Black Solidarity Day," said one Carnasie man, "then you must close the schools on Jewish Solidarity Day and Italian Solidarity Day. It's all a matter of fairness. I believe in black pride, but don't step on my Italian pride. We've all been discriminated against." Said another Canarsie man said, "Ramsey of the NAACP told us we had to pay the price for those years of slavery. But I ask you, who will pay the Jews for two thousand years of slavery? Who will compensate the Italians for all the ditches they dug?"[55]

In the 2008 campaign, both Democratic candidates tread carefully around the issue of affirmative action.[56] Famously, Obama seemed to say that his daughters should not be eligible for affirmative action. Actually, I disagree. Conventional affirmative action programs have helped create a black middle class and also have been extraordinarily important for women. Moreover, thirty years of social science, most dramatically the implicit association test, document that race and gender bias continue to shape the mini-politics of everyday life.[57]

Yet affirmative action programs have been, and remain, a flashpoint for many whites in the Missing Middle. It is not hard to see why: conventional affirmative action programs are a formal expression of the view that race and gender are the key (or sole?) axes of disadvantage in the United States. From the viewpoint of those disadvantaged by class, this is infuriatingly inaccurate.

Race and gender continue to disadvantage, but so does class—depending on the context. When it comes to the higher-paid blue-collar jobs, of which white workers still hold 90% or more, class alone does not disadvantage white working-class men. But when it comes to access to upper-middle-class institutions—notably, college and professional-managerial jobs—class alone is definitely a disadvantage. I am not saying that it would be easy to design affirmative action programs that take class disadvantage into account in an appropriate way. I am saying that it is worth the effort.[58]

Culture Wars: Religion, Gay Marriage, and "Family Values"

In the past two decades, political scientists have rediscovered the important influence of religion in politics. As of the 1960s, religion's major role fell almost entirely along faith community lines, which correlated with ethnic lines. Protestants, typically of Anglo-Saxon origin, tended to vote Republican, whereas Catholics (Southern European and Irish) and Jews (Slavic and German) typically voted Democratic.[59]

By 2000, religion again played a major role in politics, but the influence of ethno-religious lines had sharply declined. Instead, traditionalist segments of all major faith traditions increasingly aligned themselves with the Republican Party, while more liberal modernist segments of all the major faith traditions increasingly aligned themselves with the Democrats. "Traditionalists" hold traditional religious beliefs, engage in traditional religious practices, and believe in transcendent and fixed sources of moral authority. They object, on moral grounds, to abortion, gay rights, and banning prayer in the public schools. "Modernists" have limited involvement in traditional forms of worship and "a more fluid conception in which moral authority is defined relative to an individual's own judgment, historical context, and human progress." This leads modernists to advocate, on moral grounds, for abortion rights and gay marriage and to oppose prayer in public schools.[60]

The traditionalist-modernist split has class dimensions that are important for understanding the culture wars.[61] Recall the commuter trainman who decried divorce and "gayism" and strongly supported capital punishment. His insistence on "all the rights and wrongs, no grays" is an apt articulation of traditionalism, echoed in the rhetoric of George W. Bush, up to and including his farewell speech to the American people ("Good and evil exist in this world, and between the two, there can be no compromise").[62] The commuter trainman agreed. Without the guidance of religion, "there's nothing," or worse than nothing—without religion "we would have anarchy, total breakdown." Religion provides the bulwark that ensures the architecture of the settled life. The workers Lamont interviewed "are not postmodern men who recreate themselves anew every morning; their lives are lived within clearly defined parameters, within networks they know inside out and which they define as remarkably (and often too) stable." Working-class whites give more support than do professionals to "cultural fundamentalism"—"adherence to traditional mores, respect of family and religious authority, asceticism, and impulse control." Men and women alike "use traditional morality, like religion, to keep pollution at arm's length, including drugs, alcohol, promiscuity, and gambling."[63]

A long line of scientific studies reaching back to the 1920s illuminates the role of religion in the lives of middle Americans. The devout have greater impulse control and "tend to do better in school, live longer, have more satisfying marriages and be generally happier." A recent review of eighty years of research offers an explanation peculiarly suited to seculars: "The rituals that religions have been encouraging for thousands of years seem to be a kind of aerobic workout for self-control," activating parts of the brain associated with self-regulation, said psychologist Brian Willoughby. Similar benefits are not found among people who describe themselves as spiritual but not religious. "Sacred values come prefabricated for religious believers. The belief that God has preferences for how you behave and the goals you set for yourself has to be the grand-daddy of all psychological devices for encouraging people to follow through with their goals,"[64] Willoughby asserts.

The conventional path for progressives is to eschew organized religion, in favor of building one's path to "spirituality." It is worth noticing that the approach of a customized, purpose-build secular spirituality is premised on an elite type and breadth of education and also is intertwined with the elite norm of, and material access to, self-actualization. In this context, belief in traditionalist religion, or indeed in any organized religion, may be seen as distinctly déclassé. "Why is our papal blessing not on display?" asked a writer in the *New York Times,* referring to a certificate available from the Vatican. "Is it because we worry that in some circles our faith might be considered a bit—uncool? (*You actually attend Mass? Really?*)."[65]

Yet, for the working class, self-regulation is more to the point: keeping one's nose to the grindstone in order to maintain a settled life. Thriving in non-elite jobs requires dependability and consistency—as a working-class worker, you can be easily replaced. Long-term financial stability requires not having an attitude; "Question Authority," the unspoken anthem in many elite private schools, would serve only to get you fired.

In my view, a condescending attitude toward organized religion, or toward traditionalist religion, is a class act unworthy of progressives. I would rather signal consistent respect for whatever belief system people choose to cherish and hold them to their aspirations toward compassion, agape, and tikuun. As for pinched judgmentalism toward gays, I do not share it, any more than I shared the similar sentiment against unmarried couples who lived together in the 1970s. But it is an important fact of political life that shifts in sexual norms are extremely upsetting to traditionalists, which means they are tinder for class conflicts.

The uncomfortable reality is that progressives, gay and straight, need to come to terms with the fact that if the goal is to build a coalition around economic issues—including health insurance—crucial coalition partners may feel differently about gay marriage and other equality issues. If coalition building is considered an important goal, progressives will have to give our leaders the room to maneuver as they attempt to defuse cultural issues as a key political force. This includes issues we hold near and dear. For me, as a feminist, to acknowledge that abortion rights fuel class conflict is upsetting. That does not mean I will give up my own deeply held commitments, but it does mean that I talk about them differently and will go out of my way to signal respect for those who disagree with me in arenas where they and I can find common ground.

Big Guns

What does class conflict have to do with guns? A lot, Barack Obama learned, to his chagrin:

> To act like hunting, like somebody who wants firearms doesn't get it—that kind of condescension has to be purged from our vocabulary. And that's why that whole "Bittergate" episode was so bitter for *me*. It was like: Oh, this is exactly what I wanted to avoid.[66]

When guys love their pistols, what's gender got to do with it? Astute observers have pointed out that the "gender gap" in voting is not a story about women. It is a story about men, whose voting patterns have changed far more dramatically than those of women. Working-class men voted Democratic by a twenty-five-point margin forty years ago; as of 1999, they were voting Republican by a seven-point margin.[67]

The gender dynamics are not subtle. As noted before, high-school-educated men have lost more ground economically than have most other groups since 1970, and they feel under assault not only as providers but as protectors of their families. What does this have to do with guns? Polling data show that women are three times as likely as men to favor gun control. I have found no breakdowns that separate less affluent from more affluent men, but college graduates show significantly higher support for gun control (19%) than do men with less education (12%). Opposition to gun control also varies a lot by region: opposition is higher in the West and South (20%) than in the East and North (13%).[68]

Howell offers insight into the significance of hunting culture among white men in the South. He set off on a hunting trip with Barry Shackelsford, the hard-living, alcoholic, good-hearted, and ultimately heroic central character of Howell's book, *Hard Living on Clay Street*. Barry does not appear to "cling" to his guns. Hunting seems to provide him with a way of relating to nature and indulging his love of the countryside; it is a bonding experience that he enjoys sharing with close friends and his son. Gun culture no doubt reflects men choosing to define masculinity in terms of cultural practices to which they have access.

All men do this, given that masculinity is something that has to be earned, often anxiously so. Obama's mistake was to limit his analysis to the Other. He did not say, "Gee, these hedge-fund guys, they are so anxious about whether they are real men, they try to turn paper pushing into this big, macho thing." What is surprising, given Obama's highly tuned ear, is that he said the equivalent about non-elite men. What is impressive is how quickly Obama realized his mistake. He seems to get it that one key to turning this country around politically is to avoid condescending to the Missing Middle.

Family Therapy and Public Policy

The analysis presented here has concrete implications for policy design and for shifting American politics to make new policies attainable. Let's begin small, with policy design. Focusing first on child care policy, we see that—other than tax credits that chiefly benefit affluent people—the United States has only means-tested programs that pit the have-a-littles against the have-nots.[69]

Moreover, the conventional policy focus is on child care centers, yet many workers prefer either tag teaming or "family child care" (where a woman cares for a few children in her own home). No doubt this "preference" reflects existing conditions. The lack of suitable child care subsidies often means that many in the Missing Middle can afford only unappealing, care-on-the-cheap franchised McCenters. In one study, 80% of tag teaming couples mentioned money as one reason they tag teamed.[70] Nixon's 1971 veto of the Comprehensive Child Development Act, which would have provided significant federal funding for child care centers, has shaped the image of child care in a highly negative way: it now represents not a society's investment in its next generation of citizens but a family decision to consign one's child to a marketplace that transmits class disadvantage with remarkable efficiency.[71]

Given this context, parents may feel it is far better to mute the market aspects of paid child care by asking a neighbor to "watch the kids," so that the arrangement feels like a natural extension of the reciprocal relationships that characterize working-class networks. Recall that workers tend not to feel comfortable or empowered talking with teachers—and day care personnel feel more like teachers than does a neighbor. Moreover, Lamont noticed that working-class families were much more apprehensive about strangers than she was. (Her sources were concerned that she went to strangers' homes for interviews.) Anxieties about strangers also feed the distrust of child care centers. "They fear that terrible dangers await children who are cared for by strangers," concludes one author, quoting an informant who said, "I don't let people outside my family watch my kids . . . You don't know those other people. It doesn't matter that they got a sign out that says they're certified . . . There's a lot of things out there that happen to kids." Recall the deep, tight networks of working-class families. Upper-middle-class people are taught from a young age to be comfortable with strangers and to have faith in professionals. Workers, less so.[72]

In fact, precisely what upper-middle-class parents like about a (high-quality) center—that it is staffed with professionals—may feel off-putting to less affluent parents. Law professor Lucie White's study of welfare-to-work mothers in Massachusetts critiqued "the bureaucratized, monetized, professionalized, and exorbitantly expensive day care delivery model that current day care policy advocates sometimes uncritically promote." White reported ambivalence among welfare-to-work mothers about child care centers, for two reasons. First, many felt that they had received poor service in similar settings, saying that teachers and other professionals are often rude and condescending. Second, many sought a personal relationship with their caregivers and wanted "their caregivers' language and values to mirror their own." Francine Deutsch found that working-class families, too, wanted their children cared for by people who shared their values— particularly important if the goal is to raise kids who keep the world in moral order. "If I'm going to have kids . . . I'm going to be the one who instills their morals and ethics and I wasn't going to leave that to someone else," said one father. Said another, "I didn't want Marie to learn things from other people. I want her to learn from us. We are not the most intelligent people in the world, but we know right from wrong." In this context, upper-middle-class feminists' insistence on professionally staffed day care centers emerges as a source of class-based friction.[73]

A deeper point concerns the limitations of child care as a solution to work-family conflict. Child care is important, but it is only a small piece of a larger policy puzzle. Child care centers generally serve only three- to five-year-olds, and neither child care centers nor after-school programs cover all the hours parents must work in a country where adults work exceptionally long hours. Finally, significant parts of family care are fundamentally nondelegable, no matter how good the child care: appointments with doctors or social workers, school plays or sports games, holiday events, and so on.

Short-term leaves are very important—and very limited. Inside the Beltway, the key focus for decades has been to amend the Family and Medical Leave Act to create twelve weeks of paid leave. This is both vitally important and painfully limited. It takes twenty years—not twelve weeks—to raise a child. Paid sick leave, a proposal that has made significant headway in recent years, is similarly vital and similarly limited.[74] Short-term leaves are important, but the larger problem is a workplace that still assumes a workforce of breadwinners married to homemakers. The solution is what is commonly called "workplace flexibility": a new set of workplace expectations to match today's workplace to an era of single parents and tag team families.

Yet federal public policy, for decades, has focused almost exclusively on child care, short-term leaves, and child care tax credits that primarily benefit more affluent people. A key challenge for the Obama administration will be to break free of the cramped leaves-and-child-care frame that has long dominated work-family public policy at the federal level. Progressives can help make this happen. Reform-minded bloggers can raise questions about the norm of work devotion and the ideology of concerted cultivation, along the lines suggested by critiques of those outside professional-managerial circles. Bloggers and union activists can work to change the conventional wisdom that union members are only interested in wages and benefits by pointing out that no level of wages and benefits will help workers who are fired for putting family first. Feminists, in a reconstructive vein, can point out that work-family public policy needs not only to help tomboys who want to take three months off, put their kids in child care, and head back to work, but also to help femmes whose goal is to spend more time with their children without consigning themselves to the margins at work and permanent economic vulnerability. Reconstructive feminism, with its new sensitivity to different class locations, can also advocate new laws to help families who lack access to the flexible work arrangements often available to professionals, but who nonetheless need flexibility to attend a teacher's conference or take an elder to a social worker. Similar laws already exist in some states.[75]

Beyond short-term leaves and child care, easing work-family conflict in the United States requires addressing the mismatch between today's workforce and workplaces still designed for the workforce of the 1950s. Though this mismatch creates problems at every level of society, we can now see how this problem expresses itself differently in different class contexts. High-level professionals often have lots of autonomy and flexibility—they can work their sixty hours a week any time and any place they want; the norm of work devotion and the hours required to "succeed" are inconsistent with responsibilities for family caregiving. Workers in middle-wage jobs less often face long hours (although they may be required to work overtime), but typically they have rigid, highly supervised schedules where being absent or even a few minutes late can jeopardize their jobs. Low-wage workers face rotating shifts, unsocial hours, or such low wages that they hold two or three jobs at once, which makes arranging child care virtually impossible (one reason so many children are home alone).

Addressing these problems will require the implementation of working-time regulations to address working hours, location, and schedules—like those that exist in Europe. Such regulations will go nowhere without union support. Here again, an unrecognized class dynamic becomes crucial. Unions support short-term leaves, both for idealistic and for strategic reasons. Short-term leaves benefit workers whether or not they belong to unions, fulfilling unions' idealistic desire to empower all workers. Strategically, if short-term leaves are federally mandated, unions do not have to negotiate for them, leaving unions free to focus in contract negotiations on gaining additional rights.

Backing working-time regulations is a lot riskier. Hours limitations, including the right to request flexibility, collide with many unions' and union members' suspicion of part-time work.[76] Lamont found that settled-living workers considered part-time workers to be "polluting" their working environment. "[A] tin factory foreman, Jim Jennings puts himself above part-time workers, whom he views as 'dummies.'" Part-timers are seen as having low moral standards, "nothing but trouble," Lamont explains, as if "their part-time employment was to be explained by their instability, lack of character, or inability to handle responsibility." Settled living is built on a foundation of full-time work. For many union men, part-time jobs are emblematic of hard living. All this is vital background for understanding the attitude of many—although not all—unions toward part-time work. "Part-time is radioactive; I wouldn't mention it if I were you," someone at the AFL-CIO warned me when I raised the issue of part-time equity (proportional pay and benefits for part-time workers). Evidence suggests that working-class women want part-time work in higher proportions than do more privileged women, so it is not surprising that unions that represent historically female workforces (notably the Service Employees International Union) have long supported part-time equity. A union's attitude toward part-time jobs depends greatly on whether it sees its organizational center of gravity as enabling men to be effective breadwinners or as enabling women to shape jobs that allow them to do right by their families without getting fired—on whether, as it is sometimes expressed, it is a girl union or a guy union.[77]

Many unions are equally suspicious of "flexibility," the word (developed in the context of professional jobs) commonly used to discuss workplace-workforce mismatch. There are good reasons for these suspicions. Employers have used "flexibility" to claim the right to eliminate job and schedule stability for workers, requiring shifts of more than forty hours a week without overtime pay when demand is high and trimming hours when demand is low (thereby avoiding layoffs that would trigger employer contributions to unemployment). A good example is the Republican-sponsored Family Friendly Workplace Act, which, in its original form, would have given employers the "flexibility," without paying overtime, to require workers to work anywhere from twenty to sixty hours during a given week, thereby encouraging the kind of unpredictable schedules that make it nigh impossible to arrange child care. Unions, understandably, were not enthusiastic. Some unionists instinctively oppose flexibility because they see uniform rules as the only way to limit employers' power. "I do not favor flexibility," one prominent union leader told me. "If one person says, 'I have to leave because of my child,' I am going to tell her no. Because if I say yes to one, I have to say yes to everyone."[78]

An important step in widening the scope of work-family policy beyond leaves and child care is to frame arguments for working-time regulations in ways that avoid the radioactivity of flexibility and part-time work. The obvious alternative is to use the language of family values. Workers do. Said a thirty-six-year-old mother who is a sales person for a jewelry company:

> I really think the position I'm in, which is in the retail world, is totally destroying family values cause there's no way for someone to hold a position that I hold in the retail world and have a family cause they don't help you whatsoever. And they're open 363 days a year and if you're not there, someone else's going to take your job and you have to be there. You have to be there to keep your job and to keep a family you've gotta be with the family.[79]

The reframing opportunity is obvious: should an employer be able to keep you from doing right by your family? This question taps into working-class culture in ways that have significant organizing potential. These points have important implications both for shaping public policy and for union organizing.

Of course, we can design public policy until the cows come home, and it will not make a bit of difference if we cannot pass legislation. So I end where I began, with a plea, and a strategy, for political climate change. A precondition for permanent political change is a changed relationship between the white working-class and the reform-minded elite. It is disheartening that, despite thirty years of insightful books—*Hard Living on Clay Street* (1972), *Canarsie* (1985), *The Dignity of Working Men* (2000), *Women without Class* (2003)—the upper-middle class remains supremely uninterested in rethinking its relationship with the Missing Middle. Instead, a string of recent commentators offer liberals more political comfort food, most prominently Thomas Frank in his *What's the Matter with Kansas?* (2004), which was on the *New York Times* bestseller list for forty weeks. Frank paints a picture of workers too dim-witted to recognize they are being manipulated by the capitalist class. He decries

> a panorama of madness and delusion worthy of Hieronymous Bosch: of sturdy blue-collar patriots reciting the Pledge while they strangle their own life chances; of small farmers proudly voting themselves off their own land; of devoted family men carefully seeing to it that their children will never be able to afford college or proper health care; of working-class guys in Midwestern cities cheering as they deliver up a landslide for a candidate whose policies will end their way of life.[80]

While Frank aptly recognizes that what is going on is a class war, he makes little attempt to understand "credulous Kansas," duped by a business elite that may "talk Christ, but they walk corporate."[81]

Such analyses only serve to protect the reform-minded elite from the need for a frank self-assessment. This returns us to the analogy of family therapy, premised on the idea that when relationships go awry, the best approach is not to blame one family member but to change the family dynamic.[82] To improve a relationship typically both sides need to change. Family therapy requires each family member to consider what the problem looks like from the others' points of view. This approach requires the elite to learn more about what the world looks like from the viewpoint of the Missing Middle. Discarding Marxian analyses from 30,000 feet, we need to come down to learn enough about working-class life to end decades of casual insults. It is not a matter of objective truth that workers' religion is uncool, their desire for certainty pathetic, their taste excruciating. Their beliefs and lifestyles make as much sense in their context as our folkways do in ours. Our understated clothes, educational travel, and our teeny tiny portions of food—all are ways that those of us in the upper-middle class enact our higher class status for all to see.

They get the message. They sense the attitude reflected in decades of condescending studies that present the working class as fundamentally irrational, beginning with Seymour Martin Lipset's highly influential 1959 article on "working-class authoritarianism," which analyzed class location as a personality disorder. They see that we think they are dumb, as when the wildly popular *Freakonomics* casually asserts again and again that upper-middle-class people are more intelligent than the working class. They see that we think they are ignorant and pathetic, sometimes endearingly so. That is clear just from watching the longest-running television show in the

United States, *The Simpsons* (many of whose writers are known to be Harvard graduates). They know we see their folkways as irrational—all they have to do is to listen to an American whose political ear has virtually perfect pitch. If someone as astute as Barack Obama can make the arugula mistake, it is because the upper-middle-class culture he now inhabits remains sublimely clueless about the ways their everyday "truths" embed un-self-conscious class affronts.[83]

Obama has learned quickly. But his gaffes, and those of a long string of Democratic candidates since 1970, show that Democrats need to do something much deeper than re-label our chosen positions on abortion, gay rights, and so forth as "family values." We need to take several steps. The first is to institute the same kind of taboo against insulting white workers as now exists against using racial innuendo and insults. The second step is to accept the fact that class is a key axis of social disadvantage in American life and to learn more about life in the Missing Middle, so that we do not inadvertently offend potential allies by signaling that we are clueless about our class privilege. The third step is to identify aspects of non-elite culture that offer useful insights for the upper-middle class. (I have suggested the norms of work devotion and concerted cultivation, but no doubt there are others.)[84]

This is not to say that the change needs to come from only one direction. No doubt some Americans in the Missing Middle are guilty of painting upper-middle-class Americans as unpatriotic, immoral, and more. But the question is whether progressives want to insist on an apology before they begin working to change a cultural dynamic that has had disastrous political consequences. To me, the choice seems clear. Upper-middle-class progressives aptly addressed and incorporated issues of racial privilege; they should follow the same path with respect to class. The literature on white privilege shows how one can listen sensitively to the complaints of a less privileged group without insisting that they stop hurting one's feelings first.[85]

These simple steps are enough to begin to shift the poisonous political dynamic of the last forty years to a certain extent—how much we will not know until we begin the process. But we need to begin now. This entails being more willing to allow for symbolic expressions of mutual respect. Consider the flap surrounding Obama's choice of the fundamentalist preacher Reverend Rick Warren to play a key role in the Inauguration. That decision strikes me as entirely appropriate. With it, Obama signaled his willingness to engage with political opponents, who, like Warren, take risks within their own community to seek common ground. And it signals that we can respect the integrity of people who disagree with us. Note that

Obama did not propose to give Warren a policymaking role; he just asked him to say a prayer designed to bring us all together. Once the reform-minded elite start treating people who think differently with respect and begin looking for bridges to build, some of the rigid political assumptions that have hobbled real reform since 1970 will soften and, perhaps over time, disappear. It is time to take up this challenge.

Conclusion: Sarah Palin as Formula and Fantasy

NOT MANY PROGRESSIVES are crazy about Sarah Palin. Fewer feminists are. I, however, love watching Sarah Palin make the moves. I love it for the same reason I loved watching the Portland Trailblazers the only time I attended a pro basketball game. When someone is absolutely the best at what they do, a certain beauty emerges, even if the underlying activity is not to one's taste.

Palin understands just how to manipulate gender and class to tap into America's anxieties and send reassuring messages to a troubled nation. So I was determined to read her new memoir, *Going Rogue*, but equally determined not to buy it. I was on the waiting list at my local public library for weeks. Recently, I finally broke down and ordered a second-hand copy, and all I can say is—wow. It is almost as if she wrote her memoir to illustrate the themes of this book.

"Dedicated to all Patriots who share my love of the United States of America": Palin lets you know right away that she sides with Americans who feel empowered and validated by patriotism, rather than those pointy-headed liberals who do not love our country. With similar subtlety, she starts hammering in family values on page one, mentioning her disabled son, of course. Her dad was a "dedicated, family-oriented father." She and her husband, Todd, wanted children immediately when they got married—lots of them—and acted on their family values: she had been pregnant three times by the time her father was fifty-one. This lets you know that she sides with red America, whose families tend to have babies much earlier than do those of blue America.[1]

Palin is equally in sync when it comes to religion. Her mother, born Catholic—like the blue-collar voters of old—discovered charismatic fundamentalism, like the working-class Republican base today. Having played the right notes on patriotism, family values, and religion, Palin heads for another cherished working-class theme: the importance of hard work. "My siblings and I were baptized together in Big Lake's freezing, pristine waters by Pastor Paul Riley." Her mother, "the hardest-working housewife . . . worked tirelessly." "Growing up, there was always work to be done: canning, picking, cleaning, and stacking, stacking, stacking more firewood, which we burned to heat our home." Todd, Palin's future husband, "didn't come from a wealthy family but from a very hardworking family." Actually, they were upper-middle class, but Palin translates professional-managerial accomplishment (his father was in line to run the local utility company, and his stepmother would become vice president at the phone company) into the working-class religion of hard work. As for Palin's husband himself:

> Todd applied for a full-time job with BP working in the North Slope oil fields. We hoped he'd land the kind of Slope job so many young Alaskans dream of so he could work a schedule that would allow him to enjoy as many of our outdoor passions as possible while still making a good living.

In case you do not get it, Palin refers to him as "a blue-collar husband."[2]

Palin did go to college, but she takes pains to point out that she went to "a more conventional and affordable campus," the University of Idaho. Her beauty-contest past is explained as a way to get money for college. Indeed, her beauty-contest experiences are presented as further evidence of working-class sacrifice and commitment to keeping the world in moral order; they required that she "uncomfortably let my butt be compared to the cheerleaders' butts." Her parents never even allowed the kids to use the word "butt."[3]

One by one, she ticks off the touch points of working-class culture, sending reassuring signals of respect. Even when it comes to food, there are no hoity-toity grilled vegetables: "I love meat. I eat pork chops, thick bacon burgers, and the seared fatty edges of a medium-well-done steak."[4]

One conservative blogger ("a red girl in a blue state") picked up these signals, in discussing "those insider elites both from the right and the left from harvard, yale, and columbia":

> Some of the slings and arrows aimed by the elites at Palin are simply because she's an outsider. By their standards, Palin isn't pedigreed. A sheepskin from the University of Idaho might as well be a GED to them. Unlike Obama, she's

not part of their network, even indirectly. She's a practicing fundamentalist Christian, while many of the elites are secularists. She can use a gun and hunt moose. Many elites revile the 2nd Amendment and their hunting consists of finding the free-range chicken at Whole Foods.[5]

It is a very precise summary of culture wars as class conflict, seconded by a blogger of a very different stripe—a union organizer, Mike Elk, on the website truthout:

> Many white, working class people loved her because here was a politician who finally was working class and ready for a fight. They loved her even more as Ivy League liberals denounced her as basically "white trash." It felt to white, working-class people like liberal elites were calling them "white trash" too.

Elk continues, "Liberals keep playing into the class war trap," by talking down to the white working-class voters. "If I am a poor white guy," he asks, "do I want to go with the polite people (Democrats) who are going to beg for change with their sophisticated intellectual arguments that I don't understand? Or do I want to be with the party (Republicans) that embraces my anger and wants to get out in the streets to tell about how awful this economy is?"[6]

Could Palin be the next president? The deeper point is that Republicans have won elections by mobilizing class resentments. Sarah Palin is perfectly positioned to continue doing so and to continue driving voters to the Republican Party, unless progressives get savvy.

If Palin embodies this book's messages about the central role class conflict plays in American politics, she also is emblematic of my other major theme: briefly put, that the gender revolution has stalled because, while women's lives have changed a lot since 1970s, men and masculinity have changed relatively little.[7]

The dominant themes in American feminism have not helped much, in ways again illustrated by Palin. Palin paints herself as a feminist—of a certain sort. "I didn't subscribe to all the radical mantras of that early feminist era, but reasoned arguments for equal opportunity definitely resonated with me." This resonates because the equality ideal Americans agree on is equal opportunity—not equal results. Palin interprets equal opportunity to be the opportunity to live up to masculine norms to a truly rococo degree. Her return to work when her son was three days old is a classic example of the "anything you can do, I can do better" tradition. Palin looks and acts the part of a desirable woman (former beauty queen, no less) but conforms where it counts to the old-fashioned model of the ideal worker. She literally hid her pregnancy as she went about her job as governor of

Alaska and then took on an all-consuming role in the 2008 campaign at a time when a specials-needs infant and a pregnant teenager clearly needed attention. Her spouse left his job to pick up the pieces—I think. But the fact that Palin does not dwell on the impact of her choices on Todd highlights what Palin's message is *not*: that men need to change in order for women to gain equality.[8]

Palin goes out of her way to celebrate conventional masculinity, as highlighted by the way she describes Todd. "Despite his steel core, Todd was shy and quiet in demeanor, typical of Yupik men, who, unlike some others, don't feel the need to fill up the air around them with words all the time." Todd subscribes to old-time macho not because he is old-fashioned but because he is native Alaskan—try criticizing that. Todd was rarely around to help with the babies, but Palin reassures us that he did his part: "He had always been good about leaving me short love notes before he left."[9]

In Palin's version of feminism, men need not change. In addition, she herself exemplifies the conventional success strategy, which is to dress femme but act the tomboy, taking on masculine personality traits (firm, commanding, competent, confident) and roles (breadwinner). This strategy works for many professional women while they are young and child free. But it does not appeal to many women, and for many others, assimilation opportunities end abruptly once children are born. Palin so captivated many American women, in part, because she sent a reassuring message: I can be a good mother, a hot babe, and a successful leader. Nothing needs to change.

This book seeks to challenge that fantasy. As long as good jobs are designed around men's bodies and men's traditional life patterns, mothers will remain marginalized. As long as mothers remain marginalized, women will not approach equality—and a society that marginalizes its mothers impoverishes its children.

The good news is that many men seek an escape from a rigid and outmoded definition of what it means to be a "real man." Reconstructive feminism proposes not only to tap women's yearning to both care for and support their families; it also seeks to tap similar yearnings in men. The next step for feminism is to signal respect for, and willingness to work with, both tomboys and femmes—and men, to free them all from the effects of rigid and outdated masculine norms.

In the past thirty years, it has become abundantly clear that reshaping the work-family debate will require changes both in the ways we think about gender and in the ways we think about class. These changes hold the promise of a new progressive politics, in personal life, in the workplace, and in the public sphere.[10] This book, in the pragmatist tradition, has tried to sketch a new path by offering cultural criticism grounded in the moral imagination and disciplined by social science.[11] Cultural problems require cultural solutions—which begin with flights of the imagination. Then comes the hard work. Everything looks perfect from far away; it is much harder to come down and develop effective strategies for social, political, organizational—and personal—change.[12] Let's begin.

Notes

Introduction

1. The large literature on framing cannot be thoroughly reviewed here. Influential for me have been Raymond Williams, *Keywords: A Vocabulary of Culture and Society* (1975); Daniel T. Rodgers, *Contested Truths: Keywords in American Politics since Independence* (1987); *Frames of Protest: Social Movements and the Framing Process* (Hank Johnston & John A. Noakes eds., 2005).
2. See generally Janet Gornick & Marcia Meyers, *Families That Work: Policies for Reconciling Parenthood and Employment* (2003).
3. *Id.* at 81–82.
4. *Id.*
5. My focus on masculine norms is not meant to erase the existence of feminine norms. I discuss feminine norms from time to time, but my focus is on masculine norms because it is masculine, not feminine, norms that define the behaviors that are rewarded in desirable jobs.
6. S. F. Berk, *The Gender Factory* (1985); Joan Acker, "Inequality Regimes: Gender, Class, and Race in Organizations," 20 *Gender & Society* 441 (2006).
7. See, e.g., Warren Farrell, *Why Men Earn More: The Startling Truth behind the Pay Gap—and What Women Can Do about It* (2005).
8. See, e.g., Linda Hirshman, *Man up: A Manifesto for Women of the World* (2006).
9. Lisa Belkin, "The Opt-Out Revolution," *New York Times Magazine,* October 26, 2003.
10. Institute for Women's Policy Research, *Still a Man's Labor Market: The Long-Term Earnings Gap* (2004), available at http://www.iwpr.org/pdf/C366_RIB

.pdf (30% less); Christy Spivey, "Time Off at What Price? The Effects of Career Interruptions on Earnings," 59 *Indus. and Lab. Rel. Rev.* 119–140 (2005) (negative effect on wages).

11. E. J. Graff, in a *Washington Post* article reviewing the media's ongoing fascination with opting out, notes that "Belkin's piece was the most e-mailed *Times* article of the year. It drew so many outraged and laudatory letters that the *Times* ran them for four weeks. The article was critiqued on almost every prominent media Web site and online opinion magazine and was debated on countless e-mail discussion groups. Google 'The Opt-Out Revolution,' and you'll get more than 42,000 hits. The article was clearly a resounding marketing success." "The Mommy War Machine," *Washington Post,* April 29, 2007, at B1.

12. *Id.*

13. See Catharine A. MacKinnon, *Feminism Unmodified* 32 (1987).

14. Berk, *supra* note 6; Acker, *supra* note 6.

15. John W. Kingdon, *America the Unusual* 1 (1999).

16. *Id.* at 2.

17. Sheila B. Kammerman, "Europe Advanced While the United States Lagged," in *Unfinished Work: Building Equality and Democracy in an Era of Working Families* 309, 342 (Jody Heymann & Christopher Beem eds., 2005) (also citing works by Gøsta Esping-Anderson).

18. E. P. Hennock, *The Origin of the Welfare State in England and Germany, 1850–1914: Social Policies Compared* (2007); Lisa DiCaprio, *The Origins of the Welfare State: Women, Work, and the French Revolution* (2007).

19. Kammerman, *supra* note 17; Gornick & Meyers, *supra* note 2.

20. *Emergency Economic Stabilization Act of 2008,* 12 U.S.C. §§ 5201–5261 (West 2009). Congress released another $350 billion on January 15, 2009.

21. Joan C. Williams & Holly Cohen Cooper, "The Public Policy of Motherhood," 60 *Journal of Social Issues* 849, 850 (2004).

22. Gornick & Meyers, *supra* note 2 at 113–114.

23. See, e.g., National Partnership for Women and Families, *Where Families Matter: State Progress toward Valuing America's Families* (2007), http://www.nationalpartnership.org/site/DocServer/Final_2006_Round_Up.pdf?docID=2161.

24. Eastern Sociological Society, March 2003 (Philadelphia).

25. Lane Kenworthy et al., "The Democrats and Working Class Whites" 3 (June 10, 2007) (unpublished paper, available at http://www.u.arizona.edu/~lkenwor/thedemocratsandworkingclasswhites.pdf).

26. *Id.* at 1.

27. Tex Sample, *Blue Collar Resistance and the Politics of Jesus* 15 (2006).

28. For a fascinating and important analysis of the differences between black and white male workers, I highly recommend Michèle Lamont's *The Dignity of Working Men* (2000).

29. *Id.* at 17–57.

30. Cf. James T. Kloppenberg, *The Virtues of Liberalism* 82–99 (1998) (discussing John Dewey's views on the relationship between democracy and philosophy).

31. Douglas Stone, Bruce Patton, & Sheila Heen, *Difficult Conversations: How to Discuss What Matters Most* 111–112 (1999).

1. Opt Out or Pushed Out?

1. Lisa Belkin, "The Opt-Out Revolution," *New York Times Magazine*, October 26, 2003.
2. See L. Story, "Many Women at Elite Colleges Set Career Path to Motherhood," *New York Times,* September 20, 2005, at A1 (path to motherhood is "sexy"); J. Gross, "Forget the Career: My Parents Need Me at Home," *New York Times,* November 24, 2005, at A1 (opportunity, not sacrifice).
3. For the controversy following Belkin's article, see E. J. Graff, who, in a *Washington Post* article reviewing the media's ongoing fascination with opting out, notes that "Belkin's piece was the most e-mailed *Times* article of the year. It drew so many outraged and laudatory letters that the *Times* ran them for four weeks. The article was critiqued on almost every prominent media Web site and online opinion magazine and was debated on countless e-mail discussion groups. Google "The Opt-Out Revolution," and you'll get more than 42,000 hits. The article was clearly a resounding marketing success." "The Mommy War Machine," *Washington Post,* April 29, 2007, at B1. For a critique of Warren Farrell's data, see Bonnie Erbe, "Women 'Opting Out' of Work? Not in U.S.," *Deseret News,* March 12, 2006, at A5 (*New York Times'* "bizarre and predetermined effort"); F. Schumer, "The Invisible Mothers of the Suburbs," *New York Times,* May 9, 2004, at 1 (stay-at-home friends came over and cleaned); Warren Farrell, "Exploiting the Gender Gap," *New York Times,* September 5, 2005, at A21 (wage gap attributable to women's choices). Regarding the "shaky data," according to economics professor Barbara R. Bergmann, some of Farrell's statistics were figures "compiled by the Bureau of Labor Statistics, but not published, because they are based on tiny samples, which can give grossly misleading results," such as that "female transit and railroad police make ... 418 percent of what their male counterparts get," a figure Farrell "didn't quote ... because he knows nobody would believe it ... The other numbers that he presents from the same source are dubious as well" (Barbara R. Bergmann, personal communication to Council on Contemporary Families listserv, September 6, 2005); see C. Deutsch, "Behind the Exodus of Executive Women: Boredom," *New York Times,* May 1, 2005, at 3–4 (women leaving work because of boredom, not discrimination); E. Porter, "Stretched to Limit, Women Stall March to Work," *New York Times,* March 2, 2006, at A1 (got equality at work, not equality at home).
4. S. Chira, "One Who Left and Doesn't Look Back," *New York Times,* October 9, 1994, at 3–6; P. O'Crowley, "More Women Are Choosing to Make a Career out of Raising Their Children," Newhouse News Service, April 18, 2002, lifestyle section (Korkodilos).
5. For the prevalence of the opt-out story line, see V. B. Weingarten, "Case History of an Ex-Working Mother," *New York Times,* at SM-54 (1953); M. Bender, "Career Women Discover Satisfactions in the Home," *New York Times,* at 22

(1961); D. Kleiman, "Many Young Women Now Say They'd Pick Family over Career," *New York Times,* December 28, 1980, at A1; Barbara Basler, "Putting a Career on Hold," *New York Times,* December 7, 1986, at 152; Brenda Lane Richardson, "Professional Women Do Go Home Again," *New York Times,* April 20, 1988, at C1; T. Lewin, "Ideas and Trends: For Some Two-Paycheck Families, the Economics Don't Add Up," *New York Times,* April 21, 1991, at D1; Chira, *supra* note 4 (McCormick); B. Delatiner, "Once Employed, Now Discussing Problems of Coping at Home," *New York Times,* at 13L1–10 (1996); D. Bailer, "Women Leaving Medicine for Home," *New York Times,* September 21, 1997, at 13CN-12; T. Lewin, "More Mothers of Babies under 1 Are Staying Home," *New York Times,* October 19, 2001, at A14. *Time* and *Newsweek* also have featured cover stories on the opt-out trend in recent years. See, e.g., C. Wallis, "The Case for Staying Home: Caught between the Pressures of the Workplace and the Demands of Being a Mom, More Women Are Sticking with the Kids," 163 *Time* 50 (2004); M. Brenner, "Not Their Mothers' Choices," 138 *Newsweek* 48–49 (2001). For a report on the predominance of the opt-out narrative over other narratives, see Joan C. Williams, Jessica Manvell, and Stephanie Bornstein, "'Opt Out' or Pushed Out? How the Press Covers Work/Family Conflict—the Untold Story of Why Women Leave the Workforce," 5–6, San Francisco: University of California Hastings College of the Law, Center for WorkLife Law (2006), http://www.worklifelaw.org/pubs/OptOutPushedOut.pdf [hereinafter Williams et al., "'Opt Out' or Pushed Out?"].

6. Kleiman, *supra* note 5; M. Gardner, "Mothers Who Choose to Stay Home," *Christian Science Monitor,* November 14, 2001, Features, Homefront, 13.

7. Cecilia L. Ridgeway, "Gender, Status, and Leadership," 57 *J. Soc. Issues* 637, 639–641 (2001).

8. Kathleen E. Christensen, "Foreword," in *Work, Family, Health, and Well-Being,* ix (S. Bianchi, L. Casper, & R. Berkowitz King eds. 2005) (workplace-workforce mismatch).

9. See Heather Boushey, *Are Women Opting Out? Debunking the Myth,* Center for Economic and Policy Research (2005).

10. Claudia Goldin, "The Long Road to the Fast Track: Career and Family," 596 *Annals of the Am. Acad. of Pol. and Soc. Sci.* 26, 32 (2004).

11. Christine Percheski, "Opting Out? Cohort Differences in Professional Women's Employment Rates from 1960 to 2005," 73 *Am. Soc. Rev.* 510 (2008) ("child penalty"); Marin Clarkberg & Stacey S. Merola, "Competing Clocks: Work and Leisure," in *It's about Time: Couples and Careers* 41 (Phyllis Moen ed., 2003) (hours similar); Joan C. Williams, "Want Equality? Die Childless at Thirty," 27 *Women's Rights L. Rep.* 3 (2006) (similar wages).

12. Social scientists consistently find that nonemployed women, as a group, are more depressed than employed women. See Maureen Perry-Jenkins, Rena Repetti, & Ann Crouter, "Work and Family in the 1990s," 62 *J. of Marriage and the Family* 27 (2000) (reviewing the literature).

13. See B. Torpy, "Paths to Power: Women Today—Full-Time Mothers Trade Careers for Kids," *Atlanta Journal-Constitution,* April 8, 2003, at F1 (walking a

delicate balance); M. Lee, "Less Salary, More Benefits: Mothers Forgo Pay-checks to Care for Families," *Dayton Daily News,* January 23, 2005, at A1 ("you get lonely"); S. Pesmen, "At-Home Moms: New Minority Defends Old-Style Parenting Role," *Crain's Chicago Business,* April 28, 1996, at Section: Options, 73 ("I felt depressed"); D. White, "Home Is Where the Job Is: Work-ing Women Find Full-Time Mothering Creates Whole New Set of Challenges," *The Commercial Appeal,* March 22, 1998, at A2 ("I was at my wit's end"); S. Evans, "Mothers Making Themselves More at Home: Many Women Forgo Return to Working World Despite Pressures," *Washington Post,* October 2, 1989, at A1 (snubbed at dinner parties); and K. Miller, "Career Women Come Home: Mothers Find Rewards, Risks in Decision to Stay at Home," *Star Tri-bune,* May 31, 1994, at E1 (Minnesota women).

14. See Leslie Bennetts, *The Feminine Mistake: Are We Giving Up Too Much?* 52 (2007).

15. See, e.g., Susan T. Fiske et al., "A Model of (Often Mixed) Stereotype Content: Competence and Warmth Respectively Follow from Perceived Status and Competition," 82 J. *Personality & Soc. Psychol.* 878, 885–888 (2002) [herein-after Fiske et al., "A Model of (Often Mixed) Stereotype Content"]; Thomas Eckes, "Paternalistic and Envious Gender Prejudice: Testing Predictions from the Stereotype Content Model," 47 *Sex Roles* 99, 110 (2002) (housewives lumped alongside most stigmatized groups in economy); Amy Scheibe, *What Do You Do All Day?* (2006); Loretta Kaufman and Mary Quigley, *And What Do You Do? When Women Choose to Stay Home* (2000); Glenna Matthews, *"Just a Housewife": The Rise and Fall of Domesticity in America* (1987); Amy Richards, *Opting In: Having a Child without Losing Yourself* (2008); Joan K. Peters, *Not Your Mother's Life: Changing the Rules of Work, Love, and Family* (2001).

16. R. Stovsky, "Goodbye, Superwoman! Meet the Sequencers," *St. Louis Post-Dispatch,* January 20, 1991, at 8.

17. See Nina Darton, "Women and Stress on Job and at Home," *New York Times,* August 8, 1985, at C1 (higher incidence of depression among housewives); Pamela Stone, *Opting Out? Why Women Really Quit Careers and Head Home* (2007) [hereinafter Stone, *Opting Out?*] (women wish for better choices); Ben-netts, *supra* note 14 at 194–198 (higher levels of depression); Alice H. Eagly & Linda L. Carli, *Through the Labyrinth* 57 (2007) [hereinafter Eagly & Carli] (it's ego, too).

18. Percheski, *supra* note 11, table 1, at 507 (3.7% of American women); United States Department of Labor, Women's Bureau, *Women in the Labor Force in 2005* (2005) (27% American women hold blue-collar jobs, which include ser-vice occupations; production, transportation, and material moving occupa-tions; and natural resources, construction, and maintenance occupations).

19. Daphne Spain & Suzanne M. Bianchi, *Balancing Act: Motherhood, Marriage, and Employment among American Women* 184–185 (1996) (Latinas have lower employment levels); Maureen Perry-Jenkins & Amy Claxton, "Feminist Visions for Rethinking Work and Family Connections," unpublished grant proposal (on file with author) (blacks have lower work-family conflict).

20. Joan C. Williams & Heather Boushey, *The Three Faces of Work-Family Conflict: The Poor, the Professionals and the Missing Middle,* at 6–7, Table 1 & Figure 2, Report of the Center for American Progress and the Center for WorkLife Law, University of California, Hastings College of the Law (2010), available at http://www.worklifelaw.org/pubs/ThreeFacesofWork-FamilyConflict .pdf. In this report, the bottom 30% of Americans are categorized as low-income and the top 13% as professional-managerial, with Americans in the middle categorized as middle income.

21. D. A. Cotter, J. M. Hermsen, & R. Vanneman, *Gender Inequality at Work,* a volume in the series *The American People: Census 2000,* at 80 (2004) (more highly educated); Percheski, *supra* note 11 at 505–506 (55% professional women employed full-time year-round).

22. P. N. Cohen & S. M. Bianchi, "Marriage, Children, and Women's Employment: What Do We Know?" 122 *Monthly Labor Rev.* 22–31 (1999) (effect of educational level increased); Janet C. Gornick & Marcia K. Meyers, *Families That Work: Policies for Reconciling Parenthood and Employment* Table 2.3 at 47 (2003) (average hours work per week by educational level).

23. See Story, *supra* note 2 (for expectation of Ivy League women to opt out); A. Reed, "Career Women Taking 'Off-Ramp'; Temporary Leave from Jobs a Trend," *Ventura County Star,* September 5, 2005, at Main News-1 (63% of women stay in workforce).

24. Lisa Dodson et al., *Keeping Jobs and Raising Families in Low Income America: It Just Doesn't Work* (2002) (unfair household labor standard).

25. For reactions to Hekker's op-ed, see Carolyn & Philip Cowan, "Men's Involvement in Parenthood: Identifying the Antecedents and Understand the Barriers," in *Men's Transitions to Parenthood: Longitudinal Studies of Early Family Experience* 145–174 (P. W. Berman & F. A. Pederson eds.) (1987); Carolyn Cowan & Philip Cowan, *When Partners Become Parents: The Big Life Change for Couples* (1992); J. Belsky & E. Pensky, "Marital Change across the Transition to Parenthood," 12 *Marriage and Family Rev.* 133–153 (1988); Myra H. Strober & Agnes Miling Kaneko Chan, "Husbands, Wives and Housework: Graduates of Stanford and Tokyo Universities," 4 *Feminist Economics* 97–108 (1998); L. Belkin, "When Mom and Dad Share It All," *New York Times Magazine,* June 15, 2008, at 47 (wives more satisfied); T. M. Hekker, "The Satisfactions of Housewifery and Motherhood in 'an Age of Do-Your-Own-Thing,'" *New York Times,* December 20, 1977, at 35 (considered ignorant).

26. Temy Martin Hekker, "Paradise Lost (Domestic Division)," *New York Times,* January 1, 2006, at 9.9 (defending importance; "canceled"; job training at age 67); Joan C. Williams, *Unbending Gender: Why Family and Work Conflict and What to Do about It,* 122 (2000) [hereinafter Williams, *Unbending Gender*] (alimony awards low, temporary); Steven J. Haider, Alison Jacknowitz, & Robert F. Schoeni, *The Economic Status of Elderly Divorced Women,* Michigan Retirement Research Center, May 2003, at 1, available at http://www.mrrc .isr.umich.edu/publications/conference/pdf/HaiderShoeni_0208.pdf (divorced elderly women nearly five times as likely to live in poverty as elderly married women).

27. Reports examining gender bias in the courts have chronicled decisions in the Ninth Circuit as well as in the states of Missouri, Illinois, Maryland, and Washington (e.g., the Washington State Task Force on Gender and Justice in the Courts' 1989 report, "Gender and Justice in the Courts"); Hekker, *supra* note 26 (greater self-sufficiency).

28. For the portrayal by the press, see J. B. Quinn, "Prosperity Means Choice for Mothers," *Pittsburgh Post-Gazette,* August 7, 2000, at B9 (investing in husbands' careers); Lee, *supra* note 13 ("I always knew"); M. Lee & K. McCall, "More Miami Valley Women Work outside Home, Census Says; but Wealthy Areas such as Springboro Buck the Trend," *Dayton Daily News,* August 11, 2002, at A1 (some sense of values); J. Ernest, "Modern Moms Make Tough Choices," *Plain Dealer,* May 9, 1999, at K7 ("I want to be a part"); H. Auer, "Motherland; More Women Are Swearing Their Allegiances to Staying Home with the Kids, Even if It's Just Temporary," *Buffalo News,* July 21, 2003, at A7 (mother stayed at home); P. Stone & M. Lovejoy, "Fast-Track Women and the 'Choice' to Stay Home," 596 *Annals of the Am.Acad. of Pol. and Soc. Sci.* 62–83 (2004) (16%).

29. S. Bianchi, M. Milkie, L. C. Sayer, & J. P. Robinson, "Is Anyone Doing the Housework? Trends in the Gender Division of Household Labor," 79 *Social Forces* 191–234 (2000) (86% as much time with children, 82% as much child care); Eagly & Carli, *supra* note 17, at 24, 54 (only five hours a week more).

30. Howard Chudacoff, *Children at Play: An American History* 181, 207 (2007) (safeguard, enrich, and entertain; adult-created activities); Annette Lareau, *Unequal Childhoods* 238, 61, 241–242, 39 (2003) [hereinafter Lareau, *Unequal Childhoods*] (spontaneous play; hovered over them; perform in public; activities replicate workplace); see Paul Willis, *Learning to Labor: How Working Class Kids Get Working Class Jobs* (1981) (children learning to labor).

31. See Eagly & Carli, *supra* note 17 at 53, 54 (employed mothers' time interacting with children); W. Jean Yeung, John F. Sandberg, Pamela Davis-Kean, & Sandra Hofferth, "Children's Time with Fathers in Intact Families," 63 *Journal of Marriage and the Family* 136, 124, 145 (2001) (mothers spend more time on children's activities).

32. For sources on separate spheres, see Nancy Cott, *The Bonds of Womanhood* (1977); Jeanne Boydston, *Home and Work* (1990); Joan C. Williams, "Gender Wars: Selfless Mothers in the Republic of Choice," 66 *N.Y.U. L. Rev.* 1559 (1991).

33. Belkin, *supra* note 1 (nineteenth-century version of separate spheres).

34. Garey Ramey & Valerie A. Ramey, *The Rug Rat Race,* National Bureau of Economic Research Series, Working Paper 15284, available at http://www.aeaweb.org/annual_mtg_papers/2008/2008_401.pdf; *id.* at 1 (increase in child care in the mid-1990s for college educated parents); *id.* at 11 (transportation); *id.* at 3 (differences between U.S. and Canada college prestige); *id.* at 21 (the value of after-school resumes).

35. For intensive mothering, see, e.g., Judith Warner, *Perfect Madness: Motherhood in the Age of Anxiety* (2006); Alvin Rosenfeld and Nicole Wise, *The Over-Scheduled Child: Avoiding the Hyper-Parenting Trap* (2001); William

Crain, *Reclaiming Childhood: Letting Children Be Children in Our Achievement-Oriented Society* (2003); Carl Honoré, *Under Pressure: Rescuing Our Children from the Culture of Hyper-Parenting* (2009). William Celis, "Schools Crack down on Academic Overload," *Boston Globe,* October 30, 2005, available at http://www.boston.com/news/education/k_12/articles/2005/10/30/schools_crack_down_on_academic_overload/(academic overload in high schools).

36. K. S. Peterson, "Gen X Moms Have It Their Way," *USA Today,* May 7, 2003, at D1 (Gen X moms more realistic); Story, *supra* note 2 (women turning realistic).

37. J. B. Quinn, "Prosperity Means Choice for Mothers," *Pittsburgh Post-Gazette,* August 7, 2000, at B9 (no dependency worries); M. Kissinger, "Just Call Them Mom; More Women Are Leaving the Office Behind," *Milwaukee Journal Sentinel,* March 29, 1998, at Lifestyle-1 (skills will not leave); E. Bryce, "Staying at Home: Women Choose Womanhood as a Full-Time Career," *Sarasota Herald-Tribune,* May 6, 2004, at H1; Belkin, *supra* note 1 (degree insurance policy); D. Carr-Elsing, "Stay-at-Home Parents: Bucking the 'Do-It-All' Trend Can Be Hard on Self-Esteem," *Capital Times,* May 8, 1997, at F1 ("I know women who have returned"); C. L. Reed, "Moms Stand up to the Boss: Today's Mothers and Fathers Insist on Flexible Schedules, as Corporations Fear Talent Drain," *Chicago Sun-Times,* October 11, 2004, in News-24 ("I can always come back").

38. S. J. Rose & H. I. Hartmann, *Still a Man's Labor Market: The Long-Term Earnings Gap,* Institute for Women's Policy Research (2004), available at http://www.iwpr.org/pdf/C366_RIB.pdf (30% less); Christy Spivey, "Time off at What Price? The Effects of Career Interruptions on Earnings," 59 *Indus. and Lab. Rel. Rev.* 119–140 (2005) (negative effect on wages).

39. A. Reed, *supra* note 23, at 1 (talented women take off-ramps); S. A. Hewlett, C. B. Luce, P. Shiller, & S. Southwell, *The Hidden Brain Drain: Off-Ramps and On-Ramps in Women's Careers,* Center for Work-Life Policy/Harvard Business Review Research Report no. 9491 at 42 (2005) (loss of lifetime wages).

40. M. McGrath, M. Driscoll, & M. Gross, *Back in the Game: Returning to Business after a Hiatus: Experiences and Recommendations for Women, Employers and Universities,* Wharton Center for Leadership and Change and Forte Foundation at 9, 10, 8, 15, 12 (50% frustrated, 18% depressed; no work experience at all; lower position; "less than zero"; functional roles changed); S. Nance-Nash, "Those Who Step out of Careers Face Tough Re-Entry," *Women's eNews,* October 18, 2001 (hits a wall).

41. A. Nakao, "More Mothers Staying at Home: Rate of Working Moms Drops for First Time since Data Collection Began," *San Francisco Chronicle,* October 18, 2001, at A1 (tighten belts); P. B. Librach, "For Kids' Sake: Women Weigh Payoffs," *St. Louis Post-Dispatch,* July 31, 1989, at News-1 (giving up vacations, cars); Carr-Elsing, *supra* note 37 (sacrifices to be made); A. Veciana-Suarez, "Bringing up Baby on One Paycheck; Compromise, Reducing Lifestyle Crucial," *The Times Union,* June 17, 1994, at C4 (babysitter, summer camp gone).

42. Rose & Hartmann, *supra* note 38, at 2 (38% of wages of men); Gornick & Meyers, *supra* note 21, Figure 3.7 at 68 (67 cents); United States Census Bureau, *Current Population Survey, 2005 Annual Social and Economic Supplement* (2005) (two out of three of elderly poor are women); A. H. Munnell, *Why Are So Many Older Women Poor? Just the Facts: On Retirement Issues*, Center for Retirement Research at 10 (April 2004) (only 32% of retired women have pensions; only 41% of men leave pensions to wives upon death).

43. Williams et al., "'Opt Out' or Pushed Out?" *supra* note 5 at 10 (overall tone of pulls); Stone & Lovejoy, *supra* note 28 at 68 (86% of women cited work-related reasons).

44. P. Zahn, *Paula Zahn NOW* [Television series], November 16, 2001, Atlanta, GA: Cable News Network.

45. See Deborah Swiss and Judith Walker, *Women and the Work/Family Dilemma* (1993).

46. Eagly& Carli, *supra* note 17 at 142.

47. C. L. Reed, *supra* note 37.

48. M. D. Vesperi, "Stay-at-Home Moms: Back to the '50s," *St. Petersburg Times*, August 30, 1987, at D1.

49. E-mail from Anne Nolan, Operations and Customer Support Manager, WFC Resources, Inc., to Joan Williams, Distinguished Professor of Law, 1066 Foundation Chair and Director, Center for WorkLife Law (February 9, 2009) (on file with the author).

50. Shelley Correll, Stephen Benard, & In Paik, "Getting a Job: Is There a Motherhood Penalty?" 112 *Am. J. of Soc.* 1316 (2007).

51. See Cynthia Thomas Calvert, *Family Responsibilities Discrimination: Litigation Update 2010*, San Francisco: University of California Hastings College of the Law, Center for WorkLife Law (2010) available at http://www.worklifelaw .org/pubs/FRDupdate.pdf; Joan Williams & Cynthia Thomas Calvert, *WorkLife Law's Guide to Family Responsibilities Discrimination*. San Francisco: University of California Hastings College of the Law, Center for WorkLife Law (2006).

52. See *Walsh v. National Computer Systems, Inc.*, at 1155 (2003) (potential to become pregnant); Bootie Cosgrove-Mather, *Fighting Maternal Discrimination*, CBS Evening News, November 13, 2002, available at http://www.cbsnews .com/stories/2002/11/13/eveningnews/main529258.shtml.

53. See *Burlington Northern & Santa Fe Railway v. White*, at 2416 (2006).

54. C. Stocker, "Career Moms: They've Just Said No to Juggling Job and Family," *Boston Globe*, June 26, 1991, in Living-77 (do not want to be home full-time); M. Osborn, "Women Change Career Paths: More Choose to Stay Home with Children," *USA Today*, May 10, 1991, at B1 (felt forced to quit); S. Klemens, "Sometimes a Career Must Be Put Aside: The New Parents," *Washington Post*, August 27, 1984, at A21 (gave up lucrative partnership).

55. Stone, *Opting Out? supra* note 17 at 83 (all-or-nothing workplace); Belkin, *supra* note 1 (Sally Sears).

56. See Gornick and Meyers, *supra* note 21 at 62 (dual earners' work hours); K. Lynn, "She's the Boss," NorthJersey.com, January 16, 2006 (family and business

lives); D. Vincent, "Staying Home with Kids: Less Money, but More Satisfying for Some Women," *The Union Leader,* December 31, 1995, at F1 (dinner with family).

57. Percheski, *supra* note 11 at 487, 506 (highly trained mothers); *Current Population Survey: 2006 March Supplement,* United States Census Bureau (2006). Data generated by Mary C. Still for the Center for WorkLife Law, using the DataFerret. Files generated April 25, 2006, at http://dataferret.census.gov/ TheDataWeb/index.htm (5% of mothers);Williams & Boushey, *supra* note 20, at 7–8.

58. See Williams & Boushey, *supra* note 20, Table 3 at 8; A. Hochschild & A. Machung, *The Second Shift: Working Parents and the Revolution at Home* (1989).

59. Jerry A. Jacobs & Kathleen Gerson, *The Time Divide: Work, Family, and Gender Inequality* 47 (2004) (time squeeze); Clarkberg & Merola, *supra* note 11, at 39; Phyllis Moen et al., "Success," in *It's about Time: Couples and Careers* 143 (Phyllis Moen ed. 2003)(this study is based on a sample in which the upper-middle class predominated: 66% of the women and 69% of the men were professionals);Phyllis Moen et al., "Methodological Notes on *The Cornell Couples and Careers Study,*" in *It's about Time: Couples and Careers* 339 (Phyllis Moen ed., 2003) (in all the couples in the sample, at least one partner had attended college; this sample is not a perfect proxy for my definition of professionals: I define professionals as having graduated from college).

60. See Stone, *Opting Out?, supra* note 17 at 78.

61. Youngjoo Cha, "Reinforcing Separate Spheres: The Effect of Spousal Overwork on Men's and Women's Employment in Dual-Earner Households" 75 *Am. Soc. Rev.* 318 (2010)(husband's hours and likelihood of wife quitting); Stone, *Opting Out? supra* note 17 at 62 (60% of women cite husband); Phyllis Moen et al., "Success," in *It's about Time: Couples and Careers* 150 (Phyllis Moen ed., 2003).

62. See Clarkberg & Merola, *supra* note 11 at 23, 20 (common family pattern; 40% dual-career professionals); Moen et al., *supra* note 61 at 144 (lower levels of satisfaction). For the lack of coverage, see W. Jean Yeung, John F. Sandberg, Pamela Davis-Kean, & Sandra Hofferth, "Children's Time with Fathers in Intact Families," 63 *J. of Marriage and the Family* 136, 138, 153 (2001); Cowan & Cowan, *When Partners Become Parents, supra* note 25; Charlotte J. Patterson, Erin L. Sutfin, & Megan Fulcher, "Division of Labor among Lesbian and Heterosexual Parenting Couples: Correlates of Specialized versus Shared Patterns," 11 *J. of Adult Dev.* 179, 186 (2004) (men's work hours spiral up; household work spirals down); Stone, *Opting Out? supra* note 17.

63. Margaret Wise Brown, *Goodnight Moon* (1947). Fathers' lack of involvement in children's lives has been extensively documented. See Annette Lareau, "My Wife Can Tell Me Who I Know: Methodological and Conceptual Problems in Studying Fathers," in *Families at Work: Expanding the Bounds* 52 (Naomi Gerstel et al. eds., 2002) (citing eight studies).

64. Stone & Lovejoy, *supra* note 28 at 75 (husbands key influence), and Stone, *Opting Out? supra* note 17 at 65 (noting that the "unspoken backdrop against which these women's decisions to quit are negotiated and decided" is that

men's careers take precedence); Cha, *supra* note 61 at 315 (40% more likely); Belkin, *supra* note 25 at 44 (wives do three times as much housework).

65. Stone & Lovejoy, *supra* note 28 at 76.

66. Joan Williams, *Unbending Gender, supra* note 26 at 27 (percentage of women who felt that their husbands should be the primary providers); Nicholas W. Townsend, *The Package Deal: Marriage, Work, and Fatherhood in Men's Lives* 53 (2002) (good father is a good provider); Stone, *Opting Out? supra* note 17 at 86 (flexibility not a reality); Candace West and Don H. Zimmerman, "Doing Gender," 1 *Gender & Society* 121–151 (1987) (workplaces are key sites for "doing gender").

67. Michèle Lamont, *The Dignity of Working Men* 116 (2000) (doubly sacred); Mary Blair-Loy, *Competing Devotions: Career and Family among Women Executives* (2003) (devotion to work).

68. Heather Boushey, "The New Breadwinners," in *The Shriver Report: A Women's Nation Changes Everything* 33 (2009); Gornick & Meyers, *supra* note 21 at 68–69 (women contribute 28% of family income). See Jack Shafer, "Weasel-Words Rip My Flesh! Spotting a Bogus Trend Story on Page One of Today's *New York Times*," *Slate*, September 20, 2005; Reyhan Harmanci, "Women's Pages: Next Time You Read about 'What Women Want,' Check the Research— It's Likely to Be Flimsy," *San Francisco Chronicle*, January 4, 2006, at H1 (stories seep into culture).

69. Williams et al., "'Opt Out' or Pushed Out? *supra* note 5 at 31 (one in four women ages 25–44 out of workforce); "A Guide to Womenomics," *The Economist*, April 12, 2006 (women's underemployment is an important economic issue).

70. "A Guide to Womenomics," *supra* note 69.

71. See J. Heymann, "We Can Afford to Give Parents a Break," *Washington Post*, May 14, 2006, B7 (one of four countries); National Partnership for Women and Families, *Paid Leave*, available at http://www.nationalpartnership.org/Default.aspx?tabid=39.

72. See Gornick & Meyers, *supra* note 21. The twelve countries are the United States, the United Kingdom, Canada, Belgium, Germany, the Netherlands, Luxemburg, France, Finland, Denmark, Sweden, and Norway (study of work-family policies in twelve industrialized countries).

73. *Id.* at 130–132 (leave for family reasons), 128, Figure 5.2 (United States an outlier), 127–130 (alternative child care).

74. Cal. Lab. Code §233 (options for use of accrued sick leave); Stocker, *supra* note 54 (sick child in the morning); Cal. Labor Code §§ 230.7, 230.8 (participate in activities at children's school); Cal. Senate Bill No. 1661 (2002) (family leave insurance); Cal. Unemp. Ins. Code §2626. (The state's disability insurance program provides additional partial pay benefits for unpaid time off due to one's own illness or pregnancy disability.)

75. E-mail from Stephen Brand, Associate Professor (Research), NCPE-SP, University of Rhode Island, to Joan Williams, Distinguished Professor of Law, 1066 Foundation Chair and Director, Center for WorkLife Law (September 12, 2006) (on file with the author).

76. See Gornick & Meyers, *supra* note 21 at 239 (impact of paid leave); e-mail from Stephen Brand, *supra* note 75 (University of Rhode Island parental leave); Gornick & Meyers, *supra* note 21 at 242.

77. Spain & Bianchi, *supra* note 19, at 177 (1996) (citing studies).

78. Pre-K Now, "Fact Sheet: Pre-K across the Country," available at http://www .preknow.org/advocate/factsheets/snapshot.cfm (programs in Georgia, Florida, etc.); Gornick & Meyers, *supra* note 21 (Belgium and France); Sam Dillon, "Obama Stirring Great Hope for Early Education," *New York Times,* December 17, 2008, at A1.

79. See Gornick & Meyers, *supra* note 21 at 196 (twenty- to twenty-five-hour gap and estimated 39 million children), 197 (increase in summer); Afterschool Alliance, *Impossible Choices: How States Are Addressing the Federal Failure to Fully Fund Afterschool Programs* (2004), available at http://www.afterschool alliance.org/documents/Impossible_choices.pdf (more children would participate if local quality programs existed).

80. See Gornick & Meyers, *supra* note 21, at 198, 206–218 (few infants in child care), Table 7.1 (child care provisions in other countries).

81. *Id.* at 214–215, Table 7.5 (U.S. and European family income to child care).

82. *Id.* at 226 (U.S. child care staff turnover), 227 (salaries), 195 (child care center ratings), 196 (care for children under three).

83. Williams et al., "'Opt Out' or Pushed Out?" *supra* note 5 at 31.

84. Sara McLanahan, "Diverging Destinies: How Children Are Faring under the Second Demographic Transition," 41(4) *Demography* 607, 610 (2004).

85. Jody Heyman, *The Widening Gap: Why America's Working Families Are in Jeopardy—and What Can Be Done about It,* at 4 (2000) (70% of U.S. children); National Alliance for Caregiving & AARP, *Family Caregiving in the US, Findings from a National Survey* (1997) (one out of four); Katherine Mack, Lee Thompson, & Robert Friedland, The Center on an Aging Society, Georgetown University, Data Profiles, *Family Caregivers of Older Persons: Adult Children* 2 (May 2001) (more every year); Dan Hurley, "Divorce Rate: It's Not as High as You Think," *New York Times*, April 19, 2005.

86. Gornick & Meyers, *supra* note 21 at 157 (E.U. directive).

87. *Id.* at 180 (vacation time in European countries).

88. Joan Williams and Stephanie Bornstein, "The Evolution of 'FreD': Family Responsibilities Discrimination and Developments in the Law of Stereotyping and Implicit Bias," 59 *Hastings L.J.* 1311–1358 (2008); C. L. Fisk, "Employer-Provided Child Care under Title VII: Toward an Employer's Duty to Accommodate Child Care Responsibilities of Employees," 2 *Berkeley Women's L.J.* 89 (1986); Samuel Bagenstos, "The Structural Turn in Antidiscrimination Law," 94 *Cal. L. Rev.* 1 (2006); Christine Jolls, "Antidiscrimination and Accommodation," 115 *Harv. L. Rev.* 642 (2001).

89. See A. Lisk, "Home Work; Couples Choose between Dual Incomes or Having a Parent at Home with the Kid," *Star-News,* October 27, 2002, at E1, E5.

90. Eyal Press, "Family-Leave Values," *New York Times Magazine,* July 20, 2008, at 36, 38.

91. Belkin, "When Mom and Dad Share It All," *supra* note 25 at 44.

2. One Sick Child Away from Being Fired

1. Ruth Marcus, "The Family as Firing Offense; for Too Many Workers, Emergencies at Home Force Stark Choices," *Washington Post*, May 14, 2006, at B7 (epigraph). © 2006 The Washington Post. All rights reserved. Used by permission and protected by the Copyright Laws of the United States. The printing, copying, redistribution, or retransmission of the Material without express written permission is prohibited.

2. Naomi Gerstel & Dan Clawson, "Union's Responses to Family Concerns," 48 *Social Problems* 284–285 (2001).

3. ATU database: *Chicago Transit Authority,* case no. 97-0166 (Hayes, 1999) (arbitrator reinstated a female bus driver with no loss of seniority but put her on probation and gave her partial back pay, after she was discharged because of absences due to a flat tire, a family funeral, misunderstandings about a vacation day and extra board duty, a suspended driver's license, and time lost spent taking her son to a high school placement test); *Knauf Fiber Glass,* 81 LA 333 (Abrams, 1983) (arbitrator reinstated the grievant without back pay and put her on probation, concluding: "[The grievant] felt deeply about her personal obligations and responsibilities as the unwed mother of three children. While understandably her son and daughters may be of paramount importance to her, her employer can insist that she meet reasonable attendance requirements. The grievant can meet those requirements, keep her job and support her children. If she cannot meet those requirements now and in the future, she will lose her job and her children will suffer as a result. It will require great effort on her part to meet her dual responsibilities, but it certainly is worth the effort."); *Chicago Tribune Co.,* 119 LA 1007 (Nathan, 2003) (arbitrator reinstated the grievant after holding that her oversleeping, which led to her tardiness, was an FMLA-qualified event because it resulted from exhaustion from her responsibilities as primary caregiver for her mother).

4. *Interlake Material Handling Div., Interlake Material Handling Div., Interlake Conveyors Inc.,* 113 LA 1120 (Lalka, 2000) (arbitrator reinstated grievant when he was not allowed to show that he needed to stay home because his asthmatic son was sick); *Boise Cascade Corp., Insulite Div. International,* 77 LA 28 (Fogelberg, 1981) (severely handicapped son); *State of NY, Dept. of Correctional Services,* 89 LA 122 (Handsaker, 1987) (paralyzed stepson); ATU database: *Massachusetts Bay Transportation Authority* (Hodlen, 2001) (diabetic son); *Budget Rent-A-Car Systems,* 115 LA 1745 (Suardi, 2001) (son with heart condition); ATU database: *Chicago Transit Authority,* case no. 99-155 (Patterson, 2001) (child on ventilator); ATU database: *Massachusetts Bay Authority* (Dunn, 2000) (special needs child); *Tenneco Packaging, Burlington Container Plant,* 112 LA 761 (Kessler, 1999) (arbitrator reinstated with full back pay the grievant, a single parent of a mentally handicapped son, who was terminated after twenty-seven years for failing to report to work when her son's caregiver could not work); *Mercer County Association for the Retarded & American Federation of State, County and Municipal Employees AFL-CIO,* 1996 WL 492101 (Hewitt, 1996) (mentally disabled son).

5. Netsy Firestein, *A Job and a Life: Organizing & Bargaining for Work Family Issues: A Union Guide,* Labor Project for Working Families 17 (2005), available

to order at http://www.laborproject.org/bargaining/guide.html (20% caring for a child with special needs); CWA database: *Ameritech,* case no. 4-99-39 (Bell-man, 2001) (arbitrator reinstated a twenty-five-year employee, without back pay, discharged for monitoring her phone to check up on her young children, one of whom was asthmatic); Firestein, *supra* note 5, at 15 (one in ten children aged six to twelve is home alone).

6. United States Department of Labor, Bureau of Labor Statistics, *Union Members Summary,* January 28, 2009, http://www.bls.gov/news/release/union2.nro.htm. In a unionized workplace, when a worker is disciplined or fired, the union may file a grievance on the worker's behalf, arguing that the employer lacked "just cause." If the union and employer's attempts to negotiate a settlement are unsuccessful, the case goes to arbitration. Most arbitrations are not public, but in some cases the decisions are published. This chapter draws on several sources. It uses published cases analyzed in the Center for WorkLife Law's initial report on union arbitrations, *Work/Family Conflict, Union Style,* which was written by Martin H. Malin, Maureen K. Milligan, Mary C. Still, and Joan C. Williams and published on the Web in 2004. It also uses other published arbitrations we found after publication of that initial report and taps databases of unpublished arbitration made available to us through the generosity of three unions: the Communication Workers of America (CWA), the Amalgamated Transit Union (ATU), and the Teamsters (UPS database only). We are currently seeking access to other arbitration databases; please contact the author for more information.

7. Marion Crane, "Feminizing Unions: Challenging the Gendered Structure of Wage Labor," 89 *Mich. L. Rev.* 1155–1156 (1991).

8. Jody Heymann, *The Widening Gap: Why America's Working Families Are in Jeopardy and What Can Be Done about It* 115, Figure 6.1 (2000).

9. AFL-CIO, *Work and Family,* available at http://www.aflcio.org/issues/work family; Heymann, *supra* note 8 at 133 (87% have two weeks or less combined); Maureen Perry-Jenkins, Heather Bourne, & Karen Meteyer, "Work-Family Challenges for Blue-Collar Families," in *The Future of Work in Massachusetts,* 185–204, 191, 193 (Tom Juravich ed., 2007) (70% of working-class parents; "hard to get time off"; 10% of mothers).

10. Francine Deutsch, *Halving It All: How Equally Shared Parenting Works* 172, 186–189 (1999) (wives typically worked shorter hours); Janet C. Gornick & Marcia K. Meyers, *Families That Work: Policies for Reconciling Parenthood and Employment* 63 (2003) (wage penalty is 21%); Corporate Voices for Working Families (WFD Consulting), *Business Impacts of Flexibility: An Imperative for Expansion* 16 (November 2005), available for download from http://www .cvwf.org/ (higher demand for part-time work); Gornick & Meyers, *supra* note 10 at 81 (wish they had more time with family).

11. See, e.g., Jeanne M. Vonhoff & Martin H. Malin, "What a Mess! The FMLA, Collective Bargaining and Attendance Control Plans," 21 *Ill. Pub. Employee Rel. Rep.* 1 (2004).

12. Deutsch, *supra* note 10 at 170 (1999) (at least one parent working nonday shift); Heymann, *supra* note 8 at 48 (evening shift most common alternative work schedule).

13. Julia R. Henly, H. Luke Schaefer, & Elaine Waxman, "Nonstandard Work Schedules: Employer- and Employee-Driven Flexibility in Retail Jobs," 80 *Social Service Rev.* at 609, 610 (December 2006) (citing studies); *ITT Industries, Night Vision Roanoke Plant,* 118 LA 1504 (Cohen, 2003) (arbitrator reinstated grievant after the employer did not allow grievant to revoke her resignation that she had submitted after the employer changed its shift schedules).

14. Heymann, *supra* note 8 at 24–25 (30% had to cut back); *Id.* at 36, 126 (cutbacks more frequent among low-income workers).

15. *Princeton City School District Board of Education,* 101 LA 789 (Paolucci, 1993) (arbitrator held that the personal day should have been granted after grievant was denied leave when her child day care provider became sick).

16. CWA database: *General Telephone Company of Indiana,* case no. 5-80-934 (Walt, 1981) (arbitrator reinstated the grievant who was terminated after not attending an out-of-town training program that began the day she returned from maternity leave).

17. *Social Security Administration, Westminster Teleservice Ctr.,* 93 LA 687 (Feigenbaum, 1989) (arbitrator held that grievant was entitled to emergency annual leave after she was disciplined for being AWOL when her regular babysitting arrangement broke down).

18. Harriet B. Presser, "Toward a 24-Hour Economy," 284 *Science* 1778, 1779 (June 11, 1999).

19. Firestein, *supra* note 5 at 7.

20. Heather Boushey, *Tag Team Parenting,* Washington, DC: Center for Economic and Policy Research 3 (2006) (Boushey concluded that "lower income families simply cannot afford to buy formal childcare" and that "the older a family is, the more likely it is that the spouses have similar schedules"); Heymann, *supra* note 8 at 50 (average price of child care for one-year old); Gornick & Meyers, *supra* note 10 at 53 (only 10% of paid child care is developmentally enriching).

21. *U.S. Steel Corp.,* 95 LA 610 (Das, 1990) (factory worker took off work for child care because wife's employer's absentee policy was stricter, and arbitrator sustained the grievant's suspension for failure to report to mandatory overtime due to child care difficulties); *Central Beverage,* 110 LA 104 (Brunner, 1998) (arbitrator held that unilateral change of grievant's working hours violated the contract); *Jefferson Partners,* 109 LA 335 (Bailey, 1997) (arbitrator reduced a father's discharge to a one-month suspension for refusing to take an assignment because he had to pick up his daughter); *Ashland Oil, Inc.,* 91 LA 1101 (Volz, 1988) (arbitrator reduced a three-day suspension to one day for a carpenter who left job early to pick up his child from day care).

22. CWA database: *Suprenant Cable Corp.,* case no. 1-95-85 (Bornstein, 1995) (arbitrator reinstated grievant without back pay after he was discharged for excessive absenteeism due to caring for his son after his wife left him); *Interlake Material Handling Div., supra* note 4 (arbitrator reinstated grievant when he was not allowed to show that he needed to stay home because his son was sick).

23. *Naval Air Rework Facility*, 86 LA 1129 (Hewitt, 1986) (arbitrator upheld the discharge of grievant who was denied sick leave to care for a child with chicken pox); *Piedmont Airlines Inc.*, 103 LA 751, 753; *Southern Champion Tray Co.*, 96 LA 633 (Nolan, 1991) (arbitrator upheld the discharge of a mechanic whom he faulted for failing to make backup child care arrangements after two warnings from his supervisor that he needed to do so); *Sutter Roseville Medical Center*, 116 LA 621 (Staudohar, 2001) (arbitrator upheld the discharge of a nuclear medicine technician who was charged with insubordination by a new supervisor after refusing to be placed on standby because he lived far away and had to care for his son); *Town of Stratford*, 97 LA 513 (Stewart, 1991) (arbitrator upheld a five-day suspension of a police officer when she failed to report for an "orderback" because she could not without notice find child care).

24. *Simpson v. District of Columbia Office of Human Rights*, 597 A.2d 392 (D.C. Cir. 1991).

25. CWA database: *U.S. West Communications*, case no. 7-95-93 (Rinaldo, 1999) (arbitrator upheld the discharge of seven workers because they were not facing an "immediate, overwhelming threat to safety" and reduced to final warnings the dismissals of nine cases that met the threat-to-safety test); *Ameritech*, *supra* note 5 (employee monitored her phone to check on her asthmatic child); ATU database: *Chicago Transit Authority*, case no. 98-080 (Goldstein, 1997) (arbitrator reinstated without back pay a fourteen-year employee when he failed to report to work because he did not want to leave his children with his pregnant wife after she broke the phone in a fit of rage).

26. Heymann, *supra* note 8 at 73 (routine childhood illness stats); *Naval Air Rework Facility*, *supra* note 23.

27. Family and Medical Leave Act of 1993, Pub. L. No. 103-3, 107 Stat. 6 (codified at 29 U.S.C. Sect. 2601-2654 (1994)); 29 USC § 2612(b)(1), 29 CFR § 25.203(a); Susan J. Lambert & Anna Haley-Lock, "The Organizational Stratification of Opportunities for Work-Life Balance," 7 *Community, Work & Family* 179 (2004); Gornick & Meyers, *supra* note 10, at 114 (10% and 60%); ATU database: *Chicago Transit Authority*, case no. 00-373 (Gundermann, 2001) (employee failed to request FMLA leave in a way the employer could understand); *Budget Rent-A-Car Systems*, *supra* note 4 (some employees failed to provide the necessary medical documentation); *Boise Cascade Corp., Insulite Div. International*, *supra* note 4 (was unclear whether workers considered using FMLA leave).

28. Barbara Schneider & David Stevenson, *The Ambitious Generation: America's Teenagers, Motivated but Directionless* 145 (1999) (parental involvement can build self-esteem); Stanford A. Newman et al., *America's After-School Choice: The Prime Time for Juvenile Crime, or Youth Achievement and Enrichment*, Fight Crime: Invest in Kids, 2–3 (2000), available at http://www.fightcrime .org (active parental involvement can help prevent juvenile crime); ATU database: *Transit Management of Decatur* (Perkovich, 1998) (suicidal daughters); *Chicago Transit Authority*, *supra* note 27 (gang beating); *Greater Cleveland Regional Transit Authority*, 106 LA 807 (Duda, 1996) (arbitrator upheld the

discharge of a brake mechanic who did not request family and medical leave despite being notified that he could do so, did not use the resources of the Employee Assistance Program although he was repeatedly urged to do so, and failed to provide proper documentation for an illness even when given an extra two weeks to accomplish this); and ATU Database: *Regional Transit Authority* (Vernon, 1983) (daughter's drug overdose).

29. *Columbiana County Brd. of Mental Retardation & Disabilities*, 117 LA 13 (Skulina, 2002) (arbitrator upheld the county's decision to pass over grievant, a senior employee, for a position because the junior employee had a better attendance record; grievant had a significant amount of absences due to caring for her injured son); Heymann, *supra* note 8 at 166 (three of four grandmothers and nine of ten grandfathers in labor force); Presser, *supra* note 18 at 1779 (one out of three care-providing grandmothers are in labor force); Harriet B. Presser & Amy G. Cox, "The Work Schedules of Low-Income American Women and Welfare Reform," *Monthly Lab. Rev.* 26 (April 1997) (grandmothers tag team with daughters); *Dept. of Veterans Affairs Medical Ctr.*, 100 LA 233 (Nicholas, 1992) (arbitrator reduced a fourteen-day suspension to five days); *Federal Mogul Corporation*, WL. 2003: 23531172 (Cohen, 2003) (arbitrator reinstated a factory worker after her employer refused to revoke her resignation); *Mercer County Association for the Retarded*, *supra* note 4 (arbitrator upheld a three-day suspension of a residential worker in a home for the mentally handicapped who refused to work overtime because her husband was not at home and she could not leave her own mentally handicapped son alone); U.S. Census Bureau, *Who's Minding the Kids?* Table 2 (Fall 1995, issued October 2000), available at http://www.census.gov/prod/2000pubs/p70-70.pdf (21.7% of preschool-aged children are cared for by a grandparent); U.S. Census Bureau, *Grandparents Living with Grandchildren: 2000*, at 3 (2000, issued October 2003), available at http://www.census.gov/prod/2003pubs/c2kbr-31.pdf (2.4 million grandparents).

30. Heymann, *supra* note 8 at 2 (one in four families take care of elderly relatives); Mary Jo Gibson, American Association of Retired Persons, *Beyond 50.03: A Report to the Nation on Independent Living and Disability* 59 (2003), available at http://research.aarp.org/il/beyond_50_il.html (84% rely on informal arrangements); Firestein, *supra* note 5 at 16 (one in five caregivers provide forty-plus hours per week); *Id.* at 14 (4.3 years); *Sprint/Central Telephone Company of Texas, Inc.*, 117 LA 1321 (Baroni, 2002) (arbitrator upheld the discharge of a customer service representative who had cared for a dying mother because the grievant did not have the skills and temperament to do her job well); Firestein, *supra* note 5 at 14 (57% of working caregivers).

31. Gornick & Meyers, *supra* note 10 at 59 (Americans work longer hours); Mary C. Still, *Litigating the Maternal Wall: U.S. Lawsuits Charging Discrimination against Workers with Family Responsibilities*, Center for WorkLife Law Report, University of California, Hastings College of the Law (2006), available at http://www.worklifelaw.org/pubs/FRDreport.pdf (95% of mothers); Joan C. Williams & Heather Boushey, *The Three Faces of Work-Family Conflict: The Poor, the Professionals and the Missing Middle*, report by the Center for

American Progress and the Center for WorkLife Law, University of California, Hastings College of the Law, Table 3, 7–8 (2010) available at http://www .worklifelaw.org/pubs/ThreeFacesofWork-FamilyConflict.pdf (38% and 23%); Gornick & Meyers, *supra* note 10 at 156–163 (working-class men work forty-two to forty-three hours per week; in interpreting Gornick's statistics, I have defined working class as men with high school but not college degrees).

32. Joan C. Williams, *One Sick Child away from Being Fired: When Opting Out Is Not an Option,* Center for WorkLife Law Report, University of California, Hastings College of the Law (2006), available at http://www.uchastings.edu/ site_files/WLL/onesickchild.pdf.

33. *U.S. Steel Corp.,* 95 LA 610 (Das, 1990) (arbitrator sustained the grievant's suspension for failure to report to mandatory overtime due to child care difficulties).

34. *Tenneco Packaging Burlington Container Plant, supra* note 4 at 765–766.

35. *State of New York, Rochester Psychiatric Ctr.,* 87 LA 725 (Babiskin, 1986) (arbitrator reinstated grievant) (Based on information from the Rochester Psychiatric Center website, available at http://www.omh.state.ny.us/omhweb/ facilities/ropc/facility.htm, MHTA is either "Mental Hygiene Therapy Assistant" or "Mental Health Therapy Aide."); *Id.* at 726, 727; *Rock County, Wisconsin,* 1993 WL 835474 (McAlpin, 1993) (arbitrator sustained the discharge); *Fairmont General Hospital, Inc.,* 2004 WL 3422192 (Miles, 2004) (arbitrator sustained grievant's discharge for refusal to work overtime because grievant's childcare arrangement broke down and she made no effort to make alternative arrangements).

36. CWA database: *GTE California, Inc.,* case no. 11-91-86 (Miller, 1992) (Arbitrator overturned grievant's dismissal because the employee was entitled to leave rather than obeying the supervisor's order and filing a grievance later because her situation was covered by a rule concerning safety. If more than one person wanted to avoid overtime work on a given day, the rule was that they had to agree which of them would not work overtime. If they could not agree, then both had to work overtime.).

37. Gornick & Meyers, *supra* note 10 at 247 (overtime largely masculine phenomenon); *Bryant v. Bell Atlantic Maryland,* 288 F.3d 124, 129 (4th Cir. 2002) (single father construction lineman fired for refusing overtime).

38. *Marion Composites,* 115 LA 95 (Wren, 2001) (arbitrator reduced the grievant's suspension to a written warning and awarded him back pay after the grievant was suspended for insubordination for leaving after eight hours of a twelve-hour overtime shift to care for his children); *Suprenant Cable Corp., supra* note 22 at 14.

39. *Allied Paper,* 80 LA 435, 448 (Mathews, 1983) (arbitrator reduced the suspension to a written warning).

40. In *Tenneco Packaging, supra* note 4, a woman janitor did not explain to her employer that she could not work because the babysitter had not arrived to look after her disabled child. Her silence appears to have been differently motivated: the arbitrator states that the worker simply did not know that management expected an explanation.

41. *Tractor Supply Co.*, 2001 WL 1301335 (Dichter, 2001). The boy's father worked as the only manager on duty during the evening and had joint custody of his eighteen-month-old; because of the boy's medical condition, the court required that the child be cared for by a family member. Arbitrator Dichter emphasized the worker's failure to explain why he could not stay, but he found that the discharge was unreasonable in the face of the worker's need to care for the child and the confusion concerning notice the day before. He reduced the penalty to a thirty-day suspension, without back pay.

42. *Midwest Body, Inc.*, 73 LA 651, 652-653 (Guenther, 1979) (arbitrator upheld the dismissal).

43. UPS database: *UPS*, case no. 97-222(B) (McKay, 1998) (arbitrator upheld the grievant's discharge, pointing to an established arbitral history of discharge for "stolen time" and faulting grievant for lying when he claimed overtime rather than admitting he had not been at work for part of the regular workday).

44. *Ashland Oil*, supra note 21; *Tom Rice Buick, Pontiac & GMC Truck, Inc.*, 334 NLRB 785 (2001); *VA, Medical Center, Indianapolis*, 92 LA 691(Doering, 1988) (arbitrator reduced an AWOL demerit to leave without pay); *City of Columbus*, 96 LA 32, 37 (Mancini, 1990) (arbitrator sustained grievant's suspension; the worker claimed at the hearing that he had so informed his supervisor, but this claim was inconsistent with a prior statement, and the arbitrator did not believe it. The Arbitrator notes that the worker had "two recent reprimands for committing similar offenses." It is unclear from the decision whether that means that the worker had gotten into trouble for leaving for child care reasons before. If so, that may explain why he did not discuss his child care issues when they arose again.).

45. Roberta Sigel, *Ambition and Accommodation: How Women View Gender Relations* 159 (1996). Sigel argues that attitudes have shifted among younger men, but the available evidence (including her own) raises questions about the extent of that shift. See also Joan C. Williams, *Unbending Gender: Why Family and Work Conflict and What to Do about It* 159–160 (2000).

46. Gregory DeFreitas and Niev Duffy, "Young Workers, Economic Inequality, and Collective Action," in *What's Class Got to Do with It? American Society in the Twenty-First Century* 145 (Michael Zweig ed., 2004) (wages have fallen); Williams, *supra* note 45 at 153 ("A guy should be able to support his wife and kids"); Richard Sennett & Jonathan Cobb, *The Hidden Injuries of Class* (1973). For other studies that discuss working-class men's attitudes, see Lillian B. Rubin, *Worlds of Pain: Life in the Working-Class Family* 78 (1992); Ellen Rosen, *Bitter Choices: Blue-Collar Women in and Out of Work* 104 (1987); and Sigel, *supra* note 45 at 159 (Sigel argues that attitudes have shifted among younger men, but the available evidence—including her own—raises questions about the extent of that shift). See Williams, *supra* note 45 at 159–160; Michèle Lamont, *The Dignity of Working Men: Morality and the Boundaries of Race, Class, and Immigration* 34 (2000).

47. Sennett & Cobb, *supra* note 46 ("hidden injury of class"); Jeanne Boydston, *Home and Work: Housework, Wages, and the Ideology of Labor in the Early*

Republic 156 (1990); Williams, *supra* note 45 at 34–35, 156–157, 160–161 (housewife as way of signaling difference); Rubin, *supra* note 46; Lamont, *supra* note 46; Sigel, *supra* note 45; Frank S. Levy and Richard C. Michel, *The Economic Future of American Families: Income and Wealth Trends* (1991) (breadwinner ideal tied to class privilege); Williams, *supra* note 45 at 25–31, 157–160 ("walk the walk").

48. E-mail from Peter Richardson, part-time lecturer, University of Washington Bothell, to Joan Williams, Distinguished Professor of Law, 1066 Foundation Chair and Director, Center for WorkLife Law (December 23, 2008) (on file with the author) (makes sense that working-class men are less forthcoming).

49. T. D. Allen, J. E. Russell & M. C. Rush, "Effects of Gender and Leave of Absence on Attributions for High Performance, Perceived Organizational Commitment, and Allocation of Rewards," 31 *Sex Roles* 443–464 (1994) (stigma triggered when men signal involvement in family care); Michael K. Judiesch & Karen S. Lyness, "Left Behind? The Impact of Leaves of Absence on Managers' Career Success," 42 *Academy of Management Journal* 641–651 (1999) (stigma can be severe).

50. *Southern Champion Tray, supra* note 23 at 637 ("I didn't feel anything else could be worked out").

51. Studies show that fathers' knowledge about their children's lives typically is limited. See Ann C. Crouter & Melissa R. Head, "Parental Monitoring and Knowledge of Children," in *Handbook of Parenting* (Bornstein ed., 2002); Matthew F. Bumpus & Ann C. Crouter, "Work Demands of Dual-Earner Couples: Implications of Parents' Knowledge about Children's Daily Lives in Middle Childhood," 61 *J. of Marriage and the Family* 465 (1999); Annette Lareau, "My Wife Will Tell Me Who I Know: Methodological and Conceptual Problems in Studying Fathers," 23 *Qualitative Soc.* 407 (2000) (little role in arrangements); *U.S. Steel Corp., supra* note 21 (factory worker was not familiar with how to make babysitting arrangements).

52. *Tom Rice Buick, Pontiac & GMC Truck, Inc., supra* note 44 at 786.

53. Lamont, *supra* note 46 at 112 (poor quality of interpersonal relationships; "money isn't a big thing"; "He's a family man"); *Ashland Oil, supra* note 21 ("I must do what I have to do").

54. *State of New York, Rochester Psychiatric Ctr., supra* note 34 (recipe for disaster for tag-teaming parents); *GTE California, Inc., supra* note 35 (workers themselves decide when to take overtime).

55. *Knauf Fiber Glass, supra* note 3 at 336.

56. *Id.* at 336, 337.

57. *Southern Champion Tray, supra* note 23 at 637; also quoted in *Tractor Supply, supra* note 41.

58. *Social Security Administration, Westminster Teleservice Ctr., supra* note 17.

59. *Town of Stratford, supra* note 23 at 513–514 (police officer suspended; order back "firm" requirement). Fertility studies of working-class women are scarce, but from Sylvia Ann Hewlett, *Creating a Life: Professional Woman and the Quest for Children* 33 (2002) (stating that 33% of high-earning career women aged forty to fifty-five are childless, and the rate of childlessness among high-

achieving women is about twice that of the population at large), we can infer that working-class women are less likely to be childless (childless working-class couples are unusual). Phyllis Moen & Yan Yu, "Effective Work/Life Strategies: Working Couples, Work Conditions, Gender, and Life Quality," 47 *Social Problems* 3, 295, 311, 314 (2000) (spouse available for child care duties without regard for job concerns unusual in working-class couples); *City of Titusville*, 101 LA 828, 835–836 (Hoffman, 1993) (arbitrator overturned employer's finding that grievant had abused her sick leave to care for her ill son because "the uncontested facts are that every single absence during this period was known to her supervisors, approved by them, and paid for, " and thus management had waived its right to discipline).

60. Karen Kornbluh, "The Parent Trap," 291 *Atlantic Monthly* 111–114 (2003) (all adults in workforce in 70% of households with children).

61. Williams, *supra* note 45 at 93 (family-responsive workplaces maximize profits); Corporate Voices for Working Families, *supra* note 10 at 12 ("strong return" on human capital investments).

62. *Dial Corp., Bristol, Pa.*, 107 LA 879 (Robinson, 1997) (arbitrator reduced the termination to a suspension).

63. *Piedmont Airlines, Inc., supra* note 23 at 755.

64. Williams, *supra* note 45 at 93 ("How could I not be grateful?"); James L. Heskett, W. Earl Sasser, & Leonard A. Schlesinger, *The Service Profit Chain: How Leading Companies Link Profit and Growth to Loyalty, Satisfaction, and Value* (1997) (happy workers make for happy customers); Corporate Voices for Working Families, *supra* note 10 at 20 (First Tennessee Bank; companies with happy employees had larger stock increases).

65. Corporate Voices for Working Families, *supra* note 10 at 13.

66. *Id.* at 10, 18 (flexibility influenced decision to stay; flexibility "very important").

67. *Id.* at 14, 16 (effect of flexibility on employee commitment is dramatic; hourly workers likely to be in positions requiring attention to detail; lack of commitment can impact customer relations; commitment and engagement important; effects of flexibility nearly identical).

68. Williams, *supra* note 45 at 92 (flexible policies can improve productivity). For more examples of improvements in productivity, see Williams, *supra* note 45 at 84–94 and Corporate Voices for Working Families, *supra* note 10.

69. Williams, *supra* note 45 at 92 (StrideRight benefited from flexibility); Corporate Voices for Working Families, *supra* note 10 at 8, 22 (PNC's Eastwick, PA, location benefited from flexibility).

70. Williams, *supra* note 45 at 93.

71. *Id.*

72. Corporate Voices for Working Families *supra* note 10 at 15 (stress leading cause of absenteeism); Maureen Perry-Jenkins, Abbie E. Goldberg, Courtney P. Pierce, & Aline G. Sayer, "Shift Work, Role Overload, and the Transition to Parenthood," 69 *Journal of Marriage and the Family* 123, 124 (2007) (citing studies, evening and rotating hours associated with greater psychological distress); Elizabeth Gudrais, "Unequal American," *Harvard Magazine* 22, 28

(July–August 2008) (lack of flexibility correlated to increased heart disease, sleep disorders—citing study by Lisa Berkman); T. M. Beers, "Flexible Schedules and Shift Work: Replacing the "9 to 5" Workday," 123 *Monthly Labor Rev.* 839 (2000) (unsocial hours have negative effect on health); Alexander Wedderburn, *Shiftwork and Health*, European Studies on Time (BEST) (2001), cited in Vanessa R. Wight, Sara B. Raley, & Suzanne M. Bianchi, "Time for Children, One's Spouse and Oneself among Parents Who Work Nonstandard Hours," 87 *Social Forces* 243 (2008) (long hours have negative effect on health); Corporate Voices for Working Families, *supra* note 10 at 14 (stress responsible for host of workplace ills).

73. Williams, *supra* note 45 at 87.

74. *Id.* at 88 (costs of replacing hourly worker); Corporate Voices for Working Families, *supra* note 10 at 22 (costs of replacement add up); Joan C. Williams & Nancy Segal, "Beyond the Maternal Wall," 26 *Harv. Women's L.J.* 77, 89 (2003) ($2,100 to replace unskilled hotel worker).

75. *Internal Revenue Service*, 89 LA 59 (Gallagher, 1987) (arbitrator overturned dismissal for typist); ATU database: *Miami Valley Regional Transit Authority*, case no. 52-390-484-00 (Campbell, 2001) (arbitrator upheld the discharge of a bus driver whose absences were caused by problems with child care and her extended family).

76. *Miami Valley Regional Transit Authority*, *supra* note 75.

77. Maureen Perry-Jenkins et al. (in press), *Work-Family Challenges for Blue-Collar Parents* 14 (on file with author).

78. Dodson et al., *Keeping Jobs and Raising Families in Low-Income America: It Just Doesn't Work*, the Across the Boundaries Project (2002) (attrition stems from breakdowns in child-care arrangements); Julia R. Henly, H. Luke Schaefer, & Elaine Waxman, "Nonstandard Work Schedules: Employer- and Employee-Driven Flexibility in Retail Jobs," *Social Service Review* 609, 623 (December 2006) ("most of 'em leave because the schedule doesn't work around their schedule"); Williams, *supra* note 45 at 91 (workers more likely to make up time missed for family care); Ellen Galinsky, James T. Bond, & Dana E. Friedman, *The Changing Workforce: Highlights of the National Study of the Changing Workforce*, Families and Work Institute, 88 (1993) (absenteeism and tardiness reduced by flextime); Work & Family Connection, Inc., *Work & Family: A Retrospective* 130, 123, 126 (Survey by AMA, 1997) (flexibility cut absenteeism by 50%; job sharing decreased absenteeism by 81%).

79. Corporate Voices for Working Families, *supra* note 10 at 10–11 (flexible work options help recruit); Williams, *supra* note 45 at 90 (deluge of applications).

80. See also *Tenneco Packaging Burlington Container Plant*, *supra* note 4; *State of New York, Rochester Psychiatric Ctr.*, *supra* note 34.

81. See Norman Brand ed., *Discipline and Discharge in Arbitration* 105–106 (1998) (discussing when family emergency is a mitigating factor in attendance contexts). See also Roger I. Abrams & Dennis R. Nolan, "Toward a Theory of Just Cause in Employee Discipline Case," 85 *Duke L.J.* 594 (1985).

82. *Sutter Roseville Medical Center*, *supra* note 24 (arbitrator upheld the discharge of a nuclear medicine technician who was charged with insubordina-

tion by a new supervisor after refusing to be placed on standby because he lived far away and had to care for his son). It may be that the argument was made in *Sutter* but not in *Dept. of Veterans Affairs Medical Center*, *supra* note 29.

83. If sick leave is available only for care of children, workers who need to care for their parents will still find their jobs at risk. *See Puget Sound Hospital, Tacoma*, 109 LA 659 (Monat, 1997) (arbitrator upheld employer's denial of sick leave for a surgical supply coordinator who requested leave to travel out of state to care for her mother during and after a surgery).

84. *State of New York, Rochester Psychiatric Ctr.*, *supra* note 34; *Allied Paper*, *supra* note 38.

85. Corporate Voices for Working Families, *supra* note 10 at 16 (hourly workers more likely to want part-time schedule); Still, *supra* note 31 (most mothers aged twenty-five to forty-four years will need a reduced schedule).

86. For example, at Texas Instruments, over 60% of hourly workers are on compressed workweeks. Corporate Voices for Working Families, *supra* note 10 at 17.

87. Corporate Voices for Working Families, *supra* note 10 at 17 (telecommuting), 22 (GlaxoSmithKline).

88. *Id.* at 21 (flexible schedules increased productivity and coverage).

89. Alford A. Young Jr., "The Work-Family Divide for Low-Income African Americans," in *The Changing Landscape of Work and Family in the American Middle Class: Reports from the Field* 87, 94, 101 (E. Rudd & L. Descartes eds., 2008).

90. *Id.* at 102.

91. David G. Hurlburt, *One Sick Kin away from Being Fired* (2006) (on file with the author).

92. *Tom Rice Buick, Pontiac & GMC Truck, Inc.*, *supra* note 44 (NLRB upheld the dismissal of the grievant who left work fifteen minutes early to pick up his thirteen-year-old son).

3. Masculine Norms at Work

1. Peter Glick, Korin Wilk, & Michele Perreault, "Images of Occupations: Components of Gender and Status in Occupational Stereotypes," 32 *Sex Roles* 565 (2005).

2. Donald Tomaskovic-Dewey, *Gender and Racial Inequality at Work: The Sources and Consequences of Job Segregation* 62 (1993).

3. Elizabeth H. Gorman, "Gender Stereotypes, Same-Gender Preferences, and Organizational Variation in the Hiring of Women: Evidence from Law Firms," 70 *Am. Soc. R* 702, 709 (2005).

4. Joan Williams, *Unbending Gender: Why Family and Work Conflict and What to Do about It* 21 (2000) (before separate spheres); *Id.* at 22 (ideology of gender hierarchy); *Id.* (fathers as the ultimate authority in child rearing).

5. Williams, *supra* note 3 at 31–33 (equal in separate spheres).

6. *Id.*

7. Richard D. Ashmore & Frances K. Del Boca, "Sex Stereotypes & Implicit Personality Theory: Toward a Cognitive–Social Psychological Conceptualization," 5 *Sex Roles* 219, 222 (1979).

8. Peter Glick & Susan T. Fiske, "Ambivalent Sexism," in *Advances in Experimental Social Psychology* 115, 169 (Mark P. Zanna ed., 2001) (view of a typical man); Cecilia L. Ridgeway, "Gender, Status, and Leadership," 57 *J. Soc. Issues* 637, 639–641 (2001) (view of a typical woman); Arlie Hochschild, *The Managed Heart: Commercialization of Human Feeling* (1983) (typical woman suited for "emotional labor").

9. Howard Georgi, "Is There an Unconscious Discrimination against Women in Science?" *APS News Online* (January 2000), available at http://www.people .fas.harvard.edu/~jgeorgi/women/backpage.htm.

10. Alice H. Eagly and Linda L. Carli, *Through the Labyrinth* 86 (2007) ("agentic associations convey assertion and control"; "communal associations convey a concern with the compassionate treatment of others").

11. Mary Blair-Loy and Amy S. Wharton, "Mothers in Finance: Surviving and Thriving," 596 *Annals of Amer. Acad. of Pol. and Soc. Sci.* 151–171 (2004).

12. Janet E. Gans Epner, *Visible Invisibility: Women of Color in Law Firms*, ABA Commission on Women in the Profession 11 (2006).

13. See Arlie Russell Hochschild, *The Second Shift: Working Parents and the Revolution at Home* (1989) (masculinity and the gender revolution).

14. Catharine MacKinnon, *Feminism Unmodified* 36 (1987) (benefits of masculine norms);*Oncale v. Sundowner Offshore Serv., Inc.*, 523 U.S. 75, 77 (1998); Debra Meyerson et al., "Disrupting Gender, Revising Leadership," in *Women & Leadership: The State of Play and Strategies for Change* 453, 461 (Barbara Kellerman & Deborah L. Rhode eds., 2007) (workplace machismo).

15. See John M. Broder, "Schwarzenegger Calls Budget Opponents 'Girlie Men,'" *New York Times*, July 19, 2004, at A11 ("'I call them girlie men,' Mr. Schwarzenegger said of the Democrats, as hundreds of shoppers who had gathered to hear him speak roared their approval at the Ontario Mills megamall, about 40 miles east of Los Angeles.").

16. *Oncale, supra* note 13 at 77.

17. *Id.* at 82; Mary Anne Case, "Disaggregating Gender from Sex and Sexual Orientation, The Effeminate Man in the Law and Feminist Jurisprudence," 105 *Yale L.J.* 1 (1995); but see Nancy Levit, "Feminism for Men: Legal Ideology and the Construction of Maleness," 43 *UCLA L. Rev.* 1037, 1054 (1996).

18. Nick Townsend, *The Package Deal: Marriage, Work, and Fatherhood in Men's Lives* 120 (2002) (good fathers/providers); Francine Deutsch, *Halving It All: How Equally Shared Parenting Works* 90 (1999) (risk of wimpiness);Victoria L. Brescoll & Eric Luis Uhlmann, "Attitudes toward Traditional and Nontraditional Parents," 20 *Psych. of Women Q.* 436 (2005) (stay-at-home fathers); Michèle Lamont, *Money, Morals, and Manners: The Culture of the French and the American Upper-Middle Class* xxix (1992) ("men want to build their ego").

19. Williams, *supra* note 3 at 125 (30% pay difference); see Kathleen Fuegen et al., "Mothers and Fathers in the Workplace: How Gender and Parental Status

Influence Judgments of Job-Related Competence," 60 *J. Soc. Issues* 737, 749 (2004) (fathers held to lower standards); Amy J. C. Cuddy et al., "When Professionals Become Mothers, Warmth Doesn't Cut the Ice," 60 *J. Soc. Issues* 701, 712–713 (2004) (study of fatherhood and management application); Julie Holliday Wayne & Bryanne L. Cordiero, "Who Is a Good Organizational Citizen? Perceptions of Male and Female Employees Who Use Family Leave," 49 *Sex Roles* 233, 241 (2003) (men penalized by other men). For fewer rewards and lower performance ratings, see Adam B. Butler & Amie Skattebo, "What Is Acceptable for Women May Not Be for Men: The Effect of Family Conflicts with Work on Job-Performance Ratings," 77 *J. of Occupational and Org. Psych.* 553 (2004); Tammy Allen & Joyce Russell, "Parental Leave of Absence: Some Not So Family-Friendly Implications," 29 *J. of Applied Soc. Psych.* 166 (1999).

20. Deutsch, *supra* note 17 at 90.
21. UC Faculty Family-Friendly Edge, *Creating a Family Friendly Department: Chairs and Deans Toolkit* (July 1, 2007), at 17, available at http://ucfamilyedge .berkeley.edu/toolkit.html.
22. For illegality of discriminatory parental leave policies, see Title VII of the Civil Rights Act of 1964, 42 U.S.C. § 2000e (West 2008); The Family and Medical Leave Act, 29 U.S.C. § 2601–2654 (West 2008); U.S. const. amend. XIV, § 1. For illegality of retaliation, see Joan C. Williams & Cynthia Thomas Calvert, *WorkLife Law's Guide to Family Responsibilities Discrimination* (Center for WorkLife Law, University of California Hastings College of the Law, 2006).
23. Jerry A. Jacobs & Kathleen Gerson, *The Time Divide: Work, Family, and Gender Inequality* 66, 69 (2004).
24. Marin Clarkberg & Stacy S. Merola, "Competing Clocks: Work and Leisure," in *It's about Time: Couples and Careers* 35, 39, 43 (Phyllis Moen ed., 2003) (in the Cornell sample, 66% of the women and 69% of the men were professionals). In all the couples in the sample, at least one partner had attended college. *Id.* at 339. This sample is not a perfect proxy for my definition of professionals: I define professionals as having graduated from college. See also Jacobs & Gerson, *supra* note 22 at 32.
25. Eagly and Carli, *supra* note 9 at 141.
26. Ellen Galinsky, *Ask the Children: What America's Children Really Think about Working Parents* 67 (1999) (study of impact on children of absent parents); Lynne M. Casper & Suzanne M. Bianchi, *Continuity and Change in the American Family* 307 (2002) (fathers spend one hour for every three mothers do).
27. Annette Lareau, "My Wife Can Tell Me Who I Know: Methodological and Conceptual Problems in Studying Fathers," in *Families at Work: Expanding the Bounds* 32, 47, 52 (Naomi Gerstel et al. eds., 2002) (citing six other studies); Ann C. Crouter & Matthew F. Bumpus, "It's 10 P.M., Do You Know Where Your Child Is?: Parental Knowledge as a Window into Daily Processes in Dual-Earner Families" (plenary talk at "Persons, Processes, and Places: Research on Families, Workplaces, and Communities" conference, San Francisco, February 9, 2002); Matthew Bumpus et al., "Work Demands of Dual-Earner

Couples: Implications for Parents' Knowledge about Children's Daily Lives in Middle Childhood," 61 *J. of Marriage & Family* 465–475 (1999); Ann C. Crouter & Susan M. McHale, "Temporal Rhythms in Family Life: Seasonal Variation in the Relation between Parental Work and Family Processes," 29 *J. Developmental Psych.* 198–205 (1993).

28. Lareau, *supra* note 26 at 32, 47, 52.
29. Micaela di Leonardo, "The Female World of Cards and Holiday: Women, Families, and the Work of Kinship," 12 *Signs* 440, 441–442 (1987).
30. *About Schmidt* (New Line Cinema 2002).
31. Leslie Bennetts, *The Feminine Mistake* 43 (2008).
32. Sarah Fenstermaker, *The Gender Factory* (1985). see also Linda Babcock & Sarah Laschever, *Women Don't Ask: The High Cost of Avoiding Negotiation—and Positive Strategies for Change* (2007).
33. Linda R. Hirshman, *Get to Work: A Manifesto for Women of the World* 1, 62 (2006).
34. Marianne Cooper, "Being the 'Go-To Guy': Fatherhood, Masculinity, and the Organization of Work in Silicon Valley," in *Families at Work: Expanding the Bounds* 5 (Naomi Gerstel et al. eds., 2002).
35. *Id.* at 5, 7.
36. Meyerson, *supra* note 13 at 453. See also David L. Collinson & Jeff Hearn, "Men and Masculinities in Work, Organizations, and Management" in *Handbook of Studies on Men & Masculinities* 289 (Michael S. Kimmel, Jeff Hearn, & R. W. Connell eds., 2005) (more theoretical discussion of masculinity at work).
37. *Id.* at 456.
38. *Id.* at 459.
39. *Id.*
40. *Id.* at 460.
41. *Id.* at 463.
42. *Id.* at 462.
43. Shelley E. Taylor et al., "Categorical and Contextual Bases of Person Memory and Stereotyping," 36 *J. Personality & Soc. Psychol.* 778, 791 (1978).
44. Meyerson, *supra* note 13 at 461, 326.
45. *Id.* at 462.
46. *Id.* at 463.
47. *Id.* at 465.
48. Cooper, *supra* note 33.
49. *Id.* at 7.
50. *Id.* at 9.
51. *Id.* at 26.
52. *Id.*
53. *Id.*
54. *Id.* at 20.
55. Cynthia Epstein, *The Part-Time Paradox: Time Norms, Professional Life, Family and Gender* 22 (1998); Jonathon Lazear, *The Man Who Mistook His Job for a Life* (2001).

56. Cooper, *supra* note 33 at 20.

57. *Id.* at 10.

58. *Id.* at 14.

59. *Id.*

60. See Stanley Coren, "Sleep Deprivation, Psychosis and Mental Efficiency," 15 *Psychiatric Times* (March 1, 1998), available at http://www.psychiatrictimes .com/display/article/10168/54471("People who are operating with a sleep debt are less efficient, and this inefficiency is most noticeable when the circadian cycle is at its lowest ebb. Among the common consequences of a large sleep debt are attentional lapses, reduced short-term memory capacity, impaired judgment and the occurrence of 'microsleeps.'"); Editorial: Mary Corbitt Clark, "The Cost of Job Stress," Winning Workplaces, available at http:// www.winningworkplaces.org/library/features/the_cost_of_job_stress.php ("Job stress is a key driver of health care costs ... Health care expenditures are nearly 50 percent greater for workers reporting high levels of stress."); Emily Tanner-Smith & Adam Long, "The Stress-Health Connection and Its Implications for Employers," 21 *Managed Care Outlook* (May 15, 2008), reprinted in *Keeping in Touch* 2 (3rd quarter, 2008), available at http://www.villa-geeap.com/employer-resources/newsletters/3rd%20Qtr_Suprv.Newsltro8.pdf.

61. Williams, *supra* note 3 at 84–100; The Project for Attorney Retention, http:// www.pardc.org/.

62. Joan C. Williams & Cynthia Thomas Calvert, *Solving the Part-Time Puzzle: The Law Firm's Guide to Balanced Hours* 18, 151–156 (2004).

63. Keith Cunningham, "Father Time: Flexible Work Arrangements and the Law Firm's Failure of the Family," 53 *Stan. L. Rev.* 967, 969–970 (2001) (The "normal" large law firm turnover rate of 20% is over double that of other industries).

64. Cooper, *supra* note 33 at 19.

65. *Id.* at 21–22.

66. *Id.* at 21.

67. *Id.*

68. Metropolitan Corporate Counsel Association (MCCA), *Creating Pathways to Diversity: Myth of the Meritocracy—A Report on the Bridges and Barriers to Success in Large Law Firms* 40 (2003), available at http://www.mcca.com/ index.cfm?fuseaction=page.viewpage&pageid=614.

69. Deborah Tannen, *Talking from 9 to 5* 69–70 (1994).

70. Michael Kimmel, *Manhood in America* 23 (1996).

71. R. Woolfolk & F. Richardson, *Sanity, Stress, and Survival,* cited in Joseph H. Pleck, *The Myth of Masculinity* 133 (1974) (inadequacy).

72. Robert L. Griswold, *Fatherhood in America: A History* 2 (1993).

73. E-mail from Derek Bok, professor, Harvard University, to Joan Williams, Distinguished Professor of Law, 1066 Foundation Chair and Director, Center for WorkLife Law (2007) (on file with the author) (confirming statements made in 2001).

74. Tannen, *supra* note 68 at 70; Joseph A. Vandello & Jennifer K. Brown, Dov Cohen, Rochelle M. Burnaford, & Jonathan R. Weaver, "Precarious Manhood,"

95 *J. of Personality and Soc. Psych.* 1325, 1335. See also Steven Krugman, "Male Development and the Transformation of Shame," in *Toward a New Psychology of Men* 91 (Ronald F. Levant & Williams S. Pollack eds., 2003).

75. Catalyst, *The Next Generation: Today's Professionals, Tomorrow's Leaders* (2001).

76. Cooper, *supra* note 33 at 25.

77. Arlie Hochschild, *The Time Bind* 65 (1997).

78. See Janet C. Gornick & Marcia K. Meyers, *Families That Work* 58–67 (2003); Organization for Economic Co-operation and Development (OECD), OECD Stat Extracts, "Average annual hours actually worked per worker," http://stats.oecd.org/Index.aspx?DatasetCode=ANHRS (sortable data showing U.S. among top 11 countries with longest work hours and longer work hours than Japan, each year from 2000 to 2008); "Death by overwork in Japan, Japan and overwork," *The Economist*, December 19, 2007, available at http://www.economist.com/world/asia/displaystory.cfm?STORY_ID=10329261 (defining *karoshi*); Jacobs and Gerson, *supra* note 22 at 4 (elites).

79. Cooper, *supra* note 33 at 27.

80. For job requirement stereotyping, see Williams & Calvert, *supra* note 21 at 1-31-1-40; Joan C. Williams & Stephanie Bornstein, "The Evolution of 'FreD': Family Responsibilities Discrimination and Developments in the Law of Stereotyping and Implicit Bias, 59 *Hastings L.J.* 1341–1358 (2008). For better use of federal law, see Williams & Bornstein, *supra* note 79 at 1311, 1358. For physical manifestations, see Williams, *supra* note 3 at 60.

81. *Id.* at 577.

82. See, e.g., Center for WorkLife Law, "Gender Bias in Academia," available at http://www.worklifelaw.org/GenderBiasInAcademia.html (four basic patterns of gender bias); Catalyst, *Women "Take Care," Men "Take Charge": Stereotyping of U.S. Business Leaders Exposed* (2005) (perceived "lack of fit" between male jobs and women).

83. Madeline E. Heilman, "Sex Bias in Work Settings: The Lack of Fit Model," 5 *Research in Organization Behavior* 280 (1983); Catalyst, *The Double-Bind Dilemma for Women in Leadership: Damned if You Do, Doomed if You Don't* 17, 19, 21 (July 2007), available at http://www.catalyst.org/publication/83/the-double-bind-dilemma-for-women-in-leadership-damned-if-you-do-doomed-if-you-dont.

84. Steve Nadis, "Women Scientists Unite to Battle Cowboy Culture," 398 *Nature* 361 (1999).

85. Phillip Matier and Andrew Ross, "Former Chief of Building Inspection Gets Damage," *San Francisco Chronicle*, April 30, 2007, at B1 (pregnancy brain); Harvard Women's Law Association, *Presumed Equal: What America's Top Women Lawyers Really Think about Their Firms* 72 (1995), quoted in Deborah L. Rhode, "Myths of Meritocracy," 65 *Fordham L. Rev.* 585–594, 585, 588 (1996) (baby, not a lobotomy); Susan T. Fiske et al., "A Model of (Often Mixed) Stereotype Content: Competence and Warmth Respectively Follow from Perceived Status and Competition," 82 *J. Personality & Soc. Psych.* 885 (2002) (competence of housewives); Monica Biernat et al., "Stereotypes and

Standards of Judgment," 60 *J. Personality & Soc. Psych.* 485–499 (1991); Stephen Benard, In Paik, & Shelley J. Correll, "Cognitive Bias and the Motherhood Penalty," 59 *Hastings L.J.* 1378 (2008); *Id.* at 1383.

86. D. Kobrynowicz & M. Biernat, "Decoding Subjective Evaluations: How Stereotypes Provide Shifting Standards," 33 *J. of Experimental Soc. Psych.* 592 (1997).

87. For image of black and Latina mothers, see Benard et al., *supra* note 85 at 1378. For studies of the maternal wall, see studies as discussed in Benard et al., *supra* note 85 at 1383.

88. Fuegen et al., *supra* note 18 at 737–748. See also Laurie A. Rudman, "Self-Promotion as a Risk Factor for Women: The Costs and Benefits of Counter-stereotypical Impression of Management," 74 *J. Personality & Soc. Psych.* 639 (1998), citing J. Berger et al., "Status Cues, Expectations, and Behaviors," *in Advances in Group Processes* 1–22 (E. Lawler ed., 1986); Heilman, *supra* note 83 at 269; Natalie Porter & Florence L. Geis, "When Seeing Is Not Believing: Nonverbal Dues to Leadership," in *Gender and Nonverbal Behavior* (Clara Mayo & Nancy M. Henly eds., 1981).

89. Martha Foschi, "Double Standards for Competence: Theory and Research," 26 *Ann. R. Soc.* 21, 23 (2000), citing Joseph M. Berger et al., *Status Characteristics and Social Interaction: An Expectation States Approach* (1977).

90. Rhea E. Steinpreis, Katie A. Anders, & Dawn Ritzke, "The Impact of Gender on the Review of the Curricula Vitae of Job Applicants and Tenure Candidates: A National Empirical Study," 41 *Sex Roles* 509, 520 (1999).

91. Christine Wenneras & Agnes Wold, "Nepotism and Sexism in Peer Review," 387 *Nature* 341, 342 (1997).

92. Monica Biernat, "Toward a Broader View of Social Stereotyping," 58 *Am. Psychologist* 1019, 1021 (2003); Madeline E. Heilman et al., "Has Anything Changed? Current Characterizations of Men, Women, and Managers," 74 *J. Applied Psychol.* 935, 935–942 (1989); Madeline E. Heilman, "Sex Stereotypes and Their Effects in the Workplace: What We Know and What We Don't Know," 10 *J. of Soc. Behavior & Personality* 3, 16 (1995).

93. Judith G. Oakley, "Gender-Based Barriers to Senior Management Positions: Understanding the Scarcity of Female CEOs," 27 *J. Bus. Ethics* 321, 329 (2000).

94. Eagly & Carli, *supra* note 9 at 164.

95. See Kay Deaux & Tim Emswiller, "Explanations of Successful Performance on Sex-Linked Tasks: What Is Skill for the Male Is Luck for the Female," 28 *J. Personality & Soc. Psychol.* 80, 80–85 (1974). See also Janet K. Swim & Lawrence J. Sanna, "He's Skilled, She's Lucky: A Meta-Analysis of Observers' Attributions for Women's and Men's Successes and Failures," 22 *Personality & Social Psychol. Bulletin* 507, 508 (1996).

96. See Deaux & Emswiller, *supra* note 95 at 80, 80–85. See also Swim & Sanna, *supra* note 95 at 508.

97. Cecilia L. Ridgeway, "Interaction and the Conservation of Gender Inequality: Considering Employment," 62 *Am. Soc. Rev.* 218, 222 (1997).

98. Transcript of focus group performed by the Center for Worklife Law through an ADVANCE Leadership Grant, Spring 2008.

99. Foschi, *supra* note 89 at 28.
100. Joan C. Williams, "The Social Psychology of Stereotyping Using Social Science to Litigate Gender Discrimination and Defang the 'Cluelessness' Defense," 7 *Emp. Rts. & Emp. Pol'y J.* 401, 401–458 (2003) [hereinafter Williams, "Social Psychology of Stereotyping"]. See also Douglas M. McCracken, "Winning the Talent War for Women: Sometimes It Takes a Revolution," *Harv. Bus. Rev.*, December 12, 2000, available at http://hbswk.hbs.edu/item.jhtml?id=1840&t=organizations.
101. Joan C. Williams and Consuela A. Pinto, *Fair Measure: Toward Effective Attorney Evaluations* 20 (2008).
102. Marilynn B. Brewer, "In-Group Favoritism: The Subtle Side of Intergroup Discrimination," in *Codes of Conduct: Behavioral Research into Business Ethics* 65 (Ann E. Tenbrunsel ed., 1996).
103. Penelope M. Huang, *Gender Bias in Academia: Findings from Focus Groups,* Center for WorkLife Law (2008), available at www.worklifelaw.org/pubs/GenderBiasinAcademia_final.doc
104. Williams & Pinto, *supra* note 101 at 20.
105. Patricia W. Linville & Edward E. Jones, "Polarized Appraisals of Out-Group Members," 38 *J. Personality & Soc. Psych.* 689, 691–692 (1980).
106. Eagly & Carli, *supra* note 9 at 115.
107. Williams, "Social Psychology of Stereotyping," *supra* note 100 at 418. See also Monica Biernat et al., "All You Can Be: Stereotyping of Self and Others in a Military Context," 75 *J. Personality & Soc. Psych.* 301, 304; Taylor, *supra* note 42 at 785.
108. Michael I. Norton et al., "Casuistry and Social Category Bias," 87 *J. Personality & Soc. Psych.* 817, 817–831 (2004); E. L. Uhlmann & G. L. Cohen, "Constructed Criteria: Redefining Merit to Justify Discrimination," 16 *Psych. Sci.* 170 (2005).
109. See, e.g., Marianne Bertrand & Sendhil Mullainathan, "Are Emily and Greg More Employable than Lakisha and Jamal? A Field Experiment on Labor Market Discrimination," 94 *Am. Econ. Rev.* 991 (2004).
110. *Id.* at 992–993.
111. John F. Dovidio & Samuel L. Gaertner, "Aversive Racism and Selection Decisions: 1989 and 1999," 11 *Psych. Sci.* 315 (2002).
112. Gans Epner, *supra* note 11 at 8.
113. Monica Biernat, "Toward a Broader View of Social Stereotyping," 58 *Am. Psych.* 1021–1022 (2003).
114. Hope Landrine, "Race x Class Stereotypes of Women," 13 *Sex Roles* 65, 72 (1985).
115. Gans Epner, *supra* note 11 at 25.
116. Charisse Jones & Kumea Shorter-Gooden, *Shifting: The Double Lines of Black Women in America* 14 (2003).
117. Interview with Irma Herrera, Executive Director, Equal Rights Advocates, in San Francisco, CA (June 9, 2009).
118. F. T. L. Leong & J. A. Grand, "Beyond the Model Minority—More than Meets the Eye," in *Model Minority Myth Revisited: An Interdisciplinary*

Approach to DeMystifying Asian American Educational Experiences 102 (Guofang Li and Lihshing Wang eds., 2008).

119. Won M. Hurh & Kwang C. Kim, "The 'Success' Image of Asian Americans: Its Validity, and Its Practical and Theoretical Implications," 12 *Ethnic & Racial Stud.* 512, 512–588 (1989); Harry H. L. Kitano & Stanley Sue, "The Model Minorities," 29 *J. Soc. Issues* 1, 1–9 (1973); *Id.* at 83, 83–98; Stanley Sue et al., "Asian Americans as a Minority Group," 30 *Am. Psych.* 906–910 (1975); Setsuko M. Nishi, "Perceptions and Deceptions: Contemporary Views of Asian Americans," in *A Look beyond the Model Minority Image: Critical Issues in Asian America* 3, 6 (Grace Yun ed., 1989). The author is not aware of any lab studies of stereotypes of Latinas or Native American women.

120. Gans Epner, *supra* note 11 at 10.

121. Taylor, *supra* note 42 at 778, 791.

122. Eagly & Carli, *supra* note 9 at 102.

123. Holly English, *Gender on Trial: Sexual Stereotypes and Work/Life Balance in the Legal Workplace* 142 (2003).

124. *Price Waterhouse v. Hopkins,* 490 U.S. 228, 234 (1989); Eagly & Carli, *supra* note 9 at 112.

125. *Id.* at 256.

126. *Id.* at 235.

127. *Id.* at 251.

128. Eagly & Carli, *supra* note 9 at 110.

129. For more on ambivalent sexism, see Peter Glick & Susan T. Fiske, "Ambivalent Stereotypes as Legitimizing Ideologies: Differentiating Paternalistic and Envious Prejudice," in *The Psychology of Legitimacy: Emerging Perspectives on Ideology, Justice, and Intergroup Relations* (J. T. Jost & B. Major eds., 2001); Peter Glick & Susan T. Fiske, "An Ambivalent Alliance: Hostile and Benevolent Sexism as Complementary Justifications for Gender Inequality," 56 *Am. Psychol.* 109–118 (2001); Peter Glick & Susan T. Fiske, "Ambivalent Sexism," *supra* note 7 at 115–188; Peter Glick & Susan T. Fiske, "The Ambivalent Sexism Inventory: Differentiating Hostile and Benevolent Sexism," 70 *J. Personality & Soc. Psychol.* 491–512 (1996). For ambivalent sexism in the workplace, see Oakley, *supra* note 93 at 328. For competence and social approval, see Madeline Heilman, "Description and Prescription; How Gender Stereotypes Prevent Women's Ascent up the Organizational Ladder," 57 *J. Soc. Issues* 657, 661 (2001). For the double bind, see Glick & Fiske, "Ambivalent Sexism," *supra* note 7, at 115, 170.

130. Peter Glick, Jeffrey Diebold, Barbara Bailey-Werner, & Lin Zhu, "The Two Faces of Adam: Ambivalent Sexism and Polarized Attitudes toward Women," 23 *Personality & Soc. Psych. Bul.* 1323, 1330 (1997).

131. Huang, *supra* note 103 at 9.

132. Diana Burgess & Eugene Borgida, "Who Women Are, Who Women Should Be: Descriptive and Prescriptive Gender Stereotyping in Sex Discrimination," 5 *Psychol., Pub. Pol'y, and Law* 675 (1999).

133. Williams, "Social Psychology of Stereotyping," *supra* note 100 at 423.

134. Gans Epner, *supra* note 11 at vi.

135. Eagly & Carli, *supra* note 9 at 106 .

136. Heilman, "Sex Stereotypes," *supra* note 92 at 6 (citing Taylor, *supra* note 42 at 778, 778–793).

137. Joan C. Williams & Donna Norton, *Under the Elms*, published at www .worklifelaw.org.

138. Rudman, *supra* note 88 at 639, citing Alice H. Eagly et al., "Sex Differences in Social Behavior: A Social-Role Interpretation," 111 *Psychol. Bull.* 3, 3–22 (1992); Susan T. Fiske et al., "Social Science Research on Trial: Use of Stereo-typing Research in *Price Waterhouse v. Hopkins*," 46 *Am. Psych.* 1049, 1049–1060 (1991).

139. Rudman, *supra* note 88 at 642 (citing studies).

140. *Id.* at 631.

141. Fiske et al., *supra* note 85 at 885 (feminists).

142. *Ezold v. Wolf, Block, Schorr & Solis-Cohen*, 983 F. 2d 509 (3d. Cir 1992), cert. den., 510 U.S. 826 (1993).

143. Charisse Jones & Kumea Shorter-Gooden, *Shifting: The Double Lines of Black Women in America* 23 (2003).

144. Fiske et al., *supra* note 85 at 880n.3, citing Patricia G. Devine, "Stereotypes and Prejudice: Their Automatic and Controlled Components," 56 *J. Person-ality Soc. Psych.* 5–18 (1989); Patricia G. Devine & Andrew J. Elliot, "Are Racial Stereotypes Really Fading? The Princeton Trilogy Revisited," 21 *Per-sonality Soc. Psych. Bulletin* 1139, 1139–1150 (1995); Patricia G. Devine et al., "Prejudice with and without Compunction," 60 *Personality Soc. Psych. Bulletin* 817, 817–830 (1991).

145. Jones & Shorter-Gooden, *supra* note 143 at 24.

146. Fiske et al., *supra* note 85 at 880.

147. *Id.* at 885.

148. Glick & Fiske, "An Ambivalent Alliance," *supra* note 129 at 109, 113 ; Shelley E. Taylor, "A Categorization Approach to Stereotyping," in *Cognitive Pro-cesses in Stereotyping and Intergroup Behavior* 84 (D. Hamilton ed., 1981); Kay Deaux et al., "Level of Categorization and Content of Gender Stereo-types," 3 *Soc. Cognition* 145, 166 (1985). See also Williams, "Social Psychol-ogy of Stereotyping," *supra* note 100 at 419–420.

149. English, *supra* note 123 at 168.

150. Eagly & Carli, *supra* note 9 at 104

151. *Id.* at 88.

152. Peter Glick & Susan Fiske, "Ambivalent Stereotypes as Legitimatizing Ideol-ogies: Differentiating Paternalistic and Envious Prejudice," in *The Psychol-ogy of Legitimacy, supra* note 129.

153. Eagly & Carli, *supra* note 9 at 105.

154. Glick & Fiske, *The Two Faces of Adam, supra* note 130 at 1328.

155. Confidential interview (name in quote also removed for confidentiality), 2008.

156. Devon W. Carbado & Mitu Gulati, "The Fifth Black Woman," 11 *J. of Contemporary & Legal Issues* 701 (2000); Devon W. Carbado & Mitu Gu-lati, "Working Identity," 85 *Cornell L. Rev.* 1259 (2000); Devon W. Car-

bado & Mitu Gulati, "Conversations at Work," 79 *Oregon L. Rev.* 103 (2000).

157. Kenji Yoshino, *Covering: The Hidden Assault on Our Civil Rights* (2007).

158. Joan C. Williams, Stephanie Bornstein, & Tamina Alon, "Beyond the 'Chilly Climate': Eliminating Bias against Women and Fathers in Academe," *Thought & Action: The NEA Higher Education Journal* 79 (Fall 2006).

159. J. S. Bridges & C. Etaugh, "College Students' Perceptions of Mothers: Effects of Maternal Employment-Childrearing and Motive for Employment," 32 *Sex Roles* 635 (1995).

160. Phyllis Moen & Stephen Street, "Time Clocks: Couples' Work Hour Strategies," in *It's about Time* 32 (Phyllis Moen ed., 2003).

161. Douglas Stone, Bruce Patton, & Sheila Heen, *Difficult Conversations: How to Discuss What Matters Most* 111–128 (2000).

162. Katharine Graham, *Personal History* 5 (1997). See also Ronald F. Levant, "Toward the Reconstruction of Masculinity," in *A New Psychology of Men* 229 (Ronald F. Levant & Williams S. Pollack eds., 1995); Stephen J. Bergman, "Men's Psychological Development: A Relational Perspective" in *id.* at 68 (exploring masculinity and the expression of emotion).

163. Lillian Rubin, *Worlds of Pain: Life in the Working-Class Family* 124 (1992).

164. Shel Silverstein, *The Giving Tree* (1964).

165. Kris Paap, *Working Construction: Why White Working-Class Men Put Themselves—and the Labor Movement—in Harm's Way* (2006); Michael Yarrow, "The Gender-Specific Class Consciousness of Appalachian Coal Miners: Structure and Change," in *Bringing Class back in: Contemporary and Historical Perspectives* 285 (S. McNall, R. Levine, & R. Fantasia eds., 1991).

166. S. McNall, R. Levine, & R. Fantasia, *Bringing Class back in: Contemporary and Historical Perspectives* 300 (1991).

167. Eagly, et al., "Sex Differences in Social Behavior," *supra* note 138.

168. Ridgeway, *supra* note 7 at 637, 639–641.

169. Eagly & Carli, *supra* note 9 at 87.

170. Judith Butler, *Gender Trouble* 4 (1990) ("The very subject of women is no longer understood in stable or abiding terms").

171. Lareau, *supra* note 26 (healthy relationships).

172. Ann Bookman, *Starting in Our Own Backyards: How Working Families Can Build Community and Survive the New Economy* (2003).

173. Michael S. Kimmel, *The Gendered Society* 138 (2004).

174. See, e.g., Bernice Johnson Reagon, "Coalition Politics: Turning the Century," in *Home Girls: A Black Feminist Anthology* 356–368 (Barbara Smith ed., 2000); Sheryl Cashin, "Shall We Overcome? Transcending Race, Class and Identity," 79 *St. John's L. Rev.* 253–291 (2005); Sumi Cho and Robert Westley, "Critical Race Coalitions: Key Movements That Performed the Theory," 33 *U.C. Davis. L. Rev.* 1377–1427 (2000); Leslie Espinoza & Angela P. Harris, "Afterword: Embracing the Tar-Baby—LatCrit Theory and the Sticky Mess of Race," 85 *Cal. L. Rev.* 1585–1645 (1997).

175. Ann Swidler, "Culture in Action: Symbols and Strategies," 51 *Am. Soc. Rev.* 273–286 (1986) (toolkit metaphor).

4. Reconstructive Feminism and Feminist Theory

1. Trudi C. Ferguson, *Blue Collar Women: Trailblazing Women Take on Men-Only Jobs* 129 (1994) (epigraph), by permission of the publisher, New Horizon Press. For examples of second-wave feminists who reason from personal identity, see, e.g., Paula Gunn Allen, "Where I Come from Is Like This," in *The Sacred Hoop: Recovering the Feminine Side in American Indian Traditions* (1986) (experience of a biracial American Indian Woman); Audre Lorde, "The Master's Tools Will Never Dismantle the Master's House," in *Sister Outsider: Essays and Speeches* (1984) (experience of a Black lesbian feminist); Peggy McIntosh, *White Privilege and Male Privilege: A Personal Account of Coming to See Correspondences through Work in Women's Studies*, Working Paper 189 (1988), reprinted in *Feminist Frontiers* 29 (5th ed., 2001) (white woman viewing white privilege); Patricia Hill Collins, "The Social Construction of Black Feminist Thought," 14 *Signs: J. of Women in Culture and Society* 745 (1989) (experience of Black women); Roberta Galler, "The Myth of the Perfect Body," in *Pleasure and Danger: Exploring Female Sexuality* (Carole S. Vance ed., 1984) (experience of disabled woman); Yen Le Espiritu, "Ideological Racism and Cultural Resistance: Constructing Our Own Images," in *Asian American Women and Men* (1997) (experience of an Asian-American woman); Gloria Anzaldúa, "En Rapport, in Opposition: Cobrando Cuentas a las Nuestras," in *Making Face, Making Soul = Haciendo caras* (1990) (women of color and feminism); Cathy J. Cohen, "Punks, Bulldaggers, and Welfare Queens: The Radical Potential of Queer Politics?" 3 GLQ: A J. of Lesbian and Gay Studies 437 (1997) (politics of queer identities); R. W. Conell, "Gender Politics for Men," in *Feminism and Men: Reconstructing Gender Relations* (Steven P. Schact & Doris W. Ewing eds., 1998) (experience of a man exploring masculinity). For a useful review of third-wave feminism, see Bridget J. Crawford, "Toward a Third-Wave Feminist Legal Theory: Young Women, Pornography and the Praxis of Pleasure," 14 *Mich. J. Gender & L.* 99, 125–126 (2007–2008).
2. Joan C. Williams, "Notes of a Jewish Episcopalian: Gender as a Language of Class; Religion as a Dialect of Liberalism," in *Debating Democracy's Discontent: Essays on American Politics, Law, and Public Policy* (Anita L. Allen & Milton C. Regan eds., 1998).
3. See Thomas Nagel, *The View from Nowhere* (1989).
4. The argument in the text is, in essence, that looking for "a" theory of gender is an example of "language gone on holiday." Ludwig Wittgenstein, *Philosophical Investigations* I para. 38, 11; John Dewey, "The Need for a Recovery of Philosophy," in *Creative Intelligence: Essays in the Pragmatic Attitude* 3–69 (J. Dewey ed., 1917).
5. Catharine MacKinnon, *Feminism Unmodified: Discourses on Law and Life* 6 (1987) [hereinafter MacKinnon, *Feminism Unmodified*].

6. Catharine A. MacKinnon, *Toward a Feminist Theory of the State* 137 (1989) [hereinafter *Theory of the State*].
7. Judith Butler, *Gender Trouble* 6–7 (1990).
8. Nicholas Pedriana, "From Protective to Equal Treatment: Legal Framing Processes and Transformation of the Women's Movement in the 1960s," 111 *Am. J. of Soc.* 1718 (2006).
9. 29 U.S.C. § 206(d) (West 2008) (Equal Pay Act of 1963); 42 U.S.C. § 2000e (West 2008) (Title VII of the Civil Rights Act of 1964).
10. Lenore J. Weitzman, *The Divorce Revolution: The Unexpected Economic Consequences for Women and Children in America* xiv, 32–36 (1985).
11. 477 U.S. 57 (1986).
12. Alice H. Eagly & Linda L. Carli, *Through the Labyrinth* 109 (2007).
13. Minneapolis, Mn. Code § 139.10 (1983) (Minneapolis Anti-Pornography Ordinance). See Model Anti-Pornography Civil-Rights Ordinance, in Andrea Dworkin & Catharine MacKinnon, *Pornography and Civil Rights: A Day for Women's Equality* 95 (1988) (veto by mayor).
14. Indianapolis Ind. Code § 16 (1984) (Indianapolis Ordinance); *Am. Booksellers Ass'n v. Hudnut*, 771 F.2d 323 (7th Cir. 1985), *aff'd*, 475 U.S. 1001 (1986) (holding antipornography ordinance unconstitutional).
15. 42 U.S.C. 13925 *et seq.* (West 2008).
16. Butler, *supra* note 7.
17. MacKinnon, *Feminism Unmodified, supra* note 5 at 32.
18. *Id.* at 32–45.
19. See, e.g., Lisa Belkin, "The Opt-Out Revolution," *New York Times,* October 23, 2006, available at http://www.nytimes.com/2003/10/26/magazine/26WOMEN.html?ei=5007&en=02f8d75eb63908e0&ex=1382500800&partner=USERLAND&pagewanted=all&position= ; Deborah Tannen, *You Just Don't Understand* (1990); Deborah Tannen, *Talking 9-to-5* (1994); John Gray, *Men Are from Mars, Women Are from Venus* (1992). Gray has now written nine books along this theme.
20. Vicki Schultz, "Life's Work," 100 *Colum. L. Rev.* 1881 (2000) (critiquing "joint property" feminists, including Joan Williams, for what Schultz sees as their failure to recognize the dangers that face women who focus on family work); Joan Williams, "Deconstructing Gender," 87 *Mich. L. Rev.* 797, 806–810 (1989) (critiquing difference feminism, as represented by Carol Gilligan).
21. Martin H. Malin, "Fathers and Parental Leave," 72 *Tex. L. Rev.* 1047, 1064–1065, 1065 n.109 (1994).
22. *Taylor v. Louisiana*, 419 U.S. 522 (1975); *Duren v. Missouri*, 439 U.S. 357 (1979) (prohibiting the exclusion of women from juries);29 U.S.C. § 206(d) (West 2008) (Equal Pay Act).
23. See The Justices of the Supreme Court, available at http://www.supremecourtus.gov/about/biographiescurrent.pdf (Ruth Bader Ginsburg biography); *Reed v. Reed*, 404 U.S. 71 (1971) (invalidating a law that favored men over women as estate administrators); *Frontiero v. Richardson*, 411 U.S. 677 (1973) (invalidating law that required proof of dependency by wives); *Weinberger v. Wiesenfeld*, 420 U.S. 636 (1975) (invalidating law that automatically awarded

survivor's benefits to wives but not to husbands); See above, *Califano v. Gold-farb*, 430 U.S. 199 (1977) (invalidating law that required dependent husbands to show proof for survivor's benefits).

24. *Reed v. Reed, supra* note 23 (striking down as a violation of equal protection a Florida statute that appointed men rather than women as administrators of decedents' estates if a man and a women were equally qualified pursuant to existing rules); *Weinberger v. Wiesenfeld, supra* note 23 (striking down as a violation of equal protection a rule allowing spousal benefits for widows, but not widowers, of service members); *Orr v. Orr*, 440 U.S. 268 (1979) (striking down as a violation of equal protection state statutes that require husbands but not wives to pay alimony); *Mississippi Univ. for Women v. Hogan*, 458 U.S. 718 (1982) (striking down as a violation of equal protection a state nursing school that was limited to women students).

25. Cary Franklin, *Sex Roles and the Foundations of Constitutional Sex Discrimination Law* (manuscript in possession of the author).

26. Ruth Bader Ginsberg, *Gender and the Constitution*, 44 U. Cin. L. Rev. 1, 34 (1975).

27. Ruth Bader Ginsberg, *Some Thoughts on Benign Classifications in the Context of Sex*, 10 Conn. L. Rev. 813, 826 (1978).

28. Katharine T. Bartlett & Deborah L. Rhode, *Gender and Law: Theory, Doctrine, Commentary* 17 (discussing *Frontiero v. Richardson, supra* note 23 at 677, 678, 151 (4th ed., 2006)).

29. *Price Waterhouse v. Hopkins*, 490 U.S. 228, 235 (1989).

30. *Dothard v. Rolinson*, 433 U.S. 321 (1977) (prison guards); *UAW v. Johnson Controls*, 499 U.S. 187 (1991) (factory workers); *Bd. of Directors of Rotary Int'l v. Rotary Club of Duarte*, 481 U.S. 537 (1987) (Rotary club); *Isbister v. Boys' Club of Santa Cruz, Inc.*, 707 P.2d 212 (Cal. 1985) (Boys' club).

31. Mary Becker, *Prince Charming: Abstract Equality*, 1987 Sup.Ct.Rev. 201, 202.

32. Jana B. Singer, *Divorce Reform and Gender Justice*, 67 N.C. L. Rev. 1103, 1106 (1989).

33. Leslie J. Harris, Lee E. Teitelbaum, & Carol A. Weisbrod, *Family Law* 374 (1996) (documenting changing attitudes toward alimony); *Id.* at 369 (tendency to award spouse with physical custody possession of the marital home less likely today than in 1970s and 1980s). June Carbone & Margaret F. Bring, "Rethinking Marriage: Feminist Ideology, Economic Change, and Divorce Reform," 65 *Tul. L. Rev.* 953, 981 (1991).

34. See Harris et al., *supra* note 33 at 604 (for discussion of traditional standards for child custody); Harry D. Krause, Linda D. Elrod, Marsha Garrison, & J. Thomas Oldham, *Family Law: Cases and Questions* 698 (6th ed., 2007); Walter O. Weyrauch, Sanford N. Katz, & Frances Olsen, *Cases and Materials on Family Law: Legal Concepts and Changing Human Relationships* 840 (1994) (regarding how mothers trade off economic claims to get child custody).

35. Martha Albertson Fineman, "Societal Factors Affecting the Creation of Legal Rules for Distribution of Property at Divorce," in *At the Boundaries of Law: Feminism and Legal Theory* (Martha Albertson Fineman & Nancy Sweet Thomadsen eds., 1991) [herein after "Societal Factors"].

36. *Calif. Fed. S. & L. Ass'n v. Guerra,* 479 U.S. 272 (1987).
37. 42 U.S.C. 2000e(k) (West 2008). The PDA provides in pertinent part: "The terms 'because of sex' or 'on the basis of sex' include, but are not limited to, because of or on the basis of pregnancy, childbirth, or related medical conditions; and women affected by pregnancy, childbirth, or related medical conditions shall be treated the same for all employment-related purposes, including receipt of benefits . . . as other persons not so affected but similar in their ability or inability to work." *Id.*
38. See, e.g., Christine A. Littleton, *Reconstructing Sexual Equality,* 75 Calif. L. Rev. 1279 (1987); Linda Krieger and Patricia Cooney, "The Miller-Wohl Controversy: Equal Treatment, Positive Action, and the Meaning of Women's Equality," Women's L. Forum: 13 *Golden Gate Univ. L. Rev.* 513 (1983), reprinted in, *Feminist Legal Theory: Foundations* 156 (D. Kelly Weisberg ed., 1993).
39. Wendy Webster Williams, "The Equality Crisis: Some Reflections on Culture, Courts, and Feminism," 7 *Women's Rts. L. Rep.* 175 (1982).
40. Wendy Williams is a friend, but no relation, of the author.
41. Wendy Williams, *supra* note 39 at 196.
42. 29 U.S.C. § 2601-2654. See Ronald D. Elving, *Conflict & Compromise: How Congress Makes the Law* 18-21 (1995).
43. Penelope M. Huang, *Gender Bias in Academia: Finding from Focus Groups* 7, Center for WorkLife Law, 2008 (on file with the author).
44. *Id.* at 9.
45. Katherine Franke, "Cunning Stunts: From Hegemony to Desire, a Review of Madonna's Sex," 20 *N.Y.U. Rev. of L. & Social Change* 549 (1993).
46. Ginia Bellafonte, "Two Fathers, One Happy to Stay at Home," *New York Times,* November 12, 2004, at A1; Census Snapshot, *California Lesbian, Gay and Bisexual Population,* October 2008 (percentage of California gay couples with one parent at home is almost the same as among comparable heterosexual couples).
47. Bellafonte, *supra* note 46.
48. R. W. Chan, R. C. Brooks, B. Raboy, & Christine Patterson, "Division of Labor among Lesbian and Heterosexual Parents: Associations with Children's Adjustment," 12 *J. of Fam. Psychol.* 402–419 (1998); G. Dunne, "Opting into Motherhood: Lesbians Blurring the Boundaries and Transforming the Meaning of Parenthood and Kinship," 14 *Gender and Soc'y* 11–35 (2000); Christine Patterson, "Families of the Lesbian Baby Boom: Parents' Division of Labor and Children's Adjustment," 62 *J. of Marriage and the Fam.* 1052–1069 (1995); M. Sullivan, "Rozzie and Harriet? Gender and Family Patterns of Lesbian Coparents," 10 *Gender and Soc'y* 747–767 (1996); F. L. Tasker & S. Golombok, "The Role of Co-Mothers in Planned Lesbian-Led Families," in *Living Difference: Lesbian Perspectives on Work and Family Life* 49–68 (G. A. Dunner ed., 1998); Sondra Solomon, Esther Rothblum, & Kimberly Balsam, "Money, Housework, Sex and Conflict: Same-Sex Couples in Civil Unions, Those Not in Civil Unions, and Heterosexual Married Siblings," 52 *Sex Roles* 561–575 (2005); Charlotte Patterson, Erin Sutfin, & Megan Fulcher, "Division of Labor among Lesbian and Heterosexual Parenting Couples: Correlates of Specialized versus Shared Patterns," 11 *J. of Adult Dev.* 179–189 (2004); Abbie

E. Goldberg & Maureen Perry-Jenkins, "The Division of Labor and Perceptions of Parental Roles: Lesbian Couples across the Transition to Parenthood," 24 *J. Soc. & Personal Relationships* 297 (2007).

49. Judith Stacey & Timothy J. Biblarz, "(How) Does the Sexual Orientation of Parents Matter?" 66 *Am. Soc. Rev.* 159, 166 (2001).
50. Steven E. Mock & Steve W. Cornelius, "The Case of Same-Sex Couples," in *It's about Time: Couples and Careers* 275, 285 (Phyllis Moen ed., 2003); Christopher Carrington, "Domesticity and Political Economy of Lesbigay Families," in *Families at Work: Expanding the Bounds* 88 (Naomi Gerstel et al. eds., 2002).
51. Carrington *supra* note 50 at 88.
52. *Id.*; Patterson et al., *supra* note 48. In lesbian couples, the strongest influence is ideological. However, the study found that the "more the second parent wanted to be responsible for childcare, the more [she] actually participated in it." This appears to be a statement that the lesbian partner who does not want to participate in child care need not do so—which sounds pretty similar to the kind of gender privilege exercised by heterosexual men—except that lesbian "second parents," being women, may well choose more often to participate. Patterson, *supra* note 48 at 184.
53. Christopher Carrington, *No Place Like Home: Relationships and Family Life among Lesbians and Gay Men* 173 (1999).
54. *Id.* at 177.
55. *Id.*
56. *Id.* at 209. I saw many women struggling to found home-based business "in order to make a contribution" at a conference of Mothers and More, in Chicago on October 21, 2001.
57. Franke, *supra* note 45 at 572.
58. Schultz, *supra* note 20, at 1900n.60–61
59. "Be a Man: Men Compete Harder than Women," *The Economist*, June 26, 2003.
60. Janet Halley, *Split Decisions: How and Why to Take a Break from Feminism* 13 (2006).
61. Maureen Dowd, "Who's Hormonal? Hillary or Dick?" *New York Times*, February 8, 2006, at A1.
62. Maureen Dowd, "Should Hillary Pretend to Be a Flight Attendant?" *New York Times*, November 14, 2007, at 23.
63. Raymond Fisman, Sheena S. Iyengar, Emir Kamenica, & Itamar Simonson, "Gender Differences in Mate Selection: Evidence from a Speed Dating Experiment," *Quarterly J. of Econ.* 673 (May 2006).
64. Linda L. Carli, "Gender and Social Influence," 57 *J. Soc. Issues* 725 (2001).
65. Carla Marinucci, "McCain and Obama Have High Hopes for Today; Independents Expected to Hold Key in New Hampshire," *San Francisco Chronicle*, January 8, 2008, at A1.
66. Eagly & Carli, *supra* note 12 at 166 (Steel quote); Cecilia Ridgeway, "Gender, Status & Leadership," 57 *J. Soc. Issues* 637 (2001) (high-powered women set off signals of masculinity with signals of femininity); John F. Dovidio et al., "Power Displays between Men and Women in Discussions of Gender Linked Tasks," 50 *J. Personality & Soc. Psych.* 580 (1988) (women talk less than

men); Linda L. Carli, "Gender, Language, and Influence," 59 *J. of Personality and Soc. Psych.* 941 (1990) (more tentative speech patterns); Wendy Wood & Steven J. Karten, "Sex Differences in Interaction Style as a Product of Perceived Sex Difference in Competence," 50 *J. Personality and Soc. Psych.* 341 (1986) (fewer task suggestions); S. L. Ellyson, John Dovidio, & C. E. Briwn, "The Look of Power: Gender Differences and Similarities," in *Gender, Interaction, and Inequality* 50 (Cecilia Ridgeway ed., 1992) (fewer gestures that display dominance); Gardiner Harris, "If Shoe Won't Fit, Fix the Foot? Popular Surgery Raises Concern," *New York Times,* December 7, 2003, available at http://query.nytimes.com/gst/fullpage.html?res=9400E0DF133DF934A 35751C1A9659C8B63&sec=&spon=&pagewanted=all.

67. Interview with Shauna Marshall, professor of law and academic dean, UC Hastings College of the Law, in San Francisco, CA (June 2009).

68. Linda Hirshman, *Get to Work: A Manifesto for Women of the World* (2006); Leslie Bennetts, *The Feminine Mistake: Are We Giving up Too Much?* 234 (2008); S. J. Rose & H. I. Hartmann, *Still a Man's Labor Market: The Long-Term Earnings Gap,* Institute for Women's Policy Research (2004), available at http://www.iwpr.org/pdf/C366_RIB.pdf (30% less); Christy Spivey, "Time off at What Price? The Effects of Career Interruptions on Earnings," 59 *Indus. and Lab. Rel. Rev.* 119–140 (2005) (negative effect on wages).

69. Hirshman, *supra* note 68 at 34, 2, 78, 13, 79.

70. Bennetts, supra note 68 at 72–96; Joan C. Williams, Jessica Manvell, & Stephanie Bornstein, *Opt Out or Pushed Out: How the Press Covers Work-Family Conflict* 15–16, at http://www.uchastings.edu/site_files/WLL/OptOutPushed Out.pdf (press conveys the inaccurate image that it is easy for women to re-enter the workforce after a career break).

71. Bennetts, *supra* note 68 at 234, 249, 237, 239, 176, 180.

72. Jennifer Baumgardner & Amy Richards, *Manifesta: Young Women, Feminism, and the Future* (2005).

73. Crawford, *supra* note 1 at 162, 120, 121.

74. Stephanie Rosenbloom, "Evolution of a Feminist Daughter," *New York Times,* March 18, 2007, at 162 (quoted in Crawford, *supra* note 1).

75. *Id.*

76. Mignon R. Moore, "Gendered Power Relations among Women: A Study of Household Decision Making in Black, Lesbian Stepfamilies," 73 *Am. Soc. Rev.* 335, 337 (2008).

77. Riché Jeneen Daniel Barnes, "Black Women Have Always Worked: Is There a Work-Family Conflict among the Black Middle Class?" in *The Changing Landscape of Work and Family in the American Middle Class: Reports from the Field* 189 (E. Rudd & L. Descartes eds., 2008); Mary Pattillo-McCoy, "Black Picket Fences," in *Families at Work, supra* note 50 at 203.

78. Jennifer Hochschild, *Facing up to the American Dream: Race, Class, and the Soul of the Nation* 55 (1995) ("Americans are close to unanimous in endorsing the idea of the American dream. Virtually all agree that all citizens should have political equality and that everyone in America warrants equal educational opportunities and equal opportunities in general.").

79. Janet C. Gornick & Marcia K. Meyers, *Families That Work: Policies for Reconciling Parenthood and Employment* 266 (Table 8.8.) (2003) (table illustrating association of lack of family support and poverty rates).

80. Reva Siegel, "Note: Employment Equality under the Pregnancy Discrimination Act of 1978," 94 *Yale L. J.* 929 (1985). For Siegel's most recent thinking on this topic, see Reva B. Siegel, "'You've Come a Long Way, Baby': Rehnquist's New Approach to Pregnancy Discrimination in *Hibbs*," 58 *Stanford L. Rev.* 1871–1878 (2006).

81. *Calif. Fed. S. & L. Ass'n, supra* note 36 at 289, (quoting 123 Cong. Rec. 29658 (1977)).

82. *Washington v. Ill. Dep't of Revenue*, 420 F.3d 658, 662 (7th Cir. 2005) (both quotes).

83. Becker, *supra* note 31 at 209 (quote).

84. *Id.* at 206 (real physical differences), 216 (real social differences); Mary Becker, "Patriarchy and Inequality: Toward a Substantive Feminism," 999 *U. Chi. L. F.* 21, 21–22, 48–49 (defending cultural feminism, which is based on the premise of real psychological differences between men and women).

85. Bartlett & Rhode, *supra* note 28 at 208–53; *Calif. Fed. S. & L. Ass'n, supra* note 36 at 272; *Troupe v. May Dept. Stores Co.*, 20 F.3d 734 (7th Cir. 1994) (pregnant women); *Kahn v. Shevin*, 416 U.S. 351 (1974); *State v. Bachmann*, 521 N.W.2d 886 (Minn. Ct. App. 1994) (homemakers).

86. *American Nurses' Ass'n v. Illinois*, 783 F.2d 716 (7th Cir. 1986).

87. Bartlett & Rhode, *supra* note 28, at 637.

88. Butler, *supra* note 7.

89. Martha Minow, *Making All the Difference* 56–60 (1990).

90. *Los Angeles Dept. of Water & Power v. Manhart*, 435 U.S. 702 (1978).

91. Martha Albertson Fineman, "Feminist Theory in Law: The Difference It Makes," 2 *Colum. J. Gender & L.* 2 (1992) ("The lesson some of us have learned from the results of the past several decades of equality feminism, however, is that a theory of difference is necessary in order to do more than merely open the doors to institutions designed with men in mind.").

92. Martha Albertson Fineman, *The Illusion of Equality: The Rhetoric and Reality of Divorce Reform* 3 (1991).

93. See Carl E. Schneider & Margaret F. Brinig, *An Invitation to Family Law: Principles, Process, and Perspectives* 308–309 (2000) (fewer than half of divorcing husbands in a relatively wealthy sample had property worth $2,500 or more, and only a third had property worth $10,000 or more).

94. Gornick & Meyers, *supra* note 79 at 48.

95. See Mary E. O'Connell, "Alimony after No-Fault: A Practice in Search of a Theory," 23 *New Eng. L. Rev.* 437, 438 (1988); Milton C. Regan Jr., "Divorce Reform and the Legacy of Gender," 90 *Mich. L. Rev.* 1453, 1470 (1992) (book review); Cynthia Starnes, "Divorce and the Displaced Homemaker: A Discourse on Playing with Dolls, Partnership Buyouts, and Dissociation under No-Fault," 60 *U. Chi. L. Rev.* 106–119 (1993); Ann Laquer Estin, "Maintenance, Alimony, and the Rehabilitation of Family Care," 71 *N.C. L. Rev.* 721, 741 (1993); Ira M. Ellman, "The Theory of Alimony," 77 *Cal. L. Rev.* 1 (1989).

96. Joan C. Williams, *Unbending Gender: Why Family and Work Conflict and What to Do about It* 126–127 (2000).

97. Gornick & Meyers, *supra* note 79 at 48.

98. Marin Clarkberg & Stacey S. Merola, "Competing Clocks: Work and Leisure," in *It's about Time: Couples and Careers* 35, 41–42 (Phyllis Moen ed., 2003).

99. Harris et al., *supra* note 33 at 318–329.

100. "Societal Factors," *supra* note 35 at 269 ("I am not convinced that the circumstances that generated arguments for a distribution system focused on needs, however, are no longer in evidence"). The issue is not whether women remain unequal but whether "needs" is a persuasive rhetoric.

101. Hochschild, *supra* note 78 at 18.

102. Patricia J. Williams, "Alchemical Notes: Reconstructing Ideals from Deconstructed Rights," 22 *Harv. C.R.-C.L. L. Rev.* 401, 412–413 (1987).

103. See, e.g., Lynn Hecht Schafran & Norma Juliet Wikler, *Operating a Task Force on Gender Bias in the Courts* 91 (1986); Lynn Schafran, "Gender Bias in Family Courts," 17 *Fam. Advoc.* 22 (1994); *Report of the Florida Supreme Court Gender Bias Study Commission, Executive Summary* 4–10 (1990), available at http://www.floridasupremecourt.org/pub_info/documents/bias. pdf; *Achieving Equal Justice for Women and Men in California Courts, Final Report* 119–202 (1996), available at http://www.courtinfo.ca.gov/programs/access/documents/f-report.pdf. The NOW Legal Defense and Education Fund provides on its Web site a comprehensive listing of the federal and state gender bias reports as well as contact information for obtaining copies. NJEP Task Force Reports, available at http://www.nowldef.org/html/njep/report.shtml (1997).

104. Williams, *supra* note 96 at 114–144.

105. *Id.* at 120–121.

106. See, e.g., Linda K. Kerber et al., "On *In a Different Voice*: An Interdisciplinary Forum," in *Feminism in the Study of Religion* (Darlene Juschka ed., 2001); Judy Auerbach et al., "Commentary: On Gilligan's *In a Different Voice*," 11 *Feminist Stud.* 149 (1985); Debra Nails, "Social Scientific Sexism: Gilligan's Mismeasure of Man," 50 *Soc. Res.* 643 (1983); John M. Broughton, "Women's Rationality and Men's Virtues: A Critique of Gender Dualism in Gilligan's Theory of Moral Development," 50 *Soc. Res.* 597 (1983).

107. See, e.g., Sally F. Goldfarb, "Reconceiving Civil Protection Orders for Domestic Violence: Can Law Help End the Abuse without Ending the Relationship?" 29 *Cardozo L. Rev.* 1487, 1500 (2008) (citing Carol Gilligan for the proposition that women are more focused on relationships than are men). See also Bartlett & Rhode, *supra* note 28 at 637 (discussing different voice feminism); Martha Chamallas, *Introduction to Feminist Theory* 53–62 (2nd ed., 2003).

108. See Belkin, *supra* note 19 at 47 (quoting mothers attributing their decisions to leave the workforce to "evolution" and differences in men's and women's brains, and herself attributing women's decisions to biology). *Id.* at 58 ("'My first readjustments were practical . . . I wouldn't hop on a plan every morning

to explore the wilds of Texas while leaving a nursing baby at home. Quickly, though, my choices became more philosophical.' ").

109. *Id.* at 47.

110. Kingsley R. Browne, "Sex and Temperament in Modern Society: A Darwinian View of the Glass Ceiling and the Gender Gap," 37 *Ariz. L. Rev.* 971, 984 (1995).

111. *Id.* at 1065.

112. Shelley E. Taylor et al., "Categorical and Contextual Bases of Person Memory and Stereotyping," 36 *J. Personality & Soc. Psychol.* 778, 791 (1978); Wendy Wood, Nancy Rhodes, & Melanie Whelan, "Sex Differences in Positive Well-Being: A Consideration of Emotional Style and Marital Status," 106 *Psychological Bulletin* 249, 250 (1989) (citing studies).

113. See Browne, *supra* note 110.

114. *Id.*; Peter Glick & Susan T. Fiske, "Ambivalent Sexism", in *Advances in Experimental Social Psychology* 33 (Mark P. Zanna ed., 2001); Laurie Rudman, "Self-Promotion as a Risk Factor for Women: The Costs and Benefits of Counter-Stereotypical Impression Management," 74 *J. Personality & Soc. Psych.* 629 (1998).

115. Carol Gilligan, *In a Different Voice: Psychological Theory and Women's Development* 66 (1982).

116. *Id.* at 31.

117. Browne, *supra* note 110 ("a passion for success"); Peter Glick & Susan T. Fiske, "Ambivalent Stereotypes as Legitimizing Ideologies," in *The Psychology of Legitimacy: Emerging Perspectives on Ideology, Justice, and Intergroup Relations* 278, 301 (John T. Yost & Brenda Major eds., 2001) (astute commentator).

118. Susan Fiske, Jun Xu, & Amy C. Cuddy, "(Dis)respecting versus (Dis)liking: Status and Interdependence Predict Ambivalent Stereotypes of Competence and Warmth," 55 *J. Soc. Issues* 473, 476 (1999).

119. Jeanne L. Schroeder, "Feminism Historicized: Medieval Misogynist Stereotypes in Contemporary Feminist Jurisprudence," 75 *Iowa L. Rev.* 1135, 1143n.12 (1990).

120. Naomi Cahn, "Gendered Identities: Women and Household Work," 44 *Villanova L. Rev.* 525, 538 (1999).

121. Lisa Belkin, "Life's Work: The Grapes of Marital Wrath," *New York Times,* March 15, 2000, at G1.

122. Susan Schwartz, "Women Could Get More, Just by Asking," *The Gazette,* December 15, 2003; Allyce Bess, "Fear of Negotiating Can Keep Women behind on the Payroll," *St. Louis Post-Dispatch,* November 12, 2003; Alan B. Kreuger, "Economic Scene: Women Are Less Likely to Negotiate, and It Can Be Costly to Them," *New York Times,* August 21, 2003; UC Irvine Graduate School of Management, "Ground-Breaking Study: Women's Negotiating Style Leads to Lower Pay Offers than Men Receive," Ascribe Newswire, July 21, 2003; Tessa Mayes, "Selfless Women Too Backward in Coming Forward for Promotion," *London Times,* August 24, 2003; Denise Kersten, "Women

Need to Learn the Art of the Deal; The Pay Gap Is Linked to One's Negotiation Skills," *USA Today,* November 17, 2003.

123. Caroline E. Mayer, "Readings," *Washington Post,* September 21, 2003.

124. Bess, *supra* note 122.

125. Jaine Carter & James D. Carter, "Women Are More Likely to Shrink from Negotiating," Scripps Howard News Service, July 24, 2003.

126. Catherine Jones, "Shy Women Lose Thousands by Not Asking for Promotion; Failure to Negotiate Is an Expensive Trait," *Western Mail,* August 25, 2003.

127. Bess, *supra* note 122.

128. Jones, *supra* note 126.

129. Linda Babcock & Sara Laschever, *Women Don't Ask* 184 (2008).

130. *Id.* at 186.

131. Nancy F. Cott, *The Bonds of Womanhood: "Women's Sphere" in New England, 1780–1835* 69–70, 146–148 (1997).

132. Marilyn Gardner, "Women Still Find It Hard to Say, 'Let's Make a Deal,'" *Christian Science Monitor,* September 3, 2003.

133. Stephanie Earls, "His and Hers: Although Some Games Have Been Made, Women's Paychecks Remain Smaller than Men's," *The Times Union,* December 22, 2003.

134. "Be a Man," *supra* note 59.

135. Hannah Riley Bowles, Linda Babcock, & Lei Lai, "Social Incentives for Gender Differences in the Propensity to Initiate Negotiations: Sometimes It Does Hurt to Ask," 103 *Org. Behav. and Human Decision Processes* 84–103 (2007).

136. *Id.* at 98–99.

137. *Id.* at 99–100.

138. *Id.* at 84, 99.

139. *Id.* at 86.

140. Dina W. Pradel et al., *When Gender Changes the Negotiation,* Harvard Business School Working Knowledge (February 13, 2006), available at http://hbswk.hbs.edu/item/5207.html.

141. Amy E. Walters et al., "Gender and Negotiator Competitiveness: A Meta-Analysis," 76 *Org. Behav. and Human Decision Processes* 1, 4 (1998).

142. Eagly & Carli, *supra* note 12 at 170.

143. "Arguing Works," *The Sun,* October 2, 2003.

144. Babcock & Laschever, *supra* note 129.

145. *Id.* at ix.

146. *Id.* at 1.

147. *Id.* at 5.

148. *Id.* at 11.

149. Amy Joyce, "Her Pay Gap Begins Right after Graduation," *Washington Post,* April 29, 2007, at F01, available *at* http://www.washingtonpost.com/wp-dyn/content/article/2007/04/28/AR2007042800827_pf.html.

150. Kenneth Glenn Dau-Schmidt, Marc Galanter, Kaushik Mukhopadhaya, & Kathleen E. Hull, *Gender and the Legal Profession: The Michigan Alumni*

Data Set 1967–2000, Research Paper #104 (2007), available at http://ssrn .com/abstract=1017362.

151. Pia Peltola, Melissa Milkie, & Stanley Presser, "The 'Feminist Mystique': Feminist Identity in Three Generations of Women," 18 *Gender & Society* 122 (2004); Jason Schnittker, Jeremy Freese, & Brian Powell, "Who Are Feminists and What Do They Believe? The Role of Generations," 68 *Am. Soc. Rev.* 607 (2003).

152. This is described at http://www.worklifelaw.org/GenderBias_takeAction .html.

153. *Queer Eye for the Straight Guy* (Bravo Television, 2003–2007).

154. Butler, *supra* note 7.

155. Candace West & Don H. Zimmerman, "Doing Gender," and Sarah Fenster- maker & Candace West, "Power, Inequality, and the Accomplishment of Gender: An Ethnomethodological View," in *Doing Gender, Doing Differ- ence: Inequality, Power, and Institutional Change* 42–43 (Sarah Fenstermaker & Candace West eds., 2002).

156. *The Adventures of Priscilla, Queen of the Desert* (Polygram Filmed Enter- tainment, 1994).

157. *About Schmidt* (New Line Cinema, 2002).

158. Katherine Franke, "Cunning Stunts: From Hegemony to Desire," 20 *N.Y.U. Rev. L. & Soc. Change* 549 (1993–1994).

159. Katherine M. Franke, "The Central Mistake of Sex Discrimination Law: The Disaggregation of Sex from Gender," 144 *U. Pa. L. Rev.* 1 (1995).

160. MacKinnon, *Feminism Unmodified, supra* note 5 at 36.

161. *Id.* at 37.

162. MacKinnon, *Theory of the State, supra* note 6 at 3, 128–31.*Compare* Rosa- lind Dixon, "Feminist Disagreement (Comparatively) Recast," 31 *Harv. J. L. & Gender* 277, 282 ("Sex-positive feminists challenge the premises of domi- nance feminism"); Crawford, *supra* note 1 at 99, 122 ("Offering women the opportunity to shop for sex toys, to make their sexual desire primary, is an example of sex-positive feminism at work"); Brenda Cossman et al., "Gen- der, Sexuality, and Power: Is Feminist Theory Enough?" 12 *Colum. J. Gender & L.* 601, 605. See also generally carol Queen, *Real Live Nude Girl: Chron- icles Of Sex-Positive Culture* (1997).

163. MacKinnon, *Feminism Unmodified,* supra note 5 at 14, 32, 45.

164. *Id.* at 86 ("the point of view of men"). See, e.g., *id.* at 3 ("Men in particular, if not men alone, sexualize inequality, especially the inequality of the sexes."); 59 ("Men define women as sexual beings; feminism comprehends that femi- ninity 'is' sexual. Men see rape as intercourse; feminists say much inter- course 'is' rape. Men say women desire degradation; feminists see female masochism as the ultimate success of male supremacy and marvel at its failures."); 71 (One "approach available under sex discrimination doctrine views women as men view women: in need of special protection, help, or indulgence.").

165. *Id.* at 45.

166. See Chamallas, *supra* note 107 at 78–88.

167. Angela Harris, "Race and Essentialism in Feminist Legal Theory," 42 *Stan. L. Rev.* 581 (1990); Catharine A. MacKinnon, "Reflections on Sex Equality under Law," 100 *Yale L. J.* 1281 (1991).

168. Kimberlé Williams Crenshaw, "Demarginalizing the Intersection of Race and Sex: A Black Feminist Critique of Antidiscrimination Doctrine, Feminist Theory, and Antiracist Politics," 1989 *U. of Chicago L. Forum* 139–167 (1989).

169. See generally *Critical Race Feminism: A Reader* (Adrien Wing ed., 1997); Patricia A. Cain, "Stories from the Gender Garden: Transsexuals and Anti-Discrimination Law," 75 *Denv. U. L. Rev.* 1321 (1998); Patricia A. Cain, "Lesbian Perspective, Lesbian Experience, and the Risk of Essentialism," 2 *Va. J. Soc. Pol'y & L.* 43 (1994).

170. See, e.g., Amy J. C. Cuddy & C. M. Frantz, "Race, Work Status, and the Maternal Wall" (May 3, 2007) (unpublished paper presented at *Gender Roles: Current Challenges*, an invited symposium conducted at the 79th annual meeting of the Midwestern Psychological Association in Chicago, IL), as cited in Stephen Benard et al., "Cognitive Bias and the Motherhood Penalty," 59 Hastings L. J. 1359, 1377–1378 (2008); Tanya Koropeckyj-Cox et al., "Biases, Premiums, and Penalties: Students' Perceptions of Parents and Childless/Childfree Couples" (2008) (unpublished manuscript, under review), as cited in Benard et al., *supra*.

171. See Janet E. Gans Epner, *Visible Invisibility: Women of Color in Law Firms*, ABA Commission on Women in the Profession 7 (2006); Benard et al., *supra* note 170, discussing Leticia Anne Peplau & Adam Fingerhut, "The Paradox of the Lesbian Worker," 60 *J. Soc. Issues* 719 (2004); Amy J. C. Cuddy et al., "When Professionals Become Mothers, Warmth Doesn't Cut the Ice," 60 *J. Soc. Issues* 701 (2004); Rebecca Glauber, "Marriage and the Motherhood Wage Penalty among African Americans, Hispanics, and Whites," 69 *J. Marriage & Fam.* 951 (2007); Ivy Kennelly, "That Single Mother Element: How White Employers Typify Black Women," 13 *Gender & Soc'y* 168 (1999); Cuddy & Frantz, *supra* note 170; Koropeckyj-Cox et al., *supra* note 170.

172. Barnes, *supra* note 77 at 190–192.

173. *Id.* at 195.

174. *Id.* at 197.

175. *Id.* at 198.

176. *Id.* at 195.

177. *Id.* at 197.

178. *Id.*

179. Compare Pamela Stone, *Opting Out?: Why Women Really Quit Careers and Head Home* 62 (2007) (arguing that although two-thirds of her predominantly white sample of stay-at-home mothers cited their husbands as a key reason they left employment, women typically cited their children's needs as the reason they left work), with Barnes, supra note 77 at 196, 206 (arguing that for black women, being a stay-at-home mother means opting out of careers that they and their families had worked so hard to achieve and that they were not the "strong black women" they were raised to be).

180. See generally Gans Epner, *supra* note 171.
181. Maureen Perry-Jenkins et al., "A Socio-Cultural Lens on Parents' Mental Health across the Transition to Parenthood" (2008) (unpublished manuscript on file with the author).
182. See generally Charisse Jones & Kumea Shorter-Gooden, *Shifting: The Double Lives of Black Women in America* (2003).
183. See, e.g., Crawford, *supra* note 1 at 99.

5. The Class Culture Gap

1. Julie Bettie, *Women without Class: Girls, Race, and Identity* 38 (2003) (epigraph), by permission of the publisher, the University of California Press. Lane Kenworthy, Sondra Barringer, Daniel Duerr, & Garrett Andrew Schneider, *The Democrats and White Working-Class Whites* (working paper, 2007), available at http://www.u.arizona.edu/~lkenwor/thedemocratsandworkingclasswhites .pdf (fell from 60% to 40%); Ruy Teixeira & Joel Rogers, *America's Forgotten Majority: Why the White Working Class Still Matters* 32–33, 85 (2000).
2. Arlie Hochschild, "Let Them Eat War," 6 *European J. of Psychotherapy, Counseling & Health* 1– 10 (2004) (painters, furniture movers); Teixeira & Rogers, supra note 1 at 177 (7 points).
3. Hochschild, *supra* note 2 (2004 data); Teixeria & Rogers, *supra* note 1 at 117 (two-thirds); Ruy Teixeira, *New Progressive America: Twenty Years of Demographic, Geographic, and Attitudinal Changes across the Country Herald a New Progressive Majority,* Center for American Progress, March 2009, available at http://www.americanprogress.org/issues/2009/03/pdf/progressive _america.pdf. Another recent article argues that the shift of white workers away from the Democrats occurred only after 1996. David Brady, Benjamin Sosnaud, & Steven M. Frenk, *The Shifting and Diverging White Working Class in Presidential Elections, 1972–2004* (working paper, July 21, 2008), available at http://www.soc.duke.edu/~brady/web/wwc.pdf. Divergences among scholars as to when the white working class began to move away from the Democrats reflect different definitions of "working class." Although I cite Kenworthy et al., *supra* note 1, I disagree with the article's thesis that cultural issues have not played a role. The proxies used in their quantitative analysis of the impact of cultural issues are too thin to yield dependable results, in my view.
4. As always, much depends on one's definition of class, and definitions of class vary wildly. McTague defines as working class voters in the 25th to 50th percentile of income and the top one-third or one-quarter in terms of education. John McTague, *Bowling for Voters? In Search of the White Working Class in American Politics,* available at http://www.bsos.umd.edu/gvpt/apworkshop/ mctague2009.pdf (2009), at 3 (first quote), 17 (second quote), 17 (middle class more predictably Republican), 21 (both classes in the middle more predictably Republican), 15 (formula for defining class location), 18 (caution). McTague includes in the middle class voters with incomes between the 51st and 90th percentiles—in other words, he codes as middle class some voters I

include in the professional-managerial elite. Theda Skocpol, *The Missing Middle: Working Families and the Future of American Social Policy* (2000).

5. Kenworthy et al., *supra* note 1 (fell from 60% to 40%); Teixeira & Rogers, *supra* note 1 at 32–33, 85 (Democratic presidential voting declined). A more recent article argues that the shift of white workers away from the Democrats occurred only after 1996. Brady et al., *supra* note 2 (Divergences among scholars as to when the white working class began to move away from the Democrats reflect different definitions of "working class.").

6. See, e.g., Thomas Byrne Edsall & Mary Byrne Edsall, *Chain Reaction: The Impact of Race, Rights, and Taxes on American Politics* (1991) (race is chiefly responsible for the Republican Party's rise); Martin Gilens, *Why Americans Hate Welfare* (1999) (race in the welfare debate); David C. Leege, Kenneth D. Wald, Brian S. Krueger, & Paul D. Mueller, *The Politics of Cultural Differences* 199 (2002); Thomas F. Schaller, *Whistling Past Dixie* 68–115 (2006) (race and religion explain the GOP rise). For a thorough listing of the extensive political science literature pointing to race, see McTague, *supra* note 4 at 12. For a more scholarly treatment of the role of religion in recent politics, see Geoffrey C. Layman, *The Great Divide* (2001); John Michael McTague & Geoffrey C. Layman, "Religion, Parties and Voting Behavior: A Political Explanation of Religious Influence," in *Oxford Handbook on Religion and American Politics* (James Guth, Lyman Kellstedt, & Corwin Smidt eds., forthcoming).

7. See generally Gary Gerstel, *American Crucible: Race and Nation in the Twentieth Century* (2002).

8. Barbara Ehrenreich, *Fear of Falling: The Inner Life of the Middle Class* 141 (1989) (construction workers are louts).

9. *Wikipedia, the Free Encyclopedia*, s.v. "Homer Simpson," http://en.wikipedia .org/wiki/Homer_simpson (accessed May 9, 2009).

10. Michael Zweig, *What's Class Got to Do with It?: American Society in the Twenty-First Century* 166 (2004) (casually refer to "trailer trash"); Michelle M. Tokarczyk & Elizabeth A. Fay, *Working-Class Women in the Academy* 293 (1993) (last acceptable ethnic slurs), 3 (barely acknowledges); C. L. Barney Dews & Carolyn Leste Law, *This Fine Place So Far from Home* 85 (1995) (caricature), 46 (professors resented having to teach).

11. Dennis Gilbert, *The American Class Structure in an Age of Growing Inequality* 270 (6th ed., 2003); Roger Lehecka & Andrew Delbanco, "Ivy-League Letdown," *New York Times,* January 22, 2008, at A21.

12. Joan Williams et al., "'Opt-Out' or Pushed Out?: How the Press Covers Work/Family Conflict," Center for WorkLife Law 23 (2006), available at http://www.worklifelaw.org/pubs/OptOutPushedOut.pdf (graph showing occupational segregation by education); Bettie, *supra* note 1 at 38, citing Eric Olin Wright et al., "The American Class Structure," 47 *Am. Soc. Rev.* 722 (1982). Common occupations for working-class women include secretary, receptionist, cashier, hairdresser, and retail salesperson. See Abbie E. Goldberg & Maureen Perry-Jenkins, "Division of Labor and Working-Class Women's Well-Being across the Transition to Parenthood," 18 *J. of Family Psychology* 225, 228 (2004).

13. Skocpol, *supra* note 4; Michèle Lamont, *The Dignity of Working Men: Morality and the Boundaries of Race, Class, and Immigration* 10 (2000).

14. *Invasion of the Body Snatchers* (1956); Ann Swidler, "Culture in Action: Symbols and Strategies," 51 *Am. Sociological Rev.* 273, 277 (1986) (class culture default mode); Lamont, *supra* note 13 at 20 (2000) (success in moral or socioeconomic terms).

15. United States Dep't of Labor, Bureau of Labor Statistics, "Union Members Summary," January 28, 2009, available at http://www.bls.gov/news/release/union2.nro.htm.

16. Joan Williams, *Unbending Gender: Why Family and Work Conflict and What to Do about It* 29 (2000) (job allowed middle-class basics); Teixeira & Rogers, *supra* note 2 at 11 (twice as well-off), 13–14 (12% dive).

17. Teixeira & Rogers, *supra* note 1 at 55.

18. *Id.* at 55–56.

19. *Id.* at 56 ($2000–$3000 less); Monica McDermott, *Working-Class White: The Making and Unmaking of Race Relations* 5 (2006) (16%).

20. See Williams, *supra* note 16; Alice Kessler-Harris, *A Woman's Wage: Historical Meanings and Social Consequences* (1990); Nancy F. Cott, *The Bonds of Womanhood: "Woman's Sphere" in New England, 1780–1835* (1977) (family wage); Hedrick Smith, *Juggling Work and Family* (PBS 2000), transcript available at http://www.hedricksmith.com/PBSDoc/jugglingWorkTranscript.shtml; Joan C. Williams, "One Sick Child away from Being Fired: When 'Opting-Out' Is Not an Option," Center for WorkLife Law 4 (2006), available at http://www.worklifelaw.org/pubs/OneSickChild.pdf (could be fired for being a few minutes late).

21. Cott, *supra* note 20 (history); Francine Deutsch, *Halving It All: How Equally Shared Parenting Works* 180–194 (1999) (unchanged view). For a discussion of other studies, see Williams, *supra* note 20 at 157–160. See also Susan Faludi, *Stiffed* (1999).

22. Phyllis Moen & Stephen Sweet, "Time Clocks," in *It's about Time* 20 (Phyllis Moen ed., 2003) (neotraditional family life).

23. Carla Shows & Naomi Gerstel, "Fathering, Class and Gender," 23 *Gender & Society* 161, 175, 177 (2009).

24. *Id.* at 177 (quote), 175 (two-thirds).

25. Heather Boushey, *Women Breadwinners, Men Unemployed*, Washington, DC: Center for Economic and Policy Research 1 (2009); Elizabeth Eaves, "In This Recession, Men Drop Out," available at http://www.forbes.com/2009/04/09/employment-men-women-recession-opinions-columnists gender-roles.html.

26. See, e.g., Ronald Inglehart, *The Silent Revolution* (1977); Ronald Inglehart, *Culture Shift in Advanced Industrial Society* (1990); Ronald Inglehart, *Modernization and Postmodernization* (1997); Ronald Inglehart & Paul R. Abramson, "Economic Security and Value Change," 88 *Amer. Political Sci. Rev.* 336–354 (1994); Paul R. Abramson & Ronald Inglehart, "Comment: Formative Security, Education, and Postmaterialism: A Response to Davis," 60 *Public Opinion Quarterly* 450–455 (1996) (attention shift); Jeffrey Stonecash, *Class*

and Party in American Politics 149 (2000); Jeroen van der Waal, Peter Achterberg, & Dick Houtman, "Class Is Not Dead – It Has Been Buried Alive: Class Voting and Cultural Voting in Postwar Western Societies (1956–1990)," 35 *Politics and Society* 404 (2007) (class played decreasing role); Kenneth D. Duerr, *Behind the Backlash: White Working-Class Politics in Baltimore, 1940–1980* (2003).

27. Stonecash, *supra* note 26 at 103 (compared voting patterns). For a more thorough discussion of this pattern, see McTague, *supra* note 4 at 9–14.

28. Search conducted on July 2, 2009.

29. Alice O'Connor, *Poverty Knowledge: Social Science, Social Policy, and the Poor in Twentieth-Century U.S. History* (2001) (lopsided emphasis); Dorothy Ross, "Gendered Social Knowledge: Domestic Discourse, Jane Addams, and the Possibilities of Social Science," in *Gender and American Social Science: The Formative Years* (Helene Silverberg ed., 1998) (Jane Addams).

30. Theda Skocpol, *supra* note 13. See also Robin Kelley, *Race Rebels: Culture, Politics, and the Black Working Class* (1994) (arguing that poor blacks have been studied extensively; the black working class, rarely); Skocpol *supra* note 13 at 23 (puzzling), 163 (family-oriented populism).

31. Van der Waal et al., *supra* note 26 at 406 (low incomes socially conservative), 409 (less educated liberal on economic issues), 415 (cultural voting), 416 (become stronger).

32. Cowie Jefferson, "From Hard Hats to the NASCAR Dads," 13 *New Labor Forum* 1 (2004).

33. Alfred Lubrano, *Limbo: Blue-Collar Roots, White-Collar Dreams* 5 (2004).

34. Pierre Bourdieu, *The Logic of Practice* 243 (1990) (cultural repertoires), 245 (focusing solely), 4 (without predefining specific dimensions).

35. Swidler, *supra* note 14 at 274.

36. Michèle Lamont & Annette Lareau, "Cultural Capital: Allusions, Gaps and Glissandos in Recent Theoretical Developments," 6 *Sociological Theory* 153, 159 (1988).

37. Julie Bettie, "Class Dismissed? Roseanne and the Changing Face of Working-Class Iconography," 45 *Soc. Text* 125, 133 (1995), citing Eric Olin Wright et al., "The American Class Structure," 47 *Am. Soc. Rev.* 722 (1982); Goldberg & Perry-Jenkins, *supra* note 12 at 228 (majority of working class is female); Lamont & Lareau, *supra* note 36 at 159 (cultural capital); Bettie, *supra* note 1 at 108 ("use of nonstandard grammar").

38. Cultural capital is related to, but different from, social capital. Social capital is used to signal that the webs of connection available to people in socially and economically advantaged positions are readily transformable into high-level job opportunities and job offers. The need to develop this social capital plays a major role in the cultural habits of the professional-managerial class in ways explored in this chapter.

39. Lamont, *supra* note 13 at 10 (best defined negatively); Ruy Teixeira & Alan Abramowitz, *The Decline of the White Working Class and the Rise of a Mass Upper Middle Class* 2 (Brookings working paper, April 2008) (29% of Americans graduate from college).

40. Jerome Karabel, "The New College Try," *New York Times,* September 24, 2007, at A27.
41. Ehrenreich, *supra* note 8 at 15 (insecure and deeply anxious), 83 (disciplined enough), 76, 75; Annette Lareau, *Unequal Childhoods: Class, Race, and Family Life* 238 (2003) (concerted cultivation).
42. Joseph T. Howell, *Hard Living on Clay Street* 263–353 (1972) (hard living); Bettie, *supra* note 1 at 15 (2003) (study of working-class high school girls); Howell, *supra* note 42 at 258 (very routine), 255 (strict control), 257 (graduate from high school); Lamont, *supra* note 13; Maria Kefalas, *Working-Class Heroes: Protecting Home, Community, and Nation in a Chicago Neighborhood* (2003)
43. Kefalas, *supra* note 42 at 12 (people of Beltway willingly dedicate themselves), 13 (order and abundance), 21 ("white trash").
44. Bettie, *supra* note 1 at 13–14 (joy ride).
45. *Id.* at 134 ("My life is shit").
46. Lareau, *supra* note 41 at 43 (they rush home).
47. *Id.* at 35 (everyone seems exhausted), 39, 62, 65, 112, 171 (television sharply controlled, unstructured time rare).
48. *Id.* at 238.
49. Lubrano, *supra* note 33 at 10 (conformity, obedience, and intolerance); Paul Willis, *Learning to Labor: How Working Class Kids Get Working Class Jobs* (1977).
50. Bettie, *supra* note 1 at 50 (family life as crucial site).
51. Lareau, *supra* note 41, at 238 (formidable challenge).
52. *Id.* at 238 (actively fostered and assessed), table C4 at 282 (organized activities), 264 (hard to find upper-middle-class child not in organized activities).
53. *Id.* at 97 (obligation to cultivate); Lamont, *supra* note 13 at 31 (self-regulation); "Return to Childhood 2008," *This American Life* (Chicago Public Radio broadcast, March 7, 2008) (kids do not know how to play).
54. Lareau, *supra* note 41 at 79, 81, 283, tables C5–C6.
55. *Id.* at 250 (adult life as hard and pressured), 251 (I think he's not a child, dead-dog tired), 77 (sibling rivalry).
56. Tokarczyk & Fay, *supra* note 10 at 102 (not obliged to give us care).
57. Lareau, *supra* note 41 at 58 (soccer more of a priority).
58. Mark S. Granovetter, "The Strength of Weak Ties," 78 *Am. J. of Sociol.* 1360 (1973) (the strength of weak ties).
59. Pierre Bourdieu, *Distinction: A Social Critique of the Judgement of Taste* (1985) (reciprocal invitations); Marjorie L. DeVault, *Feeding the Family: The Social Organization of Caring as Gendered Work* 206 (1991) (social time with kin); Lamont, *supra* note 13 at 11 (2000) (tight networks); Lareau, *supra* note 41 at 57 (cousins play together).
60. Karen Walker, "'Always There for Me': Friendship Patterns and Expectations among Middle- and Working-Class Men and Women," 10 *Sociolog. Forum* 281 (1995) (reciprocal exchange is sex-specific).
61. Peter V. Marsden, "Core Discussion Networks of Americans," 52 *Am. Sociolog. Rev.* 129, 124 (1987) (network range grows with education); Bonnie H.

Erickson, "Culture, Class and Connections," 102 *Am. J. of Sociol.* 236 (1996) (contacts more wide-ranging); Granovetter, *supra* note 58 at 1360.

62. Lubrano, *supra* note 33 at 131 (remain near the clan); Dews & Law, *supra* note 10 at 165 (regular and close association), 175 (cultural cross-fire); Tokarczyk & Fay, *supra* note 10 at 100 (bell hooks); Lubrano, *supra* note 33 at 107 (Ohio? "It's a blue-collar thing").

63. Walker, *supra* note 60 at 280 (80% / less than 50%).

64. Lamont, *supra* note 13 at 18.

65. DeVault, *supra* note 59 at 214 (pleasure with novelty and entertainment; "all my meats the same"), 212 (steady drumbeat), 203 (reproduce meals they grew up with), 204 ("Ma, I have this and this"), 222 (meat and potatoes people), 210–212 (original and exotic).

66. Kim Severson, "What's for Dinner? The Pollster Wants to Know," *New York Times,* April 16, 2008, at D1.

67. Kefalas, *supra* note 42 at 13 (food served family style).

68. DeVault, *supra* note 59 at 205 (different cuisines), 213 (different and interesting; "feedback for experimenting"), 210–211 (creativity, novelty, and experimentation).

69. *Id.* at 208 (gatherings familiar).

70. *Id.* at 209 (unspoken law).

71. *Id.* at 210–211 (ready to be impressed), 210 (*Gourmet* magazine).

72. Bourdieu, *supra* note 59 at 194 (plain speaking, plain eating); Severson, *supra* note 66 at D1 (Red Lobster); Bourdieu, *supra* note 59 at 195 (informality is the rule of the game), 197 (freedom from rigorous time discipline).

73. There is also a gender dimension there is not space to explore here. Working-class women's jobs more often require social skills; note whose felt needs predominate. Some evidence exists that working-class women struggle to teach social skills at the table while working class men resist their efforts. DeVault, *supra* note 59 at 49.

74. Lareau, *supra* note 41 at 146 (extended verbal discussions; comfortable silences).

75. Bourdieu, *supra* note 59 at 195 (habitus of order); Dews & Law, *supra* note 10 at 269–270 (1995) (teachable moments); Kari Haskell, "A Sense of Duty Takes Shape during Dinner Table Conversations," *New York Times,* January 6, 2008, at 20.

76. Bettie, *supra* note 1 at 83 ("somethin' in an office"); Dews & Law, *supra* note 10 at 104 (manipulating the system), 269 (question them and reshape them); Lareau, *supra* note 41 at 130 (Lareau found), 110 (negotiation), 109 (banter and jousting); Lubrano, *supra* note 33 at 20 (development of curiosity), 5.

77. Lubrano, supra note 33 at 166.

78. Bettie, *supra* note 1 at 105.

79. L. M. Boyd, "The Grab Bag," *San Francisco Chronicle,* January 6, 2008, at 22.

80. Lamont, *supra* note 13 at 146–147 (worth in terms of socioeconomic status).

81. *Id.* at 18 (world in moral order), 24 (cursed; parasites).

82. *Id.* at 25 (importance of responsibility), 132 (forward-looking); Howell, *supra* note 42; Bettie, *supra* note 1; Tex Sample, *Hard Living People and Mainstream*

Christians (1993) (commentator's observations); Bettie, *supra* note 1 at 81, 100, 118, 128 (judge the hard-living harshly); Howell, *supra* note 42 at 261 ("from good families", "lower class" or "white trash").

83. Lamont, *supra* note 13 at 23 (disciplined self), 25 ($50 a week), 27 (highly dependent on actions of others).

84. *Id.* at 1 (I like people who are responsible).

85. Lubrano, *supra* note 33 at 16–17 (well-developed work ethic); Lamont, *supra* note 13 at 27, 26 (hanging in there); Jonathan Rieder, *Canarsie: The Jews and Italians of Brooklyn against Liberalism* 105 (1985) (busting chops); Willis, *supra* note 49 (rubric of self-development); Kris Paap, *Working Construction: Why White Working-Class Men Put Themselves—and the Labor Movement—in Harm's Way* 155 (2006) (paid from shoulders down).

86. Lamont, *supra* note 13 at 24 (signals moral purity); Paul Willis, "The Class Significance of School Counter-Culture," in *The Process of Schooling* (Martyn Hammersley & Peter Woods eds., 1976) (it's heavy work); Willis, *supra* note 49 at 53 (out of proportion); Lamont, *supra* note 13 at 18 (can't or won't do).

87. See, e.g., Elvia R. Arriola, "What's the Big Deal—Women in the New York City Construction Industry and Sexual Harassment Law, 1970–1985," 22 *Colum. Hum. Rts. L. Rev.* 21, 62 (1990).

88. Dews & Law, *supra* note 10 at 143 (disrespected pencil pushers); Bourdieu, *supra* note 34 at 126–127 (servitude into honor); Dews & Law, *supra* note 10 at 141 (daughter of carpenter).

89. Lamont, *supra* note 13 at 99 (my family is what I center myself around), 116 (view with suspicion); Jonathan Lazear, *The Man Who Mistook His Job for a Life: A Chronic Overachiever Finds the Way Home* (Crown 2001) (mistake job for a life); Lamont, *supra* note 13 at 110 (miss all of life; "me, me, me, me"); David Shevin, Janet Zandy, & Larry R. Smith, *Writing Work: Writers on Working-Class Writing* 61, 69 (1999) (Pride in hard work is not gender-specific. One woman recalled that "When a child was born, my grandmother would be back in the fields three days after delivery, the newborn propped under a tree close by where she could nurse him when summoned." The same woman went on to quote, approvingly, a maxim attributed to the nineteenth-century French author Colette: "'Who said you should be happy? Do your work.' The rich and super-rich ask, 'Who said we should work? Make us happy.'").

90. Tex Sample, *Blue Collar Resistance and the Politics of Jesus: Doing Ministry with Working Class Whites* 86 (2006).

91. Dews & Law, *supra* note 10 at 69 (tolerated the college boy); Sample, *supra* note 90 at 86 (2006) (the gang delights); Shevin et al., *supra* note 89 at 27, 28 (don't like to get hands dirty; Charlie).

92. Shevin et al., *supra* note 89 at 29 (needed the money), 32 (working-class background helps me deliver).

93. Lamont, *supra* note 13 at 39, 41 (18% picked religion).

94. Lamont, *supra* note 13 at 43 (more rigid moral norms), 38–39 (going to hell).

95. *Id.* at 39 (trainman); Sample, *supra* note 90 at 46 (commitment to different moral order is itself a form of resistance).

96. Sample, *supra* note 90 at 47 (not using the term "settled living").

97. Lamont, *supra* note 13 at 39 (religion to stop drinking); Sample, *supra* note 90 at 47 (good life, not using term "settled living").

98. Lamont, *supra* note 13 at 40 (I know Jesus Christ), 39 (religion gives authority), 44 (source of status).

99. Note the association of tact with femininity, perhaps reflecting the fact that like all women, appropriately feminine working-class women are expected to be amiable.

100. Lamont, *supra* note 13 at 18 (don't jerk me around); Rieder, as cited in *Id.* at 37 (straight talk); Dews & Law, *supra* note 10 at 216 (directness working-class norm); Lamont, *supra* note 13 at 36 (come talk to me); Howell, *supra* note 42 at 310 (call a spade); Lamont, *supra* note 13 at 37 (wuss and a wimp; pride).

101. R. Jackell, *Moral Mazes: The World of the Corporate Manager* (1988); Richard Abel, *American Lawyers* (1989); R. Kanter, *Men and Women of the Corporation* (1977) (ability to get along); Michèle Lamont, *Money, Morals, and Manners: The Culture of the French and the American Upper-Middle Class* (1992), at 1 (tact, friendliness), 35 (conforming).

102. Lamont, *supra* note 13 at 99 (he's a jerk), 108 (two-face).

103. *Id.* at 109 (Barbie and Ken), 108 (shirt and tie types); Bettie, *supra* note 1 at 84 (fake).

104. Lubrano, *supra* note 33 at 139 (credit hogging); Tokarczyk & Fay, *supra* note 10 at 72 (game-playing bullshit); Dews & Law, *supra* note 10 at 172 (desire to be unique).

105. Barack Obama, *Dreams from My Father* (2004).

106. Lamont, *supra* note 13 at 31 (he's got high standards), 30 (family above work).

107. *Tom Rice Buick*, 167 L.R.R.M. 1343 (2001) (Thomas Fell).

108. Lamont, *supra* note 13 at 29 (effective breadwinner), 31 (keep the wife at home), 29 (I'm old-fashioned), 26 (hard to support a wife).

109. Lamont, *supra* note 101 at 33 (work is the means); Jungmeen E. Kim, Phyllis Moen, & Hyunjoo Min, "Well-Being," in *It's about Time: Couples and Careers* 129, 131 (Phyllis Moen ed., 2003) (workplace success); Lisa Belkin, "When Mom and Dad Share It All," *New York Times*, June 15, 2008, at 44 (a way to put food on the table); Tokarczyk & Fay, *supra* note 10 at 65 (productive children).

110. Lubrano, *supra* note 33 at 108 (you're happy with your family); Lamont, *supra* note 13 at 112 (how much money), 29 (support my family).

111. Ofer Sharone, "Engineering Overwork: Bell-Curve Management in a High-Tech Firm," in *Fighting for Time: Shifting Boundaries of Work and Social Life* 191, 206 (Cynthia Fuchs Epstein & Arne L. Kalleberg eds., 2004).

112. Lamont, *supra* note 13 at 99 (my family is what I center myself around), 116 (view with suspicion); Lazear, *supra* note 89 (mistake job for a life); Lamont, *supra* note 13 at 100 (miss all of life; "me, me, me, me"); Shevin et al., *supra* note 89 at 61, 69 (1999).

113. David C. Leege, Kenneth D. Wald, Brian S. Krueger, & Paul D. Meuller, *The Politics of Cultural Differences: Social Change and Voter Mobilization Strategies in the Post-New Deal Period* 26–27 (2002).

6. Culture Wars as Class Conflict

1. William Safire, "Locavorism," *New York Times*, October 09, 2008, at MM18 (Obama arugula quote); Devlin Barrett, "Obama Bowls for Pennsylvania Voters," http://www.huffingtonpost.com/2008/03/30/obama-bowling-for-voters-_n _94097.html (last visited July 09, 2009) (Obama bowling score); Maureen Dowd, "Eggheads and Cheese Balls," *New York Times*, April 16, 2008, at A0 (Dukakis Belgian endive, Obama's arugula).

2. Marjorie L. DeVault, *Feeding the Family: The Social Organization of Caring as Gendered Work* 223 (1991) (salad greens as class acts); John McCormick, "Obama Talks Arugula-again-in Iowa," *The Swamp,* http://www.swamppoli tics.com/news/politics/blog/2007/10/obama_talks_arugula_again_in_i.html (accessed October 5, 2007).

3. Joseph T. Howell, *Hard Living on Clay Street: Portraits of Blue Collar Families* 314 (1972) (first quote); Barbara Ehrenreich, *Fear of Falling: The Inner Life of the Middle Class* 137 (1990) (second quote); Howell, *supra* note 3 at 315.

4. Annette Lareau, *Unequal Childhoods: Class, Race, and Family Life* 39, 239 (2003).

5. Michèle Lamont, *The Dignity of Working Men: Morality and the Boundaries of Race, Class, and Immigration* 103 (2000) (first quote), 104 (second quote).

6. Reeve Vanneman & Lynn Weber Cannon, *The American Perception of Class* 86–87 (1987).

7. Karen D. Pyke, "Class-Based Masculinities: The Interdependence of Gender, Class and Interpersonal Power," 10 *Gender and Soc.* 531–532 (1996) (common longing).

8. Lamont, *supra* note 5 at 104; Michelle M. Tokarczyk & Elizabeth A. Fay, *Working-Class Women in the Academy: Laborers in the Knowledge Factory* 102 (1993) (first quote); Confidential interview, Washington, D.C., 1999 (Harvard-trained public interest lawyer).

9. See Jonathan Cobb & Richard Sennett, *The Hidden Injuries of Class* (1993) (hidden injuries of class); C. L. Dews, *This Fine Place So Far from Home* 178 (1995) (first quote).

10. See Dews, *supra* note 9 at 20.

11. Alfred Lubrano, *Limbo: Blue-Collar Roots, White Collar Dreams* 109 (2004)

12. See *id.* at 66.

13. See Dews, *supra* note 9 at 4.

14. See *id.* at 1.

15. See *id.* at 304 (all quotes)

16. See *id.* at 180–181.

17. Bonney Kapp, "Obama Draws Fire for Comments on Small-Town America," FOXnews.com, http://www.foxnews.com/politics/elections/2008/04/11/obama -draws-fire-for-comments-on-small-town-america (April 11, 2008).

18. Aaron Burns, Mosheh Oinounou, & Bonney Kapp, "Clinton Team Lunges at Obama, Hunts for Opening over Small-Town America Remarks," FOXnews .com, http://www.foxnews.com/politics/elections/2008/04/12/clinton-team

-lunges-at-obama-hunts-for-opening-over-small-town-america-remarks (April 12, 2008)

19. Matt Bai, "Can Obama Close the Deal with Those White Guys?: Working for the Working-Class Vote," *New York Times Magazine,* October 19, 2008, at M40.

20. This is an occupational hazard of writing about class. Jonathan Rieder worried about the same thing: "I did not try to stick it to anyone . . . but I have written a book." Jonathan Rieder, *Canarsie: The Jews and Italians of Brooklyn against Liberalism* 8 (1985).

21. See Dowd, *supra* note 1.

22. See Dews, *supra* note 9 at 83.

23. See Dews, *supra* note 9 at 144; Tex Sample, *Blue Collar Resistance and the Politics of Jesus: Doing Ministry with Working Class Whites* 27–28 (2006) (theology professor); Lareau, *supra* note 4 at 226 (school counselor); Rieder, *supra* note 20 at 146 (hyperactivity).

24. See Rieder, *supra* note 20 at 8. (I, too, have violated this rule and, if early audiences are any indication, will encounter pushback as a result.)

25. Mosheh Oinounou & Aaron Bruns, "Obama on Guns and Religion: 'I Didn't Say It as Well as I Should Have,'" FOXNews.com, http://www.foxnews.com/politics/elections/2008/04/12/obama-on-guns-and-religion-i-didnt-say-it-as-well-as-i-should-have (April 12, 2008).

26. Mark Stricherz, *Why Democrats Are Blue: Secular Liberalism and the Decline of the People's Party* 1 (2007).

27. See *id.* at 5 (Democrats move away); Geoffrey Layman & John Michael Mc-Tague, "Religion, Parties, and Voting Behavior: A Political Explanation of Religious Influence" in *The Oxford Handbook on Religion and American Politics* 330 (James Buth, Lyman Kellstedt, & Corwin Smidt eds., (2009) (George McGovern).

28. Thomas Edsall, *Building Red America* 18 (2006).

29. See Peter Beinart, *The Good Fight: Why Liberals—and Only Liberals—Can Win the War on Terror and Make America Great Again* (2008).

30. See Lubrano, *supra* note 11 at 91 (first quote); Donna Adkins, Audience Member Comment at preliminary presentation of this material to the staff of the Center for WorkLife Law, Spring 2009.

31. See Lamont, *supra* note 5 at 35 (all quotes).

32. See Mosheh Oinounou & Bonney Kapp, "Michelle Obama Takes Heat for Saying She's 'Proud of My Country' for the First Time," FOXNews.com, http://www.foxnews.com/story/0,2933,331288,00.html (February 19, 2008).

33. Kevin Fagan, "Single Mom Charged after Refusing Duty," *San Francisco Chronicle,* January 24, 2010, at A1 (initial quote); Richard Buddin, *Tuition Assistance Usage and First Term Military Retention* (2005); Ronald Fricker & C. Christine Fair, *Going to the Mines to Look for Diamonds: Experimenting with Military Recruiting Stations in Malls* (2003) (entering service to finance college).

34. David C. Leege, Kenneth D. Walk, Brian S. Krueger, & Paul D. Mueller, *The Politics of Cultural Differences: Social Change and Voter Mobilization Strategies in the Post-New Deal Period* 230 (2002) (50% point differential); Edsall,

supra note 28 at 54 (racial code words); Leege et al., *supra* note 34 (upper-middle-class defection).

35. See Kristin Luker, *Abortion and the Politics of Motherhood* 163 (1984), cited in Joan Williams, *Unbending Gender: Why Family and Work Conflict and What to Do about It* 151 (2000) (both quotes).

36. See Edsall, *supra* note 28 at 20.

37. See Julie Bettie, *Women without Class: Girls, Race, and Identity* 110–113 (2002) (gender progress versus consolidation of class privilege).

38. I take the term "euphemized racism" from Lamont. See Michèle Lamont, *The Dignity of Working Men* 55 (2000).

39. See Lane Kenworthy et al., "The Democrats and Working Class Whites" 3 (June 10, 2007) (unpublished paper, available at http://www.u.arizona.edu/~lkenwor/thedemocratsandworkingclasswhites.pdf); *Votes for Women* 13 (Jean H. Baker ed., 2002) (diluting black vote).

40. See Lamont, *supra* note 5 at 71 (first quote); Rieder, *supra* note 20 at 59–65 (last six quotes).

41. See Monica McDermott, *Working-Class White: The Making and Unmaking of Race Relations* (2006); Bettie, *supra* note 37 at 173 (marker of progressive politics).

42. See Thomas F. Schaller, *Whistling Past Dixie: How Democrats Can Win without the South* (2006) (Southern strategy to capture formerly Democratic South).

43. See Kenworthy et al., *supra* note 39 at 38; Reider, *supra* note 20 at 70 (working-class jobs), 101 (popular on welfare soared).

44. See Rieder, *supra* note 20 at 68 (street crime, trucker, two-year probation, and indelible imprint), 98 (danger).

45. See Lamont, *supra* note 5 at 32, 33 (iron bars); McDermott, *supra* note 41; Associated Press, "Clinton Outlines $4 Billion Anti-Crime Plan," Msnbc.com, http://www.msnbc.msn.com/id/24063698/ns/politics-decision_08/ (April 11, 2008).

46. See Lillian Rubin, *Worlds of Pain* 158–159 (1976), cited in Williams, *supra* note 35 at 155.

47. See Theda Scokpol, *The Missing Middle* (2001).

48. Naomi Gerstel & Dan Clawson, "Unions' Response to Family Concerns," in *Families at Work: Expanding the Bounds* 325 (Naomi Gerstel et al. eds., 2002).

49. Joan C. Williams and Heather Boushey, Center for American Progress, & the Center for WorkLife Law, "The Three Faces of Work-Family Conflict: The Poor, the Professionals, and the Missing Middle" 8–9 (2010), available at http://www.worklifelaw.org/pubs/ThreeFacesofWork-FamilyConflict.pdf.

50. See Rieder *supra* note 20 at 106 (all quotes).

51. See *id.* at 102.

52. See Scokpol *supra* note 47 at 8–9.

53. See Rieder, *supra* note 20 at 119.

54. See *id.* at 30 (successful social programs).

55. See *id.* at 121 (matter of fairness), 112 (NAACP).

56. See Youtube.com, "Obama's views on Affirmative Action," http://www.youtube.com/watch?v=saIVafSC38k (accessed July 10, 2009).

57. For information about the implicit association test, see http://www.project implicit.net (accessed July 10, 2009).

58. See Williams, *supra* note 35 at 76.

59. See Leege et al., *supra* note 34 (influence of religion in politics); Layman & McTague, *supra* note 27 at 6 (1960s and Protestants).

60. See Layman & McTague, *supra* note 27 at 4 (traditional segments), 12 (traditionalists), 4 (modernists), 9 (leads modernists).

61. See *id.* at 4.

62. "Bush's Farewell Address: The Goods, the Bad and the Ugly," Foxnews.com, http://foxforum.blogs.foxnews.com/2009/01/15/pinkerton_bush_farewell/ (accessed July 10, 2009).

63. Lamont, *supra* note 8, at 38–39 (guidance of religion), 11 (postmodern men), 286 (cultural fundamentalism), 44 (traditional morality).

64. See John Tierney, "For Good Self-Control, Try Getting Religious about It," *New York Times,* December 30, 2008, at D2 (quotes two and three). See Michael E. McCullough & Brian L. B. Willboughby, "Religion, Self-Regulation and Self-Control: Associations, Explanations, and Implications," 135 *Psychological Bulletin* 70 (2009).

65. David Barry, "A View from My Pew," *New York Times,* http://www.nytimes .com/2008/04/13/weekinreview/13barry.html?n=Top/Reference/Times %20Topics/People/J/John%20Paul%20II (accessed July 10, 2009).

66. See Bai, *supra* note 19.

67. Karen M. Kaufmann & John R. Petrocik, "The Changing Politics of American Men: Understanding the Sources of the Gender Gap," 43 *American Journal of Political Science* 816–817 (1999).

68. See Lamont, *supra* note 5; Andrew Kohut & Carroll Doherty, Pew Research Center, "Little Boost for Gun Control or Agreement on Causes" (2007), available at http://people-press.org/reports/pdf/321.pdf (gun control polling data).

69. See Janet C. Gornick & Marcia K. Meyers, *Families That Work: Policies for Reconciling Parenthood and Employment* 188–189 (2003); Lucie White, "Quality Child Care for Low-Income Families: Despair, Impasse, Improvisation," in *Hard Labor: Women and Work in the Post-Welfare Era* 120, 133–134.

70. Francine Deutsch, *Halving It All: How Equally Shared Parenting Works* 173 (1999).

71. See Williams, *supra* note 35 49.

72. See Lamont, *supra* note 5 at 33 (Lamont noticed); Deutsch, *supra* note 70 at 175, 177 (1999) (anxieties about strangers).

73. See White, *supra* note 69 at 128–129; Deutsch, *supra* note 70 at 176 (Deutsch found).

74. See Family Medical Leave Act of 1993, 29 5 U.S.C. § 2601(2009); National Partnership for Women and Families, Paid Sick Days Campaign http://paidsick days.nationalpartnership.org/site/PageServer?pagename=psd_index.

75. See Cal. Lab. Code § 230.8.

76. Naomi Gerstel & Dan Clawson, "Unions' Response to Family Concerns," in *Families at Work: Expanding the Bounds* 324, 336 (Naomi Gerstel et al. eds., 2002).

77. See Lamont, *supra* note 5 at 136–137.

78. Susan Lampert, Comments at Women and Work: Choices and Constraints Conference, University of Massachusetts, Amherst (October 31, 2008); Family Friendly Workplace Act, S. 4, 105th Cong. Section 13a (1997). The current version of the bill eliminates the provision described in the text but still raises in unions and others the apprehension that employees would be pressured to accept comp time, which might never appear, instead of time-and-a-half pay. Family Friendly Workplace Act (H.R. 933), available at http://thomas.loc.gov/ cgi-bin/z?c111:H.R.933.IH.

79. See Maureen Perry-Jenkins and Amy Claxton, "Feminist Visions for Rethinking Work and Family Connections" 17 (unpublished paper, on file with author).

80. See Thomas Frank, *What's the Matter with Kansas?* 10 (2004) (block quote).

81. See *id.* at 6 (class war).

82. I recognize that this is a decidedly upper-middle-class analogy—but, after all, I am an upper-middle-class person seeking to reach an upper-middle-class audience.

83. See Seymour Martin Lipset, "Democracy and Working-Class Authoritarianism," 24 *American Sociological Review* 482–501 (1959); Stephen D. Levitt & Stephen J. Dubner, *Freakanomics: A Rogue Economist Explores the Hidden Side of Everything* (2005).

84. See Bai, *supra* note 19.

85. See, e.g., Stephanie M. Wildman, Margalynne Armstrong, Adrienne D. Davis, & Trina Grillo, *Privilege Revealed: How Invisible Preference Undermines America* (1996).

Conclusion

1. Sarah Palin, *Going Rogue* 11, 59 (2009); Naomi Cahn & June Carbone, *Red Families, Blue Families* (2009) (families in red states tend to have children earlier than do families in blue states).

2. Palin, *supra* note 1 at 22, 11, 17, 34, 50, 62.

3. *Id.* at 42, 43, 26.

4. *Id.* at 18.

5. *Id.;* "Blatherings: Musings, Gibberish, and Notable Thoughts from a Red Girl in a Blue State," http://blatheringsblog.com/?p=3023 (July 5, 2009).

6. Mike Elk, "Ivy League Liberal Elitism Will Make Sarah Palin President—How Only Union Organizing Can Prevent It," http://www.huffingtonpost.com/mike -elk/liberal-elistism-will-mak_b_355249.html (November 12, 2009).

7. Arlie Hochschild (with Anne Machung), *The Second Shift* 11 (1989) (stalled revolution).

8. Palin, *supra* note 1 at 29; Jennifer L. Hochschild, *Facing up to the American Dream* 55 (1995); Jodi Kantor, "Fusing Politics and Motherhood in a New Way," *New York Times,* September 7, 2008, http://www.nytimes.com/2008/ 09/08/us/politics/08baby.html (hid her pregnancy); Lorenzo Benet & Jill Smolowe, "Gov. Sarah Palin's Family Matters," *Time,* September 15, 2008, http://

www.people.com/people/archive/article/0,,20230644,00.html (special-needs infant and pregnant teenager); Marjorie Miller, "Todd Palin, Husband of Sarah Palin: A 'True Alaskan,'" *Los Angeles Times,* September 7, 2008 (husband left his job).

9. Palin, *supra* note , at 36, 50, 55.
10. Robert B. Westbrook, *John Dewey and American Democracy* 136 (1991).
11. *Id.* at 140.
12. James T. Kloppenberg, *Uncertain Victory: Social Democracy and Progressivism in European and American Thought, 1870–1920* 349 (1998); The Postal Service, "Such Great Heights," on *Give Up* (SubPop 2003) ("But everything looks perfect from far away, 'come down now,' but we'll stay").

Acknowledgments

This book would not exist without Jim Kloppenberg and Shauna Marshall. Jim, who has supported me through the ups and downs of my career, proposed me for the Massey Lectures, I think, as a way of ensuring that I write up my current thinking in academic form, given how wrapped up I have been for the last ten years in attempting to fuel social change through the Center for WorkLife Law. I have deeply treasured this opportunity to think through some new ideas at a theoretical level—given that theory is my first love and best talent—and I have found it hard to find time for it in the whirlwind of activity since the publication, nearly ten years ago, of *Unbending Gender*. I thank Jim, and Nancy Cott, for creating an opportunity to do what I love best. Thanks, too, to the many people whose efforts made the Massey Lectures a success: Harvard History of American Civilization Professor John Stauffer, who ran the lectures; those who introduced me at the lectures—James T. Kloppenberg and Nancy F. Cott, Harvard Department of History, and Christine Desan, Harvard Law School; and my commentators, Jane Mansbridge, Kennedy School of Government, Michèle Lamont, Harvard Sociology Department, and Joseph Singer, Harvard Law School. Thanks, too, to Christine McFadden, who, with extraordinary efficiency, kept the trains running even when she faced personal challenges.

The process of writing the Massey Lectures, while teaching full-time and running the Center for WorkLife Law, was a challenge. I never would have been able to make the transition from lectures to book without the unstinting support of Shauna Marshall, academic dean of my home institution, the University of California, Hastings College of the Law. The research leave Shauna arranged in the fall of 2009 kept me sane. Thanks to Shauna, and the dean, Nell Newton, for all their support. Other vital support from Hastings was from my magician-of-a-librarian, Hilary Hardcastle, and Jenny Parish, who as head of the library went to bat for me when I requested an expensive social science database that Hilary and I (and my students) use all the time.

Thanks, too, to two people who believed in my work when most experts still thought I was a bit touched: Susan Eaton of the Kennedy School, whose premature death robbed us of an important voice; and Reva Siegel of the Yale Law School, whose belief in me has sustained me during those periods when I myself wondered if I was a bit touched.

Another person without whose faith in me this book would not exist is Kathleen Christensen of the Alfred P. Sloan Foundation. Kathy pursued me after *Unbending Gender* until I submitted a grant proposal, and Sloan has funded me for ten solid years. This book owes much to Sloan Foundation support, and to Kathy's vision: in her work at Sloan, she created an entire field. Kathy also funded the *Opt Out or Pushed Out? How the Press Covers Work-Family Conflict* report, which forms the basis for Chapter 1 of this book. I am also deeply grateful to Lisa Guide of the Rockefeller Family Fund, who has allowed me to realize my dream of exploring the cross-class differences in work-family conflict and has provided general support for WorkLife Law—the only funder ever to do so. In addition, WorkLife Law owes a debt of gratitude to our other funders, including Abigail Disney, the Berger-Marks Fund, the Wallace A. Gerbode Fund, the W. K. Kellogg Foundation, the National Science Foundation ADVANCE Program, and the Novo Foundation.

Chapter 2 of this book would not exist without Hillary Wické, then a reporter with National Public Radio's *Marketplace*. Hillary's agreement to an exclusive on what became the report *One Sick Child Away from Being Fired: When Opting Out Is Not an Option* lit a fire under me actually to write it.

An earlier version of material included in Chapters 3 and 5 was published as Joan C. Williams, "Reconstructive Feminism: Changing the Way We Talk about Gender and Work Thirty Years after the PDA," 21 *Yale Journal of Law & Feminism* 80 (2009).

More generally, I would like to thank everyone at WorkLife Law whose work is embedded in this book. Thanks, first, to the chair of our board, Carolyn Lerner, whose warm and generous support has sustained me and whose wisdom has saved me from embarrassment many times. Thanks, too, to Jessica Manvell, whose extensive research and careful coding made Chapter 1 possible, and to Mary C. Still, now a professor of sociology at George Washington University, for teaching Jessica (and me) how to undertake and carry out such a project and for helping Jessica carry it out at a high level of rigor. Thanks to both for the years they worked with me at WorkLife Law while we were still at American University and to the research assistants who helped us with the report: Claire-Therese Luceno, Matthew Melamed, Angela Perone, Liana Sterling, and Emily Stratton. Thanks, too, to Stephanie Bornstein, associate director of WorkLife Law, for her unbelievable rigor, creativity, and brilliance, which guides WorkLife Law's work on union arbitrations, such as those used as the basis of Chapter 2. Many others also helped with that work, including Maureen Milligan, Professor Martin H. Malin of Chicago-Kent Law School, and Mary C. Still through their work on an earlier (2004) report on union arbitrations,

Work/Family Conflict Union Style. For additional help on *One Sick Child*, many thanks to Netsy Firestein and Stephanie Coontz, for help on the title to that report; Manar Morales, senior counsel of WorkLife Law, for help in preparing the report; and Susan Kwiatkowski and Frances Shehadeh, for research assistance. Genevieve Guertin spent many long hours on the notes to several chapters. The remainder of the staff of WorkLife Law also played vital roles in keeping things going as I was working on this book: Cynthia Thomas Calvert, deputy director and my intellectual partner for more than ten years; as well as Consuela Pinto, senior counsel; Donna Adkins, program coordinator, 2004–2009; and Rachel Allyn-Crane, program coordinator, 2009–present. Thanks also to the staff of the Project for Attorney Retention, Linda Bray Chanow, Natalie Hiott-Levine, and Linda Marks.

Thanks especially to the people who stayed late to finally put this book to bed. Stephanie Bornstein was her usually unflappable and unbelievably efficient self, and our summer clerks spent several days and evenings scrubbing up the notes, with incredible patience and precision: Alexander Felstiner, Erin Mohan, Molly Wilkens, and Veronica Williams. Rachel Allyn-Crane did, too, with her usual efficiency and good humor. At a later period, Jeremy Hessler and Tamsen Drew worked with patience to make sure the notes were in order.

Deep thanks to two colleagues who have given me generous and unstinting support for over twenty years: Naomi Cahn and Jana Singer. I regret that the book on class just completed by Naomi and her coauthor June Carbone, *Red Families v. Blue Families: Why America's Families Are in Trouble,* was not completed in time for me to incorporate their insights. My hope is that our books will complement each other and will open up new lines of inquiry and activism.

Many friends and colleagues gave generously of their time to give me comments on various chapters. Given the crazy time pressures we all face, I am very grateful for this important and generous form of support, given me by Heather Boushey of the Center for American Progress; Lisa Dodson, Boston College Sociology Department; Claudia Goldin, of the Harvard Economics Department; Annette Laureau, University of Pennsylvania History Department; Dorothy Ross, Johns Hopkins History Department (retired); Floyd Sipes; and Todd Tucker. Thanks also to Jana Singer, University of Maryland Law School, who read the *Opt Out or Pushed Out* report and gave me comments on it; and to Paula England, of the Stanford Sociology Department, who both gave comments on the report and ran some numbers for it. Thanks as well to my Hastings colleagues, who gave me helpful and rigorous comments at a faculty workshop, especially Hadar Aviram.

I also had the benefit of two rigorous and challenging edits, by Katherine Mooney and my daughter, Rachel Williams Dempsey. Chapter 1 irritated Rachel, and Chapters 5 and 6 irritated Katherine. As I said to Katherine, "better alienate a friend than an audience." I appreciate both their honesty and their expertise.

Thanks, as well, to my brother and agent, Roger S. Williams, of Publish or Perish Agency, and to Kathleen McDermott of the Harvard University Press. Both gave me extremely savvy advice about how to make this book more appealing to a trade audience.

Very special thanks for John McTague, who as a graduate student at the University of Maryland Department of Government and Politics helped me wend my way through the political science literature discussed in Chapters 5 and 6. I owe a lot to his insight, and he has a great future ahead of him as a professor. Thanks, too, to Chris Foreman, a professor at the University of Maryland School of Public Policy and my friend of many years, who was patient with my queries and who found John McTague to help me.

Last but not least, thanks to my family. My mother-in-law, Ruth Fallon Dempsey, has been part of the bedrock of my life: her joie de vivre reminds me of my own mother, and her unshakable confidence and pride in my accomplishments are a rare gift from a mother-in-law. Thanks, too, to my awesome children, Nicholas Dempsey Williams and Rachel Williams Dempsey, who have become such humane and impressive human beings: what did I do to deserve such wonderful kids? And, as always, thanks to my husband, Jim, for enriching my life for over three decades.

Index

Abortion, 195–196
About Schmidt, 82, 143
Addams, Jane, 161
Adolescent children, 51
The Adventures of Priscilla, Queen of the Desert, 112, 143
Aetna, 68
Affirmative action, class dynamics of, 202–203
After-school programs, 36–38
Aggressiveness, in workplace, 98
Alimony, 21, 111, 117, 131
Allied Paper, 56, 74
All in the Family, 153–154
All-or-nothing workplace, 30–32
Allstate Insurance, 67, 74
Amalgamated Transit Union, 53
Ambivalent sexism, 97–100, 141
American dream, 126, 259n78
Amnesty, 194–195
Anthony, Susan B., 115
Anti-essentialism, 5, 110, 144–148
Arugula, 187
Ashland Oil, 49, 58, 62, 235n21
Assertiveness, in workplace, 98
Assimilationist feminism, 115–126, 149
AstraZeneca, 67, 75

Babcock, Linda, 136–140
Baltimore Sun, 139
Barnes, Riché Jeneen Daniel, 145–146
Bartlett, Katherine, 116, 128, 133
Baumgardner, Jennifer, 109
Becker, Mary, 117, 128
Belkin, Lisa: "The Opt-Out Revolution," 2–3, 12–13, 30, 114; article on parenting, 41; on women's psychological differences, 133; E. J. Graff on, 222n11, 223n3; on reasons for opting out, 261n108
Bennetts, Leslie, 109, 124–125
Bergmann, Barbara R., 223n3
Best practices for workplace flexibility for hourly workers, 71–75
Berman, Howard, 118
Bettie, Julie, 151, 164–165, 175, 183, 198
Blair-Loy, Mary, 32–33
Bok, Derek, 89
Bourdieu, Pierre, 162, 169, 173, 174
Boushey, Heather, 15, 235n20
Bowles, Hannah Riley, 137–138
Brady, David, 152
Brand, Stephen, 36
Breadwinner ideal, 32, 59–60, 80–83, 184–185
Bristol-Myers Squibb, 67, 71
Browne, Kingsley R., 133–134

Bryant v. Bell Atlantic Maryland, 55
Bunker, Archie (fictional character), 153–154
Burden, Amanda, 123
Bush, George H. W., 195
Bush, George W., 44, 151, 183, 204
Business case for workplace flexibility for hourly workers, 64–71
Butler, Judith, 110–111, 112, 142

Cahn, Naomi, 135
CalFed. See California Federal Savings and Loan v. Guerra
California, 35–36
California Federal Savings and Loan v. Guerra, 117–118, 126–127, 257n37
Campbell, Alice, 66
Campbell, Kim, 97
Canada, 24
Cannon, Lynn Weber, 188
Carbado, Devon, 101
Caregiving: work-family conflicts and, 42–46, 233n3, 235–239; working schedules around, 50–52; mandatory overtime and, 52–56; men and, 56–61, 80–81, 239nn45,46; lessons for unions and employers on, 61–64; workplace flexibility and, 64–71; conclusions on, 75–76; masculine norms and, 89–90; welfare and, 199–201. *See also* Child care; Elder care; Ethic of care
Carrington, Christopher, 120
Casuistry, 95
Center for WorkLife Law, 13–14, 29, 43, 44
Center for Work-Life Policy, 25
Central Beverage, 49, 235n21
Chicago Transit Authority, 42, 50, 233n3, 236n25
Chicago Tribune Co., 42, 233n3
Child care: for nonprofessional workers, 4; increased time on, 22; public policy and, 36–38, 207–209; work-family conflicts and, 42–44; tag teaming and, 46–50, 235n20; mandatory overtime and, 52–56; working-class attitudes towards, 207–208; lesbian couples and, 258n52. *See also* Caregiving
"Child penalty," 15
Children: concerted cultivation and, 22–23, 24; scheduling around ill, 50–52; class and, 166–168, 240n59; family meals and, 174. *See also* Caregiving; Child care
Child support, 131

Chrysalis Performance Strategies, 69
City of Columbus, 58, 239n44
City of Titusville, 65, 241n59
Class: changing attitudes on, 6–11; opt-out news coverage and, 19; gender equality and, 59; politics and, 151–153, 192–196; different classes defined, 155; cultural difference and, 162–164; as learned identity, 166–168; injuries of, 189–192; divisions of, 226n20, 266n4; children and, 166–168, 240n59
Class acts: definition of, 6; class culture gap and, 10; gender performance as, 157–160; entertaining and leisure as, 172–175; of Democrats, 187; self-analysis and, 191–192
Class conflict: overview, 187–189; injuries of class and, 189–192; class affronts and, 192–196; race and, 196–203; religion and family values and, 203–206; firearms and, 206–207; public policy and, 207–214; Sarah Palin and, 215–217
Class culture gap: disrespect for working class and, 9–10, 153–154, 212–213; overview, 151–153; class distinction and, 155–157; gender performance and, 157–160; cultural differences and, 162–164; fear of hard living and, 164–165; learning class and, 166–168; social networks and, 169–171; food and, 171–172; entertaining and leisure and, 172–175; moral vision and, 175–186; politics and, 186
Clinton, Bill, 8, 105, 131, 192–193
Clinton, Hillary: femininity and, 91, 122–123; presidential campaign of, 104; class food preferences and, 171–172; on Obama's Bittergate, 191, 192; crime and, 199
Cobb, Jonathan, 59
Coffee, 171
Coit Tower, 153
Colette, 272n89
Columbiana County Brd of Mental Retardation & Disabilities, 52, 237n29
Competency, of women in workplace, 93–96
Comprehensive Child Development Act, 207
Concerted cultivation, 22–23, 24, 164, 166, 167–168
Consumer safety, 66
Cooper, Marianne, 86–87, 90

Corporate Voices for Working Families, 67–68
Cosby, Bill, 108
Crenshaw, Kimberlé, 144–145
Crime, 198–199
Cultural capital, 162–164, 269n38
Cultural voting, 161
Culture, class and, 6, 162–164, 186
Culture wars: overview, 10, 187–189; injuries of class and, 189–192; class affronts and, 192–196; race and, 196–203; religion and family values and, 203–206; firearms and, 206–207; public policy and, 207–214; Sarah Palin and, 215–217
Curie, Marie, 104

Daddy days, 36
Dean, Howard, 162, 187
Democrats/Democratic Party, 187–188, 193, 266n3, 267n5
Denmark, 35
Department of Labor, 44
Department of Veterans Affairs Medical Center, 52, 72
Deutsch, Francine, 158–159, 208
DeVault, Marjorie, 169, 171, 172–173
Dial Corp., Bristol, Pa., 66
Difference feminism, 111, 128–136
Different-voice feminism, 114, 133–135, 149
Directness, 182–184
Disabled workers, 39
Disciplined self, 176–180
Discrimination: against women, 27–29, 101, 136–140; against male caregivers, 80–81. *See also* Gender bias
Divorce, 20–21, 49, 117, 131–133
Domesticity. *See* Separate spheres
Dominance feminism, 143–144
Dorn, Kelley, 16
Double binds, 96–99
Double jeopardy, 93, 95, 99. *See also* Intersectionality
Dowd, Maureen, 122, 191
Dukakis, Michael, 187
Dworkin, Andrea, 112

Easterbrook, Frank, 127
Economics: opting out and, 24–26; women's employment and, 33–34
Economist magazine, 34, 137
Edsall, Thomas, 193, 196

Education: opt-out news coverage and, 19–20; occupational segregation by, 20 (table); class and, 163–164
Ehrenreich, Barbara, 164, 188
Elder care, 52
Elk, Mike, 217
Ely, Robin, 83–84
Emotions, 103–104
Employee loyalty, 66–68
Employers, lessons for, 61–64
Employment: education and, 19–20; of women, 33–34, 121, 224n12, 225n18, 271n73
Entertaining, 172–175
Epstein, Cynthia Fuchs, 87
Equality, 126, 131–133, 259n78, 260n91. *See also* Formal equality
Equal Pay Act, 115
Equal Protection, 129–130
Erbe, Bonnie, 13
Ethic of care, 149–150
Ethnicity. *See* Race
Europe: family supports in, 6–7; short-term leaves and, 35; child care in, 37; workplace flexibility in, 38

Fair Labor Standards Act (FLSA), 38
Fairmont General Hospital, Inc., 55, 238n35
Family: as "gender factory," 2, 83; gay couples and, 119–121; settled, 164–165, 181; class identity and, 166–168; family meals, 172–174; importance of, 184–186
Family and Medical Leave Act (FMLA), 8, 51, 62, 72–73
Family Friendly Workplace Act, 211, 278n78
Family values, 203–206, 211
Farrell, Warren, 13, 223n3
Fathers. *See* Men
Fell, Thomas, 184
Feminine norms, 221n5
Femininity: evolution of, 90–91; double binds and, 96–99; as problematic, 103–107; difference feminism and, 134–135
Feminism: overview, 5; workplace discrimination and, 99; identity and, 109–110; evolution of, 110–112; difference feminism, 111, 128–136; sameness feminism, 111, 114; assimilationist feminism, 115–126, 149; dominance feminism, 143–144; third-wave

Feminism *(continued)*
  feminism, 148–149; Sarah Palin and, 217–218; Martha Fineman on, 260n91. *See also* Reconstructive feminism
Femmes: overview, 5; assimilationist feminism and, 118–119; difference feminism and, 135–136; salary negotiation and, 141; third-wave feminism and, 149
Fenstermaker, Sarah, 83
Fineman, Martha, 117, 131, 260n91
Finland, 35
Firearms, 206–207
First Tennessee Bank, 66–67
Fiske, Susan, 100
Fisman, Ray, 123
Flexibility. *See* Workplace flexibility
Flexwork, 74–75
FMLA (Family and Medical Leave Act), 8, 51, 62, 72–73
Food, 171–175, 187
Formal equality, 115–126, 128. *See also* Assimilationist feminism
Frank, Steven M., 152
Frank, Thomas, 212
Franke, Katherine, 119, 121
Frey, William, 24–25
Friedan, Betty, 109
Friendship, class culture gap and, 170–171
Frontiero v. Richardson, 115

Gay couples, 119–121, 205, 258n52
Gender: workplace norms and, 2, 77–79, 91–92; changing attitudes on, 4–5; traditionalism and, 21–24; divisions among, 107–108; work-family axis of, 113–115; gender performance as class act, 157; work ethic and, 178; guns and, 206–207
Gender bias: maternal wall, 92–93; prove it again!, 93–96; double binds, 96–100; gender wars, 100–102; divorce and, 132; women of color and, 145–148. *See also* Ambivalent sexism; Intersectionality
Gender flux, 106–107
Gender performance, 142, 157–160
Gender privilege, 82–83, 144
Gender theory, 110–115
Gender wars, 100–103, 118–122, 140–142
General Telephone Company of Indiana, 47
Generational conflicts, 101–102, 141
Gerson, Kathleen, 31

Gerstel, Naomi, 159
Gilbert, Dennis, 155
Gilligan, Carol, 111, 114, 134
Ginsberg, Ruth Bader, 115–116
GlaxoSmithKline, 75
Glick, Peter, 77, 100
Goldin, Claudia, 15
Goldstein, John, 48
Goodnight Moon syndrome, 31–32
Gore, Al, 151
Gornick, Janet, 8–9, 35, 36, 37
Graff, E. J., 222n11, 223n3
Graham, Katharine, 103
Grandparents, 51–52
Gray, John, 136
Greater Cleveland Regional Transit Authority, 51, 236n28
Griswold, Robert, 89
GTE California, Inc., 55, 62, 238n36
Gulati, Mitu, 101
Gun control, 206–207

Halley, Janet, 121–122
Hard living, 165–166, 176–177, 181, 197, 199–200. *See also* Settled living
Harrington, Michael, 161
Hays, Sharon, 23
Health coverage, 39–40, 69, 104, 202
Hekker, Terry Martin, 21
Hewlitt, Sylvia Ann, 25
"Hidden injuries of class," 59
High heels, 123
Hippies, 193–194
Hirshman, Linda, 83, 124–125
Hochschild, Arlie, 90
hooks, bell, 168, 170
Hopkins, Ann, 97
Household work, 120–121, 135–136
Howell, Joseph T., 164, 182, 206
Hughey, Tammy, 22
Husbands, as push factor for opting out, 31–33, 265n179
Hutchinson, Alexis, 194–195

Identity: through work, 16–17; generational divisions and, 102; feminism and, 109–110, 121; class and, 162, 167
Illness, scheduling work around, 50–52
Income, class distinction and, 155
Indianapolis Ordinance, 112
Injuries of class, 189–192
Insurance, 39–40, 69, 104, 202
Integrity, 182–184

Intelligence, 122–123
Intensive mothering, 3, 23–24
Interlake Conveyors, 49
Internal Revenue Service, 69–70
Intersectionality, 5, 144–148

Jackson, Henry (Scoop), 193
Jacobs, Jerry, 31
Jefferson Partners, 49, 235n21
Jenkins, Maureen Perry, 147–148
Jennings, Jim, 210
Job sharing, 68–71, 74
Job turnover, 69–71
Joint property, 117, 121, 131–133, 255n20

Kefalas, Maria, 165, 172
Kennedy, Duncan, 122
Kennedy, John F., 152
Kerry, John, 187
King, Martin Luther, Jr., 108
Kingdon, John W., 6, 8
Knauf Fiber Glass, 62–64, 233n3
Korkodilos, Debbie, 14
Krieger, Linda Hamilton, 118

Lai, Lei, 137–138
Lamont, Michèle: on working class, 10, 61–62, 156–157, 177, 184; on class and workplace, 32; on class and social networks, 169; moral vision and, 176–177; on patriotism, 194; on part-time employment, 210
Lareau, Annette: on child rearing, 22–23, 166–168; concerted cultivation and, 164; on class and social networks, 169; on working class, 174; on class conflict, 188
Laschever, Sara, 136–137, 139–140
Law and order, 198–199
Lear, Norman, 153–154
Leaves, 35–36, 73, 208–209. *See also* Maternity leave
Leege, David C., 186, 195
Leisure, 175
Leniency bias, 94–95
Lesbian couples, 120, 258n52
Life span, 129–130
Lipset, Seymour Martin, 212
Littleton, Christine, 118
Los Angeles v. Manhart, 129–130
Loyalty, employee, 66–68
Lubrano, Alfred, 166, 183, 185
Luker, Kristin, 195–196

MacKinnon, Catharine, 110, 112, 143–144, 264n162
Madonna, 143
Mandatory overtime, 52–56, 62
Marcus, Ruth, 42
Marion Composites, 56, 238n37
Marital property, 117, 121, 131–133, 255n20
Marquette Electronics, 68
Marshall, Thurgood, 126–127
Masculine norms: feminism and, 2, 5, 107–108, 127, 128–129; overview, 2, 77–79, 149; create "real gender differences," 5, 129–33; breadwinner ideal and, 59–60; influence on men, 79–91; influence on women, 91–103; gender wars and, 118–122; in divorce proceedings, 132–133; feminine norms and, 221n5
Masculinity: working-class, 9, 83–86, 56–61, 80; professional-managerial, 31–44, 81–83, 86–88; forged at work, 83–91, 178; as problematic, 103–107; formal equality and, 121–122; Sarah Palin and, 217–218
Maslon, Edelman, Barman, and Brand, 68, 71
Maternal wall, 27–29, 92–93
Maternity leave, 7, 27–29, 35, 117–118, 126–127
McCain, John, 191
McCormick, Mary Ellen, 14
McDermott, Monica, 198
McGovern, George, 193
McNeeley, Jennifer, 22
McTague, John, 151–152, 266n4
Men: as push factor for opting out, 31–33, 265n179; tag teaming childcare and, 48–49, 239n45,46; mandatory overtime and, 55–56; work-family conflict and, 56–61; masculine workplace norms and, 79–91; physical differences of women and, 129–130; salary negotiation and, 141. *See also* Masculine norms
Mercer County Association for the Retarded, 52, 237n29
Meritor Savings Bank v. Vinson, 111–112
Meyers, Marcia, 35, 36, 37
Meyerson, Debra, 83–84
Miami Valley Regional Transit Authority, 70
Middle class, defining, 155–156
Midwest Body, Inc., 57

Military, 194–195
Milton, John, 78
Minneapolis Anti-Pornography Ordinance, 112
Minow, Martha, 129
Missing Middle, 156. *See also* Working class
Mississippi Univ. for Women v. Hogan, 256n24
Modernists, 204
Moen, Phyllis, 31
Molofsky, Robert, 53
Morality, 180–182
Moral vision of the working class, 175–186
Motherhood (wage) penalty, 24–26,
Mr. Mom, 105

Naufus, Penni, 30
Naval Air Rework Facility, 51, 236n23
Negotiation, 136–140
Nevada Department of Human Resources v. Hibbs, 127
New Deal, 153
New Deal Coalition, 7, 151, 193
New York Times, 13, 18, 20, 21
New York Times Magazine, 3, 12–13, 40–41
Nicholson, Jack, 82
Nixon, Richard, 7, 193, 198, 207
No-fault progressive discipline systems, 45–46, 62–64
Nolan, Ann, 28
Nolan, Dennis, 64
Norway, 35, 36

Obama, Barack: challenges of, 2, 10–11; childhood education and, 37; race division and, 108; class and, 151, 184, 187, 190–191; patriotism and, 194; affirmative action and, 203; firearms and, 206–207; inauguration of, 213–214
Obama, Michelle, 124, 194
O'Hare-Blumberg, Kristin, 22
Oil platforms, masculinity and, 83–86
Oncale, Joseph, 79–80
Oncale v. Sundowner Offshore Services, 79–80
One Sick Child report, 44
Opting out: misconceptions about, 2–4, 14–15; media coverage on, 12–14, 17–21; drawbacks to, 16–17, 224n12; traditionalism and, 21–24; economic consequences of, 24–26; push and pull factors of,

27–33, 265n179; public policy and, 33–40; tax policy and, 40; conclusions on, 40–41, 75–76; sameness-difference debate and, 114; Lisa Belkin and, 222n11, 223n3, 261n108
Overtime: mandatory, 52–56, 62; alternative systems for, 73–74

Palin, Sarah, 183, 215–218
Palin, Todd, 215, 216, 218
Panley-Pagetti, Julia, 27
Parental leave, 36
Part-time work, 37, 38–39, 45, 74–75, 210
Patriotism, 194–195
Pella Corporation, 70
Performativity, 142, 157–160
Perreault, Michele, 77
Physical differences, of women, 129–130
Piedmont Airlines, 66
PNC Operations Center, 68
Politics: reframing, 1–2; creating family supports through, 6–9; class and, 151–153, 160–161, 186, 192–196; culture wars and, 187–189; injuries of class and, 189–192; race and, 196–203; religion and family values and, 203–206; firearms and, 206–207. *See also* Public policy
Pollack, Jackson, 104
Pornography, 112
Potuchek, Jean L., 32
Poverty, 160–161
Pragmatism, 1, 110, 113, 155, 219
Pregnancy, 27, 92, 118, 127–129
Pregnancy Discrimination Act, 118, 257n37
Presenteeism, 68–69
Price Waterhouse v. Hopkins, 116
Princeton City School District Board of Education, 47
Problem of the poor and the privileged, 160–161
Professional-managerial class: defined, 155; childrearing in, 166–168; social networks in, 169–171; food culture in, 171–172; entertaining in, 172–175. *See also* Masculinity
Project for Attorney Retention, 87–88, 147
Prove it again!, 93–96
Psychological differences, of women, 133–136, 149
Public policy: opting out and, 33–34; short-term leaves, 35–36; child care, 36–38; workplace flexibility, 38–39;

universal health coverage, 39–40; culture wars and, 207–214. *See also* Politics
Puget Sound Hospital, Tacoma, 243n83

Queen bees, 101
Queer theory, 112, 142–143
Quinn, Sally, 22

Race: opt-out news coverage and, 18–19; merit standards and, 95–96; ambivalent sexism and, 99; discrimination and, 101; divisions among, 107–108; assimilationist feminism and, 126; anti-essentialism and, 144–148; culture wars and, 196–203
Racism, class and, 196–198
Ramey, Garey, 24
Ramey, Valerie A., 24
Reagan, Ronald, 7, 183, 195
Reconstructive feminism: overview, 5, 126–127; goals of, 106–107; difference feminism and, 128–136; queer theory and, 142–143; dominance feminism and, 143–144; anti-essentialism and, 144–148; third-wave feminism and, 148–149; conclusions on, 149–150; public policy and, 209; next steps for, 218–219
Recruitment, 69–71
Reed v. Reed, 115, 256n24
Religion, role of, in working-class culture, 180–182; in class politics, 203–206
Responsibility, 176–180, 196
Rhode, Deborah, 116, 128, 133
Richards, Amy, 109
Richardson, Peter, 60
Rieder, Jonathan, 177–178, 182, 197, 199, 275n20
Rivers, Caryl, 34
Robinson, Elena, 28
Rochester Psychiatric, 62, 74
Roediger, David, 196–197
Rosenfeld, Alvin, 24
Rubin, Lillian, 103, 200

Safety, workplace, 66
Salary: effects of opting out on, 24–26; negotiating, 136–140; class distinction and, 155; drop in working-class, 157–158
Sameness-difference debate, 5, 113–115, 136–140, 149–150
Sameness feminism, 111, 114
Scheduling: opting out and, 29–33; caregiving and, 46–52; mandatory overtime, 52–56; masculine norms and,

86–88, 90; as adverse employment action, 127; public policy and, 209–211. *See also* Workplace flexibility
Schmidt, Warren (fictional character), 82
Schreiber Foods, 68–69
Schultz, Vicki, 121
Schwarzenegger, Arnold, 79–80, 244n15
Sears, Sally, 30
Self-actualization, 163, 167, 175, 181, 191, 196
Self-analysis, 191–192
Self-employment, 188
Self-promotion, 98–99, 139, 183
Self-regulation, 164, 165, 167, 181, 196, 204–205
Sennett, Richard, 59
Separate spheres: assumptions on gender and, 4–5; gender roles and, 23; maternal wall and, 28, 93; workplace norms and, 78–79; gender theory and, 113–115; assimilationist feminism and, 115–117; difference feminism and, 134–135; negotiation and, 137; reconstructive feminism and, 149
Settled living, 164–165, 175–177, 180–181, 193, 196, 199, 204,
Sexism, ambivalent, 97–100, 141
Sex-positive feminism, 144, 264n162
Sexual harassment, 111–112
Sexual orientation, 112. *See also* Gay couples
Shackelsford, Barry, 206
Shafer, Jack, 34
Shaughnessy, Kathy, 109
Short-term leaves, 35–36, 208–209
Shows, Carla, 159
Siegel, Reva, 126, 127
Sigel, Roberta, 239n45, 46
Silicon Valley, 86–87, 90
Simpson, Homer (fictional character), 154
Simpson v. District of Columbia Office of Human Rights, 50
Skocpol, Theda, 156, 161, 201, 202
Sleep, 86–87, 247n60
Social capital, 189–190, 269n38
Social networks, 169–171
Social Security Administration, Westminster Teleservice Center, 47–48
Solis, Joe, 120–121
Sosnaud, Benjamin, 152
Southern Champion Tray Co., 60, 236n23
Sports, 175
Spragins, Ellyn, 24

Springsteen, Bruce, 153
Sprint/Central Telephone Co. of Texas, 52, 237n30
Stanton, Elizabeth Cady, 115
State of New York, Rochester Psychiatric Center, 54–55
Status negotiations, 88–89
Stay-at-home fathers, 80
Stay-at-home mothers: by race and family income, 18 (table); assimilationist feminism and, 117, 124–126; racialization of gender bias and, 145–146; motivation for, 265n179
Steel, Dawn, 123
Steinbeck, John, 153
Stereotyping, 105–106
Stone, Pamela, 17, 22, 31, 32, 265n179
Stonecash, Jeffrey, 160
Story, Louise, 13, 20, 34
"Straight talk," 182–184
Stress, workplace flexibility and, 69, 247n60
StrideRight, 68
Substantive equality, 131–133
Suprenant Cable Corp., 56, 235n22
Sutter Roseville Medical Center, 71–72, 236n23, 242n82
Sweden, 8, 35
Sweet, Stephen, 31
Swidler, Ann, 162

Tag teaming, 46–50, 52, 53, 207, 235n20
Tannen, Deborah, 88–89, 100
Tax policy, 40–41
Teixeira, Ruy, 152
Telephone lines, tapping, 43, 50, 234n5
Tenneco Packaging Burlington Container Plant, 53–54, 238n40
Therapy, 191–192
Third-wave feminism, 148–149
Tomboys: overview, 5; double binds and, 96–97; assimilationist feminism and, 116–119, 122, 126; difference feminism and, 135–136; salary negotiation and, 140–141
Town of Stratford, 64–65, 236n23
Tractor Supply Co., 57, 239n41
Traditionalism, 21–24, 203–205

Unions: arbitration and, 43–44, 234n6; lessons for, 60–64, 76; workplace flexibility and, 71, 210–211; working class and, 157

United States: politics and work-family conflict in, 7–9; women's employment in, 33–34; short-term leaves and, 35; child care in, 37–38
Universal health coverage, 39–40, 104, 202
University of Michigan, 142
Unsocial hours, 46–50
UPS, 57–58, 239n43
U.S. Steel Corp., 49, 53, 60–61, 235n21
U.S. West Communications, 50, 236n25

Vacations, 175
VA Medical Center of Indianapolis, 58
Vandello, Joseph A., 89
Vanneman, Reeve, 188
Vietnam War, 193–195
Violence Against Women Act, 112
Visible Invisibility: Women of Color in Law Firms, 145, 147
Voting, cultural, 161

Waismel-Manor, Ronit, 31
Walker, Alice, 126
Walker, Rebecca, 125–126
Walsh, Shireen, 29
Warner, Judith, 24
Warren, Rick, 213
Warwick, Bob, 40
Washington, Chrissie, 29
Washington Times, 18
Washington v. Illinois Department of Revenue, 29, 127
Waters, Alice, 172
Webster, Scott, 83
Weinberger v. Weisenfeld, 115, 256n24
Welfare, 199–202
West, Candace, 142
White, Lucie, 208
"White trash," 154, 176
Wiggins, Patsy, 17
Wilk, Korin, 77
Williams, Patricia, 132
Williams, Wendy Webster, 118
Willis, Paul, 178
Willoughby, Brian, 204–205
Wise, Nicole, 24
Women: opting out and, 2–4, 14–15; domesticity and, 4–5; employment and, 33–34, 121, 224n12, 225n18, 271n73; caregiving and, 60; workplace norms and, 78–79, 91–103; social relationships and,

82; physical differences of, 129–130; differences in lives of, 130–133; psychological differences of, 133–136; negotiation and, 136–140; in blue collar jobs, 225n18

Women Don't Ask: Negotiation and the Gender Divide (Babcock & Laschever), 136–137, 139–140

Work: pride in, 176–180, 272n89; working-class attitudes on, 185–186

Work-family axis of gender, 113

Work-family conflict: public policy and, 1–2, 209–211; in working class, 6–11, 42–46; in professional-managerial class, 30–33; interaction of working-class work schedules and child care, 46–50, 52–56; interaction of working-class work schedules and family crises, 50–52, 233n3, 235–239; impact of mandatory overtime, 52–56; lessons for unions and employers on, 61–64; racialization of gender bias and, 145–146

Working class: defined, 155–156; sharp drop in men's wages, 157–160; settled

versus hard living, 164–166; childrearing in, 166–168; social networks in, 169–171; food culture in, 171–172; entertaining in, 172–175; the disciplined self, 176–177; "hanging in there," 177–180; religion and traditional morality, 180–182; "straight talk," 182–184; "family comes first," 184–186. *See also* Masculinity; Missing Middle

Working hours. *See* Scheduling

Workplace flexibility: public policy and, 38–39, 209–211; work-family conflict and, 44–45; mandatory overtime and, 52–56; arguments for, 64–71, 241n67; steps for improving, 71–75

Workplace safety, 66

Works Progress Administration, 153

Yamashita, Laura, 16

Yoshino, Kenji, 101

Young, Alfred, Jr., 75

Zamora, Henry, 120–121

Zimmerman, Don, 142